THE COMPLETE OLYMPIC GAMES–COUNTRY BY COUNTRY

2024 EDITION

INTRODUCTION 3

CHAPTER ONE - Northern America (United States, Canada, Mexico, Bermuda) 6

CHAPTER TWO - Central America (Costa Rica, Panama, Guatemala, Nicaragua, Honduras, El Salvador, Belize) 15

CHAPTER THREE - Caribbean, Greater Antilles (Cuba, Jamaica, Bahamas, Dominican Republic, Puerto Rico, Haiti, Cayman Islands) 20

CHAPTER FOUR - Caribbean, Lesser Antilles (Trinidad & Tobago, Grenada, US Virgin Islands, Barbados, British Virgin Islands, St Kitts & Nevis, St Lucia, Antigua & Barbuda, Dominica, Aruba, St Vincent & the Grenadines) 28

CHAPTER FIVE - South America, North & West (Colombia, Venezuela, Ecuador, Peru, Suriname, Guyana) 35

CHAPTER SIX - South America, South & East (Brazil, Argentina, Chile, Uruguay, Paraguay, Bolivia) 41

CHAPTER SEVEN - British Isles (Great Britain, Ireland) 46

CHAPTER EIGHT - Scandinavia (Sweden, Norway, Finland, Denmark, Iceland) 51

CHAPTER NINE - Latin Europe (France, Italy, Spain, Portugal, San Marino, Monaco, Malta, Andorra) 62

CHAPTER TEN - Western Central Europe (Germany, Netherlands, Switzerland, Austria, Belgium, Liechtenstein, Luxembourg) . 72

CHAPTER ELEVEN - Eastern Central Europe (Hungary, Czech Republic, Poland, Slovakia) 88

CHAPTER TWELVE – Balkans (Romania, Bulgaria, Greece, Serbia, Croatia, Slovenia, Kosovo, North Macedonia, Montenegro, Albania, Bosnia & Herzegovina) 98

CHAPTER THIRTEEN - Former USSR, European (Russia, Ukraine, Belarus, Estonia, Georgia, Azerbaijan, Lithuania, Latvia, Armenia, Moldova) 109

CHAPTER FOURTEEN - Middle East, northern (Turkey, Iran, Israel, Syria, Jordan, Kuwait, Lebanon, Cyprus, Iraq, Palestine) 122

CHAPTER FIFTEEN Middle East, southern (Qatar, Bahrain, United Arab Emirates, Saudi Arabia, Oman, Yemen) 130

CHAPTER SIXTEEN - Northern Africa (Egypt, Morocco, Algeria, Tunisia, Libya) 135

CHAPTER SEVENTEEN Western Africa, west coast (Senegal, Sierra Leone, Liberia, Guinea-Bissau, Mauritania, Gambia, Guinea, Cape Verde) 140

CHAPTER EIGHTEEN - Western Africa, central & south (Nigeria, Ivory Coast, Ghana, Niger, Burkina Faso, Togo, Mali, Benin) 144

CHAPTER NINETEEN - Middle Africa (Cameroon, Gabon, Congo, Angola, Central African Republic, Chad, Congo DR, Sao Tome & Principe, Equatorial Guinea) 149

CHAPTER TWENTY - Eastern Africa, north (Kenya, Ethiopia, Uganda, Sudan, Eritrea, Djibouti, Seychelles, Somalia, South Sudan) 154

CHAPTER TWENTY-ONE - Eastern Africa, south (Zimbabwe, Burundi, Mozambique, Tanzania, Zambia, Mauritius, Madagascar, Malawi, Rwanda, Comoros) 160

CHAPTER TWENTY-TWO - Southern Africa (South Africa, Namibia, Botswana, Lesotho, Eswatini) 167

CHAPTER TWENTY-THREE - Former USSR, Asian (Kazakhstan, Uzbekistan, Tajikistan, Kyrgyzstan, Turkmenistan) 170

CHAPTER TWENTY-FOUR - Southern Asia (India, Pakistan, Sri Lanka, Afghanistan, Nepal, Bangladesh, Bhutan, Maldives) .. 174

CHAPTER TWENTY-FIVE - Eastern Asia (China, Japan, South Korea, North Korea, Chinese Taipei, Mongolia, Hong Kong) ... 179

CHAPTER TWENTY-SIX - South-Eastern Asia (Thailand, Indonesia, Philippines, Vietnam, Singapore, Malaysia, Myanmar, Cambodia, Laos, Timor-Leste, Brunei) 192

CHAPTER TWENTY-SEVEN - Australasia & Melanesia (Australia, New Zealand, Fiji, Papua New Guinea, Solomon Islands, Vanuatu) 200

CHAPTER TWENTY-EIGHT - Micronesia & Polynesia (Samoa, Tonga, American Samoa, Nauru, Micronesia, Kiribati, Cook Islands, Marshall Islands, Tuvalu, Palau, Guam) 207

CHAPTER TWENTY-NINE - Other Teams 213

CHAPTER THIRTY - Top 5s 214

CHAPTER THIRTY-ONE - Full Olympic Rankings 217

CHAPTER THIRTY-TWO - Summary of Olympic Games 221

INTRODUCTION

There are a number of books about the history of the Olympics. Several of those list medal winners. However, this is, as far as I am aware, the first book that looks at each country in turn, and discovers their Olympic record. How successful have they been, in proportion to their population? Which sports have they excelled at? And, if they are one of the many countries that have never won an Olympic medal, how close have they got?

The idea for researching this information first came to me when I read that Alessandra Perilli's 4th-place finish in the 2012 women's trap Shooting event was the highest ever position achieved in an Olympic event by a competitor from San Marino. It made me wonder – had San Marino ever got near 4th place before? How many countries have never even managed that? Are there any countries that have never reached the top eight of an event? Or the top 16? (The answer is yes, plenty – indeed, there is just one country which has never even finished in the top 32 of any Olympic event – read on to find out which!). And what about countries like the US Virgin Islands, or Togo; they have won just one medal each, but was it a flash in the pan? Or the climax of years of getting close? This book seeks to provide the answers.

From reading each country's entry in the book, you will find the following information:
- Which Games that country has competed in
- Which years have seen that country's peak Olympic performances
- Who the top-performing Olympians from that country have been
- What the best sports have been for that country
- How that country has fared specifically in Athletics and Swimming – the two biggest sports of the Games
- …and much more

I have made the decision to allocate every medal ever won in Olympic competition amongst the 206 currently competing Olympic nations. That means, in particular, the following:
- Medals won by both West and East Germany have been added to Germany
- Medals won by the Soviet Union (and the 1992 Unified Team) have been added to Russia
- Medals won by Yugoslavia have been added to Serbia
- Medals won by both Czechoslovakia and Bohemia have been added to the Czech Republic
- Medals won by the Netherlands Antilles have been added to the Netherlands
- Medals won by the British West Indies have been added to Jamaica

For determining each country's Olympic rank, I have simply expanded the criteria which makes up Olympic medal tables, i.e. the first tie-breaker is number of golds, followed by silvers, bronzes, 4th places, 5th places etc. In many sports, there is an official final ranking, but in some sports there is not. I have worked out a top eight for each of the 6,668 Olympic events to have taken place, using the official rankings where available, and devising what I deem to be the fairest ranking system otherwise. Each sport has its own format, so I have tried to be as consistent as possible when determining final positions. Some of the main criteria I have used are these:
- In knockout events (e.g. Football or Tennis), losing quarter-finalists are ranked according to how narrowly they lost their quarter-final. In sports such as Boxing or Judo, I rank people eliminated in the same round by how long they lasted in the bout before losing.
- In events with heats, where the criteria for the final was, for example, top four in each heat qualify, I rank the rest of the competitors by heat position, followed by time. In events where the criteria for the final was, for example, top three in each plus two fastest losers qualify, I rank the rest of the competitors purely by time.

For determining each country's best sport(s), I have gone with the one where they have won the highest percentage of all the gold medals ever won in that sport. For example, there have been 34 gold medals ever awarded in Basketball, and the United States have won 26 of them – 76.47%. If no golds have been won, then it goes to a percentage of all medals. If no medals have been won, I have gone with the sport in which that country achieved their highest finishing position.

In terms of each country's entry in this book, I have taken a slightly different approach to the 22 most successful Olympic nations (those that have won 75 or more golds). These countries are analysed sport-by-sport (in each case starting with the most successful sports first), whereas other countries are given an overall summary of their Olympic history.

I have used a large number of books and websites in researching this information, but I must pay particular tribute to www.olympedia.org, a truly magnificent piece of work. Populations figures have been taken from the CIA website.

In the early years of the Olympics, athletes did not compete as part of national teams, and therefore determining nationalities can sometimes be tricky. Where medals in early Olympics were won by teams with mixed nationalities, I have added them to the country with a majority of the team's members. If there is no majority, I have split the medals. You can find a full list in Chapter 29.

The 1900 and 1904 Games were effectively sideshows to major world's fairs, and it is often difficult to determine which events to include. Some of the events had entries restricted to home athletes, for example, so definitely shouldn't be included, but I have gone with the majority and most pragmatic view where relevant. The 1906 Intercalated Games are not recognised by the IOC; however, they were a much more truly international "Olympic" event than either 1900 or 1904 (indeed, without it, the entire Olympic movement might have died in its infancy). I have therefore included all medals won in 1906. I have, however, not included the Olympic Art medals won between 1912 and 1948, for a number of reasons. They were very sporadic and irregular, they recognised achievements created outside of the timeframe of the Olympics themselves, and in a number of events, silvers and/or bronzes were awarded but no golds. In some events, only one medal was awarded.

In the last few years, a large number of medals, particularly from 2008 and 2012, have been rescinded and re-allocated following re-testing of doping samples. It can be an especially onerous task in keeping up with all the updates, especially as often it takes a long period of appeals, counter-appeals etc. before disqualifications are confirmed, and can take even longer for the medals to be re-allocated (sometimes they simply aren't). And the IOC are not always the most reliable for updating their own website. But I have been as meticulous as I can, and all info should be accurate as of 4th October 2023.

There are currently 206 "countries" recognised by the IOC. They are the 193 full members of the United Nations, plus 13 others:
- 1 UN observer state   (Palestine)
- 4 US territories   (American Samoa, Guam, Puerto Rico, US Virgin Islands)
- 3 British overseas territories   (Bermuda, British Virgin Islands, Cayman Islands)
- 1 overseas "country" of the Netherlands   (Aruba)
- 1 associated state of New Zealand   (Cook Islands)
- 1 special administrative region of China   (Hong Kong)
- 2 states with limited international recognition (Chinese Taipei, Kosovo)

For the most part, these countries were given Olympic status before the rules were tightened in 1996, so are allowed to continue to send their own teams to the Olympics.

Please note also that, in the pages that follow, **PWDS** stands for pre-war discontinued sports. These were:
- Tug of War   6 events (1900, 1904, 1906, 1908, 1912, 1920)
- Polo   5 events (1900, 1908, 1920, 1924, 1936)
- Croquet   3 events (all in 1900)
- Motor Boating   3 events (all in 1908)
- Lacrosse   2 events (1904 & 1908)
- Rackets   2 events (both in 1908)
- Cricket   1 event (1900)
- Pelota Basque   1 event (1900)
- Roque   1 event (1904)
- Jeu de Paume   1 event (1908)

One final note: throughout the book, numbers in the format (e.g.) 4-3-2 indicates 4 gold medals, 3 silver medals and 2 bronze medals.

The full list of 37 Summer and 15 Winter sports (not including the PWDS listed above) is as follows:

Athletics	(1896, and every Games thereafter)
Cycling	(1896, and every Games thereafter)
Fencing	(1896, and every Games thereafter)
Gymnastics	(1896, and every Games thereafter)
Swimming	(1896, and every Games thereafter)
Wrestling	(1896, and every Games thereafter except for 1900)
Shooting	(1896, and every Games thereafter except for 1904 & 1928)
Tennis	(1896 to 1924, and every Games since 1988)
Weightlifting	(1896, and every Games thereafter except for 1900, 1908 & 1912)
Rowing	(1900, and every Games thereafter)
Football	(1900, and every Games thereafter except for 1932)
Water Polo	(1900, and every Games thereafter except for 1906)
Sailing	(1900, and every Games thereafter except for 1904 & 1906)
Equestrianism	(1900, and every Games thereafter except for 1904, 1906 & 1908)
Archery	(1900, 1904, 1908, 1920, and every Games since 1972)
Rugby/ Rugby Sevens	(1900, 1908, 1920, 1924, 2016 & 2021)
Golf	(1900, 1904, 2016 & 2021)
Diving	(1904, and every Games thereafter)
Boxing	(1904, and every Games thereafter except for 1906 & 1912)
Hockey	(1908, and every Games thereafter except for 1912 & 1924)
Modern Pentathlon	(1912, and every Games thereafter)
Basketball	(1936, and every Games thereafter)
Canoeing	(1936, and every Games thereafter)
Handball	(1936, then 1972, and every Games thereafter)
Volleyball	(1964, and every Games thereafter)
Judo	(1964, and every Games thereafter except for 1968)
Artistic Swimming	(1984, and every Games thereafter)
Table Tennis	(1988, and every Games thereafter)
Badminton	(1992, and every Games thereafter)
Baseball/Softball	(1992, and every Games thereafter except for 2012 & 2016)
Beach Volleyball	(1996, and every Games thereafter)
Taekwondo	(2000, and every Games thereafter)
Triathlon	(2000, and every Games thereafter)
Karate	(2021)
Skateboarding	(2021)
Sport Climbing	(2021)
Surfing	(2021)

Figure Skating	(1908 & 1920 Summer Games, and every Winter Games since 1924)
Ice Hockey	(1920 Summer Games, and every Winter Games since 1924)
Speed Skating	(1924, and every Games thereafter)
Nordic Combined	(1924, and every Games thereafter)
Nordic Skiing	(1924, and every Games thereafter)
Ski Jumping	(1924, and every Games thereafter)
Bobsleigh	(1924, and every Games thereafter except for 1960)
Biathlon	(1924, then 1960, and every Games thereafter)
Curling	(1924, then 1998, and every Games thereafter)
Skeleton	(1928 & 1948, then 2002, and every Games thereafter)
Alpine Skiing	(1936, and every Games thereafter)
Luge	(1964, and every Games thereafter)
Short Track Speed Skating	(1992, and every Games thereafter)
Freestyle Skiing	(1992, and every Games thereafter)
Snowboarding	(1998, and every Games thereafter)

I hope you find reading this book as interesting as I found researching it. If you have any questions, comments, or indeed corrections, please contact me at peteblac17@hotmail.com.

CHAPTER ONE - Northern America (United States, Canada, Mexico, Bermuda)

UNITED STATES   **Olympic Rank 1st**
Population: 339,665,118 (rank 3rd)
Olympic rank/ population differential: +2
Population per gold: 286,154 (rank 32nd)
Population per medal: 113,714 (rank 41st)

Summer: 1074 gold, 836 silver, 744 bronze (total 2654)
Winter: 113 gold, 123 silver, 96 bronze (total 332)
Total: 1187 gold, 959 silver, 840 bronze (total 2986)
(plus mixed team: 0 gold, 0.5 silver, 0.5 bronze (total 1))

Best sports: Basketball (26 golds, 76.47%, 1st)
                      Golf (5 golds, 62.50%, 1st)
                      Beach Volleyball (7 golds, 50.00%, 1st)

The United States's domination of Summer Olympic history can best be summed up by the fact that Tokyo 2021 saw them win the lowest proportion of available gold medals (11.47%) that they have managed in any Games, yet they still topped the medal table anyway. Only in 1976 and 1988 have they finished lower than 2nd (they finished 3rd both times; they famously boycotted in 1980). Their most dominant Games, in terms of proportion of golds won were St Louis 1904 and Los Angeles 1984, followed by Paris 1924 (winning 45 golds out of 126).

They are the 4th most successful nation in Winter Olympic history. Their most golds won is 10 (in 2002), and their most medals won is 37 (in 2010). They have won at least one gold at every Winter Games. They have topped the table once (Lake Placid 1932), with a lowest finish of 9th (1968 & 1988). They have finished in the top five at every other Games since 1968.

SUMMER
Basketball (26-2-3, 1st). The US won the first seven men's Basketball titles, winning 63 matches in a row leading up to the 1972 final, which they were to lose in hugely controversial circumstances, when a dispute over the timing of the final buzzer led to the Soviet Union being given an extra three seconds to score the winning basket. Even since then, they have only failed to win gold twice – in 1988 and 2004, when they won bronze both times. The women have only failed to win gold twice; they lost the final to the Soviets in 1976 (the inaugural event), and the semi-final to the Unified Team in 1992 (they won bronze). The women even won the inaugural 3x3 event in 2021 for good measure. Two men, Carmelo Anthony and Kevin Durant, have won three golds each, whilst two women, Diana Taurasi and Sue Bird, have won five golds each.

Golf (5-3-5, 1st). Americans won 3 golds, 3 silvers and 4 bronzes in the 4 events held in 1900 and 1904. They include Margaret Abbott, who was America's first female Olympic champion, although she would never know the competition she had won was part of the Olympics. The US won both men's and women's golds in 2021.

Beach Volleyball (7-2-2, 1st). The US has won four of the last five golds in the women's event, but their last men's medal was gold in 2008. Kerri Walsh and Misty May won golds in 2004, 2008 and 2012 (Walsh won bronze in 2016 too). Karch Kiraly won gold in 1996, having won indoor Volleyball golds in 1984 & 1988.

Surfing (1-0-0, 1st=). Carissa Moore won the women's event in 2021. Kolohe Andino came 5th in the men's.

Swimming (259-180-144, 1st). Surprisingly, the US didn't win any Swimming medals in 1896 or 1900, but have won golds at every Games since. Having won just two in 1956, they have won at least 8 at every Games since; their record is 21 golds in 1968 & 1984. In 1968, they won a record 52 medals in total; their lowest post-war medals total is nine in 1952. The most successful swimmers in Olympic history have all been American. There have been seven golds each for Katie Ledecky (2012-21) and Caeleb Dressel (2016-21), eight for Matt Biondi (1984-92) and Jenny Thompson (1992-2000), nine for Mark Spitz (1968-72), and a ludicrous 23 for Michael Phelps (2004-16; the next best total for any Olympian in any sport is the 10 won by US athlete Ray Ewry).

Diving (48-45-45, 1st). The US utterly dominated Diving at one time, winning 32 golds out of 37 between 1924 and 1964 (and taking silver in four of the other five). They still won at least one gold at every Games after that until 1992, but by that time the Chinese were beginning their own long domination, and the US have won just two golds since. Greg Louganis won platform and springboard doubles in both 1984 & 1988 and is the only man ever to win four Diving golds. Pat McCormick also did the double double on the women's side in 1952 & 1956.

Baseball/Softball (4-3-2, 1st). After finishing 4th in the first Baseball event (1992), they have won one gold (2000), one silver (2021) and two bronzes (1996 and 2008) since. The women won the first three Softball titles (1996 to 2004) before losing the finals of 2008 and 2021 to Japan.

Athletics (354-277-220, 1st). The fewest golds the US have ever won at a Games is six (1972 & 1976). The most they have won is 23 (1904) followed by 16 (four times pre-war, plus 1956 & 1984). The fewest medals they have won is 16 (2000). At the other end of the scale, they won 68 in 1904, 42 in 1912 and 40 in 1984. Their best events have been the men's 110m hurdles, 400 metres and shot put (20 golds in each), and the 400m hurdles and pole vault (19 golds in each). They won every pole vault gold from 1896 to 1968, apart from 1906. Ray Ewry won 10 golds in the now-defunct standing jump events (1900-08) to become Athletics' leading Olympian of all time, Carl Lewis won nine golds (1984-96), Allyson Felix won an all-time female record of seven (2008-21, six of which were in relays) and Martin Sheridan won five in discus and shot events (1904-08).

Tennis (21-6.5-12.5, 1st). The US have won 14 gold medals since Tennis's return in 1988, including four golds each for Serena and Venus Williams (they shared the women's doubles titles of 2000, 2008 and 2012, with Venus also taking singles gold in 2000, and Serena likewise in 2012).

Artistic Swimming (5-2-2, 2nd). Since 2000, the Russians have won every gold going, with the US having to settle for a couple of bronzes in 2004. Prior to that, though, they dominated the event (along with Canada), winning 5 golds and 2 silvers in the 7 events between 1984 and 1996. Tracie Ruiz won solo and duet in 1984.

Rugby (2-0-0, 2nd=). They entered 15-man Rugby twice, and surprisingly won both times, beating France in both finals (1920 and 1924). Daniel Carroll was in their squad in 1920, having previously won gold with Australasia in 1908. Since Sevens was introduced in 2016, the women have come 5th and the men 6th.

Archery (14-10-9, 2nd). There were six Archery events in 1904, all of which had all-American entry lists. Hence, 16 of the 33 American medals came in that year (the team event had just the one entry, so no silver or bronze medal awarded). When Archery returned to the Games in 1972, the US dominated, taking all the individual golds in both 1972 and 1976, and the men's title again in 1984, 1988 and 1996. The latter Games also saw them take the men's team title, but there have been no further golds since.

Shooting (57-31-28, 1st). The last time that the US failed to win a Shooting gold was 1988 (just one silver). The last they failed to win a medal at all was 1936. Their best year was 1920, when they won 13 of the 21 golds available. Six men have won five golds each, of which four are American (Alfred Lane, Carl Osburn, Morris Fisher and Willis Lee), all of them pre-war. Kim Rhode is the only woman from any country to win three Shooting golds (double trap in 1996 & 2004, and skeet in 2012).

Boxing (50-27-40, 1st). The US were particularly successful in 1984, winning 9 of the 12 events, as well as a silver and bronze (which went to Evander Holyfield, who was controversially disqualified in the semi-finals). The only time they didn't win a medal was 1908. Their many gold medal winners include Oliver Kirk (who uniquely won bantamweight and featherweight in 1904, having lost 10lbs in 2 weeks between his bouts), Floyd Patterson, Cassius Clay, Joe Frazier, George Foreman, Leon Spinks, Sugar Ray Leonard and Oscar de la Hoya.

Volleyball (4-3-4, 3rd). The men won gold in 1984, 1988 and 2008, and the women in 2021.

Wrestling (55-44-39, 2nd). Only 15 of the US's 138 medals have come in Greco-Roman, including just three golds – two in 1984, and Rulon Gardner's famous win over Aleksandr Karelin in 2000. They last failed to win a Wrestling gold in 1968, and last failed to win a medal in 1912. In freestyle super heavyweight, Bruce Baumgartner won two golds, a silver and a bronze (1984-96).

Rowing (33-32-24, 2nd). The 2021 Games saw the US fail to win a medal for the first time since 1912. Their four golds this century have all come in eights. Jack Kelly (father of Grace) and Paul Costello won three golds each, including double sculls together in 1920 and 1924.

PWDS (3-4-3, 3rd). They were the only country entering the 1904 Roque tournament, thereby winning all three medals. They won all three Tug of War medals the same year, as well as Lacrosse silver. They won Jeu de Paume gold in 1908, and Polo bronze (1920) and silver (1924).

Water Polo (4-6-5, 3rd). It is debatable whether the 1904 Water Polo event should be considered an official Olympic event. Only three teams entered, and they were all American, hence their only men's gold medal in the sport. Women's Water Polo has been played 6 times, and the US have 3 golds, 2 silvers and a bronze. The last men's medal was a silver in 2008.

Football (4-2-2, 1st). The all-conquering US women's team took four of the first five golds available – 1996, 2004, 2008 and 2012. They also won silver in 2000 and bronze in 2021, but in 2016 they lost to Sweden in the quarter-finals. Four Americans (Christie Rampone Pearce, Heather Mitts, Heather O'Reilly and Shannon Boxx) have an Olympic record three Football golds each). In 1904, three (male) teams entered; two of them were American but both lost heavily to the Canadian team, and had to settle for silver and bronze. Nonetheless, they remain the only US medals in men's football; the closest they have come since is 4th in 2000.

Gymnastics (38-43-37, 2nd). Of the first 62 US Gymnastics medals, 59 of them were won at home in 1904, 1932 and 1984 (27,16 and 16 medals respectively), but they have been better on foreign soil since. Anton Heida won five golds and a silver in 1904, whilst Simone Biles took seven medals (4-1-2) in 2016 & 2021.

Sailing (19-23-19, 2nd). 1984 was the USA's best year, winning three golds and three silvers. The US last won gold in 2008, and have won just one bronze since then.

Triathlon (1-1-2, 4th=). Gwen Jorgensen won women's gold in 2016. The mixed relay team took silver in 2021.

Equestrianism (11-23-20, 5th). Six golds in three-day eventing, and five in jumping. They have won eight medals in dressage, all in the team event, but none of them gold.

Weightlifting (16-17-11, 3rd). Only one gold medal since 1960 – for Tara Nott in women's flyweight in 2000. The best record is that of Tommy Kono (two golds and one silver, 1952-60, all at different weights).

Cycling (17-22-21, 6th). The US won all 21 medals on offer in 1904, when virtually no other nationalities entered. Marcus Hurley won four golds and a bronze that year; only five people have ever matched or beaten his four golds (four of them British). The US didn't win a single Cycling medal between 1912 and 1984. Kristin Armstrong won the women's road time trial in 2008, 2012 and 2016.

Taekwondo (3-2-5, 3rd). Steven Lopez won featherweight gold in 2000, and welterweight gold and bronze in 2004 and 2008. Remarkably, his siblings Mark and Diana also both won medals in 2008. Anastasija Zolotic won the other gold, in women's featherweight in 2021.

Canoeing (6-5-6, 11th). Greg Barton won two golds in 1988 (men's K1 and K2 1000m). He also won bronzes in 1984 and 1992. Nevin Harrison's 2021 gold in women's C1 200m was the first US canoeing gold since 1992.

Fencing (4-11-18, 10th). After Albertson van zo Post's gold in the men's single sticks in 1904, the US had to wait 100 years for another gold. It came to Mariel Zagunis in the women's individual sabre; she then retained her title in 2008, and Lee Kiefer won women's foil in 2021. Only eight medals were won between 1904 and 2004, but 15 have been won since. Van zo Post won five medals in 1904, although one of those was as part of a team representing Cuba.

Judo (2-4-8, 15th). Half-heavyweight Kayla Harrison has won both American judo golds – in 2012 and 2016.

Skateboarding (0-0-2, 4th). Jagger Eaton (street) and Cory Juneau (park) won bronzes in the 2021 men's events. The US came 4th and 6th respectively in the women's equivalents.

Sport Climbing (0-1-0, 4th). Nathaniel Coleman won silver in the 2021 men's event, with Colin Duffy 7th. Brooke Raboutou came 5th in the women's.

Modern Pentathlon (0-6-3, 12th). The US have won three silvers and a bronze in the now-defunct men's team event. Emily deRiel won silver in the women's event in 2000 – the most recent medal.

Karate (0-0-1, 15th=). Ariel Torres got bronze in the men's kata in 2021, one of three top-eight finishes.

Hockey (0-0-2, 17th=). Bronzes in the two LA Games – men in 1932 and women in 1984. The men have not appeared since 1996, but the women have competed more often in recent years, albeit with no further medals.

Handball – Six men's entries and four women's entries, but both last entered in 1996. The men's best is still 6th place in 1936, whilst the women came 5th in 1984.

Table Tennis – Entered every time since 1988; their two quarter-finals both came in 2008 (women's singles and women's team). All three players involved were born in China.

Badminton – Entered every time since 1992, but only one quarter-final so far (men's doubles in 2008).

WINTER

Snowboarding (17-8-10, 1st). The US have won more than twice as many medals, and more than twice as many golds, as any other nation. Shaun White won the men's halfpipe in 2006, 2010 and 2018.

Skeleton (3-4-1, 1st). The first gold was won in 1928, the others both in 2002 (Jim Shea Jr, men's, and Tristan Gale, women's).

Freestyle Skiing (11-13-9, 2nd). They have won medals at every Games going. Their only multi-champion is David Wise (men's halfpipe gold in 2014 & 2018, and silver in 2022).

Figure Skating (16-17-21, 2nd). They have medalled at every post-war Games. Only one American has won two golds – Dick Button (men's champion in 1948 and 1952).

Bobsleigh (8-11-9, 3rd). The US have won medals at every Games since 2002, having previously been without a medal since 1956.

Speed Skating (30-22-19, 2nd). No man has ever won more golds than Eric Heiden, who won all five events in 1980. Bonnie Blair also has five golds (and a bronze, 1988 to 1994).

Ice Hockey (4-12-2, 3rd). Probably the most fondly remembered of all 1187 US gold medals was the 1980 "Miracle on Ice", when the US college players beat the mighty Soviets, and then clinched gold with a win over Finland. They had also won gold in 1960. The women won gold in 1998 and 2018, the only two not won by Canada. The men last won a medal in 2010 (silver); the women have never failed to win a medal.

Alpine Skiing (17-21-10, 3rd). Two golds each for Andrea Mead-Lawrence, Ted Ligety and Mikaela Shiffrin, but six medals in total (1-3-2) for Bode Miller (2002-14).

Short Track Speed Skating (4-7-9, 4th). Apolo Anton Ohno has won 8 medals (2002-2010), including both male golds for the US. Both female golds were won by Cathy Turner (1992 & 1994).

Curling (1-0-1, 6th). The men took bronze in 2006 and gold in 2018. The women's best is 4th in 2002.

Nordic Combined (1-3-0, 7th). All four medals came in 2010, Bill Demong with a gold, Johnny Spillane with two silvers, and a team silver which included both of them.

Nordic Skiing (1-2-1, 13th=). Only a single silver prior to 2018, but then gold in the women's team sprint for Kikkan Randall and Jessie Diggins, followed by a silver and bronze for Diggins in 2022 as well.

Luge (0-3-3, 5th). Silvers in 1998, 2002 and 2018; bronzes in 1998, 2002 and 2014.

Ski Jumping (0-0-1, 13th=). In 1924, Anders Haugen, who had emigrated from Norway, finished 4th for the US. However, 50 years later a miscalculation was discovered, and it turned out he had actually finished 3rd, ahead of Norwegian Thorleif Haug (who had won three golds in other events). Haug's daughter presented the by-now elderly Haugen with his rightful bronze, which is still the US's only Ski Jumping medal. They came 4th in 1984.

Biathlon – 6th in relay events three times (1972, 2014, 2018). Deedra Irwin came 7th in the women's 15km in 2022, the best for an American in an individual event. The only winter sport in which the US have not medalled.

CANADA   **Olympic Rank 13th**

Population: 38,516,736 (rank 38th)
Olympic rank/ population differential: +25
Population per gold: 258,502 (rank 31st)
Population per medal: 69,651 (rank 29th)

Summer: 71 gold, 111 silver, 145 bronze (total 327)
Winter: 78 gold, 72 silver, 76 bronze (total 226)
Total: 149 gold, 183 silver, 221 bronze (total 553)

Best sports: Ice Hockey (14 golds, 43.75%, 1st)
                                            Curling (6 golds, 35.29%, 1st)
                                            Freestyle Skiing (12 golds, 21.05%, 1st)

Canada have entered every Winter Games, and every Summer Games besides 1896 and 1980 (which they boycotted). The 1984 Games were by far their most successful Summer Games, winning 10 golds and 44 medals in total. They finished 6th in the medal table – their only post-war top-10 finish (their highest overall is 3rd in 1904). They won 7 golds in both 1992 and 2021, with a total of 24 medals in the latter. They have won medals in every Games in which they have competed. The last time they failed to win a gold at a Summer Games was, embarrassingly, their own Montreal Games of 1976.

Incredibly, their most recent gold-less Winter Games was also at home, in Calgary in 1988. Their best three Winter Games were 2010 (in Vancouver, where they well and truly laid their hosting hoodoo to rest), 2014 and 2018. In 2010, they topped the medal table for the only time, with 3rd-place finishes in the other two. They won 14, 10 and 11 golds, and 26, 25 and 29 medals respectively.

SUMMER
Artistic Swimming (3-4-1, 3rd). Carolyn Waldo won solo and duet golds in 1988, and Sylvie Frechette was eventually awarded solo gold in 1992, after a judge's inputting error had originally cost her.

Golf (1-0-0, 3rd=). George Lyon took gold in 1904. Their best position since the 2016 reintroduction is 7th.

PWDS (2-0-1, 4th). Canada took both Olympic Lacrosse titles (1904 and 1908); they took bronze in 1904 too, represented by the Mohawk Indians, and including players such as Man Afraid Soap and Rain in Face.

Triathlon (1-1-0, 6th=). Simon Whitfield took gold in 2000 and silver in 2008. These remain the only top-eight finishes for Canada.

Football (2-0-2, 8th). Took women's bronze in 2012 and 2016, and gold in 2021. The men took gold in 1904, since when they have participated only in 1976 and 1984, when they came 5th.

Rowing (10-17-16, 9th). Regular medallists ever since 1904, but Canada's only two golds this century have both been in eights (men in 2008 and women in 2021). Kathleen Heddle and Marnie McBean both won three golds – pairs and eights in 1992, and double sculls in 1996.

Canoeing (4-11-11, 17th). The last of their four golds was won by Adam van Koeverden in 2004. They have won medals at every Games since 1996.

Athletics (17-18-33, 13th). Percy Williams (1928) and Donovan Bailey (1996) are the two Canadians to have won men's 100m golds (given that Ben Johnson was of course disqualified in 1988). They are also the two Canadians to have won two Athletics golds – Williams also took the 200m in 1928, whilst Bailey won the 4x100m relay in 1996. They have not won a women's gold since 1928, despite 12 women's medals since then.

Swimming (9-18-28, 10th). George Hodgson (1912, men's 400m and 1500m freestyle) and Alex Baumann (1984, men's 200m and 400m individual medley) won two golds each. 17 medals this century, but only 2 golds. One of those went to Penny Oleksiak, who won 7 medals in all in 2016 and 2021, a Canadian record in all sports, Summer and Winter.

Shooting (4-3-2, 20th). Only one medal since 1956 – a gold for Linda Thom in women's sport pistol in 1984.

Tennis (1-0-0, 17th=). Men's doubles gold for Sebastien Lareau and Daniel Nestor in 2000. Aged 43, Nestor then came 4th in the doubles in 2016, Canada's only other top-4 finish.

Equestrianism (2-2-3, 13th). Gold in 1968 (team jumping) and 2008 (individual jumping, Eric Lamaze). Lamaze also took team silver that year, and individual bronze in 2016. In 2008, 61-year old Ian Millar, attending the ninth of his record ten Olympics, won his only medal – a team jumping silver.

Boxing (3-7-7, 18th). The only gold since 1932 was won in 1988 by British-born Lennox Lewis, who soon returned to Britain and became professional world champion. Canada's last Boxing medal came in 1996.

Gymnastics (4-3-2, 17th). Only one medal prior to 2000 – Lori Fung's gold in the rhythmic all-around in 1984. Only one medal ever in artistic Gymnastics – Kyle Shewfelt's gold in men's floor exercises in 2004. The other 7 medals have all come in trampolining, including two golds for Rosannagh MacLennan (2012 & 2016).

Weightlifting (2-2-1, 24th). All five medals have come in middleweight. Two men's silvers (1952 and 1984) preceded a bronze (2008) and gold (2012) for Christine Girard, and a gold for Maude Charron (2021).

Diving (1-5-8, 10th). Sylvie Bernier (women's springboard, 1984) is the only champion. All but one of the other medals have come since 1996.

Cycling (2-5-9, 15th). Both golds came in women's sprint – Lori-Ann Muenzer (2004) and Kelsey Mitchell (2021). No men's medals since 1996.

Wrestling (3-7-7, 23rd). All 17 medals have been in freestyle. Daniel Igali won men's gold in 2000; all six medals since then have been for women, including golds for Carol Huynh and Erica Wiebe.

Rugby (0-0-1, 8th=). Women's bronze in 2016. The men came 8th in 2021.

Baseball/Softball (0-0-1, 8th=). Softball bronze in 2021, and 4th in 2008. Came 4th in Baseball in 2004.

Beach Volleyball (0-0-1, 11th=). John Child & Mark Heese got men's 1996 bronze. Also 6 quarter-final losses.

Sailing (0-3-6, 28th). Only one medal since 1992 – silver in the men's Star in 2004.

Judo (0-2-5, 31st=). Won men's silvers in 1964 and 2000. The 2021 Games saw the first two women's medals.

Taekwondo (0-1-1, 25th=). A bronze in 2000 and silver in 2008, both for women. No male top-eight finish yet.

Basketball (0-1-0, 13th=). Silver (1936) for the men, who came 4th in 1976 & 1984, as did the women in 1984.

Fencing – Nine top-eight finishes, covering years from 1932 to 2021. They came 4th in the men's team épée in 1984, and 4th in the women's equivalent in 2004.

Volleyball – The Canadian men came 4th in 1984, and 8th in 2016 and 2021. The women's best is 8th (1976 and 1984).

Badminton – Only one top-eight finish – Alex Bruce and Michelle Li came 4th in women's doubles in 2012.

Hockey – The women came 5th in 1984, and 6th and 7th in the two Games after that. The men's best is 10th (achieved four times).

Archery – Three top-eight finishes, but none since 1976. Lucille Lemay's 5th place that year is the best.

Water Polo – All three top-eight finishes were achieved by the women (5th in 2000, and two 7th places). The men's best is 9th in 1976.

Handball – Entered only in 1976, when they were the host nation. Both men and women lost every game – the men came 11th and the women 6th (only 6 entered).

Karate – Canada's only entrant, Daniel Gaysinsky, came 7th in the 2021 men's >75kg event.

Table Tennis – Chinese-born Johnny Huang won four matches in the 1996 men's singles on his way to 7th place. It remains Canada's only appearance in the last eight of an Olympic Table Tennis event.

Modern Pentathlon – The men's team came 10th in 1988. Melanie McCann came 11th in the women's in 2012.

Skateboarding – Four entrants in 2021, the best of whom was Micky Papa (10th in men's street).

Sport Climbing – 14th in the women's event in 2021, and 17th in the men's.

Surfing – never entered

WINTER
Ice Hockey (14-6-3, 1st). Canada's national obsession. From the sport's introduction in 1920 (in the Summer Games), Canada won six of the first seven titles, but after 1952, it took them until 2002 to win gold again (also taking the title in 2010 and 2014). Canada are more dominant in the women's event. It was introduced in 1998; in the seven finals since then, they have won five (beating the USA in four of them), and lost to the USA in the other two. Jayna Hefford, Hayley Wickenheiser and Caroline Ouellette won four golds each.

Curling (6-3-3, 1st). The men have only failed to medal once since 1998, and won gold in 2006, 2010 and 2014, remarkably with entirely different players each time. The women have only failed to medal twice in that time, and won gold in 1998 and 2014. In 2018, John Morris and Kaitlyn Lawes won the inaugural mixed doubles, making them the first Canadians to win two golds (having previously won in 2010 and 2014 respectively).

Freestyle Skiing (12-12-6, 1st). Alexandre Bilodeau won men's moguls in both 2010 and 2014.

Short Track Speed Skating (10-13-14, 3rd). Canada have medalled at every Games since 1992. Charles Hamelin won four golds between 2006 and 2022, a record for any Canadian outside of Ice Hockey.

Skeleton (2-1-1, 4th). Men's golds for Duff Gibson (2006) and Jon Montgomery (2010). A single women's bronze was gained in 2006.

Snowboarding (5-5-7, 3rd). Max Parrot has one medal of each colour (2018-22). The first gold went to Ross Rebagliati, who originally lost it after testing positive for cannabis, only for the medal to be restored on appeal.

Bobsleigh (5-2-4, 4th). Golds in four-man (1964), two-man (1998 & 2018) and two-woman (2010 & 2014).

Figure Skating (6-11-12, 5th). Canada's stand-out stars are Tessa Virtue and Scott Moir, who combined for ice dance golds in 2010 and 2018, and both won team gold in 2018 as well.

Speed Skating (10-16-16, 6th). Gaetan Boucher (1984) and Catriona Lemay-Doan (1998 & 2002) have two golds each. Canada have medalled in each Games since 1994.

Alpine Skiing (4-1-7, 10th). All four golds went to women, the most recent being Kerrin Lee-Gartner in 1992. Just three bronzes since then, all for men.

Biathlon (2-0-1, 8th). All three medals won by Miriam Bedard – bronze in 1992, and two golds in 1994. The best in a men's event is 5th.

Nordic Skiing (2-1-0, 10th). Golds for Beckie Scott (2002) and Chandra Crawford (2006), and women's team silver in 2006. Canada have twice (2010 and 2018) finished 4th in men's events.

Luge (0-1-1, 7th). Both medals came in 2018 – Alex Gough with women's single bronze, and she also helped the mixed relay team take silver.

Ski Jumping (0-0-1, 13th=). Won mixed team bronze in 2022. The only other top-eight finish was 7th in the men's large hill in 1988.

Nordic Combined – The only Winter sport in which Canada have never won a medal – and they've never come close. Jostein Nordmoe came 10th in the men's event in 1932. Their best since then is 25th.

MEXICO   **Olympic Rank 45th**
Population: 129,875,529 (rank 10th)
Olympic rank/ population differential: -35
Population per gold: 9,990,425 (rank 86th)
Population per medal: 1,779,117 (rank 96th)

Summer: 13 gold, 24 silver, 36 bronze (total 73)
Winter: *no medals (best finish: 11th)*
Total: 13 gold, 24 silver, 36 bronze (total 73)

Best sports: Taekwondo (2 golds, 4.17%, 6th)
                                          Football (1 gold, 2.86%, 20th=)
                                          Equestrianism (2 golds, 1.31%, 14th)

Mexico, hosts of the 1968 Summer Games, have by some distance the fewest gold medals of any nation ever to have hosted an Olympics; they have 13, whereas the next fewest is Brazil's 37 (it should be noted that Bosnia & Herzegovina haven't won any, though they were part of Yugoslavia when they hosted the 1984 Winter Games). The first Mexicans to compete in the Olympics were a men's Polo team in Paris in 1900, consisting of three Mexican brothers and a fourth player who may have been either Mexican or American. They lost their only match 8-0, but have been retrospectively awarded a joint bronze medal anyway. They next appeared at the Olympics in 1924; they failed to win a medal either then or in 1928, but have won medals at every Games since.

Mexico's most successful Games were, probably not surprisingly, their home Games of 1968. With 3 golds, 3 silvers and 3 bronzes, it was their highest total of golds, and of overall medals, and highest medal table position (15th). In overseas Games, the most medals they have won is 8 (2012), the most golds is 2 (1948, 1984 and 2008), and their highest position 17th (1948 and 1984). However, they can be hit and miss – there have been several Games, most recently 1996, when they have won only a single medal, and in Tokyo in 2021 they won only four bronzes, but no golds or silvers.

Impressively, Mexico do not rely on one or two sports for their success. Their 73 medals have been won across 16 different sports. The most golds they have won in one sport is 3 in Athletics. All of them came in the walking events, for Daniel Bautista in 1976, and Ernesto Canto and Raul Gonzalez both in 1984. In fact, of Mexico's 11 Athletics medals, only one was not in a walking event – a silver in the women's 400 metres in 2004.

In 2008, they won two Taekwondo golds, meaning Taekwondo became one of three sports where they have won two golds, following Equestrianism (both in 1948) and Boxing (both in 1968). The two Equestrian golds were won by Humberto Mariles in the individual jumping, and by Mariles's team in the team event. It means Mariles is the only Mexican ever to have won two Olympic golds. He was later given 25 years in prison for shooting a man, then released by presidential pardon, only to be arrested for drug smuggling; he died whilst awaiting trial.

The sport to have produced most medals overall for Mexico is Diving – 1 gold, 7 silver and 7 bronze spread between 1948 and 2021. The first four of them were all won by Joaquin Capilla; in men's platform he won bronze in 1948, silver in 1952 and gold in 1956, beating his American rival by 152.44 points to 152.41. He also won springboard bronze in 1956, making him the most decorated Mexican Olympian, with four medals in all. Mariles won three, as did Maria Espinoza in women's heavyweight Taekwondo (gold in 2008, bronze in 2012 and silver in 2016). Diving does not appear on the list of best sports above due to there being only 1 gold, but it has provided 67 top-eight finishes for Mexico, the next most being the 39 in Athletics.

Mexico's most recent gold was in men's Football, beating Brazil in the final in 2012. There have been just two medals in Swimming, both in their home Games of 1968. Felipe Munoz won a surprise gold in the men's 200m breaststroke, perhaps the most fondly remembered of all Mexican golds (it was the only gold of their home Games besides the two in Boxing), and there was a bronze in the women's 800m freestyle as well. The only sport thus far unmentioned to have produced gold is Weightlifting (one in 2000), whilst medals have also come in Archery, Basketball, Cycling, Fencing, Modern Pentathlon, Shooting and Wrestling.

Mexico entered the four-man Bobsleigh at the Winter Games of 1928, finishing 11th out of 23. But this would remain their only Winter participation until 1984. They have entered all Games since then other than 1998 and 2006, but have not come close to emulating that position of 1928 (the best they have managed in any event since is 22nd, in men's Figure Skating in 2022).

BERMUDA   **Olympic Rank 99th**

Population:	72,576 (rank 195th)
Olympic rank/ population differential:	+96
Population per gold:	72,576 (rank 8th)
Population per medal:	36,288 (rank 15th)
Summer:	1 gold, 0 silver, 1 bronze (total 2)
Winter:	*no medals (best finish: 19th)*
Total:	1 gold, 0 silver, 1 bronze (total 2)
Best sports:	Triathlon (1 gold, 7.69%, 8th=)
	Boxing (1 bronze, 61st=)
	Sailing

Bermuda have a strong claim to be one of the biggest Olympic overachievers anywhere in the world. Given their tiny population, and the fact that, as a British Overseas Territory, they are not even an independent country, their record really is remarkable.

Their Olympic debut came as long ago as 1936, when a number of swimmers took part. Since then, they have competed in all Summer Games except the boycotted Moscow Games of 1980. Since that 1936 debut, Bermuda have competed in Swimming in most Olympics, but have never finished higher in any event than their 14th place in the men's 4x200m freestyle relay on that first appearance (this was out of a field of 18).

One of Bermuda's impressive achievements is that they have managed no fewer than 11 top-eight finishes in Olympic competition, and those came in four different sports. Their first was in 1964, finishing 5th in Sailing's Dragon class. Sailing also produced another 5th place in 1984 (in the Tornado), and 4th and 8th in the Star, in 2000 and 2004 respectively, for the pairing of Peter Bromby and Lee White.

Bermuda have only entered four Olympic Boxing competitions. They began with a first-round exit in 1972, before two quarter-finals in 1976. One (Robert Burgess in the light-heavyweight) happened by default, as he received a bye into the last 16, followed by a walkover as his Ethiopian opponent was withdrawn due to the African boycott. But the other was Clarence Hill, who beat opponents from Iran (with a knockout in the last 16) and Belgium (with a unanimous quarter-final decision) to earn a bronze medal. It made Bermuda the least populated country ever to earn an Olympic medal, a record they would hold until 2021. Their last Boxing appearance was in 1988, when they got through the first round but no further.

There have been three top-eight finishes in Athletics. In 1988, Nick Saunders finished 5th in the men's high jump. In 1992 and 1996, Brian Wellman finished 5th and 6th respectively in the men's triple jump. But the real Bermudan glory has been produced by triathlete Flora Duffy. Born in Bermuda to parents who hailed from Barrow-in-Furness and Burnley, both in England's north-west, she first entered Olympic Triathlon in 2008, aged 20, when she failed to finish after being lapped during the cycling section. In 2012, she finished 45th, improving to 8th in 2016 and, finally, taking a historic gold in Tokyo in 2021. A few days later, a Shooting bronze for San Marino robbed Bermuda of their position as the least-populated medalling nation, but they are still the least-populated gold medalling nation. Duffy's achievement earned her a damehood.

Other sports Bermuda have entered in the Summer Games are as follows: Equestrianism (every Games from 1984 to 2012, highest finish of 29th equal); Diving (three times, highest finish of 10th in 1948); Rowing (three times, highest finish of 16th in both 1972 and 2016); Tennis (one entry in 1988, but lost in straight sets in the first round); and Cycling (road race entries in 1984 and 1996, but none of them managed to finish).

Bermuda have even taken part in every Winter Games from 1992 to 2018 too, albeit with just one participant each time – and in 2022 they missed out on the Winter Games for the first time in over 30 years. Simon Payne took part in Luge in 1992 and 1994, Patrick Singleton in the same event in 1998 and 2002, before switching to Skeleton for 2006, and Tucker Murphy entered the Nordic Skiing in 2010, 2014 and 2018. Their highest finish is Singleton's Skeleton placing of 19th out of 27.

CHAPTER TWO - Central America (Costa Rica, Panama, Guatemala, Nicaragua, Honduras, El Salvador, Belize)

COSTA RICA	**Olympic Rank 91st**
Population:	5,256,612 (rank 124th)
Olympic rank/ population differential:	+33
Population per gold:	5,256,612 (rank 75th)
Population per medal:	1,314,153 (rank 88th)
Summer:	1 gold, 1 silver, 2 bronze (total 4)
Winter:	*no medals (best finish: 41st)*
Total:	1 gold, 1 silver, 2 bronze (total 4)
Best sports:	Swimming (1 gold, 0.17%, 30th)
	Cycling
	Taekwondo

Costa Rica's Olympic medal-winning history is very much a family affair. Their first medal, won 52 years after the country first entered the Olympics, was a silver medal in the 1988 women's 200m freestyle Swimming, won by 17-year old Sylvia Poll, finishing behind Heike Friedrich of East Germany. Her sister Claudia, two years younger, followed in Sylvia's footsteps, and went on to outdo her big sister on the Olympic stage.

In 1996, Claudia secured a shock gold medal in the same event (200m freestyle) – Costa Rica's only gold medal in Olympic history to date. It was also the first gold medal ever won by any Central American country – only Irving Saladino of Panama (2008) has added to the region's tally since. Claudia carried on to Sydney in 2000, where she won a bronze in the same event, as well as another bronze in the 400m freestyle. These remain Costa Rica's only four Olympic medals.

Furthermore, Sylvia finished 5th in the 100m freestyle and 6th in the 100m backstroke in 1988, and 7th in the 200m backstroke in 1992. Claudia also finished 5th in the 400m freestyle in 1996. In all, Costa Rica have secured 14 top-eight finishes in Olympic history. Eight of those, as we have seen, have gone to the Poll sisters, and there was another in women's Swimming too – Maria Paris finished 7th in the 100m butterfly in 1980.

The other five top-eight finishes for Costa Rica have come in four different sports. In Cycling, they finished 6th in the 1996 men's cross-country, and 4th in the 2021 men's BMX freestyle – Kenneth Tencio missing out narrowly on what would have been Costa Rica's first ever non-Swimming, non-Poll sister medal (he scored 90.50, with the British bronze medallist getting 90.80).

Meanwhile, Kristopher Moitland finished 6th in the 2008 men's heavyweight Taekwondo (he was originally 7th, but moved up a place when the Cuban competitor was disqualified for deliberately kicking the referee in the face). Costa Rica also finished 7th in the 2021 women's Surfing event, and 8th in the men's Football in 2004. The nation's best ever finish in an Athletics event was the 9th place achieved by Andrea Vargas in the women's 2021 100m hurdles (she was just 0.02 seconds off a place in the final).

Costa Rica's first ever Olympian was Bernardo de la Guardia, who entered the men's sabre Fencing in 1936, winning one bout (against a Greek) and losing five. He remained his nation's only Olympian until 1964, when a couple of men entered the Judo competition. They have entered every Summer Games since then.

Costa Rica's greatest Winter Olympian is Arturo Kinch. Born in Costa Rica, he went to college in the USA, where he played Football and Basketball, but then turned to Alpine Skiing, and became Costa Rica's first ever Winter Olympian in 1980, finishing 41st in the downhill, which is still Costa Rica's highest finish in a Winter event. In 1984 and 1988, he competed in both Alpine Skiing and Nordic Skiing, before returning to compete in Olympic Nordic Skiing again in 2002 and 2006 (by which time he was 49 years old, and finished 95th in the 15km event). The only other Winter sport they have entered is Biathlon, and the only time Costa Rica have entered the Winter Olympics without Kinch on the team was 1992 (they have not competed at all since 2006).

PANAMA   **Olympic Rank 98th**

Population:	4,404,108 (rank 128th)
Olympic rank/ population differential:	+30
Population per gold:	4,404,108 (rank 71st)
Population per medal:	1,468,036 (rank 93rd)
Summer:	1 gold, 0 silver, 2 bronze (total 3)
Winter:	*never participated*
Total:	1 gold, 0 silver, 2 bronze (total 3)
Best sports:	Athletics (1 gold, 0.10%, 60th)
	Weightlifting
	Boxing

Panama's first Olympian was Adan Gordon, who entered two Swimming events in 1928 and went out in the first round of both. After a 20-year gap, their second Olympian entered in 1948, and he was a revelation. Lloyd LaBeach was the only Panamanian in the Olympics that year; he entered the 100 and 200 metres, and won the bronze medal in each. Born and initially raised in Panama, his family later moved to Jamaica (where they were initially from), and he then honed his Athletics ability at the University of California. He had in fact broken the 200-metre world record shortly before the 1948 Games.

In 1952, again Panama was represented by a single individual – in this case weightlifter Carlos Chavez, who finished last after failing to complete his lifts. After not travelling to Melbourne for the 1956 Games, Panama entered the Games in 1960, with a bigger contingent this time, and have entered every Summer Games since, with the exception of Moscow 1980. They have never entered the Winter Games.

Since the exploits of LaBeach in 1948, Panama have only won one further Olympic medal. Irving Saladino had finished 36th in the men's long jump in 2004, and would fail even to register a mark in qualifying in 2012. But in 2008 things fell nicely and he won the gold medal itself (he had also won gold in the World Championships in 2007). In both Olympic and World Championship history, he remains Panama's only gold medallist. On returning from the 2008 Games, he was a national hero, with government offices and schools closed in his honour.

In all, Panama have finished in the top eight of an Olympic event eleven times. Eight of those eleven have come in Athletics. Besides their three medals, they finished 7th in the women's 4x100m relay in 1960, 5th in the men's 100 metres in 1976 (Guy Abrahams), 5th in the men's 400m hurdles in 2004 (Bayano Kamani), 7th in the men's 200 metres in 2016 (Alonso Edward – who is Panama's only other medallist in the Athletics World Championships, winning a silver behind Usain Bolt in 2009) and 7th in the women's 400m hurdles in 2021 (Gianna Woodruff).

The other three top-eight finishes came in three different sports. In 1984, Jose Diaz came 7th in the men's flyweight Weightlifting. In 2012, Carolena Carstens came 8th in the women's flyweight Taekwondo by default; she lost in the first round, but the fact that the person who beat her ended up in the final meant that Carstens ended up in the repechage, guaranteeing her a top-eight finish despite the fact that she lost in the first round of that as well. Finally, in 2021, Atheyna Bylon beat an Australian in the first round to reach the last eight of the women's middleweight Boxing – she finished 8th in the end.

Other than the four sports in which Panama have finished in the top eight, the other sports that they have contested down the years have been Basketball (1968 only), Canoeing (1996 only), Gymnastics (2016 only), Cycling (2021 only), Swimming, Wrestling, Judo, Fencing and Shooting. In Swimming, their best finish has been 14th in the women's 50m freestyle in 2004.

GUATEMALA   **Olympic Rank 119th**
Population: 17,980,803 (rank 69th)
Olympic rank/ population differential: -50
Population per gold: n/a
Population per medal: 17,980,803 (rank 129th)

Summer: 0 gold, 1 silver, 0 bronze (total 2)
Winter: *no medals (best finish: 27th)*
Total: 0 gold, 1 silver, 0 bronze (total 2)

Best sports: Athletics (1 silver, 78th=)
                                            Taekwondo
                                            Badminton

Guatemala made their Olympic debut in 1952, entering a sizeable team. But they didn't enter again until 1968, since when they have entered all Summer Games. They took 60 years in all to win their first and, to date, only Olympic medal when Erick Barrondo won a silver in the men's 20km walk in 2012. It was perhaps a surprise that Athletics provided their long-awaited medal, given that they have never finished higher than 12th in any other Athletics event.

They have finished fourth in Olympic events three times – Oswaldo Mendez in show jumping (1980), Heidy Juarez in women's welterweight Taekwondo (2004) and the celebrated Kevin Cordon in men's singles Badminton (2021). In all, they have secured 15 top-eight finishes, with the other eleven coming in Taekwondo and Shooting (three times each), Football, Boxing, Sailing, Swimming and Wrestling. The Football was their first ever top-eight finish (in 1968), whilst their national best in Swimming came in 2021 (Luis Martinez came 7th in the men's 100m butterfly).

Guatemala made their Winter Olympic debut in 1988, entering no fewer than six competitors (four Alpine skiers and two Nordic skiers) but have, strangely, never entered since. Fiamma Smith finished 27th in the women's slalom, and 29th in the giant slalom, for their best two finishes.

NICARAGUA   **Olympic Rank 141st**
Population: 6,359,689 (rank 110th)
Olympic rank/ population differential: -31

Summer: *no medals (best finish: 4th)*
Winter: *never participated*

Best sports: Baseball
                                            Weightlifting
                                            Taekwondo

Nicaragua first entered the Olympics in 1968, and have entered every Summer Games since, with the exception of 1988, which they opted not to enter. They have never entered the Winter Games. The closest they have ever come to a medal was in the 1996 Baseball competition (the only time they have qualified for the Olympic Baseball). Four wins out of seven in the group stage put them into the semi-finals, but predictably heavy defeats to Cuba in the semis and the US in the bronze medal match meant they had to settle for 4th.

They have had two other top-eight finishes. Lucia Castaneda originally finished 9th out of 10 in the women's middleweight Weightlifting in 2012, but re-testing of samples several years later led to three disqualifications and Castaneda being bumped up to 6th. The other was in the men's heavyweight Taekwondo of 2000 (the only time Nicaragua have ever entered Olympic Taekwondo). Carlos Delgado lost both his matches, but the tournament format meant he secured 7th place (out of 12 entrants) anyway.

Nicaragua's best Athletics finish is 18th in the 1968 men's shot put (there were 19 entries, with El Salvador finishing 19th). Their best in Swimming is 20th in the 1996 men's 200m individual medley. Nicaragua have also competed in Boxing, Shooting, Judo, Cycling, Rowing and Wrestling.

HONDURAS   Olympic Rank 143rd
Population: 9,571,352 (rank 95th)
Olympic rank/ population differential: -48

Summer: *no medals (best finish: 4th)*
Winter: *no medals (best finish: 50th)*

Best sports: Football
                                               Weightlifting
                                               Taekwondo

Honduras made their Olympic debut in 1968. They fielded six people, all in men's Athletics, and all went out in the first round. They didn't enter in 1972, stuck to men's Athletics again in 1976, and stayed at home again in 1980. Swimming and Judo were added in 1984, Boxing in 1988, Weightlifting and Fencing in 1992, Football in 2000, Table Tennis in 2004, Taekwondo and Rowing in 2008 and Wrestling and Shooting in 2012.

Honduras's greatest achievements in the Olympics have come in men's Football – the particular entry requirements (under-23 squads with three overage players) suit them well, as they have never been particularly competitive in the World Cup. They have qualified for every tournament since 2000 (except for 2004), finishing 10th in 2000, 7th in 2012 and 4th in 2016 (they sensationally eliminated Argentina in the group stage and beat South Korea in the quarter-finals, but lost 6-0 to Brazil in the semis and 3-2 to Nigeria in the bronze medal match). Their only other top-10 finish was a 10th place in men's middle-heavyweight Weightlifting in 2012. They have finished 12th in both Taekwondo and Wrestling. In Swimming, their best is 16th (out of 16) in women's 200m butterfly in 2021. In Athletics, their best finish is 27th in the men's 20km walk in 1976.

In Albertville in 1992, Jenny Palacios-Stillo represented Honduras in three events in Nordic Skiing. In all three of them, she was the slowest finisher by some distance, but in each case was ranked ahead of various non-finishers. Nobody else has ever represented Honduras in a Winter Games.

EL SALVADOR   Olympic Rank 148th
Population: 6,602,370 (rank 109th)
Olympic rank/ population differential: -39

Summer: *no medals (best finish: 5th)*
Winter: *never participated*

Best sports: Cycling
                                               Shooting
                                               Wrestling

El Salvador have shown commendable aptitude in a wide variety of Olympic sports since their debut in 1968 (they have competed every time since except 1976 and 1980), but have never competed in the Winter Games. They have recorded top-16 finishes in Cycling, Shooting, Wrestling, Weightlifting, Judo, Boxing, Football, Swimming, Athletics and Rowing. But unfortunately, taking that next step has proved difficult, and they have only breached the top eight twice.

The first of these came in 1996, when San Francisco-born cyclist Maureen Kaila finished fifth in the women's points race. The other came in 2008, when Luisa Maida finished eighth in the women's sport pistol event in Shooting.

In Swimming, their best finish has been 14th (in the women's 4x100m medley relay in 1968 and the men's 4x100m freestyle relay in 1972). Their best finish in an individual Swimming event is 20th. In Athletics, their best again came on debut in 1968 – shot putter Rosario Martinez finishing 14th (and last, 2½ metres behind the next-to-last finisher) in the women's event. El Salvador's best four finishes in Athletics have all come last in their events – the best finish that didn't equate to last place was 24th in the men's 50km walk in 2012.

BELIZE   **Olympic Rank 188th**
Population: 419,137 (rank 173rd)
Olympic rank/ population differential: -15

Summer: *no medals (best finish: 12th)*
Winter: *never participated*

Best sports: Athletics
                                     Taekwondo
                                     Cycling

For a country that has never finished higher than 12th in any Olympic event, Belize have entered a lot of competitors over a lot of Games. Although they have never entered the Winter Olympics, they have entered every Summer Games since their debut in 1968, with the exception of Moscow 1980.

They have entered eight sports in all although, strangely, Swimming is not amongst them. Athletics has seen their biggest successes – reaching the men's 400m hurdles semi-finals twice (Jonathan Williams came 12th in 2008, and Kenneth Medwood 17th in 2012). Belize have entered Taekwondo only once, in the men's flyweight in 2008. Alfonso Martinez lost in the first round, but lost only 2-1, which placed him 12th overall out of 16. They entered Cycling in 1968, and again from 1984 to 1996; their best finish is 19th in the men's sprint in 1988.

They entered two Judo events, one each in 2012 and 2016, losing in the first round both times. They entered Shooting between 1968 and 1976, but never finished higher than 47th. They entered a single weightlifter in 1968, who finished 19th, a single boxer in 1984, who lost in the first round, and a single canoeist in 2021, who finished 23rd and 25th in the two events he entered.

CHAPTER THREE - Caribbean, Greater Antilles (Cuba, Jamaica, Bahamas, Dominican Republic, Puerto Rico, Haiti, Cayman Islands)

CUBA   **Olympic Rank 20th**

Population: 10,985,974 (rank 85th)
Olympic rank/ population differential: +65
Population per gold: 129,247 (rank 17th)
Population per medal: 46,551 (rank 22nd)

Summer: 85 gold, 69 silver, 82 bronze (total 236)
Winter: *never participated*
Total: 85 gold, 69 silver, 82 bronze (total 236)

Best sports: Baseball/Softball (3 golds, 27.27%, 3rd)
Boxing (41 golds, 15.47%, 2nd)
Volleyball (3 golds, 10.00%, 6th)

Cuba are that rarest of specimens – a communist country whose Olympic record has stayed steady since the 1970s, and continues to be most impressive. They are by far the most successful country in Olympic history never to have participated in the Winter Games – nobody else has won more than 8 Summer golds without participating at least once in Winter competition, let alone the 85 that Cuba have won.

They first entered the Games in 1900, when their only competitor, Ramon Fonst, took a gold and silver in Fencing. Fonst returned to take a further two individuals golds in 1904, with fellow fencer Ramon Diaz also taking one, and both contributing to a team gold too. Their only other entrant that year was Felix Carvajal, who came 4th in the marathon (the top non-American), despite turning up in his street clothes (he had his trousers cut off at the knee just before the race started), and getting stomach cramp from eating bad apples during the race.

The only other pre-war Games Cuba entered were 1924 and 1928, when their small teams did not win any medals. Since the war, they have entered all Games other than their boycotts in 1984 (in opposition to the USA) and 1988 (in solidarity with North Korea). They won silver medals in 1948, 1964 and 1968 and, although it took until 1972 to win their first gold since 1904, they have prospered since then. In Barcelona in 1992, they won a record 14 golds and 31 medals overall. They finished 5th in the medal table that year, having finished 4th in 1904 (4 golds) and 1980 (8 golds). In fact, they finished in the top ten of all the Games they entered from 1976 to 2000, and have had top-20 finishes at all Games since.

SUMMER
Baseball/Softball (3-2-0, 3rd). Due to the US not using major league players at the Olympics, Cuba were the pre-eminent force when Baseball entered the Olympics in 1992. They won the first two golds, before surprisingly losing the 2000 final to the US. They won again in 2004, but lost the 2008 final to South Korea. Baseball was then dropped from the Games; it returned in 2021, but Cuba weren't there, having lost to Venezuela and Canada in qualifying. They entered Softball only in 2000, coming 7th.

Boxing (41-19-18, 2nd). Cuba won no Boxing medals until 1968, but won 3 golds in 1972, and have become synonymous with Olympic Boxing ever since. No fewer than nine Cubans have won two Olympic golds each, and a further two true legends, Teofilo Stevenson (heavyweight, 1972 to 1980) and Felix Savon (heavyweight, 1992 to 2000) have won a barely credible three in a row. Only one non-Cuban (Hungarian Laszlo Papp) has ever done likewise. Since 1972, the only year that they failed to win a gold was 2008, but they did win four silvers and four bronzes instead. Overall, Boxing has accounted for very nearly half of all Cuba's gold medals.

Volleyball (3-0-2, 6th). Cuba's women had a great run of three successive golds in 1992, 1996 and 2000 (when they came from 2 sets down in the final against Russia), followed by bronze in 2004 (having narrowly lost to China in the semi-final). Six women were part of all three gold-winning teams. The men have had to make do with a single bronze in 1976.

Judo (6-15-16, 6th). Won their first Judo medal in 1976, and have won medals at every Games they've entered since then. Their six golds have all gone to different people, including women's heavyweight Idalys Ortiz, who won bronze in 2008, gold in 2012, and silvers in 2016 and 2021.

Wrestling (11-6-10, 6th). It took until 1992 for Cuba to win a Wrestling medal, but they have won plenty since. Feliberto Ascuy won back-to-back golds in 1996 and 2000, but his achievement is dwarfed by that of the sensational Mijain Lopez, who has won four Greco-Roman super-heavyweight golds in a row (2008 to 2021). He is the only male wrestler ever to do so, and won his last three finals by shutout.

Fencing (5-3-3, 9th). After 5 golds and a silver in 1900 and 1904 (mostly by Ramon Fonst – see above), the other five medals came between 1992 and 2000.

Taekwondo (1-2-3, 14th=). The only gold was won in 2000 by Angel Matos. But in a bronze medal match in 2008, Matos was disqualified for taking too long on a medical timeout, kicked the referee in the face in anger, and was banned from the sport for life.

Athletics (11-14-20, 17th). Their first medal was a silver for Enrique Figuerola in the men's 100 metres in 1964. Cuba won silvers in both sprint relays in 1968, and their first two golds both came in 1976, when Alberto Juantorena won the men's 400m/800m double (still the only person since 1906 to do so). Cuba have continued to produce Athletics stars – 1992 high jump champion Javier Sotomayor is still the world record holder, sprint hurdle champions Anier Garcia (2000) and Dayron Robles (2008) are household names across the world, as is 2000 long jump champion Ivan Pedroso. Their most recent Athletics gold medallist is Yipsi Moreno (women's hammer, 2008).

Weightlifting (2-1-5, 25th). Daniel Nunez (1980) and Pablo Lara (1996) have won gold. Lara previously won a silver in 1992. All four Cuban medals since 1996 have been bronze.

Canoeing (1-3-0, 25th). After two silvers in 2000 and one in 2004, Cuba's first gold came in 2021, courtesy of Serguey Torres and Fernando Jorge (men's C2 1000m).

Shooting (1-1-3, 34th). The 3 bronzes came in 1980, 2004 and 2008. The gold and silver were both won by Leuris Pupo in men's rapid-fire pistol (2012 and 2021 respectively).

Basketball (0-0-1, 19th=). The men won bronze in 1972 with a 66-65 win over Italy, but haven't competed since 1980. The women (who came 4th in 1992) last competed in 2000.

Sailing (0-1-0, 34th=). Three top-eight finishes, all for Carlos de Cardenas in the Star. He won silver alongside his son (also Carlos) in 1948, and in 1952 they came 4th. In 1956, he partnered his other son, Jorge, coming 6th.

Cycling (0-1-0, 35th=). Their four top-eight finishes were all between 2008 and 2016, and all in women's track events. Yoanka Gonzalez won silver in the points race in 2008.

Swimming (0-1-1, 42nd=). First entered in 1948, they have participated in most, but not all, Games since. They have only ever won two medals, and incredibly they were in the same event, in the same year. Rodolfo Falcon and Neisser Bent came 2nd and 3rd respectively behind American Jeff Rouse in the men's 100m backstroke in 1996. Their next best finish is 7th, achieved in 1956, 1992 and 2012.

Diving – 4th in the men's synchronised springboard in 2004; their five best finishes were all between 2004 and 2012.

Rowing – Six top-eight finishes between 1980 and 2016; their best was 5th in the 1980 men's coxed pairs.

Gymnastics – Three of their five top-eight finishes came in 1980, when the competition was devalued by boycotts. The other two were earned by Manrique Larduet in 2016, including their best finish yet – 5th in the men's parallel bars.

Water Polo – Five entries for the men from 1968 to 1992; their best finish was 5th in 1980.

Beach Volleyball – Have only missed one Games since the sport was introduced in 1996. Came 5th in the men's event in 2016, their best finish yet.

Archery – First entered in 2000. Juan Carlos Stevens became Cuba's only quarter-finalist, finishing 5th in 2008.

Hockey – Only entered once – in the men's competition in 1980. A competition decimated by boycotts, Cuba were drafted in at the last minute; they beat the one team even weaker than them – Tanzania – but lost heavily to the other four countries, and finished 5th out of 6.

Football – Two entries, both for the men; out in the group stage in 1976, and a quarter-final defeat in 1980, following group stage victories over Zambia and Venezuela.

Handball – Their only two entries were in the men's competitions of 1980 and 2000; finished 11th both times.

Modern Pentathlon – They finished 15th on their first entry, in the 2008 men's competition; they have not finished as high in their entries since.

Table Tennis – Despite a number of entries, they had never reached the last 16 of any event until 2021, when they were one of 16 pairs in the mixed doubles; they lost in straight sets.

Artistic Swimming – Just one entry; they came 18th in the duet in 2000.

Badminton – Their only entry was in men's singles in 2016; they won the first match but lost the second, and failed to reach the round of 16.

Equestrianism, Golf, Karate, Rugby, Skateboarding, Sport Climbing, Surfing, Tennis, Triathlon, PWDS – never entered

WINTER
Alpine Skiing, Biathlon, Bobsleigh, Curling, Figure Skating, Freestyle Skiing, Ice Hockey, Luge, Nordic Combined, Nordic Skiing, Short Track Speed Skating, Skeleton, Ski Jumping, Snowboarding, Speed Skating – never entered

JAMAICA   **Olympic Rank 35th**

Population:	2,820,982 (rank 140th)
Olympic rank/ population differential:	+105
Population per gold:	108,499 (rank 12th)
Population per medal:	31,344 (rank 13th)
Summer:	26 gold, 36 silver, 26 bronze (total 88) *(plus British West Indies: 2 bronzes)*
Winter:	*no medals (best finish: 9th)*
Total:	26 gold, 36 silver, 26 bronze (total 88) *(plus British West Indies: 2 bronzes)*
Best sports:	Athletics (26 golds, 2.48%, 8th)
	Cycling (1 bronze, 39th=)
	Swimming

Jamaica earned their independence from the UK in 1962, but by then they had already competed in several Olympic Games. They made their debut in 1948, and have competed at all Summer Games since, although in 1960 they competed alongside athletes from Trinidad & Tobago and Barbados as part of the British West Indies team. That team won two medals that year, both bronze, one of which was an individual bronze for a Jamaican and the other of which was for a relay team consisting of three Jamaicans and a Barbadian. Therefore, I have allocated these medals to Jamaica for the purposes of this book. Including those two medals, Jamaica have won 90 Olympic medals in all; 89 of those have come in Athletics. Of those 89, 53 have come in the three sprint events of 100 metres, 200 metres, and the 4x100m relay. A further 31 have come in the 400 metres, 4x400m relay, 400m hurdles and 100/110m hurdles. There have also been three medals in the 800 metres and two in the long jump (none of them gold), but none at all in any longer running distance, or any other field event.

Jamaica's first Olympic champion was medical student Arthur Wint, who took the men's 400 metre title in 1948. That title was retained for Jamaica in 1952 by George Rhoden who, along with Wint, also helped them win the 4x400m relay. In 1956 there were no medals at all, in 1960 they won two bronzes for the British West Indies as mentioned earlier, and in 1964, there were again no medals. They have medalled at all Games since, but in ten Olympics from 1956 to 1992 they won just one gold – Don Quarrie in the 200 metres, thus making up for the disappointment of being pipped to gold in the 100 metres by Trinidad & Tobago's Hasely Crawford.

In 1996, Jamaica won one gold – Deon Hemmings in the women's 400m hurdles, but in 2000 they won 6 silvers and 3 bronzes, but no golds. Their reputation as being an Olympic "nearly" team was summed up by Merlene Ottey. She appeared in seven Olympic Games, more than anybody else in Athletics, starting in 1980 and not ending until 2004, when she was 44 and competing for Slovenia. She won nine medals for Jamaica, but none of them gold. Jamaica's emergence as a force in Olympic sprinting events only began as recently as 2004. The person who kick-started this charge was Veronica Campbell (later Campbell-Brown), who came home from Athens with golds in the women's 200 metres and 4x100m relay, and a bronze in the 100 metres. Retaining her 200-metre title in 2008, she finished her Olympic career with 3 golds, 3 silvers and 2 bronzes. Jamaica's other highly decorated Olympians have included Elaine Thompson-Herah, who won the 100/200m double in both Rio 2016 and Tokyo 2021, and has 5 golds and a silver so far, and her great rival Shelly-Ann Fraser-Pryce (women's 100m champion in 2008 and 2012, and a medal record of 3 golds, 4 silvers and a bronze).

But Jamaica's (and possibly the world's) greatest Olympian is the incomparable Usain Bolt. Charismatic and universally popular, he burst onto the scene in 2008, winning the 100 metres in a world record time despite running with his shoelace undone and slowing down to showboat well before the finish. He also won the 200 metres and 4x100m relay, both in world record times too. In London 2012, he retained all three titles, and in Rio 2016, he retained all three titles again. Unfortunately, he has since lost the 2008 relay gold due to the doping infringement of his teammate, but he still has eight Olympic medals, all of them gold. A true legend.

Jamaica's best Olympics by golds is 2016 (6), their best by total medals is 2012 (12), and their best by position in the medal table is 1952 (13th). David Weller is the only Jamaican to win a medal in anything other than Athletics, taking a bronze in Cycling's men's 1km time trial in 1980. He also finished 6th in 1984. The only other top-eight finishes have been three in Boxing, and four in Swimming, including 4th places in women's 400m freestyle (2000) and women's 100m breaststroke (2012). Jamaica made their Winter Olympic debut in 1988, when they famously competed in Bobsleigh, finishing 30th out of 40 in the two-man event. They have competed in all Winter Olympics since, other than 2006, mainly in Bobsleigh but also in Freestyle Skiing (2010), Skeleton in (2018) and Alpine Skiing (2022). Their best finish is an impressive 9th for Errol Kerr in Freestyle Skiing's men's ski cross in 2010.

BAHAMAS   **Olympic Rank 54th**
Population: 358,508 (rank 176th)
Olympic rank/ population differential: +122
Population per gold: 44,814 (rank 4th)
Population per medal: 22,407 (rank 7th)

Summer: 8 gold, 2 silver, 6 bronze (total 16)
Winter: *never participated*
Total: 8 gold, 2 silver, 6 bronze (total 16)

Best sports: Athletics (7 golds, 0.67%, 27th)
                                         Sailing (1 gold, 0.52%, 26th)
                                         Tennis

By the measure of Olympic rank/ population differential, the Bahamas are the biggest overachievers in this book. Ranked 176th by population, they are 54th on the all-time medal table. They are not one-trick ponies either. Yes, the vast majority of their success has come in Athletics, but they have produced top-eight finishes in four other sports as well.

They first entered the Games in 1952, more than 20 years before they gained full independence from the United Kingdom. Since then, they have missed only the boycotted 1980 Moscow Games, although they have never entered the Winter Olympics. On their debut, they entered only Sailing, and their best achievement was 5th place in the Star class for Durward Knowles and Sloane Farrington. The pair had finished 4th in the previous event in London in 1948, representing Great Britain. In 1956, they paired up again, finishing 3rd this time and winning the Bahamas's first Olympic medal. In 1960, they finished 6th. In 1964 Knowles, now partnering Cecil Cooke, won gold in a thrilling tight finish against the Americans. But Knowles wasn't finished yet. He returned to the Olympics, with different partners each time, in 1968, 1972 and, at the age of 70, 1988. He is one of the very few sportsmen to have competed in Olympics 40 years apart. He died, aged 100, in 2018, a true Bahamian legend.

The Bahamas never finished in the top-eight of a Sailing event after 1968, as Athletics took over. They had reached the men's 100 metre final in 1964, but in 1992 they won their first Olympic medal in the sport, as well as their first in any sport for 28 years – a bronze for Frank Rutherford in the men's triple jump. Since then, they have won a further 13 Olympic medals – all in Athletics. They have won at least one Athletics medal at every Games in that period.

In 1996, they won silver in the women's sprint relay. In 2000, Pauline Davis-Thompson won gold in both the women's 200 metres and sprint relay – the nation's first golds since Knowles and Cooke in 1964. The sprint relay gold was perhaps not surprising, given that the Bahamas had three women in the individual 100-metre final. There was also a men's 4x400m bronze, which meant 2000 was the only year to see the Bahamas win three Olympic medals. In 2004, Tonique Williams-Darling won the women's 400 metres, and Debbie Ferguson won bronze in the 200 metres. Ferguson, having been part of the sprint relay teams of 1996 and 2000, now had three Olympic medals, sharing the Bahamian record with Davis-Thompson, who was also part of both sprint relays. The 2008 Games were the only ones this century without a gold, but there was a silver for the men's 4x400m team and a bronze for Leevan Sands in the men's triple jump.

The only medal from London 2012 was a gold for the men's 4x400m team, defeating the US team in a thrilling finish, in an event the US pretty much always won. Shaunae Miller then won the women's 400 metres in 2016 and, having married and amended her name to Shaunae Miller-Uibo, defended the title in 2021. It made her the second Bahamian, after Davis-Thompson in 2000, to win two Olympic golds. Steven Gardiner won the men's race too, to complete a Bahamian 400-metre double.

Just three of their 55 top-eight finishes have come in sports other than Athletics or Sailing. In 2000, Mark Knowles and Mark Merklein finished 5th in men's doubles Tennis (losing their quarter-final 14-12 in the final set), in 2008 Toureano Johnson came 8th in men's welterweight Boxing, and in 2012 Arianna Vanderpool-Wallace came 8th in women's 50m freestyle Swimming.

DOMINICAN REPUBLIC   **Olympic Rank 68th**

Population: 10,790,744 (rank 86th)
Olympic rank/ population differential: +18
Population per gold: 3,596,915 (rank 68th)
Population per medal: 899,229 (rank 80th)

Summer: 3 gold, 5 silver, 4 bronze (total 12)
Winter: *never participated*
Total: 3 gold, 5 silver, 4 bronze (total 12)

Best sports: Boxing (1 gold, 0.38%, 39th)
                    Athletics (2 golds, 0.19%, 43rd=)
                    Taekwondo (1 silver, 1 bronze, 25th=)

The Dominican Republic have participated in every Summer Games since their initial foray back in 1964, but have never yet participated in the Winter Games. For the first 20 years, they did not really make a name for themselves, and failed to manage a top-eight finish in any of the sports they entered. However, they have done pretty well since then. In 1984, they saw two of their boxers reach the quarter-finals. One of them, Pedro Nolasco, won four fights in a row to earn himself a bronze in men's bantamweight – his nation's first Olympic medal. By the time they won another, Nolasco would be dead – murdered during an attempted robbery in 1995. The Dominican Republic had another Boxing quarter-finalist in 1988, and two more in 1992, the same year in which their men's team finished 6th in the inaugural Olympic Baseball competition. In 1996, they again finished out of the top eight in all their events, whilst in 2000, they managed just a single top-eight finish (8th in women's heavyweight Weightlifting).

Since 2004, in contrast, they have won medals at every Games. This run was kicked off in Athens by the most celebrated Dominican sportsperson in history. Going into the Games, Felix Sanchez had not lost in the men's 400m hurdles for three years, and he comfortably kept that run going with gold in Athens. He had been born in New York and raised in California, but he proudly wore the shirt of his parents' country throughout his career. Injuries led to a lack of form in 2008, but he returned to form in London 2012, and regained gold in impressive fashion.

Besides Sanchez's two golds, the Dominican Republic have won three other Athletics medals. Luguelin Santos took silver in the men's 400 metres in 2012, and Marileidy Paulino won silver in the women's 400 metres in 2021. The two then teamed up as part of the mixed 4x400m relay team that took silver behind Poland in the event's inaugural Olympic showing in Tokyo in 2021. This made Santos and Paulino (with two silvers each) the only Dominicans besides Sanchez (with two golds) to win more than one Olympic medal.

The country's other Olympic gold medal was won by Felix Diaz, in men's light-welterweight Boxing in 2008. Diaz turned professional the following year, and his medal remains the only one (of any colour) won by the Dominican Republic in Boxing since Bolasco in 1984. Also in 2008, Yulis Gabriel Mercedes took silver in men's flyweight Taekwondo, with Luisito Pie taking bronze in the same event eight years later.

Besides those already mentioned in Athletics, Boxing and Taekwondo, the Dominican Republic have won a further three Olympic medals, all in 2021. Two of these were in Weightlifting – Zacarias Bonnat in men's light heavyweight (silver), and Crismery Santana in women's heavyweight (bronze). The other was a bronze medal in men's Baseball, on that sport's return to the Games. They beat South Korea 10-6 in the bronze medal match. This made it five medals in all in Tokyo; the most they had ever won at any previous Games was two. As only nine nations have ever won medals in Baseball/ Softball, this is the only sport where the Dominican Republic are in the top 20 of the medal table.

Other than their five medal-winning sports, the Dominican Republic have also had top-eight finishes in women's Table Tennis (2008), women's Gymnastics (2012), men's Judo (2016) and women's Volleyball (2012 and 2021). In Swimming, they have never finished higher than 27th (women's 200m backstroke in 2021).

PUERTO RICO **Olympic Rank 79th**

Population:	3,057,311 (rank 138th)
Olympic rank/ population differential:	+59
Population per gold:	1,528,656 (rank 54th)
Population per medal:	305,731 (rank 56th)

Summer:	2 gold, 2 silver, 6 bronze (total 10)
Winter:	*no medals (best finish: 24th)*
Total:	2 gold, 2 silver, 6 bronze (total 10)
Best sports:	Tennis (1 gold, 1.33%, 17th=)
	Athletics (1 gold, 0.10%, 61st=)
	Boxing (1 silver, 5 bronzes, 48th)

Although Puerto Rico is not an independent country (it is still owned by the United States), they have been sending a team to the Olympic Games ever since 1948. They have not missed a Summer Games since then. In that time, they have won ten medals, all won by different athletes in individual events.

The first six of these ten medals all came in men's Boxing. The trailblazer was Juan Venegas, who claimed bronze in bantamweight in 1948. This was the last year in which losing semi-finalists in Boxing had to compete for bronze, rather than both being given medals; Venegas beat his Spanish opponent to claim Puerto Rico's first Olympic medal. Bronzes have also been claimed by Orlando Maldonado (1976 light flyweight), Aristides Gonzales (1984 middleweight), Anibal Acevedo Santiago (1992 welterweight) and Daniel Santos (1996 welterweight). One Puerto Rican, however, went one better – Luis Ortiz reached the final of the 1984 lightweight event with victory over his Cameroonian semi-final opponent, but lost to American Pernell Whitaker in the final and settled for silver.

Since then, Puerto Rico's Boxing performances have fallen off, but other sports have come to the fore. In 2012, they won two medals in one Games, an achievement they have only managed on one other occasion (1984). Jamie Espinal became the second Puerto Rican to win a silver. He beat Soslan Gattsiev of Belarus to reach the final of the men's freestyle light-heavyweight Wrestling, but lost to Sharif Sharifov of Azerbaijan in the final. This was only the second time Puerto Rico had managed a top-eight finish in Wrestling. In the same year, they won their first Olympic Athletics medal, courtesy of Javier Culson's bronze in the men's 400m hurdles (he had twice won silvers in the world championships).

In both 2016 and 2021, they won just one medal each time, but on both occasions it was gold – the first two Olympics golds they have ever won. The first of them was something of a sensation, as it was won in the women's singles Tennis by Monica Puig, who only once reached the last 16 of a grand slam event throughout her career (and never further). Along the way she defeated three recent grand slam champions – Garbine Muguruza (Spain), Petra Kvitova (Czech Republic) and Angelique Kerber (Germany). After the Games, her form fell away almost immediately, and she never scaled such heights again, but she remains the only Puerto Rican even to reach the last 16 in an Olympic Tennis event, and will always remain the first Puerto Rican ever to win an Olympic gold. In 2021, Jasmine Camacho-Quinn was amongst the favourites for the women's 100m hurdles, and won easily. American born and raised, she qualified for Puerto Rico through her mother.

In Swimming, Puerto Rico have reached the last eight three times. Ricardo Busquets did it twice in 1996 (finishing 7th and 8th), but the closest to a medal was Carlos Berrocal, who came 4th in the men's 100m backstroke in 1976. Puerto Rico have also clocked up top-eight finishes in men's Basketball five times, as well as Baseball, Softball, Diving, Gymnastics, Sailing, Shooting, Skateboarding, Taekwondo and Weightlifting.

Puerto Rico entered the Winter Olympics from 1984 to 2002, and again in 2018 and 2022. The most recent Games have provided their best finish – 24th (out of 25) in the women's Skeleton.

HAITI   **Olympic Rank 117th**

Population:	11,470,261 (rank 83rd)
Olympic rank/ population differential:	-34
Population per gold:	n/a
Population per medal:	5,735,131 (rank 113th)
Summer:	0 gold, 1 silver, 1 bronze (total 2)
Winter:	*no medals (best finish: 34th)*
Total:	0 gold, 1 silver, 1 bronze (total 2)
Best sports:	Athletics (1 silver, 78th=)
	Shooting (1 bronze, 56th=)
	Boxing

Haiti were one of the earliest countries to embrace the Olympics, entering a couple of fencers into the 1900 Paris Games, neither of whom progressed beyond the first round. However, at the same Games the Haitian-born Constantin Henriquez was part of France's gold-medal winning Rugby team. He played his club rugby in France, and is generally considered the first black person to compete, let alone win gold, in the Olympics.

By coincidence, the next Games Haiti entered, in 1924, were again in Paris. Competing in Shooting and Athletics, they won their first medal, a bronze in the team free rifle (3 positions) event. Four years later, Sylvio Cator won silver in the men's long jump. At this point, Haiti couldn't have imagined that, nearly a century later, this would still be the most recent Haitian Olympic medal.

Strangely, despite their Shooting medal in 1924, they never entered Olympic Shooting again. In 1928 and 1932, they stuck to Athletics, and didn't enter again until a solitary weightlifter in 1960. They next entered in 1972, and have entered all Summer Games since, except 1980. Between 1928 and 2000, their only top-eight finish was in Boxing in 1976. The only other sport to produce a top-eight finish for Haiti has been Taekwondo.

The best Athletics achievement since the 1928 silver is Dudley Dorival's 7th place in the 2000 men's 110m hurdles. In Swimming they have never managed better than 37th. Haiti's only Winter Olympian thus far is Richardson Viano, who competed in two Alpine Skiing events in 2022, finishing 34th in one and failing to finish in the other.

CAYMAN ISLANDS   **Olympic Rank 164th**

Population:	65,483 (rank 196th)
Olympic rank/ population differential:	+32
Summer:	*no medals (best finish: 8th)*
Winter:	*no medals (best finish: 69th)*
Best sports:	Athletics
	Swimming
	Sailing

The Cayman Islands were governed as part of Jamaica until the latter's independence in 1962, since when they have been a British Overseas Territory. They have entered all Summer Olympics since 1976, apart from 1980. In 1976, they entered just one event, in Sailing. They have since debuted in Cycling (1984), Athletics (1988), Swimming (2004) and Gymnastics (2021). They have also produced one Winter Olympian – Dow Travers, who entered one Alpine Skiing event in 2010 and two in 2014, but only finished one of them – in 69th place.

Probably the best-known Caymanian Olympian is sprinter Cydonie Mothersill, who finished 8th in the women's 200m in 2008 – the Islands' only top-eight finish in Olympic history. She also won a world championship bronze in 2001. Brett Fraser is the Islands' most successful swimmer, finishing 12th in the men's 200m freestyle in 2012. Their best finish in any of the other three summer sports in which they've entered is 19th in Sailing in 1996.

CHAPTER FOUR - Caribbean, Lesser Antilles (Trinidad & Tobago, Grenada, US Virgin Islands, Barbados, British Virgin Islands, St Kitts & Nevis, St Lucia, Antigua & Barbuda, Dominica, Aruba, St Vincent & the Grenadines)

TRINIDAD & TOBAGO **Olympic Rank 67th**
Population: 1,407,460 (rank 156th)
Olympic rank/ population differential: +89
Population per gold: 469,153 (rank 38th)
Population per medal: 74,077 (rank 32nd)

Summer: 3 gold, 5 silver, 11 bronze (total 19)
Winter: *no medals (best finish: 28th)*
Total: 3 gold, 5 silver, 11 bronze (total 19)

Best sports: Athletics (3 golds, 0.29%, 38th)
  Weightlifting (1 silver, 2 bronzes, 47th=)
  Swimming (1 bronze, 48th=)

Trinidad & Tobago did not gain independence from the UK until 1962, but had by then already competed at the Summer Olympics of 1948, 1952 and 1956, and as part of the British West Indies team of 1960. They have not missed a Summer Games since, and have finished in the top eight of at least one event each time.

The first Trinidadian Olympic hero was weightlifter Rodney Wilkes, who took silver in the featherweight category in 1948, and bronze in 1952. With Lennox Kilgour's bronze in middle heavyweight in 1952, Weightlifting looked like the national speciality, but after a 4th place and a 7th place in 1956, they have not finished in the top eight of any Weightlifting event since.

T&T have won 16 Olympic medals since then, and 15 of them have come in Athletics. The first three all came in 1964 – Wendell Mottley (silver in men's 400 metres), Edwin Roberts (bronze in men's 200 metres) and a bronze in the men's 4x400m relay. After that glut of medals, the next seven Games produced only one more medal between them – but it was the biggest one of the lot. Don Quarrie of Jamaica was the favourite for the 1976 men's 100-metre final, but in a thrilling finish, he was pipped on the line by Hasely Crawford, who duly became Trinidad and Tobago's first Olympic champion, and later had his country's national stadium named after him.

After a 20-year gap, a further four medals followed in 1996 and 2000, and all four were won by the nation's next sprinting hero, Ato Boldon. In 1996, he won bronzes in both the men's 100 and 200 metres, and followed that with further medals in 2000, a silver in the 100 and another bronze in the 200. He is the only T&T athlete to have four Olympic medals. The only medal in 2004 came not in Athletics but in Swimming – a bronze for George Bovell in the men's 200m individual medley. This was one of only two top-eight finishes Trinidad & Tobago have managed in Swimming – the other was also courtesy of Bovell, in the 50m freestyle in 2012.

Back to Athletics, and 2008 saw two medals. In the men's 100 metres, Richard Thompson finished a distant 2nd behind Usain Bolt, whilst the sprint relay team also finished a distant 2nd behind Bolt's Jamaica team. However, the latter silver was later upgraded to gold when Bolt's teammate Nesta Carter was retroactively found guilty of doping offences. With a silver in the sprint relay in 2012, it made Thompson, with one gold and two silvers, statistically the most successful Trinidad & Tobago Olympian of all time. The 2012 Games also saw bronzes for Lalonde Gordon in the men's 400 metres, and for the men's 4x400m relay team, as well as a gold – T&T's third Olympic gold – for Keshorn Walcott in the men's javelin – not an event with any kind of Caribbean pedigree whatsoever. It made 2012 the country's most successful Games yet (1 gold, 1 silver, 2 bronzes). Walcott followed it up with a bronze in 2016.

Besides their three medal sports, Trinidad & Tobago have achieved top-eight finishes in just two other sports – Taekwondo once, and Cycling eight times (three in the sprint, four in the 1km time trial, and one in the keirin). They have been to the Winter Olympics four times (1994, 1998, 2002 and 2022), but on each occasion entered only the two-man Bobsleigh event. Their best finish is 28th out of 30 in 2022, beating the teams of Brazil and Jamaica.

GRENADA   Olympic Rank 95th

Population:	114,299 (rank 185th)
Olympic rank/ population differential:	+90
Population per gold:	114,299 (rank 13th)
Population per medal:	38,100 (rank 17th)

Summer:	1 gold, 1 silver, 1 bronze (total 3)
Winter:	*never participated*
Total:	1 gold, 1 silver, 1 bronze (total 3)
Best sports:	Athletics (1 gold, 0.10%, 55th=)
	Taekwondo
	Boxing

Grenada's Olympic pedigree is all about one man – the man who has won all three of their Olympic medals. The nation first entered the Olympics in Los Angeles in 1984. They have entered all Summer Games since, but never yet ventured to the Winter Games. Their best performer on that first occasion was welterweight boxer Bernard Wilson, who got through one contest before losing in the last 16. Over the next four Games (1988 to 2000), Grenada only had one top-16 finish, and even that was a boxer who didn't have to win a match to get that far.

In 2004 however, they had a semi-finalist in the women's 400 metres, as well as a finalist in the men's 400 metres. Alleyne Francique had to settle for fourth place in that final, behind three Americans. There were no particularly noteworthy achievements in Beijing in 2008, but then came London. Andrea St Bernard finished 8th in women's welterweight Taekwondo, albeit doing so by default without winning a match, as her first-round conqueror reached the final, thus dropping St Bernard into the repechage and guaranteeing a top-eight finish. It remains Grenada's only top-eight finish in a sport other than Athletics. But 2012 was all about Grenada's first ever Olympic medal – and a gold at that.

Kirani James was born in Grenada and had shown immense talent in a number of prestigious international youth events before being recruited by the University of Alabama. Once in the US, he improved still further, and comfortably won the 400 metres final in London. He would medal again in the same event in the next two Games. In Rio in 2016, he won silver behind Wayde van Niekerk of South Africa. The race was a historic one for Grenada, as they had two athletes in the line-up – Bralon Taplin finished 7th. James went on to secure bronze in Tokyo in 2021. He was awarded a CBE in 2022.

The gold medal of 2012 made Grenada, at the time, the smallest country (by population) ever to win a Summer Olympic gold medal (Liechtenstein, which is less populous, has won two Winter golds). Grenada's record was usurped by Bermuda in 2021, though Grenada is still the least populous independent country ever to win a Summer gold.

Grenada have secured a total of seven top-eight finishes in Olympic competition. Besides the three for James, and the aforementioned ones for Francique, St Bernard and Taplin, the other was Lindon Victor's 7th place in the 2021 men's decathlon.

Grenada have only ever entered four Olympic sports. Besides Athletics (which they have entered every time since 1984), Taekwondo (in which St Bernard's 8th place is their only entry so far), and Boxing (which they have entered in 1984, 1988 and 2008, but only ever won one match), their other entries have been in Swimming. They have entered in every Games since 2000, other than 2008, and never yet finished higher than 41st.

US VIRGIN ISLANDS   **Olympic Rank 128th**
Population:						104,917 (rank 187th)
Olympic rank/ population differential:		+59
Population per gold:				n/a
Population per medal:				104,917 (rank 38th)

Summer:						0 gold, 1 silver, 0 bronze (total 1)
Winter:						*no medals (best finish: 16th)*
Total:						0 gold, 1 silver, 0 bronze (total 1)

Best sports:					Sailing (1 silver, 34th=)
						Athletics
						Boxing

The US Virgin Islands have sent a number of athletes to every Summer Games since debuting in 1968, with the exception of Moscow 1980, when they joined the boycott led by their mother country, the United States. They have entered Athletics every time, Sailing every time except 2021 and Swimming every time since 1976. They have also participated in Boxing, Shooting, Equestrianism and Cycling in multiple Games, as well as Weightlifting (1968), Wrestling (1976), Fencing (1984) and Archery (2021) once each.

Sailor Peter Holmberg is the Virgin Islands' only Olympic medallist, winning silver in the Finn in 1988; he had also finished 11th in the event in 1984, the country's second-best Sailing performance. Their only other top-eight performance was the 8th place achieved by LaVerne Jones in the women's 200m in 2012 (she actually finished 9th, missing out on the final, but one of the finalists subsequently failed a drugs test). The nation's best Swimming finish is 13th in the men's 4x200m freestyle relay in 1988.

The Virgin Islands have competed in all Winter Games since 1988 with the exception of 2010 and 2018. They have competed in four sports in total – Alpine Skiing (best finish 28th), Bobsleigh (best finish 28th), Skeleton (best finish 25th) and Luge, which has provided their best five Winter Olympic performances, four of them by Anne Abernathy in the women's singles, including the national best of 16th in 1988.

BARBADOS   **Olympic Rank 131st**
Population:						303,431 (rank 178th)
Olympic rank/ population differential:		+47
Population per gold:				n/a
Population per medal:				303,431 (rank 55th)

Summer:						0 gold, 0 silver, 1 bronze (total 1)
Winter:						*never participated*
Total:						0 gold, 0 silver, 1 bronze (total 1)

Best sports:					Athletics (1 bronze, 88th=)
						Swimming
						Cycling

Most of the top Barbadian sportspeople of all time have been cricketers (Gary Sobers and Malcolm Marshall to name but two). But in the Olympic sphere, nobody can touch Obadele Thompson. He finished 4th in the 200 metres in two Games running (1996 and 2000 – he missed out on a medal in the latter by less than 0.01 seconds), but he did win the bronze in the 100 metres in 2000, his nation's only Olympic medal to date. He later married US drug cheat Marion Jones. The best Olympic finish by any other Barbadian is 5th, achieved by Leah Martindale (women's 50m freestyle Swimming in 1996) and Ryan Brathwaite (men's 110m hurdles in 2012). The only other sport in which they have had a top-eight finish is Cycling (Barry Forde came 6th in the sprint in 2004). They have competed in ten other sports over the years at the Summer Olympics, but have never competed at the Winter Games.

Barbados have competed in every Summer Games since 1968, with the exception of the Moscow boycott. In 1960, the British West Indies competed at the Games, representing Jamaica, Trinidad & Tobago and Barbados. They won two bronze medals, including one in the men's 4x400m relay, where Barbadian Jim Wedderburn competed alongside three Jamaicans.

BRITISH VIRGIN ISLANDS   **Olympic Rank 144th**
Population: 39,369 (rank 200th)
Olympic rank/ population differential: +56

Summer: *no medals (best finish: 4th)*
Winter: *no medals (best finish: 27th)*

Best sports: Athletics
                   Sailing
                   Freestyle Skiing

The British Virgin Islands have entered every Summer Games since 1984, but have only competed in three sports in that time – Athletics (every time), Sailing (1984 to 1996) and Swimming (2016 and 2021). In Sailing, their best finish is 17th out of 24 (in the Soling class in 1992). Both of their Swimming entries have been by Elinah Phillip in the women's 50m freestyle; she finished 48th in 2016, and improved to an impressive 34th (out of 81) in 2021.

Most of their Olympic entries, though, have been in Athletics. They have entered the 100, 200, 400 and 800 metres, the 4x100m and 4x400m relays, and the high jump, long jump, shot put and discus. They have twice finished within the top 16 of an Athletics event, both in 2021. Chantel Malone qualified for the final of the women's long jump in 5th place, but finished 12th in the end. Meanwhile, Kyron McMaster finished 4th in the men's 400m hurdles, so his nation's wait for a first Olympic medal goes on.

The BVI have, rather unfathomably, also entered the Winter Olympics twice. In 1984, Erroll Fraser entered two Speed Skating events (he is thought to have been the only black competitor in Olympic Speed Skating in the 20th century), whilst in 2014 Peter Crook secured the nation's highest Winter finish of 27th out of 28 in the Freestyle Skiing halfpipe event.

SAINT KITTS & NEVIS   **Olympic Rank 152nd**
Population: 54,817 (rank 197th)
Olympic rank/ population differential: +45

Summer: *no medals (best finish: 6th)*
Winter: *never participated*

Best sports: Athletics

Saint Kitts and Nevis first entered the Olympics in 1996, and have entered every Summer Games since. However, they have not only never entered the Winter Games (unsurprising in itself), but remarkably they have never entered any Summer sport besides Athletics. The only other country to share this "feat" is South Sudan, but in their case, they have only been competing since 2016. In fact, their involvement has been even more restrictive than that – only ever entering races over 100, 200 and 400 metres, as well as the 4x100m and 4x400m relays.

Their biggest Olympic star, of course, has been sprinter Kim Collins. He has won five world championship medals, including the 100 metres gold in 2003, but on the Olympic stage he has sadly been less successful. Nonetheless, his finishes of 7th and 6th in the 100 metres of 2000 and 2004 respectively, and 6th in the 200 metres of 2008, are the only top-eight finishes his country have ever achieved on the Olympic stage. He first competed in the Olympics in 1996, and didn't bow out until 2016, by which time he was 40 years old. Despite his age, he still reached the semi-finals of the 100 metres. The best finish by St Kitts in any event not featuring Kim Collins was 13th by Tiandra Ponteen in the women's 400 metres in 2004.

SAINT LUCIA   **Olympic Rank 155th**
Population: 167,591 (rank 182nd)
Olympic rank/ population differential: +27

Summer: *no medals (best finish: 6th)*
Winter: *never participated*

Best sports: Athletics
                           Sailing
                           Swimming

Saint Lucia also first entered the Olympics in 1996, and have also never competed in the Winter Games. They have, however, entered other sports besides Athletics, albeit only Sailing (1996, and 2012-21) and Swimming (2000-21). In Sailing, they have stuck to men's laser and women's laser radial, and never finished higher than 28th. In Swimming, they have stuck to races of 50 or 100 metres, and never finished higher than 36th.

Most of their entries, though, have been in Athletics. They have entered a variety of events – 100 and 400 metres, 4x400m relay, marathon, high jump, pole vault, long jump and javelin. Their best four finishes in Olympic history have all been achieved by the same woman – high jumper Levern Spencer. First entering in 2008, she has finished 24th, 18th, 6th and 24th respectively. In 2016, she was just four centimetres short of the gold medallist (1m93 as compared to 1m97). In 2018, she won her nation's first ever Commonwealth Games gold medal in any sport.

ANTIGUA & BARBUDA   **Olympic Rank 171st**
Population: 101,489 (rank 188th)
Olympic rank/ population differential: +17

Summer: *no medals (best finish: 9th)*
Winter: *never participated*

Best sports: Athletics
                           Canoeing
                           Sailing

Antigua and Barbuda gained full independence in 1981, but had by then already participated in the 1976 Games. They missed 1980, but have entered all Summer Games since 1984. They have never entered the Winter Games. They have competed in Athletics (every time), Cycling (every time up to 1996, but not since), Canoeing (1996 only), Boxing (1988 and 2021), Sailing (1984 to 2000, and returning in 2021), and Swimming (2004 onwards).

All of their best performances have come in Athletics. Brendan Christian came 9th in the men's 200 metres in 2008, missing out on the final by one place. That equalled Antigua's best ever finish, previously set at the 1984 Games by the women's 4x400m relay team, who came 9th out of 10, ahead of Ghana. Other relay teams have previously finished 11th, 12th, 13th and 14th.

Antigua's best ever finish in any other sport came in men's C2 1000 metres Canoeing in 1996, when their pair came 17th – and last by some distance. In Boxing, they have never won a bout. In Cycling, their best is 23rd out of 25 (two were disqualified). Their best in Sailing is 23rd (out of 24). Finally, their best in Swimming is 44th out of 47 in the men's 200m freestyle in 2016 – finishing ahead of swimmers from Aruba, Samoa and Palestine.

DOMINICA   **Olympic Rank 177th**
Population: 74,656 (rank 194th)
Olympic rank/ population differential: +17

Summer: *no medals (best finish: 10th)*
Winter: *no medals (best finish: 91st (DNF))*

Best sports: Athletics
                                    Swimming
                                    Nordic Skiing

Dominica made their Olympic bow in 1996, and have entered every Summer Games since. On the first two occasions, they entered Athletics and Swimming; since then, they have confined themselves to Athletics. On the two occasions they did enter Swimming, they never entered a race longer than 50 metres, and never finished higher than 60th. But in Athletics, they have had three impressive displays, by three different people. Two of them came in 1996 – Jerome Romain qualified for the men's triple jump final in 10th place, but failed to register jump in the final so finished 12th overall, whilst Dawn Williams finished 10th in the women's 800 metres, narrowly missing a place in the final. Twenty-five years later, Thea LaFond reached the women's triple jump final in Tokyo as the 3rd best qualifier, but finished 12th after two fouls and one effort that was over two metres shorter than her qualifying effort.

Dominica made a surprising, and controversial, sortie into the Winter Olympics in 2014 – the only time they have entered. Their team consisted of New Yorker Gary di Silvestri and his Italian wife Angelica, who used several loopholes to gain not only their Dominican citizenship, but entry into the Games as well. Both were in their late 40s and had never skied to anything like a challenging standard. Entered into one Nordic Skiing event each, Angelica was injured in a training run and failed to start, whilst Gary was one of 91 entrants in the 15km event, but one of four who failed to finish (he had gastroenteritis, and pulled out after around 300 metres).

ARUBA   **Olympic Rank 184th**
Population: 123,702 (rank 183rd)
Olympic rank/ population differential: -1

Summer: *no medals (best finish: 11th)*
Winter: *never participated*

Best sports: Taekwondo
                                    Artistic Swimming
                                    Weightlifting

Prior to 1986, Aruba was part of the Netherlands Antilles, and competed in the Olympics as such. It then seceded, though still comes under the jurisdiction of the Netherlands. They have competed in every Summer Olympics since 1988 in their own right; they have yet to debut in the Winter Games.

Unlike many of the smaller nations, they have competed in a wide variety of sports, though they have never achieved a top 10 finish in any of them. In Athletics, they have only entered the 100m, 200m and marathon, and have not entered at all since 2004; they have never finished in the top 32. Their best swimmer has been Mikel Schreuders, finishing the 100m and 200m freestyle events in 2021 in equal 30th and 33rd respectively.

Technically, their best-placed finisher in any sport came in their one entry in Taekwondo. In 2016, flyweight Monica Pimentel lost in the first round, but only by a single point, seeing her finish 11th out of 16. Their next best is 15th, achieved in the Synchronized Swimming duet in 1988, but that was (by some distance) last place. In Weightlifting, Carl Henriquez finished 16th in the 2012 super-heavyweight; again that was a long way behind anybody else (barring one DNF and 2 disqualifications). They have also, over the years, entered Boxing, Cycling, Fencing, Judo, Sailing and Shooting.

ST VINCENT & THE GRENADINES   **Olympic Rank 186th**
Population: 100,804 (rank 189th)
Olympic rank/ population differential: +3

Summer: *no medals (best finish: 11th)*
Winter: *never participated*

Best sports: Athletics
                                    Swimming

St Vincent & the Grenadines first arrived at the Olympics in 1988. They have competed at every Summer Games since, but have never entered the Winter Games.

They have only ever competed in two sports – Athletics and Swimming, and Athletics has been by far the most successful of the two. Their most successful athlete by some distance has been Eswort Coombs, a 1995 World Student Games gold medallist. In the 1996 400 metres, he finished sixth in his semi-final (11th overall). St Vincent's two next best Olympics finishes of all time were in the 4x400m relays of 1992 and 1996 – Coombs was part of the team both times.

They first entered Swimming in 2000, and have competed every time since bar 2008. All their entries have come in 50m freestyle except one – the 2016 women's 100m breaststroke, in which Izzy Joachim achieved St Vincent's best Swimming finish of 39th (out of 44).

St Vincent did actually once enter another sport in the Olympics. In 1988, Hudson Nanton was named as an entry in the light-heavyweight boxing event, but his opponent was given a walkover – apparently because Nanton was overweight at the weigh-in.

CHAPTER FIVE - South America, North & West (Colombia, Venezuela, Ecuador, Peru, Suriname, Guyana)

COLOMBIA   **Olympic Rank 60th**
Population: 49,336,454 (rank 29th)
Olympic rank/ population differential: -31
Population per gold: 9,867,291 (rank 84th)
Population per medal: 1,451,072 (rank 91st)

Summer: 5 gold, 13 silver, 16 bronze (total 34)
Winter: *no medals (best finish: 20th)*
Total: 5 gold, 13 silver, 16 bronze (total 34)

Best sports: Weightlifting (2 golds, 0.87%, 22nd)
                                Cycling (2 golds, 0.74%, 17th)
                                Athletics (1 gold, 0.10%, 50th)

In the 1900 men's Tug of War, the silver medal was won by France, whose team included Francisco Henriquez de Zubiria, who was born in France to Colombian parents, and appears to have been a Colombian citizen until 1917. The first Colombian to compete under his own flag at the Olympics was Jorge Perry, who entered the men's marathon in 1932 in Los Angeles, but fainted after 10km and failed to finish.

Colombia have entered all Summer Olympics since then, with the exception of 1952. They had a slow start, and prior to 1972 they had only managed two top-eight finishes, both in Cycling (in 1956 and 1964). In 1972, they won their first Olympic medals. The first was a silver, won by Helmut Bellingrodt in Shooting's running game target event. Two Boxing bronzes followed later in the same Games. It was 12 years before another medal followed – another silver for Bellingrodt in the same event. There was another Boxing bronze in 1988, and a bronze in the women's 400 metres in 1992 for Ximena Ristrepo – the first Athletics medal for Colombia. The 1996 Games would be the last so far in which they failed to win a medal – their best finish that year was 5th.

There was only one medal in Sydney 2000, but it was Colombia's first ever gold medal. It was won in women's heavyweight Weightlifting by Maria Isabel Urrutia, who later entered politics and became an MP. In each Games since 2004, Colombia have won at least two medals. They have won a further four golds in that time – one in 2012 and three in 2016. Colombia's greatest Olympian is BMX racer Mariana Pajon. A prodigy from a very young age, Pajon claimed gold in both 2012 and 2016, and a silver behind Great Britain's Beth Shriever in 2021. She is the only Colombian with two golds, the only Colombian with three medals, and the only person from any country with three medals in BMX.

The other two golds in 2016 were won by Oscar Figueroa in men's featherweight Weightlifting (meaning that Colombia's two Weightlifting golds come from opposite ends of the weight spectrum) and Caterine Ibarguen in the women's triple jump. These three golds, as well as two silvers and three bronzes, put Colombia in 22nd place in the 2016 medal table – their best Games to date. In terms of overall medals, however, they did slightly better in 2012, with one gold, three silvers and five bronzes – nine in total.

Other than Pajon, the other Colombians to have won two Olympic medals are Figueroa and Ibarguen (both of whom also won silver in 2012), Bellingrodt (see above), Jackeline Renteria (Wrestling bronzes in 2008 and 2012), Yuri Alvear (Judo bronze in 2012 and silver in 2016), Luis Javier Mosquera (Weightlifting bronze in 2016 and silver in 2021) and Carlos Ramirez (bronzes in BMX, 2016 and 2021). The only sport not mentioned so far in which Colombia have medalled is Taekwondo. In Swimming, their best is 6th place in the 1984 men's 200m breaststroke.

Colombia have entered the Winter Olympics in 2010, 2018 and 2022, participating in Alpine Skiing on all three occasions, and Nordic Skiing and Speed Skating on the latter two. Their best finish is 20th, achieved in two Speed Skating events in 2018 – the men's 500 metres and the women's mass start.

VENEZUELA   **Olympic Rank 66th**

Population:	30,518,260 (rank 50th)
Olympic rank/ population differential:	-16
Population per gold:	10,172,753 (rank 88th)
Population per medal:	1,606,224 (rank 95th)
Summer:	3 gold, 7 silver, 9 bronze (total 19)
Winter:	*no medals (best finish: 28th)*
Total:	3 gold, 7 silver, 9 bronze (total 19)
Best sports:	Fencing (1 gold, 0.43%, 22nd=)
	Boxing (1 gold, 0.38%, 31st)
	Athletics (1 gold, 0.10%, 55th=)

Venezuela appeared at the Olympic Games for the first time in London in 1948. They were represented on that occasion by a single cyclist, but have been well represented at every Summer Olympics since (they were one of a handful nations that boycotted neither 1980 nor 1984). Just four years after their debut, they won their first medal – Arnoldo Devonish claiming bronze in the men's triple jump.

Initially they won medals at eight-year intervals – a bronze in 1960, a gold in 1968 (their first Olympic gold – won by renowned amateur boxer Francisco Rodriguez in the light flyweight), and another Boxing medal (silver this time) in 1976. Medals then came a bit more regularly; another Boxing silver in 1980 was followed by three medals in 1984, which included what is to date still the only Venezuelan medal ever won in Swimming – a bronze for Rafael Vidal in the 200m butterfly.

But then the well ran dry. Having never previously gone consecutive Summer Games without a medal, they now suffered four such ignominies in a row (although in 1992 they did win a couple of medals in the demonstration Taekwondo event). The nation finally found its way back onto the medal podiums in 2004, and have won at least one medal in every Games since. In 2012, Ruben Limardo won Fencing gold in the épée, the nation's second ever gold. Their third came in 2021, courtesy of Yulimar Rojas in the women's triple jump. Having previously won silver in the same event in 2016, Rojas is currently Venezuela's only Olympic multi-medallist in any sport. She has also been crowned world champion no fewer than four times.

Rojas's gold was one of four Venezuelan medals at the 2021 Games – the first time they have won that many at a single Games. It put them joint 46th in the medal table; in contrast, they won just a single medal (albeit gold) in 1968, and finished joint 29th.

In terms of specific sports, six of their 19 medals have come in Boxing, but the other 13 have spread across seven sports – three in Athletics and Weightlifting, two in Cycling and Taekwondo, and one in Fencing, Shooting and Swimming. Further top-eight finishes have come in Judo (seven times, without winning a medal), Gymnastics, Karate, Softball, Tennis and Wrestling.

Venezuela's Winter Olympic experience has been limited. In 1998, 2002 and 2006, they entered the Luge competition – their best finish of 28th being achieved on their debut. Since then, they have only entered one event – the 2014 men's giant slalom Alpine Skiing event – in which they failed to finish.

ECUADOR Olympic Rank 71st

Population:	17,483,326 (rank 70th)
Olympic rank/ population differential:	-1
Population per gold:	5,827,775 (rank 77th)
Population per medal:	3,496,665 (rank 106th)

Summer:	3 gold, 2 silver, 0 bronze (total 5)
Winter:	*no medals (best finish: 108th)*
Total:	3 gold, 2 silver, 0 bronze (total 5)
Best sports:	Weightlifting (1 gold, 0.43%, 36th=)
	Cycling (1 gold, 0.37%, 26th=)
	Athletics (1 gold, 0.10%, 57th=)

Ecuador sent three athletes to the 1924 Games in Paris, but then disappeared from the Olympic scene until 1968. They've entered all Summer Games since then. It took until 1996 for them to win their first medal, but when it came it was a memorable gold in the men's 20km walk for Jefferson Perez. Up to the end of the century, Ecuador had only secured three top-eight finishes in Olympic history. Other than Perez, the other two were both achieved by swimmer Jorge Delgado in the men's 200m butterfly (4th in 1972 and 7th in 1976). Delgado, in fact, still has all five of Ecuador's best Olympic swimming positions (the others were 12th, and two 14ths).

Since the turn of the 21st century, Ecuador have improved hugely, and have managed a further 22 top-eight finishes. Jefferson Perez returned to the 20km walk, finishing 4th in both 2000 and 2004, before securing Ecuador's (and his) second Olympic medal with a silver in 2008. It took until 2021 for anybody other than Perez to win a medal for Ecuador, but they made up for lost time in Tokyo by winning two golds and a silver. Two female weightlifters – Neisi Dajomes (light-heavyweight) and Tamara Salazar (heavyweight) won gold and silver respectively, and Richard Carapaz won the prestigious men's Cycling road race gold as well. In all, 11 of their top-eight finishes have come in Weightlifting (ten of those eleven have been won by women, including four for lightweight Alexandra Escobar, finishing 7th, 4th, 7th and 4th from 2004 to 2016).

Their other top-eight finishes have come in Boxing (3), BMX Cycling (1), and women's freestyle Wrestling (2), as well as one by an athlete besides Jefferson Perez – it was Alex Quinonez, finishing 7th in the men's 200 metres in 2012. Their exploits in Tokyo were enough to rank them 38th in the medal table that year.

Ecuador are the only country ever to have competed in the Winter Olympics without managing to finish in the top 100 of any event. They have only had two entrants – Klaus Jungbluth (who finished 108th in the men's 15km Nordic Skiing in 2018) and Sarah Escobar (who failed to finish in the 2022 women's Alpine Skiing giant slalom).

PERU   **Olympic Rank 88th**

Population: 32,440,172 (rank 46th)
Olympic rank/ population differential: -42
Population per gold: 32,440,172 (rank 95th)
Population per medal: 8,110,043 (rank 120th)

Summer: 1 gold, 3 silver, 0 bronze (total 4)
Winter: *no medals (best finish: 44th)*
Total: 1 gold, 3 silver, 0 bronze (total 4)

Best sports: Shooting (1 gold, 0.33%, 33rd)
Volleyball (1 silver, 15th)
Swimming

The first Peruvian Olympian was Carlos de Candamo, a fencer whose uncle would become President of Peru; he competed in Paris in 1900. The first appearance of an official Peruvian delegation, though, came in Berlin in 1936. They were the victims of some outrageous shenanigans in the Football; having seemingly beaten Austria 4-2 in the quarter-finals (despite having three goals disallowed), the Austrians made dubious allegations of violence by Peruvian players and fans (one allegedly carrying a revolver). Probably under duress from the Nazis, the authorities ordered the match replayed, but the entire Peruvian Olympic team went home in protest. This also meant Peru withdrawing from the Basketball quarter-final.

In 1948, Peru won what is still their only ever Olympic gold medal – Edwin Vasquez comfortably taking the men's 50m free pistol Shooting title. They missed the Games in 1952, but returned in 1956, and have contested every Summer Games since. In that time, they have won three more medals – all silver, and two of them in Shooting again. Francisco Boza in the 1984 trap, and Juan Giha in the 1992 skeet were the men in question (uniquely, Giha was beaten by a Chinese woman, in what was an open event but usually dominated by men).

Their other medal really caught the imagination of the Peruvian public. It was won by the 1988 women's Volleyball team – Volleyball having become a really popular sport back home. In the semi-final against Japan, Peru threw away a two-set lead, but took the decider 15-13 to guarantee themselves a medal. In the final against the Soviets, Peru again threw away a two-set lead, and this time they suffered an agonising defeat after losing the decider 17-15. This was the fifth time in 20 years that Peru reached the last eight of the women's Volleyball, but it hasn't happened since.

In all, Peru have managed 27 top-eight finishes in Olympic competition. These have come in Shooting (9), Volleyball (5), Boxing, Swimming, Taekwondo and Weightlifting (2), and Basketball, Football, Karate, Skateboarding, Surfing (1 each). The last three of those were all sports that debuted at the Olympics in 2021. All of the Volleyball, Weightlifting and Karate ones, and one of the Taekwondo ones, were achieved by women.

One sport that Peru have never managed a top-eight finish in is Athletics; their best finish being the 12th place achieved by Eduardo Jalve in the 1948 men's discus. In 2022, they won their first ever medals in the World Athletics Championships – golds for Kimberly Garcia in both women's walks, so there are high hopes that this may translate onto the Olympic stage before long. Peru's best four Swimming performances have all come from the same man – Juan Carlos Bello, who came 4th in the 200m individual medley in 1968, and 7th in the same event in 1972.

Three Peruvians thus far have competed in the Winter Olympics. The best finish they have achieved is 44th by Ornella Oettl (who was born in Munich to a German father and a Peruvian mother), in the women's Alpine Skiing slalom event in 2022. She had previously competed in 2010 and 2014, as had her brother Manfred (also in Alpine Skiing), as well as Nordic skier Roberto Carcelen (the only one of the three who was born in Peru).

SURINAME   **Olympic Rank 102nd**

Population: 639,759 (rank 168th)
Olympic rank/ population differential: +66
Population per gold: 639,759 (rank 43rd)
Population per medal: 319,880 (rank 59th)

Summer: 1 gold, 0 silver, 1 bronze (total 2)
Winter: *never participated*
Total: 1 gold, 0 silver, 1 bronze (total 2)

Best sports: Swimming (1 gold, 0.17%, 33rd=)
Cycling
Athletics

The exploits of Anthony Nesty in Seoul in 1988 had many people around the world reaching for their atlases, wondering where exactly Suriname is. But let's start at the beginning. Suriname first entered the Olympics in Rome in 1960, when their team consisted of just one man, 800-metre runner Wim Esajas. But disaster was to strike – he was apparently told the wrong time for his heats, and turned up late, before returning home to Suriname having not even competed.

The country didn't compete in Tokyo in 1964, so it was in Mexico City in 1968 that Suriname first actually competed in the Olympics. Again, just one man travelled – this time it was Eddy Monsels, who snuck through the first round of the 100 metres, but finished last in his quarter-final heat.

In both 1972 and 1976, they entered both Athletics and Judo, with no particular success. In 1980, they declined to compete in Moscow. In 1984, they returned to Athletics and Judo, and added Swimming for the first time too (in fact, Anthony Nesty himself entered two events, finishing 21st and 49th). Then came 1988. Suriname added Cycling to their Olympic roster that year, but it was in the swimming pool that they caused a global sensation.

Anthony Nesty was actually born in Trinidad, but moved to Suriname as a baby. After his performances in Los Angeles in 1984 (when aged just 16), he enrolled in a school in Florida to concentrate on developing as a swimmer. He was not one of the favourites in Seoul, but won gold in the 100m butterfly by 0.01 seconds from American Matt Biondi, becoming the first black swimmer to win an Olympic gold medal, as well as a national hero. A few days later, he came 8th in the 200m butterfly. In 1992, Nesty attempted to defend his title but had to settle for bronze, Suriname's second and, to date, last Olympic medal. He has spent the years since as an in-demand Swimming coach in the USA.

Remarkably, Suriname have only entered one new sport in all the years since 1992, namely Badminton, which they entered in 1996, and again in 2012, 2016 and 2021. But other than Nesty's three Olympic finals, Suriname have only ever finished in the top eight of an Olympic event on one other occasion. That came in 2021, when Jair Tjon En Fa came 4th in the men's keirin Cycling event – he was edged out of the medals by a cyclist from the Netherlands, the country which had, until independence was gained in 1975, governed Suriname. He remains, nonetheless, Suriname's best-performing native-born Olympian.

Suriname have yet to compete in the Winter Olympics.

GUYANA **Olympic Rank 136th**

Population: 791,739 (rank 165th)
Olympic rank/ population differential: +29
Population per gold: n/a
Population per medal: 791,739 (rank 74th)

Summer: 0 gold, 0 silver, 1 bronze (total 1)
Winter: *never participated*
Total: 0 gold, 0 silver, 1 bronze (total 1)

Best sports: Boxing (1 bronze, 61st=)
Athletics
Weightlifting

Guyana did not gain independence from Britain until 1966, but had already competed in five Summer Olympics by then, competing as British Guiana. The only Summer Olympics they have missed since their debut in 1948 has been 1976. They have never entered the Winter Olympics. In all their appearances, they have only competed in seven sports – Athletics, Cycling, Weightlifting and Boxing were their only sports prior to 2004, when they entered Swimming for the first time. They have since added Judo (2012) and Table Tennis (2021).

They have managed a top-eight finish on three occasions. In 1964, Martin Dias finished 8th in the men's bantamweight Weightlifting. In 2016, Troy Doris came 7th in the men's triple jump – he was born in Chicago, but turned to Guyana (through his ancestry) after failing to qualify for the US team.

But Guyana's one Olympic medallist is Michael Anthony, who beat opponents from Nigeria, Syria and Mexico to take bronze in the men's bantamweight Boxing in 1980. Their best performance in Cycling is 10th, in Swimming it is 42nd (achieved both in 2012 and 2016). Their only Olympic judoka lasted just 12 seconds before being defeated, and their one Table Tennis player failed to reach the last 48.

CHAPTER SIX - South America, South & East (Brazil, Argentina, Chile, Uruguay, Paraguay, Bolivia)

BRAZIL **Olympic Rank 31st**
Population: 218,689,757 (rank 7th)
Olympic rank/ population differential: -24
Population per gold: 5,910,534 (rank 78th)
Population per medal: 1,457,932 (rank 92nd)

Summer: 37 gold, 42 silver, 71 bronze (total 150)
Winter: *no medals (best finish: 9th)*
Total: 37 gold, 42 silver, 71 bronze (total 150)

Best sports: Surfing (1 gold, 50.00%, 1st=)
Beach Volleyball (3 golds, 21.43%, 2nd)
Volleyball (5 golds, 16.67%, 2nd)

Brazil first competed in the Olympic Games in 1920, when they won a gold, silver and bronze, all in Shooting. They failed to win any medals in 1924, 1932 or 1936 (they didn't take part in 1928). But since 1948, they have won medals at every Summer Games. Inevitably, for a southern hemisphere nation, they have been less successful at Winter Games. They have entered all of them since 1992, but have never done better than the 9th place taken by Isabel Clark Ribeiro in Snowboarding in 2006.

Gold medals were once a rare commodity for Brazil in the Olympics – only 12 in their first 80 years of participation. But they have added a further 25 since 2004, with their home games of Rio 2016 producing a record seven golds, which was equalled in Tokyo in 2021. The Tokyo Games also saw Brazil's highest ever total of medals (21 – 7 golds, 6 silvers, 8 bronzes) and their highest ever position in a medal table (12th).

The two most decorated Brazilian Olympians of all time are both sailors. Robert Scheidt won five medals across Laser (golds in 1996 & 2004, silver in 2000) and Star (silver in 2008, bronze in 2012), whilst Torben Grael also won five medals, coming in Soling (silver in 1984) and Star (golds in 1996 & 2004, bronze in 1988 & 2000). They are two of 15 Brazilians to have won two golds; nobody has yet managed three. The other two-time Olympic champions consist of nine Volleyball players, another three sailors, and triple jumper Adhemar Ferreira da Silva, Brazil's top track & field star, who won the title in 1952 and 1956. Triple jump has been responsible for six of Brazil's 19 Athletics medals, although nobody since da Silva has won the gold. Three other Brazilians have taken golds in other Athletics events – the men's 800 metres (1984) and pole vault (2016), and the women's long jump (2008).

The one sport that Brazil is associated with more than any other, of course, is Football. But for many years when the competition was dominated by the communist nations and their dubious "amateur" teams, Brazil never got a look-in. The rules were changed in 1984, and Brazil won their first medal that year; it was silver, after losing to France in the final. More medals followed in 1988, 1996, 2008 and 2012, and for the women's team in 2004 and 2008, before the men finally broke their "jinx" with gold in 2016. Pleasingly, they beat Germany on penalties in the final, with poster-boy Neymar scoring the winning kick, in revenge for Germany's unfathomable 7-1 win in Brazil's own World Cup two years earlier. Brazil then retained their Olympic title in 2021. Team sports have generally proved fruitful, with the men's Volleyball team winning medals in six of the last 10 games, and the women doing so in five of the last seven. Beach Volleyball is another iconic Brazilian sport – 2021 was the first time they ever failed to win a medal in the sport.

The sport which has provided the most medals for Brazil overall, however, is Judo with 24 medals, albeit 17 of them have been bronze (helped by the fact that Judo is one of the sports which provides two bronzes per event). Sailing has provided the most golds, with eight (and 19 medals overall), although this is a lower overall proportion than the "Best sports" listed above. Two new sports in 2021 – Surfing and Skateboarding – could prove fruitful to Brazil in years to come, with a Surfing gold and three Skateboarding bronzes already in the bag (putting them equal 1st, and 3rd, in the sports' respective medal tables at this embryonic stage). Brazil have been winning Swimming medals ever since 1952, but have only ever won two golds – Cesar Cielo Filho in the men's 50m freestyle in 2008, and Ana Marcela Cunha in the women's marathon swim in 2021.

ARGENTINA   **Olympic Rank 39th**

Population:	46,621,847 (rank 33rd)
Olympic rank/ population differential:	-6
Population per gold:	2,220,088 (rank 62nd)
Population per medal:	605,479 (rank 68th)
Summer:	21 gold, 26 silver, 30 bronze (total 77)
Winter:	*no medals (best finish: 4th)*
Total:	21 gold, 26 silver, 30 bronze (total 77)
Best sports:	Football (2 golds, 5.71%, 6th)
	Basketball (1 gold, 2.94%, 4th)
	Hockey (1 gold, 2.86%, 7th)

The first Argentine Olympian was Francisco Camet, who was studying in Paris at the time of the 1900 Games, and came 5th in the men's épée Fencing. They had one entrant in 1908 (in Figure Skating(!)) and one in 1920 (in Boxing), before entering a full team in 1924. They have entered all Summer Games since, except for 1980.

Argentina's first six Olympic medals came in 1924 including one gold – in men's Polo. They found themselves amongst the golds at every Games after that up to and including 1952, including three each in 1928, 1932 and 1948 – a total that has since been emulated only in 2016. In 1928, 1936 and 1948, they won seven medals each time – that total has never since been emulated. All six of their top-20 finishes in the medal table came in the six Games between 1924 and 1952, with 11th in 1932 being the best.

After 1952, when their one gold came in men's double sculls Rowing, they had a dramatic decline in Olympic performances, not winning another gold for 52 years. That huge drought ended on 28th August 2004 with victory in the men's Football and, incredibly, they also won the men's Basketball later the same day. A far cry from 1976 and 1984, when they didn't win a medal at all. In recent years, they have had more success, and have done best in the team sports – retaining their Football title in 2008 (which saw Javier Mascherano become the only Argentine to win two Olympic golds), and winning men's Hockey in 2016. The 2021 Games were the first since 2000 not to produce a gold, but they did manage a silver and two bronzes – in Hockey, Rugby Sevens and Volleyball. Other golds this century have been won in Cycling (men's madison in 2008), Taekwondo (Sebastian Crismanich in 2012), and Judo (Paula Pareto) and Sailing (mixed Nacra-17 team) in 2016.

The only sport to provide more than two gold medals for Argentina is Boxing, which has produced seven. It has also produced 24 medals in total (the next most is Sailing with ten). However, the last of those golds came back in 1948, and since 1968 there has been only a single bronze (in 1996). Two gold medals have been won in Polo (1924 and 1936), Football (2004 and 2008) and Athletics. Both of the Athletics golds came in the men's marathon – for Juan Carlos Zabala in 1932 and Delfo Cabrera in 1948. They have won three other Athletics medals, all silvers – one more in the men's marathon, and one each in long jump and triple jump. The last of those was in 1952. Swimming has provided only three medals – gold for Alberto Zorrilla in men's 400m freestyle in 1928, and a silver and bronze in 1936 and 2004 respectively.

Two Argentines have won four Olympic medals each, both doing so in four consecutive Games. Carlos Espinola won windsurfing silvers in 1996 and 2000, before switching Sailing events to Tornado, and taking bronze in 2004 and 2008. He was later elected to the national Senate. Meanwhile, the women's Hockey team was medalling in four consecutive Games – silver in 2000 and 2012, and two bronzes in between. Luciana Aymar was the only player to feature in all four. She was named as best female Hockey player in the world eight times in 13 years (2001 to 2013), and is often considered the best of all time. Argentina have taken Hockey medals at every Games since 2000.

Argentina first participated in the Winter Games in 1928, competing only in the four-man Bobsleigh. They had two crews entered, and finished 4th and 5th. They then didn't compete again until 1948. They have competed at all Winter Games since then, other than 1956, but have never bettered the positions of those two Bobsleigh crews. Their only other top-eight finish was 8th, also in the four-man Bobsleigh, in 1952 (although they finished 7th in Figure Skating at the 1908 Summer Games). Their best Winter position this century is 17th.

CHILE   Olympic Rank 77th

Population: 18,549,457 (rank 65th)
Olympic rank/ population differential: -12
Population per gold: 9,274,729 (rank 83rd)
Population per medal: 1,426,881 (rank 90th)

Summer: 2 gold, 7 silver, 4 bronze (total 13)
Winter: *no medals (best finish: 11th)*
Total: 2 gold, 7 silver, 4 bronze (total 13)

Best sports: Tennis (2 golds, 2.67%, 10th)
                   Equestrianism (2 silvers, 22nd)
                   Athletics (2 silvers, 72nd=)

Chile may or may not have taken part in the inaugural modern Olympics of 1896. It is certainly true that Luis Subercaseaux, a member of a famous family of Chilean diplomats, was entered into four events – three Athletics and one Cycling. However, there remains no conclusive evidence that he actually competed in any of them.

They next entered in 1912, and have entered every Summer Games since then, with the exception of 1932 and 1980. Their first top-eight finishes came in 1924, when Carlos Abarca reached a Boxing quarter-final and Manuel Plaza came 6th in the men's marathon. Four years later, Plaza became Chile's first Olympic medallist, winning marathon silver. No more medals would follow for over 20 years, before there was a brief lucrative period in the 1950s. In Helsinki in 1952, Oscar Cristi won silver in the individual show jumping, and also led his team of three to silver in the team event. These remain Chile's only Equestrianism medals.

In Melbourne in 1956, Chile won four medals – the most they have won at a single Games. Three of them came in Boxing – they remain Chile's only three Boxing medals at the Olympics. They were a silver for Ramon Tapia (who had reached the final by default after his opponent was declared unfit to fight), and bronzes for Claudio Barrientos and Carlos Lucas. Chile's other medal that year was a silver of Marlene Ahrens in the women's javelin. Remarkably, Ahrens later also represented Chile at both Tennis and Equestrianism (albeit not in the Olympics). These medals put Chile 27th in the medal table – the highest they have finished in any year.

After that spell of six medals in four years, it would be a further 32 years until Chile won another one. In Seoul in 1988, Alfonso de Iruarrizaga won a silver in Shooting's skeet event, finishing just one shot off the East German victor. In 1992 and 1996, Chile didn't even manage a top-eight finish, but they added to their medal tally in Sydney in 2000, winning bronze in men's Football (the only other time they had reached the quarter-finals in Olympic Football was 1984).

So, going into the Athens 2004 Games, Chile had been competing for 108 years, and had won six silvers, three bronzes, but no golds. But in Tennis that year, some remarkable things took place. Both Fernando Gonzalez and Nicolas Massu made it to the semi-finals of the men's singles. Gonzalez lost to American Mardy Fish, but Massu made it to the final with a win over another American, Taylor Dent. Gonzalez then took bronze, beating Dent 16-14 in the final set. Just over an hour later, he was back on court, partnering Massu in the men's doubles final. They saved multiple match points in the fourth set against Germans Nicolas Kiefer and Rainer Schuttler, before prevailing in a five-set thriller, which didn't finish until nearly 3am. The next day, Massu returned for another five-setter, again ending triumphant in the singles final against Fish. These two gold medals are still the only ones Chile have ever won in the Olympics. All the more amazing given that Massu, who won both of them, never progressed beyond the last 16 of a Grand Slam singles event in his entire career. Gonzalez even reached the Olympic singles final in 2008 as well, but lost to Rafael Nadal and settled for silver (making him the only Chilean with three Olympic medals). The gold medals of 2004 helped put Chile into 39th place in that year's medal table.

The best Chile have done in any event since 2008 is a couple of 4th places in Gymnastics in 2012. They have, over the years, also had top-eight finishes in Basketball, Cycling, Diving, Golf, Modern Pentathlon, Rowing, Sailing, Taekwondo, Triathlon, Weightlifting and Wrestling. Kristel Kobrich is by far Chile's most successful Olympic swimmer of all time – she entered all Games from 2004 to 2021, placing 14th in both the 800m freestyle in 2012 and 1500m freestyle in 2021. Chile have entered every Winter Games since 1948, other than 1972 and 1980. All of their entries until 1998, and the vast majority of those since, have been in Alpine Skiing. Their best finish yet is 11th by Thomas Grob in men's combined in 1998.

URUGUAY   **Olympic Rank 80th**

Population: 3,416,264 (rank 133rd)
Olympic rank/ population differential: +53
Population per gold: 1,708,132 (rank 58th)
Population per medal: 341,626 (rank 60th)

Summer: 2 gold, 2 silver, 6 bronze (total 10)
Winter: *no medals (best finish: 24th)*
Total: 2 gold, 2 silver, 6 bronze (total 10)

Best sports: Football (2 golds, 5.71%, 9th)
Rowing (1 silver, 33rd)
Cycling (1 silver, 35th=)

Uruguay first entered the Olympics in Paris in 1924, and their influence was immediate. They entered Boxing and Fencing without much success, but in men's Football they stormed to the gold medal, beating Switzerland 3-0 in the final, and having scored 20 goals and conceded just two throughout the tournament. They had surprised the European spectators, who hadn't realised how good South Americans were. Four years later, in Amsterdam, Uruguay only entered one event – men's Football – and they won gold again. Amidst great interest, they beat the hosts in the first round, but overall found it tougher going this time. They needed a replay to see off bitter rivals Argentina in the final. Nonetheless, the success of the tournament led directly to the creation of the World Cup, which has become the only international sporting event to rival the Olympics for global appeal. It was created to allow professional players to play in an international tournament (the Olympics, of course, was only for amateurs). The first World Cup, in 1930, was hosted and won by Uruguay, who fielded many of their Olympic gold-medallists, including Hector Scarone, who had scored the gold-winning goal against Argentina. Despite their seminal role in Olympic Football, Uruguay have only participated in it once since then – in 2012, when they were eliminated in the group stages.

In 1932, Uruguay once again entered just one event. This time, it was the men's single sculls Rowing, but again they came away with a medal – a bronze for Guillermo Douglas. The 1936 Berlin Games were the first in which Uruguay failed to win a medal, though they did have top-eight finishes in Boxing (twice), Rowing and Basketball. In 1948, a further two Rowing medals were won – silver in the men's single sculls for Eduardo Risso, and bronze in the men's double sculls for William Jones and Juan Antonio Rodriguez. The latter teamed up with a new partner, Miguel Seijas, for another bronze in 1952. There were also successive bronzes for the men's Basketball team in 1952 and 1956, the former being particularly satisfying as the defeated the Argentines in the bronze medal match. Uruguay in fact managed top-eight finishes in men's Basketball six times in succession from 1936 to 1964, but only once since (1984). The Games of 1948 and 1952 were the only ones in which Uruguay won more than one medal.

After this, Uruguayan Olympic performance fell into decline. In 1960, 1964 and 1968, there were a smattering of top-eight finishes in Basketball, Rowing, Boxing (which included a bronze for Washington Rodriguez in 1964) and Swimming. In the case of the latter, it was two 8th-place finishes for Ana Maria Norbis in the 100m and 200m breaststroke for women; these are still Uruguay's only top-eight finishes in Swimming. Between 1972 and 1992, they didn't manage any top-eight finishes in any sports (they boycotted the 1980 Games, the only Summer Games they have missed since their debut).

Since then, they have only managed seven top-eight finishes, and only one medal. Milton Wynants got it, in Cycling's men's points race in 2000 (having finished 7th in the same event in 1996). Emiliano Lasa finished 6th in the men's long jump in 2016 – Uruguay's only ever top-eight finish in Athletics. Meanwhile, Gabriel Hottegindre came 24th in men's slalom (Alpine Skiing) in 1998; it remains the only Winter Olympic event a Uruguayan has ever entered. Overall, a number of Uruguayan footballers (1924 & 1928) and basketballers (1952 & 1956), as well as rower Rodriguez (1948 & 1952) have won two Olympic medals – no Uruguayan has yet won three.

PARAGUAY   Olympic Rank 126th

Population: 7,439,864 (rank 104th)
Olympic rank/ population differential: -22
Population per gold: n/a
Population per medal: 7,439,864 (rank 118th)

Summer: 0 gold, 1 silver, 0 bronze (total 1)
Winter: *no medals (best finish: 17th)*
Total: 0 gold, 1 silver, 0 bronze (total 1)

Best sports: Football (1 silver, 25th=)
                Tennis
                Boxing

Paraguay's first Olympian was foil fencer Rodolfo da Ponte, who lost all five of his bouts in 1968. Since then, they have entered all Summer Games apart from 1980. They have entered numerous sports – Athletics, Swimming, Shooting, Football, Cycling, Rowing, Judo, Boxing, Sailing, Golf, Tennis and Table Tennis; all of them – except for Cycling – more than once.

They have qualified for Olympic Football just twice (both on the men's side), and on both occasions reached the last eight, something they have never done in any other Olympic sport even once. In 1992, they lost their quarter-final after extra-time to Ghana. In 2004, a win over Italy saw them win their group; they then beat South Korea in the quarters, and a 3-1 win over fellow surprise package Iraq in the semis guaranteed them their first (and so far only) Olympic medal. They lost 1-0 to Argentina in the final.

Paraguay have also achieved top-16 finishes in Boxing (Oppe Pinto in 1984), Tennis (Rossana de los Rios in 2000, helped by a walkover against an injured Lindsay Davenport) and Athletics. Just one Paraguayan has done it in Athletics, Ramon Jimenez-Gaona, but he did it twice, finishing 16th in the discus in 1992 and 1996. Julio Abreu twice finished 25th in Swimming events in 1976, and no other Paraguayan swimmer has finished as high as that. The only Paraguayan ever to compete at a Winter Olympics is Julia Marino, who came 17th out of 22 in the women's slopestyle Freestyle Skiing in 2014.

BOLIVIA   Olympic Rank 191st

Population: 12,186,079 (rank 79th)
Olympic rank/ population differential: -112

Summer: *no medals (best finish: 13th)*
Winter: *no medals (best finish: 32nd)*

Best sports: Athletics
                Wrestling
                Canoeing

Bolivia are the only one of South America's 12 nations never to have won an Olympic medal. Despite first entering the Games as long ago as 1936, and entering a very wide variety of sports over the years, they've never really come close. A single swimmer entered the Berlin Games, and the nation did not return to the Summer Olympics until 1964. Thereafter, they've missed only the 1980 Games. Their best finish in an Olympic event is 13th, which they have done twice. In 1984, Leonardo Camacho became the first, and so far only, Bolivian wrestler ever to compete at the Games. In the men's freestyle featherweight, he lost both his bouts, but gained enough points to finish 13th out of 16. In 1992, they were one of 14 countries entered in the women's 4x400m relay. Cuba were disqualified and, of the remaining 13, Bolivia finished 22 seconds slower than anyone else. It's the only time they've entered a relay.

Their only other top-16 finishes have been in Canoeing (15th out of 15 in 1964) and Weightlifting (16th out of 19, but only 16 finished, in 2008). In Swimming, they've never managed better than 35th. Bolivia have also entered the Winter Games of 1956, 1980 to 1992, 2018, and 2022. Their highest finish yet is 32nd in the 2018 men's slalom by Austrian-born Alpine skier Simon Breitfuss Kammerlander.

CHAPTER SEVEN - British Isles (Great Britain, Ireland)

GREAT BRITAIN   **Olympic Rank 4th**
Population: 68,138,484 (rank 22nd)
Olympic rank/ population differential: +18
Population per gold: 221,589 (rank 25th)
Population per medal: 69,465 (rank 28th)

Summer: 294 gold, 328 silver, 315 bronze (total 937)
Winter: 13 gold, 7 silver, 21 bronze (total 41)
Total: 307 gold, 335 silver, 336 bronze (total 978)
(plus mixed team: 0.5 gold, 0.9 silver, 1.5 bronze (total 2.9))

Best sports: Tennis (17.5 golds, 23.33%, 2nd)
                           Triathlon (3 golds, 23.08%, 1st)
                           Skeleton (3 golds, 21.43%, 2nd)

The name of the Great Britain & Northern Ireland team is usually misleadingly shortened to Great Britain or Team GB – really, they should be called United Kingdom. They are one of only three nations (along with France and Switzerland) that have competed at every Olympic Games, Summer and Winter, since 1896. They only just achieved this feat – in St Louis in 1904, they did not enter a team; however, two Irish athletes made their own way, and won medals whilst making clear they felt no allegiance to Britain (Ireland did not achieve partial independence until the 1920s). Two other US-based men born in Britain competed in Fencing and Golf. And in 1980, Britain did not join the US-led boycott *en masse*, although in some sports the British authorities did refuse to send a team. Thanks to Irish nationalist Tom Kiely winning the 1904 decathlon, Britain are the only nation to win a gold at every Summer Games. The other Games to see only a single British gold were 1952 (a team show jumping gold, won on the very last day of the Games) and 1996 (Redgrave and Pinsent in coxless pairs Rowing).

By far Great Britain's most successful Games were the London 1908 Games – hardly surprising, given that few foreigners could afford the trip at the time. They won 55 golds, and 140 medals in total. In every Summer Games up to 1924 (apart from 1904), they finished in the top five, finishing 4th in Paris in 1924 with 9 golds. There then followed decades of relative under-achievement. In the 16 games between 1928 and 1996, Britain never finished higher than 8th, and only once won more than 5 gold medals (1956, when they won 6), which is poor, especially considering the number of big nations boycotting in 1980 and 1984 in particular. They finished 18th in 1952, but reached their nadir in Atlanta in 1996, finishing 36th.

But a huge injection of lottery funds from the late 1990s onwards transformed Britain's Olympic fortunes. They won 11 golds in Sydney in 2000, finishing 9th – their best Games since the 1920s. After a 10th-place finish in 2004, they stepped up another level, finishing 4th, 3rd, 2nd and 4th in the years after that, reaching 29 golds in London 2012 and 67 medals in total in Rio 2016 (both totals are second only to 1908).

Inevitably, their Winter performances have been much more modest. They have never won more than one gold in a Games, and their highest medal total is five (in 2014 & 2018). Their last top-10 finish in the medal table was in 1952 (8th), but that was on the basis of a single gold medal. They have not won gold in a men's event since 1980. They failed to win any medals at all in 1932, 1956, 1960, 1968, 1972, 1988 and 1992. The 1988 Games were the worst, in the sense that their highest finish that year was a mere 8th (in Alpine Skiing).

Britain's five most successful Olympians (5 golds or more) are the Cycling quartet of Jason and Laura Kenny, Bradley Wiggins and Chris Hoy, and rower Steve Redgrave. Lizzy Yarnold is their only 2-time Winter Olympic champion.

SUMMER
PWDS (10-10-6, 1st). Great Britain beat France to win the only Olympic Cricket title in 1900. They won two of the three Motor Boating classes in 1908. They won all the medals in Rackets (both singles and doubles) when it was held in 1908. They won the first three Polo titles (1900, 1908 and 1920) before Argentina took over as champions. And they were Tug of War champions in 1908 and 1920 as well.

Tennis (17.5-14.5-13.5, 2nd). Exactly half of the gold medals between 1896 and 1920 (15.5 out of 31) went to Great Britain. Reggie Doherty won three of them (men's doubles in 1900 and 1908, and mixed doubles in 1900). There have been just four British medals since the sport's return in 1988, including two singles golds (2012 & 2016) and a mixed doubles silver for Andy Murray.

Triathlon (3-3-2, 1st). Alistair Brownlee won men's gold in 2012 and 2016 (the only triathlete to win two golds). Brother Jonny won bronze and silver in those events, then won gold with the mixed team relay in 2021.

Sailing (30-21-12, 1st). Ben Ainslie is the most successful Olympic sailor of all time – he took Laser silver in 1996 and gold in 2000, before switching to Finn and winning golds in 2004, 2008 and 2012. Apart from 1980 (when they didn't compete in Sailing), Britain have won medals at every Games since 1964.

Cycling (40-38-27, 2nd). When Chris Boardman won individual pursuit gold in 1992, it was Britain's first Cycling gold for 72 years, and first Cycling medal of any colour for 16 years. But after further successes in 2000 and 2004, they began to utterly dominate from 2008 onwards; they have won 28 golds in just four Games since. Bradley Wiggins won eight medals (5-1-2, 2000 to 2016) and Chris Hoy won a historic six golds and one silver (2000-12). But even their achievements have been overshadowed by Jason Kenny (7 golds and 2 silvers, 2008-21), not to mention his wife Laura Kenny (née Trott, 5 golds and 1 silver, 2012-21). The only cyclists from any country to have won five or more golds have been the four Britons – Wiggins, Hoy and the two Kennys.

Golf (1-1-1, 2nd). All three medals were won in the men's event – silver and bronze in 1900, and gold for Justin Rose in 2016. The best women's finish is equal 7th.

Water Polo (4-0-0, 5th). GB won four of the first five events, between 1900 and 1920. They entered regularly up to 1956, but since then have only competed as hosts in 2012, when both men and women lost every game. Paul Radmilovic, who won in 1908, 1912 & 1920, also took a Swimming gold in 1908 (4x200m freestyle relay).

Hockey (4-2-7, 5th). Gold was won easily in 1908 and 1920. Since then, they have generally been contenders, but have added only two more golds – men in 1988 and women in 2016.

Rowing (31-25-14, 3rd). Great Britain were prominent in Rowing pre-war, with Jack Beresford winning medals in five successive Games (3 golds and 2 silvers, 1920-36). In 1948, Rowing provided Britain with two of the three golds they won at their home Games, but they would not win another gold until 1984 – the start of their new age of success. Steve Redgrave won golds at five successive Games (1984-2000), with Matthew Pinsent winning four golds (1992-2004), the first three of which were with Redgrave; they are the two most successful male rowers in Olympic history. The 2021 Games saw GB's first failure to win gold since before 1984.

Modern Pentathlon (4-2-3, 4th). The men's team won in 1976, and Steph Cook won the inaugural women's event in 2000. Joe Choong and Kate French then completed a GB male/female double in 2021.

Football (3-0.4-0, 3rd). Britain comfortably won gold in 1900, 1908 and 1912. They continued to enter up to 1960, but eventually stopped competing due to political pressure from the four home nations. Eventually, they agreed to compete as hosts in 2012, but both the men and women lost in the quarter-finals. The women returned in 2021, and lost in the quarter-finals again.

Equestrianism (13-12-15, 4th). Great Britain won medals at every Games from 1936 to 1972, with Richard Meade winning three golds in three-day eventing (1968 & 1972 team, 1972 individual). But they didn't win another gold until 2004. Their first ever dressage medals came in 2012, and Charlotte Dujardin has won three golds in the discipline (2012 & 2016 individual, 2012 team).

Boxing (20-15-27, 4th). Two British boxers have won two Olympic golds – Harry Mallin (men's middleweight, 1920 & 1924) and Nicola Adams (women's flyweight, 2012 & 2016). Having won only three Boxing golds between 1928 and 1996, Britain have won a further eight since 2000.

Athletics (59-88-73, 4th). Great Britain have won Athletics medals at every Summer Games of the modern era. They have failed to win golds only in 1896, 1948, 1952, 1976, 1988, 1996 and 2021. There have been numerous two-time champions (Alfred Tysoe, Charles Bennett, John Rimmer, George Larner, Albert Hill, Douglas Lowe, Daley Thompson, Sebastian Coe and Kelly Holmes), but only one person has won more – Mo Farah, who did the men's 5000 & 10000m double in both 2012 and 2016. Apart from 1908, when they won 7 Athletics golds, their biggest Athletics gold haul has been four – achieved in 1900, 1920, 1964 (when it accounted for their entire Games gold haul), 1980 (accounting for 4 of their 5 golds that year), and 2012 (when three of them were won within an hour on "Super Saturday").

Shooting (15-15-21, 7th). There are two British two-time Shooting gold medallists – William Pimm (1908 & 1912, both in small-bore rifle team events) and Malcolm Cooper (men's small-bore rifle, 3 positions, 1984 & 1988). The six medals won since 1988 have all been in trap or double trap. Only two medals were won between 1928 and 1980. No woman has finished higher than 6th.

Taekwondo (2-3-4, 4th). Jade Jones won women's featherweight gold in both 2012 & 2016.

Swimming (21-33-33, 8th). Henry Taylor won 1500m freestyle gold in 1906, and won the same title in 1908, as well as men's 400m freestyle and 4x200m freestyle relay. He was the last Briton to win three golds in a Games until cyclist Chris Hoy in 2008. The next most successful British swimmer is Adam Peaty (100m breaststroke gold in 2016 & 2021, and a medley relay gold in 2021 too). Britain have medalled at every post-war Games apart from 2000. Six of their last 11 golds have been in breaststroke; they have never won a butterfly gold. After 1908, they did not win another male gold until 1976.

Archery (2-2-5, 6th). Both golds (won by William Dod and Queenie Newall), both silvers and one bronze were won in 1908. The other bronzes came in 1988, 1992 (twice) and 2004 (the latter for Alison Williamson).

Canoeing (5-8-6, 15th). No medals until 1992, and no flatwater medals until 2000. There have, though, been medals at every Games since. Tim Brabants won the first gold, in the men's K1 1000m in 2008.

Diving (2-3-8, 8th). Three medals pre-war, and two in 1960; the other eight have all come since 2004, including both golds (Chris Mears and Jack Laugher in 2016, and Tom Daley and Matty Lee in 2021).

Gymnastics (3-4-11, 18th). Prior to 2008, there was only a silver for Walter Tysal in 1908, and team bronzes in 1912 & 1928. Louis Smith broke the 80-year drought, and now has four medals, whilst Max Whitlock has six, including all three golds (men's pommel horse 2016 & 2021, and floor 2016).

Wrestling (3-4-10, 25th). All 17 medals have been in freestyle. 11 of them came in 1908, including all three golds, and there have been only two since the war (Kenneth Richmond in 1952, and Noel Loban in 1984).

Weightlifting (1-4-3, 28th=). Great Britain's first ever Olympic gold medal (in any sport) went to Launceston Elliot in the one-handed lift. It is still their only ever Weightlifting gold. He also won silver in the two-handed lift. Only two medals since 1964 – a bronze for David Mercer (1984) and silver for Emily Campbell (2021).

Fencing (1-9-0, 16th). Four medals in women's foil, most recently Gillian Sheen's gold in 1956, and six medals in men's épée, most recently a silver for Bill Hoskyns in 1960.

Rugby (0-3-0, 6th). British men won silvers behind France in 1900 and Australasia in 1908, and in Sevens behind Fiji in 2016. The women have finished 4th in both their Games (2016 & 2021).

Skateboarding (0-0-1, 5th). Sky Brown, aged 13, won bronze in women's park in 2021. Born in Japan, she became Britain's youngest ever medallist.

Judo (0-8-12, 30th). Only Poland in Canoeing have won as many Olympic medals in one sport without ever taking gold. Neil Adams is the most successful British judoka, taking two silvers (1980 & 1984).

Badminton (0-1-2, 9th=). Mixed doubles bronze in 2000 and silver in 2004, and men's doubles bronze in 2016.

Artistic Swimming – Caroline Holmyard and Carolyn Wilson came 4th in the inaugural duet event in 1984. There have been six other top-eight finishes, most recently the team in 2012 (6th out of 8).

Table Tennis – Just one quarter-final appearance – the men's team in 2016, courtesy of a dramatic last-16 win over France. They finished 8th.

Basketball – Have only ever participated as hosts. In 1948, they came 20th out of 23 in the men's event. In 2012, they finished 9th out of 12 in the men's, and 11th out of 12 in the women's.

Beach Volleyball – Entered both events as hosts in 2012 without making the top-16. Just one other entry – Audrey Cooper and Amanda Glover in 1996, who finished 9th.

Volleyball – Entered only as hosts in 2012. The men came last (12th), whereas the women managed one win, against Algeria, and finished 10th.

Sport Climbing – Shauna Coxsey came 10th in the women's event in 2021.

Handball – Entered only as hosts in 2012, when they finished 12th and last in both events.

Baseball/Softball, Karate, Surfing – never entered

WINTER

Skeleton (3-1-5, 2nd). Medalled in the women's event in every Games from 2002 to 2018, including golds for Amy Williams (2010) and Lizzy Yarnold (2014 & 2018). Won men's bronzes in 1928, 1948 and 2018.

Curling (3-2-1, 3rd). Men's gold in 1924 and silvers in 2014 and 2022. The women took gold in 2002 and 2022, and bronze in 2014.

Figure Skating (5-3-7, 6th). Won the women's in 1908 and 1952, and the men's in 1976 and 1980. Torvill and Dean won the ice dance in 1984, and returned as professionals in 1994 to take bronze; still GB's last medal.

Ice Hockey (1-0-1, 7th). With the help of many British-born, Canadian-based players, GB took a shock gold in 1936. They won bronze in 1924, but have not competed since 1948 (when they came 5th).

Bobsleigh (1-1-3, 7th=). Gold in the two-man bob (Tony Nash and Robin Dixon) in 1964. Two medals since then – four-man bronzes in 1998 and 2014 (the latter finished 5th but two Russian crews were subsequently disqualified for doping).

Snowboarding (0-0-2, 22nd). Bronzes for Jenny Jones in 2014 (Britain's first ever Winter medal on snow as opposed to ice), and Billy Morgan in 2018.

Freestyle Skiing (0-0-1, 19th=). Bronze for Izzy Atkin in 2018. The best men's finish (4th) was in the same year.

Short Track Speed Skating (0-0-1, 12th=). Bronze for Nicky Gooch in 1994 (men's 500 metres). The best women's finish (4th) was in the 500 metres in 2018.

Alpine Skiing – Alain Baxter won bronze in the men's slalom in 2002 – Britain's first ever medal on snow. However, it was soon rescinded due to failing a drugs test having taken an over-the counter nasal spray. Therefore, Britain's best remains the 4th place of Gina Hathorn in the women's slalom in 1968 (0.03 seconds off a medal).

Speed Skating – Terry Monaghan came 5th in the men's 10000 metres in 1960, and Terry Malkin came 8th in the same event in 1964. The next best is 9th in the men's 1000 metres in 2022.

Nordic Skiing – Andrew Musgrave is the only top-eight finisher, coming 7th in the 30km skiathlon in 2018.

Biathlon – Came 11th in 1972 in both the men's 20km and men's relay. Britain's best this century is 19th.

Luge – 14th in the men's doubles in 1980. The best this century is 16th.

Nordic Combined – Only ever entered once, the men's individual in 1936, when Percy Legard came 45th. He also competed in Modern Pentathlon in the Summer Games of 1932 (finishing 8th) and 1936.

Ski Jumping – The first British Olympic ski jumper was Eddie "the Eagle" Edwards, who came last by a huge margin in both his events in 1988 (55th and 58th). The only other entrant is Canadian-born Glynn Pedersen (2002), who came 55th and 62nd (but, unlike Edwards, he beat several jumpers in both events).

IRELAND   **Olympic Rank 47th**

Population: 5,323,991 (rank 123rd)
Olympic rank/ population differential: +76
Population per gold: 483,999 (rank 41st)
Population per medal: 152,114 (rank 46th)

Summer: 11 gold, 10 silver, 14 bronze (total 35)
Winter: *no medals (best finish: 4th)*
Total: 11 gold, 10 silver, 14 bronze (total 35)

Best sports: Boxing (3 golds, 1.13%, 19th)
Swimming (3 golds, 0.50%, 18th=)
Athletics (4 golds, 0.38%, 33rd)

When the modern Olympics began in 1896, the whole of Ireland was still part of the United Kingdom. In 1904, Great Britain didn't send a team; however, two Irishmen, Tom Kiely and John Daly, travelled independently and won gold and silver respectively. Those medals have both been retrospectively awarded to Great Britain, despite very vocal claims from Kiely in particular that he was Irish, not British. The southern part of Ireland broke away from the UK in 1922, and Ireland have sent a team to every Summer Games from 1924 onwards, with the exception of 1936. Prior to World War II, Ireland won three medals, all of them gold, and all of them in Athletics. Pat O'Callaghan won the first, in the men's hammer in 1928, and he retained his title in 1932. Merely an hour before O'Callaghan's second gold, Bob Tisdall took the men's 400m hurdles title.

Soon after the resumption of the Olympics, Ireland's affinity with Boxing really took hold. Between 1948 and 1992, Ireland won 12 medals, of which 9 were in Boxing. John McNally won the first, a bantamweight silver in 1952, before a further one silver and three bronzes followed in 1956. There was also a gold in 1956, Ireland's fourth in Olympic history, and again it was in Athletics. Ronnie Delany was the recipient this time, beating local favourite John Landy in the men's 1500 metres in Melbourne. Since then, Ireland have won two silvers in Athletics and, more recently, one bronze (in the men's 50km walk in 2012).

Going into the 1992 Games, Ireland had not won a gold for 36 years, and had still never won one outside of Athletics. But Michael Carruth changed all that, beating reigning world champion and strong favourite, Juan Hernandez of Cuba, in the welterweight final. Boxing has again dominated Irish medal wins in recent years, with 9 of the 15 medals won since 2008 coming in the sport, including two more golds, both in women's lightweight – Katie Taylor in 2012 and Kellie Harrington in 2021.

By far the most successful Irish Olympian, however, is swimmer Michelle Smith. She had competed in seven events across the 1988 and 1992 Games, never finishing better than 17th. However, a sudden huge improvement in the lead-up to the 1996 Atlanta Games led to whispers about doping, especially as her husband, a Dutch discus thrower who was now also her coach, was serving a four-year ban for a doping violation (which he denied). Smith obliterated the field in Atlanta, winning golds in the 200m and 400m individual medleys as well as the 400m freestyle, with a bronze in the 200m butterfly for good measure. No other Irish swimmer, before or since, has ever finished higher than 8th (that was in 2021). In 1998, a urine sample provided by Smith was found to have been tampered with, and she too was banned for four years. Given that she had never actually failed a test, though, her Olympic achievements still stand, and her three golds and four medals are both Irish records.

Ireland's only other gold medal has come in Rowing – Fintan McCarthy and Paul O'Donovan taking the men's lightweight double sculls title in 2021. The latter meant 2021 saw two Irish golds, the same as in 1932 and one fewer than 1996 (when all of Ireland's medals were won by Michelle Smith). Their final position of 16th in 1932 is yet to be emulated. The most medals they have won in one Games is six (1-1-4) in 2012. The last time they failed to win a medal at all was 2004. On that occasion, they did actually claim a gold in Equestrianism, only to be stripped when the horse failed a drugs test.

The only other sports in which Ireland have medalled are Sailing (silvers in 1980 and 2016) and Equestrianism (a bronze in 2012). Ireland first entered the Winter Games in 1992, returning in 1998, and every Games since. They have only once finished higher than 12th. This was in the 2002 men's Skeleton, when 4th place went to Clifton Wrottesley who, as Baron Wrottesley, is a peer in the British House of Lords.

CHAPTER EIGHT - Scandinavia (Sweden, Norway, Finland, Denmark, Iceland)

SWEDEN   **Olympic Rank 8th**

Population:	10,536,338 (rank 88th)
Olympic rank/ population differential:	+80
Population per gold:	49,120 (rank 5th)
Population per medal:	15,193 (rank 5th)

Summer:	146 gold, 180 silver, 185 bronze (total 511)
Winter:	68 gold, 53 silver, 61 bronze (total 182)
Total:	214 gold, 233 silver, 246 bronze (total 693)

(plus mixed team: 0.5 gold, 0 silver, 0 bronze (total 0.5))

Best sports: Curling (4 golds, 23.53%, 2nd)
                                               Modern Pentathlon (9 golds, 21.43%, 3rd)
                                               Nordic Skiing (32 golds, 17.58%, 3rd)

Sweden have only ever missed one Olympics, Summer or Winter (St. Louis 1904). Of the Games they have entered, they have only failed to win a medal once (1896, when they finished 4th in the high jump). Their best Games, neatly enough, were the 1912 Games that they hosted in Stockholm. They won 23 golds and 65 medals in total (their best in any other Games were 17 and 61 respectively, both in 1920). On both those occasions, as well as in 1948, they finished 2nd in the medal table. They also finished 3rd in 1908, and 4th in 1928, 1932 and 1952. Their last top-10 finish came in 1956. The most golds they have won at any Summer Games since then is four, and in 1988 and 2008 they didn't win any.

They have, however, won medals at every Summer and Winter Games since 1906 (only Finland can join them in that boast, with the US boycotting in 1980, and France failing to win a medal in the 1956 Winter Games). As with the Summer Games, Sweden's best Winter medal table positions came in the first half of the 20th century. They shared top spot with Norway in 1948, and finished 3rd in 1928, 1932 and 1936. In 2022, they achieved their highest totals of golds (8) and medals (18), and finished 5th.

SUMMER

Modern Pentathlon (9-7-5, 3rd). Amazingly, eight of the first nine individual Modern Pentathlon titles (1912-56) went to Swedish athletes; seven different men took gold, with only Lars Hall (1952 & 1956) winning twice. Their last gold came in 1968, with only a team bronze (1980) and an individual silver (1984) since then.

Equestrianism (18-13-14, 2nd). 10 of their golds came in the 1912-24 period, with another 7 coming in 1952 & 1956. Henri Saint Cyr won all four dressage golds in these Games (two individual and two team). In 2021, Sweden won team jumping gold – their first Equestrian gold since 1956, and their first jumping gold since 1924.

Wrestling (28-27-31, 5th). The majority of medals (58 out of 86, including 20 out of 28 golds) have come in Greco-Roman events. They have not won a men's freestyle medal since 1972, and no gold since 1952, but they did win two women's freestyle bronzes in 2016. They have only won one Greco-Roman gold since 1952 (Mikael Ljungberg in 2000). In 1948, they won five of the eight Greco-Roman events. In 1932, Ivar Johansson won golds in both freestyle and Greco-Roman events, one of only two people ever to do both in the same year.

Canoeing (15-11-4, 4th). Gert Fredriksson is Sweden's most successful Olympian of all time, taking 6 golds, as well as a silver and a bronze, between 1948 and 1960, mostly in K1 events (but one gold was in a K2 event). He is also the most successful male canoeist from any country. Sweden's most recent medal was gold in the men's K2 1000m in 2004.

PWDS (1.5-0-1, 6th). A combined Swedish-Danish team took Tug of War gold in 1900. Sweden took bronze in the same event in 1906, and gold in 1912.

Sailing (10-14-13, 8th). Won the men's Star in 2012, their only Sailing gold since 1976.

Shooting (15-25-19, 6th). Only three golds since the war (one in 1972 and two in 2000). In 1912, Oscar Swahn won gold at the age of 64, making him the oldest Olympic champion ever. In 1920, now aged 72, he became the oldest Olympic competitor ever, and won a silver medal too (in the team running deer double shot event).

Diving (6-8-7, 5th). Sweden had much success between 1908 and 1928, but only three medals since then, all for Ulrika Knape (1 gold and 2 silvers, 1972 & 1976).

Football (1-2-2, 13th). The women have been ever-presents since 1996, winning silvers in 2016 and 2021. The men, in contrast, have only competed once since 1992, but won gold in 1948, and bronzes in 1924 and 1952.

Table Tennis (1-1-1, 4th). All three medals came in men's singles. Jan-Ove Waldner won gold in 1992 and silver in 2000; Erik Lindh having won bronze in 1988.

Athletics (22-27-46, 11th). Eric Lemming won four golds from 1906-1912, two in regular javelin and two in javelin (free style). Strangely, Sweden swept the podium in the 1948 men's 3000m steeplechase, though they have only ever won one other medal in the event (in 1976). Five of Sweden's six medals this century have been gold, in five different events (high jump, long jump, pole vault, discus and heptathlon).

Swimming (9-16-14, 11th). Two golds each for Hakan Malmroth in 1920 and Gunnar Larsson in 1972, but only four medals since 2000, all of them for Sarah Sjostrom (including gold in the 2016 women's 100m butterfly).

Cycling (4-5-8, 13th). Amazingly, none of their 17 medals have come on the track. There have been 7 in the road race, 5 in the now-defunct team road race, and 4 in road time trial events. The other, and most recent, was a gold for Jenny Rissveds in the 2016 women's cross-country; only their fourth Cycling medal this century.

Gymnastics (5-2-1, 8th). The "Swedish System" team event was held twice (1912 & 1920), and it is no surprise that Sweden won gold both times. They also won the regular team gold in 1908 and the women's "portable apparatus" (effectively rhythmic gymnastics) team gold in 1952. Their other gold was also in 1952, a floor gold for William Thoresson. The three lesser medals were all won in 1956. The last top-eight finish in any Gymnastics event was in 1964.

Fencing (2-3-2, 14th). All seven medals came in épée, including team gold in 1976 and individual gold for Johan Harmenberg in 1980. The most recent medal came in 1984.

Handball (0-4-0, 9th). Silvers for the men in 1992, 1996, 2000 & 2012. The women came 4th in 2021.

Golf (0-1-0, 6th=). Henrik Stenson took silver in 2016; the only Swedish top-eight finish so far.

Tennis (0-3-5, 19th). Five of the eight medals came in 1908 and 1912 (four of which were in indoor events). Stefan Edberg won bronzes in singles and doubles in 1988, and there was a men's doubles silver in 2008.

Water Polo (0-1-2, 15th). The medals came in 1908, 1912 and 1920. The only entry since 1952 came in 1980. The women have never entered.

Triathlon (0-1-0, 11th=). In the 2012 women's event, Lisa Norden missed out on gold in an incredible photo finish (both athletes clocked 1:59:48). That remains Sweden's only top-eight finish in Triathlon.

Boxing (0-5-6, 40th). Three medals since 1952 – a bronze in 1972, and a silver and bronze in 1988.

Archery (0-2-0, 18th). Men's individual silvers for Gunnar Jervill (1972) and Magnus Petersson (1996).

Weightlifting (0-0-4, 59th). The last medal came in 1972 (although there was a 4th place in 2021). Albert Pettersson finished joint 2nd in 1920, but apparently lots were drawn for the silver, and he lost.

Rowing (0-2-0, 32nd). The silvers came in 1912 and 1956. There was a single sculls 4th place in 2012.

Taekwondo – Roman Livaja came 4th in 2000, and there have been a further five top-eight finishes.

Judo – Five top-eight finishes, but no semi-finals as yet.

Badminton – Two quarter-finals which have both ended in defeat – the 1992 women's doubles (6th) and the 2004 mixed doubles (8th).

Volleyball – Only one entry – the 1988 men's event, when they won 3 matches out of 7, and came 7th.

Artistic Swimming – The only entrant was Maria Jacobsson, who was 9th in the solo event in 1988.

Basketball – Came 10th out of 12 on their only appearance – the 1980 men's event.

Beach Volleyball – Three entries, all by men. A last-16 defeat in 2004 (14th place) is their best showing.

Skateboarding – Came 17th in their only entry in 2021.

Baseball/Softball, Hockey, Karate, Rugby, Sport Climbing, Surfing – never entered

WINTER
Curling (4-3-4, 2nd). Women's golds in 2006, 2010 & 2018. Men's gold in 2022. Both men and women have won medals in each of the last three Games.

Nordic Skiing (32-27-25, 3rd). Only in 1924 and 1994 have Sweden failed to win a medal in the sport. Four golds have been won by each of Sixten Jernberg (who won nine medals in total, 1956-64), Thomas Wassberg (1980-88) and Gunde Svan (1984 & 1988). Charlotte Kalla (2010-18) has also won nine medals.

Ice Hockey (2-4-5, 4th). Men's golds in 1994 (on penalties) and 2006. The last male medal was in 2014; the last female medal was in 2006 (silvers in both cases).

Biathlon (6-6-6, 5th). Sisters Hanna and Elvira Oberg have three medals each (2018 & 2022). Hanna is the only Swedish biathlete with two golds.

Figure Skating (5-3-2, 7th). Gillis Grafstrom won the men's title in 1920, 1924 & 1928, and took silver in 1932. He is the only male skater to win three individual golds. Ulrich Salchow, who famously had a jump named after him, won gold in 1908, and Magda Julin took the women's title in 1920. No Swedish medals since 1936.

Alpine Skiing (8-2-9, 8th). Ingemar Stenmark (1980) and Pernilla Wiberg (1992 & 1994) won two golds each. Anja Parson won six medals, including 1 gold, from 2002 to 2010.

Speed Skating (9-4-5, 7th). Tomas Gustafsson won 3 golds and a silver in 1984 & 1988 (in men's 5000m and 10000m). The two medals since then were both gold, and both won in 2022 by Nils van der Poel (in the same two events).

Freestyle Skiing (2-1-3, 9th). Four medals in 2022, including golds for Walter Wallberg and Sandra Naslund.

Nordic Combined (0-1-1, 10th). Silver in 1956 and bronze in 1948. No Swedish entries since 1972.

Ski Jumping (0-1-1, 11th=). Silver in 1936 and bronze in 1952. The last top-eight finishes came in 1988.

Snowboarding (0-1-0, 19th=). Silver in men's parallel giant slalom in 2002 for Richard Richardsson.

Bobsleigh – Four top-eight finishes. The most recent (and joint best) was 6th in 1972.

Luge – The only top-eight finish was 6th in 1992.

Short Track Speed Skating – Martin Johansson is the only Swedish Olympian in the sport; he entered seven events between 1994 and 2002, finishing 7th in the 1994 men's 500 metres.

Skeleton – never entered

NORWAY   Olympic Rank 9th

Population: 5,597,924 (rank 118th)
Olympic rank/ population differential: +109
Population per gold: 26,657 (rank 2nd)
Population per medal: 9,821 (rank 2nd)

Summer: 62 gold, 51 silver, 49 bronze (total 162)
Winter: 148 gold, 136 silver, 124 bronze (total 408)
Total: 210 gold, 187 silver, 173 bronze (total 570)

Best sports: Nordic Combined (15 golds, 37.50%, 1st)
                                          Nordic Skiing (52 golds, 28.57%, 1st)
                                          Biathlon (22 golds, 22.92%, 2nd)

It will come as no surprise to learn that Norway have been considerably more successful in the Winter Games than the Summer Games. They are one of five countries that have won more Winter golds than Summer, and one of only three to have won more Winter medals overall than Summer (Austria and Liechtenstein are the others, but Norway have the biggest majority of Winter medals over Summer). The only country that has outperformed Norway in Winter Olympic history is Germany, and even then only if one adds in both West German and East German medals as well.

Norway have entered every Winter Games, finishing top of the medal table in 1924 and 2022, as well as several times in between. In 2022, in fact, they set a new all-time Winter record of 16 golds, and fell just short of the all-time Winter record for total medals (39), which Norway themselves set in 2018. They have finished outside the top 10 just twice – 1988, when they shockingly won no golds at all, and 2006, when they won just two.

They first entered the Summer Games in 1900, and since then have missed only the 1980 Games. By far their most successful Games were the 1920 Antwerp Games, when they won 13 golds (their next best is 5) and 28 medals in total (their next best is 10). They came 6th in the medal table, equalling their best, set in 1904, when they won just 2 golds. All but one of those 13 golds in Antwerp came in Sailing and Shooting.

Norway have twice left a Games empty-handed – 1932 and 1964. But they have won at least two golds at every Games since 1988, with the exception of 2016 (when they won just four bronzes).

SUMMER
Sailing (17-11-4, 4th). Norway dominated the 1920 Sailing regatta, winning 7 of the 13 events, although it has to be said that in five of them they were the only entrants, and in the other two they only had Belgium for competition. Crown Prince Olav (who later became King of Norway) won gold at the 1928 Games as part of the crew in the 6-meter class. The only two golds since 1960 have both come in the women's Europe class – Linda Andersen (1992) and Siren Sundby (2004).

Handball (2-2-3, 7th). All 7 medals have been won by the women since 1988, including golds in 2008 and 2012. The men have only competed twice, finishing 7th in 2021.

Triathlon (1-0-0, 8th=). Kristian Blummenfelt took men's gold in 2021. The best women's finish is 24th.

Beach Volleyball (1-0-0, 5th). Men's gold in 2021 for Anders Mol and Christian Sorum. Norway's previous top-eight finish was in 1996.

Shooting (13-9-11, 9th). Ole Lilloe-Olsen won five golds and a silver in 1920 and 1924, all in various running deer events. Otto Olsen won eight medals across the same two Games (4-3-1). 25 of their 33 medals came in or before 1924, and their last gold came in 1988. Their last medal was a silver in 2008.

Football (1-0-2, 18th=). The women took bronze in 1996 and gold in 2000. The men knocked Germany out in 1936, to the disgust of the watching Adolf Hitler, and eventually won bronze. The men last entered in 1984.

Canoeing (6-4-4, 12th). Only 4 medals prior to 1992. Then 6 medals (3-2-1) in 1992-2000, all in K1 events for Knut Holmann; and 4 medals (2-1-1) in 2004-12, all involving Eirik Veras Larsen.

Rowing (3-7-8, 15th). Golds in double sculls (1976), and in single sculls for Olaf Tufte (2004 & 2008).

Wrestling (4-2-2, 22nd). Jon Ronningen took Greco-Roman flyweight golds in 1988 and 1992. The only medal since then was a bronze in 2016. The other two golds were both in 1904, both by wrestlers previously thought to be American, but have since been shown to have been Norwegian citizens.

Athletics (8-7-8, 24th). Four of their first six golds came in javelin, including two (2004 & 2008) for Andreas Thorkildsen. Two golds in 2021, for Karsten Warholm (400m hurdles) and Jakob Ingebrigtsen (1500m).

Cycling (2-0-2, 18th=). Knut Knudsen's men's pursuit gold in 1972 remains the only track medal. Gunn-Rita Dahle won the women's cross-country in 2004, and Norway took men's road race bronzes in 1984 and 2012.

Gymnastics (2-2-1, 26th). All five medals came in team events, the last of which was in 1920. The only top-eight finish since then was a pommel horse 5th place in 1964. The winning team in 1906 included Flisa Andersen, who had also won men's pole vault bronze in 1900.

Weightlifting (1-0-0, 42nd). Leif Jensen took light-heavyweight gold in 1972. A 6th place in 2008 in women's middleweight was the only other top-eight finish.

Boxing (1-2-2, 34th). Otto von Porat (1924) took the gold. The last medal came in 1936, and the last top-eight finish in 1992.

Taekwondo (0-2-0, 24th). Silvers in women's events in 2000 and 2008. The best men's finish is 6th.

Tennis (0-0-1, 26th=). Molla Bjurstedt took women's singles bronze in 1912. She later emigrated to America and became an eight-time Grand Slam champion. No top-eight finishes since 1924.

Equestrianism (0-1-0, 24th=). Three-day event team silver in 1928. No higher finish than 8th since 1956.

Fencing (0-1-0, 25th=). Bartosz Piasecki (born in Poland but raised in Norway) won men's épée silver in 2012. The other three top-eight finishes have all come in team épée.

Swimming (0-1-1, 42nd=). Both medals came in breaststroke in 2008 (Alexander Dale Oen silver and Sara Nordenstam bronze).

Archery – Martinus Grov came 4th in the men's event in 1992; the only top-eight finish so far.

Diving – Two 7th place finishes – one in 1920, one in 1988. Both were in women's events.

Golf – The best women's finish is 10th; the best men's finish is equal 14th.

Modern Pentathlon – Entered only in 1912, 1920 and 1924, with a best finish of 13th.

Judo – Entered only in 1984 and 1992, with one last-16 appearance.

Badminton – 16th place in the men's singles in 2004 is the best of their three entries so far.

Artistic Swimming, Baseball/Softball, Basketball, Hockey, Karate, Rugby, Skateboarding, Sport Climbing, Surfing, Table Tennis, Volleyball, Water Polo, PWDS – never entered

WINTER
Nordic Combined (15-12-8, 1st). Jorgen Graabak is the only 4-time gold medallist in the history of Nordic Combined, taking large hill and team golds in both 2014 and 2022. He also has two silvers.

Nordic Skiing (52-43-34, 1st). Norway have, not surprisingly, won medals in Nordic Skiing in every single Winter Games. Two people can boast achievements that eclipse all others. Bjorn Daehlie won 8 golds and 4 silvers (1992-98), whilst Marit Bjorgen's 15 medals (8-4-3) between 2002 and 2018 make her the most decorated Winter Olympian of all time. Johannes Hosflot Klaebo has won 5 golds, 1 silver and 1 bronze (2018-22) so far, and may well add more in the future.

Biathlon (22-18-15, 2nd). A number of Norwegians have won numerous Biathlon medals, including Johannes Thingnes Bo (5-2-1, 2018-22), Emil Hegle Svendsen (4-3-1, 2010-18) and Marte Olsbu Roiseland (3-2-2, 2018-22), but all pale into relative insignificance behind Ole Einar Bjorndalen (8-4-1, 1998-2014). He and his compatriots Marit Bjorgen and Bjorn Daehlie are the only people ever to win 8 Winter golds.

Ski Jumping (12-10-14, 1st). Birger Ruud is the only Norwegian to have more than one gold – taking the men's title in 1932 and 1936, before adding a silver in 1948.

Speed Skating (28-29-30, 3rd). Norway have only failed to medal in the sport three times (1988, 2006 & 2014). Ivar Ballangrud (1928-36) and Johann Koss (1992-94) have won four golds each.

Freestyle Skiing (4-2-4, 6th). Norway have only once (2014) failed to medal in Freestyle Skiing. Golds have gone to Stine Lisa Hattestad, Kari Traa, Oystein Braten and Birk Ruud.

Alpine Skiing (11-14-15, 7th). Norway virtually refused to involve themselves in Alpine Skiing for many years, believing Nordic to be superior. Between 1936 (the sport's introduction to the Olympics) and 1988, they won just four medals. But they have prospered hugely since then, with Kjetil Andre Aamodt the star, winning 8 medals (4-2-2) between 1992 and 2006.

Curling (1-2-2, 5th). The men took gold in 2002 (as well as 1998 bronze and 2010 silver). There has been a silver and bronze in mixed doubles. The best finish in the women's event is 4th.

Figure Skating (3-2-1, 10th). All three golds went to the legendary Sonja Henie (1928, 1932 & 1936; she is the only three-time champion in the women's event). The other three medals all came in 1920. No top-16 finishes since 1952.

Snowboarding (0-4-1, 15th). Two silvers in 1998, and further medals in 2006, 2014 and 2022.

Luge – Their only top-eight finish (4th) came in 1964. Have only competed in one Games this century (2014).

Bobsleigh – The best 3 positions (5th, 7th and 10th) all came in 1948. Last entered in 2002.

Short Track Speed Skating – Finished 6th, 9th and 11th in 1994, but have not entered since.

Ice Hockey – The men are regular entrants, and came 8th in 1972 and 2018. The women have never competed.

Skeleton – Their best finish is 9th in the women's 2006 event. Their best men's finish is 14th (2002).

FINLAND   **Olympic Rank 15th**

Population:	5,614,571 (rank 117th)
Olympic rank/ population differential:	+102
Population per gold:	37,936 (rank 3rd)
Population per medal:	11,600 (rank 3rd)
Summer:	102 gold, 86 silver, 120 bronze (total 308)
Winter:	46 gold, 65 silver, 65 bronze (total 176)
Total:	148 gold, 151 silver, 185 bronze (total 484)
Best sports:	Ski Jumping (10 golds, 18.52%, 2nd)
	Nordic Skiing (22 golds, 12.09%, 4th)
	Nordic Combined (4 golds, 10.00%, 3rd)

Finland have entered every Summer Games since their debut in 1908, and every Winter Games since it started in 1924. Up until 2000, they had won golds in every Summer Games they had entered. Since then, though, they have won just one gold in five Games (Satu Makela-Nummela in women's trap shooting in 2008). They won 15 golds in 1920, and 14 in 1924 (taking 37 medals in total that year, and finishing 2nd). They also finished 3rd in 1920 and 1928. In 2016, in contrast, they won just a single bronze (in Boxing).

Finland finished 2nd in the inaugural Winter Games of 1924, with four golds – a total they have matched in 1984, 1988 and 2002. Their highest medal count is 13 (in 1984). They have won medals at every Winter Games, only failing to win gold four times – most recently in 2010.

Their most successful medal-winners have been Paavo Nurmi (Athletics) with 12 and Heikki Savolainen (Gymnastics) with 9. Four Winter Olympians have won 7 – Clas Thunberg (Speed Skating), and three Nordic skiers listed below. The most golds have been won by Nurmi (9), Thunberg (5) and Ville Ritola (5).

SUMMER
Wrestling (27-29-29, 6th). Finland won multiple Wrestling medals in every Games from 1906 to 1956, but their success tapered off after that. Jouko Salamaki was their most recent gold medallist (in 1984), whilst their last medal came in 2004. Their most successful wrestlers, with 2 golds and 1 silver each, are Verner Weckman (1906-08) and Kustaa Pihlajamaki (1924-36).

Athletics (49-36-31, 5th). Most of Finland's Athletics success came pre-war, with 30 of their 49 golds coming between 1912 and 1928. The biggest star was Paavo Nurmi, with 9 golds and 3 silvers (1920-28) in various middle-distance races. Hannes Kolehmainen won 3 golds and 1 silver in similar events in 1912, plus a fourth gold in 1920, this time in the marathon. Likewise, Ville Ritola won 5 golds and 3 silvers in similar events in 1924 and 1928. In 1972 and 1976, Lasse Viren won back-to-back 5000m/ 10000m doubles, another remarkable achievement. The last gold came in 2000 (Arsi Harju in men's shot put), and there have been no medals since 2012. Of the 12 medals since 1984, nine have been won in javelin.

Gymnastics (8-5-12, 11th). Paavo Aaltonen and Veikko Huhtanen won three golds each in 1948. Heikki Savolainen won a total of nine Olympic medals between 1928 and 1952 (when he was aged 44) – two of them were gold. All three of them shared gold in the 1948 men's pommel horse. Finland's last gold was in the 1960 men's pommel horse (Eugen Ekman), whilst their most recent medal was in 1968 (also men's pommel horse).

Canoeing (5-2-3, 16th). Nine of their ten medals were won in 1948 & 1952; the other was a gold for Yrjo Kolehmainen in the men's K1 500m in 1992.

Archery (1-1-2, 9th=). Gold for Tomi Poikolainen in the men's individual in 1980; the last medal was a silver for the men's team in 1992.

Shooting (4-7-10, 17th). Pentti Linnosvuo won two of the golds (1956 & 1964). The last medals were a gold and bronze in 2008.

Rowing (3-1-3, 18th). Pertti Karppinen won men's single sculls in 1976, 1980 and 1984 (one of only two men to win three in a row in the event). The only medal since was a 2008 silver (women's lightweight double sculls).

Sailing (2-2-7, 19th). Golds in 1980 (when Esko Rechardt became the only Finn to win the Olympic Finn title) and 2000 (Jyrki Jarvi and Thomas Johanson in the men's 49er).

Boxing (2-1-13, 27th). Sten Suvio (1936) and Pentti Hamalainen (1952) won gold. Only two medals since 1992, both were bronzes won by Mira Potkonen in women's lightweight (2016 & 2021).

Weightlifting (1-0-2, 39th). Gold in 1968 for Kaarlo Kangasniemi, and two bronzes in 1984.

Modern Pentathlon (0-1-4, 13th). Three medals in 1956, and team bronzes in 1952 and 1972. The last top-eight finish was in 1980.

Swimming (0-1-4, 41st). Jani Sievenen won silver in 1996 (men's 200m individual medley). The only medal since was a bronze in 2021 for Matti Mattsson (men's 200m breaststroke).

Football – Came 4th in 1912, their only top eight finish; they have also competed in 1936, 1952 and 1980.

Equestrianism – Six top-eight finishes – five in dressage (all in involving Kyra Kyrklund, stretching from 1980 to 2008, and including three 5th places) and one in three-day eventing (in 1928).

Diving – Three 5th places, the last of which was in 1928. No top-eight finishes since then.

Cycling – Six top-eight finishes. The best was 5th in the 1912 men's team road race; the last were in the women's points race and road time trial in 1996.

Taekwondo – Two Finnish women have come 6th – in 2000 and 2012.

Judo – Two equal 7th finishes, in 1980 and 1988. The 2021 Games were the first they have missed since 1964.

Fencing – Came 8th in men's individual épée in 1956. Last entered in 1996.

Basketball – Entered only in 1952 and 1964; finishing 15th and 11th respectively.

Badminton – The best finish is 12th place in the men's singles in 2008.

Hockey – On their only entry (in 1952), they came last out of 12.

Tennis – Only competed in the last 16 once (1924 men's doubles, after a walkover).

Skateboarding – Entered the women's park in 2021, finishing 14th.

Golf – Used their full complement of four players in both 2016 and 2021; their best finish is equal 18th.

Artistic Swimming – The only entry was in the 1992 solo event; Finland finished in 19th place.

Table Tennis – Only one entry (2016 men's singles) – won one match, but failed to reach the last 32.

Baseball/Softball, Beach Volleyball, Handball, Karate, Rugby, Sport Climbing, Surfing, Triathlon, Volleyball, Water Polo, PWDS – never entered

WINTER
Ski Jumping (10-8-4, 2nd). The biggest star of Finnish Ski Jumping has been Matti Nykanen, who took four golds and a silver in 1984 & 1988. Their success seems to be fading now; they have not won a medal since 2006, or a gold since 1998.

Nordic Skiing (22-27-37, 4th). Four Finns have won 3 golds each – Veikko Hakulinen (3-3-1, 1952 to 1960), Eero Mantyranta (3-2-2, 1960 to 1968), Marja-Liisa Kirvesniemi-Hamalainen (3-0-4, 1984 to 1994), and Iivo Niskanen (3-1-1, 2014 to 2022).

Nordic Combined (4-8-2, 3rd). Samppa Lajunen won three golds (1998 men's individual, 2002 men's sprint and team). The last medal was a men's team bronze in 2006.

Speed Skating (7-8-9, 8th). Clas Thunberg won five silvers, a gold and a bronze in 1924 & 1928, including medals in all five Speed Skating events in 1924. The last four medals were all won by Kaija Mustonen, back in 1964 & 1968.

Ice Hockey (1-2-8, 6th). After medalling at 6 of the previous 9 Games, the men finally took gold in 2022 with a 2-1 win over Russia. The women have won four bronzes (1998, 2010, 2018, 2022).

Freestyle Skiing (1-2-1, 10th). All four medals came in men's moguls. Janne Lahtela won 1998 silver and 2002 gold.

Figure Skating (1-1-0, 14th=). Ludowika Jakobsson and husband Walter took gold in the 1920 pairs event, and silver in 1924. Finland's post-war best is 4th place in the ice dance in 1994.

Snowboarding (0-2-2, 17th). Two men's halfpipe medals, and two women's slopestyle medals (both for Enni Rukajarvi, 2014 & 2018).

Biathlon (0-5-2, 12th). The last of the five silvers was in 1976. The bronzes came in 1992 and 1998.

Curling (0-1-0, 9th=). The men won silver in 2006 and came 5th in 2002. Finland also came 7th in mixed doubles in 2018.

Alpine Skiing (0-1-0, 19th=). Three top-six finishes, all for Tanja Poutiainen, including women's giant slalom silver in 2006.

Bobsleigh, Luge, Short Track Speed Skating, Skeleton – never entered

DENMARK　　　　　　　　　　**Olympic Rank 25th**

Population:				5,946,984 (rank 114th)
Olympic rank/ population differential:	+89
Population per gold:			115,475 (rank 14th)
Population per medal:			27,986 (rank 11th)

Summer:			51 gold, 80 silver, 80 bronze (total 211)
Winter:			0 gold, 1 silver, 0 bronze (total 1)
Total:			51 gold, 81 silver, 80 bronze (total 212)
			(plus mixed team: 0.5 gold, 0 silver, 0 bronze (total 0.5))

Best sports:		Handball (4 golds, 15.38%, 3rd)
			Sailing (13 golds, 6.70%, 5th)
			Badminton (2 golds, 5.13%, 4th)

Denmark have entered every Summer Olympics with just one exception – the 1904 Games of St Louis, which most countries opted to miss, largely due to travel difficulties. Back in 1896, they finished 9th in the medal table with three medals each for Viggo Jensen (two, including a gold, in Weightlifting and one in Shooting) and Holger Nielsen (two in Shooting and one in Fencing). They have never failed to win at least one medal in any Summer Games since. The closest they came was in Munich in 1972, when they only won one – but at least it was a gold (Niels Fredborg in the men's 1km Cycling time trial). They have only failed to win gold four times – 1908, 1932, 1936 and (surprisingly, given the boycotts) 1984.

Denmark's most successful Olympics came in London in 1948. They secured their highest number of golds (five) and their highest number of overall medals (20), coming in 10th in the medal table. Other top-10 finishes in medal tables were achieved in 1896 (9th), 1900 (9th), 1906 (9th) and 1920 (10th). The 15 medals they won in 2016, and the 11 in 2021, were the first times they have reached double figures since 1948.

Two Danes have won three or more Olympic golds. Eskild Ebbesen was part of a lightweight coxless four Rowing crew which medalled at five consecutive Olympics (three golds and two bronzes between 1996 and 2012). The Danes won silver in the same event, without Ebbesen, in 2016. The other is sailor Paul Elvstrom, who won gold in the Finn class four times in a row (1948 to 1960). He remained the only person ever to win four Sailing golds until emulated by Great Britain's Ben Ainslie in 2012. He competed across 40 years of Olympics, from 1948 to 1988, and was later named Denmark's Sportsman of the Century.

Prior to Elvstrom's fourth gold in 1960, no other Danish sailor had ever won Olympic gold. But they have now won 13, making it their most lucrative sport. They have also won 9 silvers and 9 bronzes in Sailing, for a total of 31 medals. In terms of pure numbers, their other most successful sports have been Cycling (29 medals including 8 golds) and Rowing (25 medals including 7 golds). But, in the less played sports of Handball and Badminton, the Danes have also excelled. Their women's Handball team enjoyed a golden period of three successive Olympics titles from 1996 to 2004. The men have since won gold in 2016 and silver in 2021. Meanwhile, their nine medals in Badminton (2 gold, 3 silver and 4 bronze) make them by far the most successful Badminton nation outside of Asia. They have won medals in all five events (men's and women's singles, and men's, women's and mixed doubles).

In contrast, Denmark have, remarkably, never won a gold medal in Athletics. They have only won four silvers and three bronzes. One of each was claimed by Kenyan-born 800 metres runner Wilson Kipketer, who won his medals in 2000 and 2004, and would have been strong favourite for gold in 1996, but was unable to compete as his Danish citizenship wasn't complete in time. They have won 15 medals in Swimming, including three golds – all for women (Greta Andersen and Karen Harup in 1948, and Pernille Blume in 2016). Other sports to have produced golds for Denmark have been Football, Canoeing, Shooting, Diving, Wrestling, Fencing, Boxing and Gymnastics. They also shared gold in the 1900 Tug of War with Sweden (they had three tuggers each on the team). There have been silvers and/or bronzes in Equestrianism, Hockey, Tennis and Table Tennis.

Surprisingly for a Scandinavian nation, they have only ever won one Winter Olympic medal, despite having competed in 1948, 1960, 1964, 1968, and every Games since 1988. That medal was silver, won by the women's Curling team in 1998. Five of Denmark's seven top-eight finishes in Winter Games have come in Curling – the others in Speed Skating (2018) and Ice Hockey (2022).

ICELAND Olympic Rank 107th

Population:	360,872 (rank 175th)
Olympic rank/ population differential:	+68
Population per gold:	n/a
Population per medal:	90,218 (rank 36th)

Summer:	0 gold, 2 silver, 2 bronze (total 4)
Winter:	*no medals (best finish: 11th)*
Total:	0 gold, 2 silver, 2 bronze (total 4)
Best sports:	Athletics (1 silver, 1 bronze, 75th=)
	Handball (1 silver, 12th=)
	Judo (1 bronze, 46th=)

Iceland's first Olympian was Johannes Josefsson, a well-known versatile fighter who came fourth in Greco-Roman Wrestling (middleweight) in 1908. After sending one wrestler and one athlete to the Games of 1912, they were absent from the Games until 1936, but have competed in every Summer Games since then. They have won two silver medals in that time – Vilhjalmur Einarsson (men's triple jump 1956) and the men's Handball team in 2008; and two bronzes – Bjarni Fridriksson (Judo in 1984) and Vala Flosadottir (women's pole vault 2000). In 2021, their best finish was 22nd, making it their worst Games ever – they'd had at least a top-10 finish in every Games since 1976 until then.

Athletics and Handball have produced 12 of their 20 top-eight finishes. The others have come in Gymnastics, Judo, Weightlifting, Wrestling (twice, but not since 1912) and Swimming (three times – their best was Orn Arnason, who came fourth in the men's 200m backstroke in 2000).

Since debuting in the Winter Games in 1948, they have only been absent once (1972). However, their record is remarkably poor, given the Icelandic climate. They have not competed in any event besides Alpine Skiing and Nordic Skiing since 1960, and their best finish is 11th, in Nordic Skiing's 4x10km relay for men in 1952.

CHAPTER NINE - Latin Europe (France, Italy, Spain, Portugal, San Marino, Monaco, Malta, Andorra)

FRANCE   **Olympic Rank 6th**
Population: 68,521,974 (rank 21st)
Olympic rank/ population differential: +15
Population per gold: 242,127 (rank 28th)
Population per medal: 73,020 (rank 31st)

Summer: 242 gold, 262 silver, 295 bronze (total 799)
Winter: 41 gold, 42 silver, 55 bronze (total 138)
Total: 283 gold, 304 silver, 350 bronze (total 937)
(plus mixed team: 0 gold, 1.4 silver, 0 bronze (total 1.4))

Best sports: Fencing (47 golds, 20.35 %, 2nd)
                                Cycling (42 golds, 15.56%, 1st)
                                Handball (4 golds, 15.38%, 2nd)

France have competed in every Olympics, both Summer and Winter, although their only entrant in 1904 was Albert Corey, a US-based French immigrant, who had seemingly not changed citizenship (he won a silver medal in the marathon). The only other Summer Games without a French gold was Rome in 1960. They did not win a medal of any colour in the 1956 Winter Games (they had two 4th places). There have been various Winter Games without a gold, most recently in 1994.

In what was, in many events at least, virtually a domestic championship, France won 111 medals, including 31 golds, in Paris in 1900. That apart, their highest total of golds was 15, set both in 1906 and 1996. Their highest medal total since 1900 was 43, set in 2008 (strangely, the only Games this century with fewer than 10 golds). They topped the medal table in 1900 and 1906, and last failed to finish in the top 10 in 1984. France's best Winter Games were in Grenoble in 1968, finishing 3rd with over 10% of all gold medals (four in total). They won five (from a much bigger programme) in 2018 and 2022, and won 15 medals in total in 2014 and 2018.

SWIMMING
Fencing (47-44-37, 2nd). A French Summer Olympic record of four golds each for Lucien Gaudin (1924-28) and Christian d'Oriola (1948-56). In men's team foil, France only missed out on a medal once between 1920 and 1984, and they have medalled in team épée 18 times out of 26. Two more fencers, Philippe Cattiau (1920-36) and Roger Ducret (1920-28), won a French record eight medals each.

PWDS (4-4-3, 2nd). Three Croquet events took place in Paris in 1900 (doubles, 1-ball singles and 2-ball singles), and France were the only country that entered; thereby winning 3 gold, 2 silver and 2 bronze by default. They also won a Motor Boating gold in 1908, Polo bronze in 1900, and two silvers in 1900 in events when only two teams entered – they lost to a joint Swedish/Danish team in Tug of War, and lost to Great Britain at Cricket.

Cycling (42-28-30, 1st). France won 5 golds in both 1996 and 2000, but have won only four golds since then, three in cross-country and one in BMX. Three golds each for Paul Masson (1896), Robert Charpentier (1936), Daniel Morelon (1968-72), Felicia Ballanger (1996-2000) and Florian Rousseau (1996-2000).

Handball (4-2-1, 2nd). The men won bronze at their first attempt, in 1992. The nation then entered a golden era starting in 2008; the men won three of the next four golds, with a silver in 2016, and the women, having also won silver in 2016, made it a golden double in 2021. Michael Guigou and Nikola Karabatic are the most successful Handball Olympians of all time (three golds and a silver each).

Rugby (1-3-0, 4th). The French women took a surprise Sevens silver in 2021. They medalled on all three occasions they entered pre-war, but then there were never more than 3 entrants anyway. They won gold in 1900.

Karate (1-0-0, 5th=). Steven Da Costa won the 2021 men's <67kg. The other French karatakas came 7th and 9th.

Tennis (8-8-8, 3rd). Three golds in 1906 (all featuring Max Decugis – men's singles and doubles, and mixed doubles). Three golds in 1912. Two golds in 1920 (Suzanne Lenglen in women's singles, and Lenglen and

Decugis in mixed doubles). Since reintroduction, France have won two singles medals (Arnaud di Pasquale bronze and Amelie Mauresmo silver), and men's doubles silver and bronze in 2012.

Judo (16-13-28, 2nd). They've won medals at every Games since 1972. Heavyweight Teddy Riner is the most decorated Olympic judoka in history (2 golds and 2 bronzes, 2008-21, as well as a team gold in 2021).

Archery (7-11-7, 4th). Sebastien Flute's gold in 1992 was one of just three medals won since 1920.

Equestrianism (15-15-13, 3rd). Three golds this century, all in team events. No dressage medals since 1988.

Sailing (17-14-20, 3rd). 26 of the 51 medals were won in 1900 alone, when all the events were of dubious international merit. Two golds this century (2004 & 2016), both in women's windsurfing.

Shooting (13-15-14, 8th). 22 of the 42 medals were won pre-World War I. Two golds this century.

Weightlifting (9-3-4, 7th). All 9 golds were won between 1920 and 1936, including two for Louis Hostin (light heavyweight, 1932 & 1936; he also won silver in 1928). Just three medals since then – 1956, 1976 and 2008.

Volleyball (1-0-0, 10th). Having never previously finished higher than 8th in any Volleyball event, they took gold in the men's event in 2021, with a thrilling 5-set victory over Russia.

Canoeing (8-9-19, 8th). Tony Estanguet won men's C1 slalom in 2000, 2004 and 2012. Other than one gold in 1952, all of the others have come since 1996.

Rowing (9-17-16, 10th). The coxed pairs of 1952 was the only gold won between 1906 and 2000. Five golds won this century. Nobody has yet won gold more than once.

Water Polo (1-0-3, 10th). France beat Belgium 3-0 to win the title in Paris in 1924. Two separate French teams shared bronze in 1900, and bronze was won in 1928 as well. Their last top-eight finish was in 1948, although they competed as recently as 2016; they have never entered the women's competition.

Football (1-1.4-0, 15th). The 1984 Games saw professionals (albeit with heavy restrictions) allowed to enter for the first time; this, together with the Soviet-led boycott, meant that communist domination ended, and it was France who took advantage, beating Brazil 2-0 in the final. They had previously won silver in 1900, and contributed to the team that took silver in 1906 too. The women played for the first time in 2012, finishing 4th.

Boxing (6-9-10, 11th). Three golds before the war, and three since (Brahim Asloum in 2000, and Tony Yoka and Estelle Mossely in 2016).

Athletics (15-27-30, 15th). Only one gold this century (Renaud Lavillenie in pole vault in 2012). Marie-Jose Perec won three golds in 200 and 400 metres (1992 & 1996). Their first Olympic Athletics champion, Michel Theato (1900 men's marathon), is often claimed by Luxembourg, the country of his birth.

Swimming (8-16-20, 12th). France won four golds in 2012, having won only two in their entire history prior to 2004 (in 1900 and 1952; the one in 1900 was in the underwater Swimming event).

Gymnastics (5-10-11, 14th). Pierre Paysse won two golds in 1906. Only 8 of the 26 medals have come since 1924, including just one gold – Emilie Lepennec (women's asymmetrical bars) in 2004.

Wrestling (4-4-10, 20th). Steeve Guenot's gold in 2008 (men's Greco-Roman welterweight) is France's only title since 1936, although a number of other medals have been won in that time.

Basketball (0-4-1, 6th=). Silvers were won by the men in 1948, 2000 and 2021, and the women in 2012. The women won bronze in 2021. The USA won gold on all five of those occasions.

Taekwondo (0-3-5, 23rd). France have won at least one medal every time Taekwondo has been contested – six different women have won one each, while Pascal Gentil has won two (both bronzes) on the men's side.

Triathlon (0-0-1, 14th=). Won mixed relay bronze in 2021; their best individual finish has been 4th.

Modern Pentathlon (0-1-2, 14th). Team bronzes in 1968 & 1984; women's silver for Elodie Clouvel in 2016.

Artistic Swimming (0-0-1, 8th). Competed every time since 1984; their one medal was in the 2000 duet.

Table Tennis (0-1-1, 9th=). Jean-Philippe Gatien got a men's singles silver in 1992 and doubles bronze in 2000. France finished 4th in mixed doubles in 2021.

Diving (0-1-0, 16th). The medal went to Mady Moreau in women's springboard in 1952. Their best in recent times was a 4th place in 2016.

Hockey – 4th in 1920 and 1936, France have not competed since 1972, and never in the women's event.

Golf – The 1900 women's bronze medallist Abbie Pratt is sometimes listed as French (she played for a French club), but she was a US national. The ladies finishing 4th and 6th were French, though. None of the French entrants since 1900 have finished in the top 20.

Skateboarding – Vincent Milou came 4th in men's street in 2021.

Badminton – Just one quarter-finalist so far, Chinese-born Hongyan Pi (5th in women's singles in 2008).

Sport Climbing – Mickael Mawem came 5th in the men's in 2021; Anouck Jaubert came 6th in the women's.

Surfing – Michel Bourez came 6th in the men's event in 2021.

Beach Volleyball – Entered in 1996, 2000 and 2004, but never finished inside the top 12.

Baseball/Softball – never entered

WINTER
Biathlon (12-9-12, 4th). Martin Fourcade won five golds (an all-time French record) and a silver (2014-18).

Alpine Skiing (16-17-18, 5th). By far France's biggest star is Jean-Claude Killy, winner of 3 golds in 1968.

Snowboarding (4-5-4, 5th). Golds for Pierre Vaultier (men's snowboard cross) in 2014 & 2018.

Freestyle Skiing (3-6-6, 8th). Golds in men's moguls (1992) and ski cross (2014), and women's moguls (2018).

Nordic Combined (2-1-1, 6th). Golds for Fabrice Guy in 1992 and Jason Lamy Chappuis in 2018.

Figure Skating (4-3-7, 8th). Pairs golds in 1928 and 1932 (both for married couple Andree and Pierre Brunet), and ice dance golds in 2002 and 2022. A steady stream of silvers and bronzes in between.

Curling (0-0-1, 12th=). In 1924, only three teams entered. France lost 18-10 to Sweden and 46-4 to Great Britain, so "won" the bronze. Have only entered twice since then (both men), finishing 7th in 2010.

Nordic Skiing (0-1-4, 15th). A silver for Roddy Darragon in sprint in 2006, and four bronzes since then.

Bobsleigh (0-0-1, 12th=). Tied for bronze in 1998, finally winning a medal in the sport after 74 years of trying.

Ski Jumping (0-0-1, 13th=). Coline Mattel won bronze in the women's event in 2014.

Speed Skating – 4th-place finishes in 1984 and 2010. Have not entered a women's event since 1988.

Short Track Speed Skating – Five 5th-place finishes between 1992 and 2010, four of which were in relays.

Ice Hockey – Came 5th in 1920 and 6th in 1924. Their post-war best is 8th in 1992. Never entered the women's.

Luge – Their best two finishes are 11th in 1968 and 15th in 2002.

Skeleton – The best finish so far is 14th in 2006. Never entered the women's competition.

ITALY	**Olympic Rank 7th**
Population:	61,021,855 (rank 24th)
Olympic rank/ population differential:	+17
Population per gold:	229,405 (rank 26th)
Population per medal:	78,738 (rank 33rd)
Summer:	224 gold, 194 silver, 216 bronze (total 634)
Winter:	42 gold, 43 silver, 56 bronze (total 141)
Total:	266 gold, 237 silver, 272 bronze (total 775)
Best sports:	Fencing (49 golds, 21.21 %, 1st)
	Cycling (38 golds, 14.07%, 3rd)
	Luge (7 golds, 13.46%, 2nd)

Italy have competed in every Olympic Games. They officially missed the 1904 Games, but cyclist Frank Bizzoni, a New York resident, was not granted US citizenship until 1917, so should be considered Italian. He did not win a medal, nor did the one Italian to compete in 1896 (a shooter), but Italy have won golds at every other Summer Games. Italy's lowest medal table position is 14th (in 1976); they have only missed the top 10 four times (most recently in 1992). They finished 2nd in 1932, and 3rd in Rome in 1960. They set national records of 14 golds in 1984, and 40 medals in total in 2021. They have finished 9th or 10th at each of the last four Games.

Their best Winter Games was Lillehammer 1994, when they won 20 medals, including 7 golds, and came 4th (they also came 4th in 1968). It took until 1948 for Italy to win a Winter medal, but they have medalled at all Games since then, and won golds at all of them except 1960, 1964, 1980 and 2014.

SUMMER
Fencing (49-47-36, 1st). Italy have won medals at every Games since 1906. The 2021 Games were the first without a gold since 1980. Three Italians have won six golds – Nedo Nadi (who won one in 1912, and five of the six golds on offer in 1920), Edoardo Mangiarotti (6 gold, 5 silver, 3 bronze, 1936-60) and Valentina Vezzali (6-1-2, all in foil, 1996-2012). Vezzali is the only female fencer ever to win more than 4 golds, and all three are the only Italians in any sport to win more than 4 golds.

Cycling (38-16-12, 3rd). Francesco Verri won three golds in 1906. Their golden era was probably 1948-68, during which time they won 16 Olympic titles.

Karate (1-0-1, 3rd=). Four top-eight finishes in 2021, including gold for Luigi Busa (men's <75kg) and bronze for Viviana Bottaro (women's kata).

Water Polo (4-3-3, 4th). The men won gold in 1948, 1960 and 1992. Their last medal was bronze in 2016. The women won gold in 2004 and silver in 2012.

Boxing (15-15-18, 5th). The most recent gold medallist was super-heavyweight Roberto Cammarelle in 2008.

Rowing (15-15-17, 5th). Medals have been won in the vast majority of Games since 1906, but it took until 2021 for a women's medal (a gold in lightweight double sculls).

Shooting (16-17-11, 5th). Niccolo Campriani won three golds and a silver (2012 & 2016) in rifle events.

Modern Pentathlon (2-2-3, 6th). They won a bronze in 1936, followed by six medals between 1984 and 1992. Carlo Massulo was involved in five of them – the team won gold in 1984, silver in 1988 and bronze in 1992, with Massulo also taking an individual silver and bronze; his compatriot Daniele Masala took gold in 1984.

Equestrianism (7-9-7, 7th). No medals since 1980. Raimondo and Piero d'Inzeo (1956-72) each won four team and two individual medals in jumping.

Taekwondo (2-1-1, 9th=). Carlo Molfetta (2012) and Vito Dell'Aquila (2021) won gold; men won all four medals.

Gymnastics (14-9-12, 9th). All 14 golds were won by men, and only 3 since 1932. They won the team event in 1912, 1920 and 1924. Giorgio Zampori featured in all three, and also won the 1920 individual all-around.

Football (1-0-2, 18th=). They beat Austria to win the 1936 final, and won bronzes in 1928 and 2004. They have never contested the women's competition.

Archery (2-3-4, 5th). Marco Galiazzo won the men's individual in 2004, and was part of the men's team that won gold in 2012. Lucilla Boari won individual bronze in 2021, becoming the first Italian woman to medal.

Judo (4-4-9, 9th). They have won medals every year since 1976, except for 1988. They took golds in 1980, 2000, 2008 and 2016.

Canoeing (6-7-4, 10th). Other than a silver in 1960, all their medals have come since 1992. Antonio Rossi won 5 medals (3-1-1) from 1992 to 2004.

Diving (3-5-3, 6th). Klaus Dibiasi was the greatest diver of his era. He took platform gold in 1968, 1972 and 1976, and silver in 1964, as well as springboard silver in 1968. Franco Cragnotto won four medals from 1972 to 1980. Only two other medals have been won, both in 2016 and both involving Cragnotto's daughter Tania.

Athletics (24-15-26, 9th). In 2016, Italy finished without an Athletics medal for the first time since 1956. But in 2021, they more than made up for that, winning five golds, including the 100 metres and 4x100m relay for Marcell Jacobs. Ugo Frigerio won three golds and a bronze in walking events (1920-32).

Weightlifting (5-6-7, 12th). Four of Italy's five golds were won in 1920 and 1924. The other was won by heavyweight Norberto Oberburger in 1984. Since that year, only three more medals have been won, all in 2021.

Sailing (4-3-8, 14th). Five of Italy's eight medals up to 1984 were won in the Star class. Four of their seven medals since then have been won by Alessandra Sensini in women's windsurfing (1996 bronze, 2000 gold, 2004 bronze, 2008 silver).

Wrestling (7-4-11, 14th). Only 3 of the 22 medals were in Freestyle, which includes two since the last Greco-Roman medal (which came in 2008). Vincenzo Maenza won two golds and a silver in light-flyweight (1984-92).

Swimming (5-7-17, 14th). No medals at all until 1972, when Novella Calligaris won a silver and two bronzes in the same Games. The first three golds all arrived in 2000, with Domenico Fioravanti winning both the 100m and 200m breaststroke for men, and Massimiliano Rosolino winning gold, silver and bronze that year too. Two golds since then – Federica Pellegrini in 2008 and Gregorio Paltrinieri in 2016.

Volleyball (0-3-3, 11th). All 6 medals have gone to the men, all between 1984 and 2016, but no golds yet.

Beach Volleyball (0-1-0, 7th=). Plenty of quarter-finals, but only one medal so far – Paolo Nicolai and Daniele Lupo taking silver in the 2016 men's event.

Basketball (0-2-0, 9th). The men were 4th in 1960 and 1972, and won silver in 1980 and 2004. The women's best is 6th.

Tennis (0-0-1, 26th=). Uberto de Morpurgo took men's singles bronze in 1924, beating Jean Borotra 7-5 in the fifth set in the bronze medal match. Since re-introduction in 1988, Italy have reached 11 quarter-finals, but lost them all.

Artistic Swimming – Italy came 5th in the team event in 2016 and 2021.

Baseball/Softball – Entered Baseball four times and Softball three times. Their best finish is 5th (Softball 2000).

Triathlon – Nadia Cortassa came 5th in the 2004 women's event. In 2021, Italy came 7th in the women's event, and 8th in the mixed relay.

PWDS – Entered Tug of War in 1920, finishing last of the five teams competing.

Hockey – Only entered twice, finishing 11th in 1952 and 13th in 1960, both in the men's event.

Surfing – Only one entry in 2021 (in the men's event), finishing 11th.

Skateboarding – Their best finish in 2021 was 12th in men's park.

Table Tennis – Their best finish is 14th (women's doubles in 2004).

Sport Climbing – Their best finishes in both the men's and women's events in 2021 were 15th.

Golf – Four entries in 2016 and four in 2021; their best finish is equal 27th.

Badminton – Have only entered three events (all women's singles), and lost every match they've played.

Handball, Rugby – never entered

WINTER
Luge (7-4-7, 2nd). Armin Zoggeler won medals in the men's single-seat event in six consecutive Olympics (1994-2014), including golds in 2002 & 2006. His bronze in 2014 made him the first person in Olympic history to win medals in the same individual event, Summer or Winter, six times in a row.

Alpine Skiing (14-11-11, 6th). Italy have medalled at every Games since 1984 apart from 2006. Alberto Tomba (1988-92) and Debbie Compagnoni (1992-98) won three golds each.

Bobsleigh (4-4-4, 5th). Three medals since 1972 – bronzes in 1994 and 2006, and gold for the two-man in 1998.

Skeleton (1-0-0, 7th=). Nino Bibbia took men's gold in 1948. Since the 2002 re-introduction, Italy's best finish is 5th (women's in 2006).

Curling (1-0-0, 7th). Took mixed doubles gold in 2022; their previous best finish in any event had been 7th.

Nordic Skiing (9-14-13, 5th). 31 of their 36 medals were won between 1992 and 2006, including 10 (2-3-5) for Stefania Belmondo.

Short Track Speed Skating (3-6-6, 5th). Between 2006 and 2022, Arianna Fontana has won 11 medals (2-4-5), more than any other Italian bar fencer Edoardo Mangiarotti.

Snowboarding (1-2-2, 11th). Gold for Michela Moioli (women's snowboard cross) in 2018.

Speed Skating (2-1-4, 13th). No medals until 2006, but Italy won 2 golds and a bronze that year, all involving Enrico Fabris.

Biathlon (0-1-6, 15th). Their first medals were won in 1988. The silver went to Pier Alberto Carrara in 1998.

Nordic Combined (0-0-1, 11th=). Alessandro Pittin won bronze in 2010 and came 4th in 2014.

Figure Skating (0-0-2, 20th). Bronze in the ice dance in 2002, and for Carolina Kostner in 2014.

Freestyle Skiing – Two 5th places in 2022 are the best finishes so far.

Ski Jumping – Evelyn Insam came 5th in the 2014 women's event – Italy's best so far.

Ice Hockey – The men have a best finish of 7th in 1956. Their only entry this century was as hosts in 2006. The women only entered in 2006, finishing 8th out of 8.

SPAIN   Olympic Rank 26th

Population: 47,222,613 (rank 32nd)
Olympic rank/ population differential: +6
Population per gold: 963,727 (rank 48th)
Population per medal: 271,394 (rank 53rd)

Summer: 48 gold, 72 silver, 49 bronze (total 169)
Winter: 1 gold, 1 silver, 3 bronze (total 5)
Total: 49 gold, 73 silver, 52 bronze (total 174)

Best sports: Sport Climbing (1 gold, 50.00%, 1st=)
                 Karate (1 gold, 12.50%, 2nd)
                 Sailing (13 golds, 6.70%, 7th)

Spain's Olympic record was, for nearly a century, very poor indeed. Then, they hosted the 1992 Games in Barcelona, and everything changed. They first entered the Games in 1900, then returned in 1920, since when they have competed in every Summer Games except 1936 (they also boycotted in 1956, protesting the Soviet invasion of Hungary, though they did compete in the Equestrian events, held earlier that year in Stockholm).

Prior to hosting in 1992, their all-time Olympic record read 6 golds, 12 silvers and 10 bronzes. Their golds had been in Pelota (1900), Equestrianism (1928), Alpine Skiing (1972), and Sailing (1980, 1984 and 1988). In 1924, 1956, 1964 and 1968, they had won no medals at all. And yet in Barcelona, they won 22 medals in total, including an astonishing 13 golds. These included four more Sailing golds, two Athletics golds for Fermin Cacho (1500 metres) and Daniel Plaza (20km walk), a first Swimming gold (Martin Lopez-Zubero in the 200m backstroke), and prestigious golds for the men's football and women's hockey teams. They finished sixth in the medal table. They have won at least three golds in each Summer Olympics since then, and reached double figures in total medals won every time. Barcelona apart, their best Games for golds has been Rio 2016 (seven golds), their best for medals have been Athens 2004 and London 2012 (20 each), and their best for medal table position has been Atlanta 1996 (13th).

Two Spanish Olympians have won five medals each, and they are both canoeists. They are David Cal in the C1 events (gold in the 1000m in 2004, and silver in the same event in 2008 and 2012, plus two more silvers in the 500m in 2004 and 2008), and Saul Craviotto in kayaking (2008 gold in K2 500m, 2012 silver in K1 200m, 2016 bronze in K1 200m and gold in K2 200m, 2021 silver in K4 500m). Craviotto is one of six Spaniards to have won two golds. The others are Luis Doreste (Sailing 470 class 1984 and Flying Dutchman 1992), Teresa Zabell (Sailing 470 class 1992 & 1996), Gervasio Deferr (Gymnastics vault 2000 & 2004), Joan Llaneras (Cycling points race 2000 & 2008) and Rafael Nadal (Tennis singles 2008 and doubles 2016).

With 13 golds, Sailing is by far Spain's most lucrative Olympic sport. Next on the list are Canoeing and Cycling with five each. The most traditional Olympic sports have been less rewarding – just three golds in Athletics, and just two in Swimming. In Sailing, their best events have been 470 (seven medals) and Finn (five medals). In Cycling, they have won seven of their 16 medals either on the road or the cross-country track. Of their nine track medals, four have been in the points race and one in the madison (effectively a team points race).

Since 1992, their only Athletics gold was won by Ruth Beitia in the 2016 high jump, and their only Swimming gold came in the same year for Mireia Belmonte Garcia in the 200m butterfly. Besides Sailing, they are in the all-time top 10 for a number of other sports. These are Sport Climbing and Karate (both of which debuted in 2021), Water Polo (men's gold in 1996), Hockey (women's gold in 1992), Tennis (two golds, both for Nadal as above), Badminton (just one medal – a gold for Carolina Marin in 2016), and three sports in which they have yet to win gold – Basketball (four silvers puts them 6th equal), Artistic Swimming (three silvers puts them 6th), and Beach Volleyball (one silver puts them 7th equal).

Spain's first two Olympic medals both came in sports which have long since been discontinued. In 1900, they won gold in the Olympic Games' only ever pelota event – and they won it by default when the only other team that entered – France – withdrew shortly before it was due to start. Twenty years later, they won a silver in Polo. Meanwhile, they have entered every Winter Games since their debut in 1936. Their first two medals were won by siblings Francisco and Blanca Fernandez Ochoa in the Alpine Skiing slalom events (1972 gold and 1992 bronze respectively). Three more medals have followed (bronzes in Snowboarding and Figure Skating in 2018, and a silver for snowboarder Queralt Castellet in the women's halfpipe in 2022).

PORTUGAL   **Olympic Rank 61st**

Population:	10,223,150 (rank 91st)
Olympic rank/ population differential:	+30
Population per gold:	2,044,630 (rank 60th)
Population per medal:	365,113 (rank 61st)
Summer:	5 gold, 9 silver, 14 bronze (total 28)
Winter:	*no medals (best finish: 21st)*
Total:	5 gold, 9 silver, 14 bronze (total 28)
Best sports:	Athletics (5 golds, 0.48%, 31st)
	Sailing (2 silvers, 2 bronzes, 29th)
	Equestrianism (3 bronzes, 27th)

Portugal may have a positive rank/population differential, but given their status as a relatively wealthy nation from Western Europe, their overall Olympic record is desperately disappointing. Their population, after all, is comparable to that of Belgium, who have won 46 Summer golds, and Switzerland, who have won 57. Portugal, on the other hand, have only ever won five gold medals in their history – all in Athletics, and all in different Games, despite having entered every Summer Games since 1912. In their six pre-war appearances, they won just three medals, all of them bronze (two in team show jumping, and one in team épée Fencing). In 1948, they won their first silver, in Sailing's Swallow class, as well as another bronze, but then had just one silver and one bronze to show for the next six Games. Two more silvers followed in 1976, before another failure to win a medal (Moscow 1980). Then in 1984, Carlos Sousa Lopes scored an impressive win in the men's marathon to finally win his nation's first ever gold – it had taken them 72 years.

In Tokyo 2021, Portugal won four medals in one Games for the first time – a gold for Pedro Pichardo in the men's triple jump, a silver in the women's triple jump, and bronzes in Canoeing and Judo. Their best finishing position in a medal table is 23rd equal (in both 1924, when they won just a single bronze, and 1984, when they won Lopes's gold as well as two bronzes). Since 1980, they have had one Games where they have failed to win a medal at all – that was the Games of 1992, hosted by neighbouring Spain.

Athletics has provided Portugal with 12 of their 28 Olympic medals – seven in long-distance races (5000m, 10000m and marathon), three in triple jump, one in 100m (a silver for Francis Obikwelu in 2004) and one in 1500m. Medals have been won in eight other sports – four in Sailing, three in Equestrianism and Judo, two in Canoeing, and one each in Cycling, Fencing, Shooting and Triathlon. In addition, they have had 4th-placed finishes in Beach Volleyball, Football and Rowing, and other top-eight finishes in Gymnastics, Skateboarding, Surfing, Table Tennis, Taekwondo and Swimming – where their sole top-eight finisher was Alexandre Yokochi, who finished 7th in the 200m breaststroke in 1984.

A total of five Portuguese sportspeople have won two Olympic medals each – Luiz Mena e Silva (team bronzes in show jumping in 1936 and dressage in 1948), Fernando Pimenta (canoeing silver in 2012 and bronze in 2021 in K2 1000m and K1 1000m respectively), and three long-distance runners. They are Fernanda Ribeiro (1996 gold and 2000 bronze in the 10000 metres), Rosa Mota (1984 bronze and 1988 gold in the marathon) and – statistically the best Portuguese Olympian – Carlos Sousa Lopes (silver in the 1976 10000 metres, and gold in the 1984 marathon). Apart from Ribeiro, Mota, Lopes and the aforementioned Pichardo, Portugal's other Olympic champion is Nelson Evora, who won the triple jump title in 2008.

Portugal's Winter Olympic record has been predictably poor. They entered a single Alpine skier in 1952, who finished 69th, and didn't enter again until 1988. They entered Bobsleigh that year, missed out in 1992, entered Alpine Skiing in 1994, and Freestyle Skiing and Speed Skating in 1998. Having missed out again in 2002, they have since entered Nordic Skiing (2006 and 2010), Alpine Skiing (2014), and both in 2018 and 2022. Their one Freestyle Skiing entrant, Mafalda Queiroz Pereira in 1998, is their highest finisher, managing 21st out of 24.

SAN MARINO   **Olympic Rank 113th**
Population: 34,892 (rank 201st)
Olympic rank/ population differential: +88
Population per gold: n/a
Population per medal: 11,631 (rank 4th)

Summer: 0 gold, 1 silver, 2 bronze (total 3)
Winter: *no medals (best finish: 40th)*
Total: 0 gold, 1 silver, 2 bronze (total 3)

Best sports: Shooting (1 silver, 1 bronze, 45th=)
                    Wrestling (1 bronze, 52nd=)
                    Judo

San Marino, arguably the oldest independent country in the world, and certainly one of the smallest, have been entering the Olympics since 1960. They have entered every Summer Games since then, other than 1964, and every Winter Games since 1976, other than 1980 and 1998. The only sport they have entered every time they've entered the Summer Games is Shooting, and it is that sport which has provided by far their most success. Six of their seven top-eight finishes have come in the sport, beginning with 5th place in the men's small-bore rifle in 1984. Trap shooter Alessandra Perilli achieved San Marino's first 4th place in 2012, before winning a historic bronze in 2021. Two days later, she teamed up with Gian Marco Berti to win silver in the new mixed trap event.

As if that wasn't enough glory for the tiny microstate, they won a third medal a few days later – Myles Amine (who was a US citizen but qualified for San Marino through his great-grandfather) taking bronze in the freestyle light heavyweight Wrestling. He was the first wrestler to compete for San Marino for 61 years. San Marino have not finished in the top 16 in any other sports. Their best Athletics performance is 21st in the men's 4x100m in 1992. Their best in Swimming is 29th. Their best in any Winter event is 40th (in Alpine Skiing in 1984).

MONACO   **Olympic Rank 153rd**
Population: 31,597 (rank 202nd)
Olympic rank/ population differential: +49

Summer: *no medals (best finish: 10th)*
Winter: *no medals (best finish: 6th)*

Best sports: Bobsleigh
                    Rowing
                    Taekwondo

Monaco hold the record for most Olympic appearances without winning a medal (currently 21 Summer Games and 11 Winter). It should, however, be noted that Monegasque architect Julien Medecin did win a bronze medal in the Olympic Art competitions of 1924, but these awards are not historically recognised by the IOC). They have competed in all Summer Games since 1920, except for 1932, 1956 and 1980; and all Winter Games since 1984. Their one and only top-eight finish came in the Winter Games of 2022 – Rudy Rinaldi and Boris Vain finishing 6th in the 2-man Bobsleigh.

For many years, their Olympic entries were dominated by Shooting events, yet they have never finished higher than 31st in any of them. They have managed top-16 finishes in a variety of sports – Rowing (10th out of 11 in the 1928 men's coxed fours), Taekwondo (10th in 2000 despite losing his only match 15-1), Judo, Gymnastics, Alpine Skiing (the only Winter sport they have ever entered besides Bobsleigh), Weightlifting and Athletics. Their best finish in the latter is 15th by Edmond Medecin. He was not thought to be related to the aforementioned Julien Medecin, although he was the brother of Gaston Medecin, the second-best finisher for Monaco in any Athletics event. The best they have managed in a Swimming event is 28th.

MALTA   Olympic Rank 160th

Population: 467,138 (rank 172nd)
Olympic rank/ population differential: +12

Summer: *no medals (best finish: 8th)*
Winter: *no medals (best finish: 21st)*

Best sports: Shooting
Water Polo
Sailing

Despite not gaining independence until 1964, Malta entered the Olympics for the first time in 1928. They entered only Water Polo that year, beating Luxembourg 3-1 in the first round but losing 16-0 to France in the quarter-finals and finishing 8th. They have entered most Summer Games since – the last one they missed was in 1976. Their most common sports have been Athletics, Swimming, Shooting, Sailing and Judo; they have also competed in Archery, Weightlifting, Cycling, Wrestling and Badminton.

They have only once emulated that 8th place finish in 1928. This happened when William Chetcuti finished 8th in the men's double trap Shooting in 2008. Chetcuti also finished 9th in the same event in both 2004 and 2012, and is undoubtedly Malta's best Olympian of all time. Peter Bonello finished 9th in men's windsurfing in 1984.

Malta's best in Athletics is 23rd (out of 23, in the women's javelin in 1984); they have never got past round one in any Athletics event. In Swimming, their best is 22nd (women's 400m freestyle in 2021). They entered the Winter Olympics for the first time in 2014, entering Alpine Skiing in 2014 and 2018, and Snowboarding in 2022. The latter produced their highest finish so far – 21st out of 22.

ANDORRA   Olympic Rank 170th

Population: 85,468 (rank 192nd)
Olympic rank/ population differential: +22

Summer: *no medals (best finish: 9th)*
Winter: *no medals (best finish: 9th)*

Best sports: Alpine Skiing
Cycling
Canoeing

Andorra have entered every Olympics (Summer and Winter) since debuting in both in 1976. In that time, well over half of their entries have come in the same sport – Alpine Skiing. They never entered another Winter sport until 2006 (Nordic Skiing), also adding Snowboarding in 2010 and Biathlon in 2014. As far as Summer sports are concerned, they have had a number of entries in Athletics, Swimming, Shooting (mostly trap events) and Judo, as well as more sporadic appearances in Boxing, Sailing, Cycling and Canoeing.

Emili Perez finished 9th in the men's Cycling road race in 1988. This best finish was emulated by Joan Verdu in the men's Alpine Skiing giant slalom event in 2022. Both of these have managed their 9th-place finishes in very crowded fields (Verdu was 9th out of 87, Perez 9th out of 136). Andorra have also had 11th-place finishes in Boxing (1976) and slalom Canoeing (2021). They have never progressed beyond the first round of any Athletics event. In Swimming, their best finish is 29th (men's 400m individual medley, 2008).

CHAPTER TEN - Western Central Europe (Germany, Netherlands, Switzerland, Austria, Belgium, Liechtenstein, Luxembourg)

GERMANY   **Olympic Rank 3rd**
Population: 84,220,184 (rank 18th)
Olympic rank/ population differential: +15
Population per gold: 139,322 (rank 19th)
Population per medal: 45,859 (rank 21st)

Summer: 232 gold, 266 silver, 288 bronze (total 786)
Winter: 113 gold, 105 silver, 70 bronze (total 288)
Total: 345 gold, 371 silver, 358 bronze (total 1074)
(plus mixed team: 0.5 gold, 0 silver, 0 bronze (total 0.5))

plus East Germany: Summer (153-129-127 tot 409); Winter (39-36-35 tot 110); Total (192-165-162 tot 519)
plus West Germany: Summer (56-67-81 tot 204); Winter (11-15-13 tot 39); Total (67-82-94 tot 243)

Combined totals: Summer: 441.5 gold, 462 silver, 496 bronze (total 1399.5)
           Winter: 163 gold, 156 silver, 118 bronze (total 437)
           Total: 604.5 gold, 618 silver, 614 bronze (total 1836.5)

Best sports: Luge (38 golds, 73.08%, 1st)
           Bobsleigh (22 golds, 41.51%, 1st)
           Nordic Combined (12 golds, 30.00%, 2nd)

Germany were one of the main early drivers of the Olympics, sending a relatively sizeable team to Athens in 1896, particularly in Gymnastics. After the first World War, they were banned from participating in 1920 or 1924, but returned in 1928, when they made their Winter debut too. Banned from entering following war again in 1948, the country then split into East and West Germany. However, the two Germanys continued to compete as one team between 1952 and 1964. The short-lived independent state of Saarland entered their own team in 1952 (they had two top-eight finishes in Rowing, finishing 7th in both the men's single sculls – Gunther Schutt – and men's coxless fours). East and West Germany competed as separate nations for just twenty years (1968-88). They each entered six Winter Games and five Summer Games in that time (they boycotted a Summer Games each, the West in 1980 and the East in 1984). Germany was then reunified, and has entered every Games since.

In their pre-war appearances, Germany's lowest medal table position was 9th (Los Angeles 1932). They finished 3rd in 1896, 2nd in 1904 and 1928, and topped the medal table in the Nazi Games of 1936 with 33 golds (the USA came 2nd with 24). In their first post-war Summer Games (Helsinki 1952), they achieved the bizarre feat of winning 24 medals, with not a single gold amongst them (7 silver, 17 bronze). The most medals any other country has won at a single Games without a gold is 12 (Brazil in 2000). This put them 28th in the medal table, by far their lowest-ever position (the only one outside the top ten), and the only time they have failed to win a gold at a Summer Games. The combined German team then finished 7th, 4th and 4th in the following Games.

The countries then split. West Germany finished 8th in 1968, but finished in the top 5 every time after that. Their best was in 1984, when they won 17 golds, 59 medals in total, and came 3rd. The East came 5th in 1968 and 3rd in 1972, but then 2nd behind the Soviets in each of their other three Games. Their gold totals in those three Games were 40, 47 and 37, and their medal totals were 90, 126 and 102. For context, the best a united Germany have ever managed is 33 golds and 89 medals in total (in 1936). The East's performance in just 20 years was absolutely phenomenal, but clearly it was largely achieved via nefarious means. The reunified Germany came 3rd in both 1992 and 1996, winning 33 golds in the former. They have slipped a bit since then, with Tokyo 2021 being their worst Games since reunification, finishing 9th with just 10 golds.

No unified German team has ever finished outside the top 10 in a Winter Games, and they have not failed to win a gold since 1932. Their best Games prior to splitting were in 1936 in Garmisch, and in 1960, when they came 2nd both times. Again, the East outperformed the West in the divided era, topping the medal table in 1984 and coming 2nd four times. The reunified Germany topped the medal table in 1992, 1998 and 2006, and have only finished outside the top three once (coming 6th in 2014). Their record gold tally is 14 (2018), and they won 36 medals in total in 2002.

Throughout this chapter, GDR means East Germany and FRG means West Germany.

SUMMER

Equestrianism (44-24-27, 1st). Germany have won 44 golds; no other country has won more than 18. The two top gold medallists in dressage are both German – Isabell Werth (7 golds and 5 silvers, 1992-2021, making her the most-decorated German Olympian of all time) and Reiner Klimke (6 golds and 2 bronzes, 1964-88). So too are the two top gold medallists in show jumping – Hans-Gunter Winkler (5 golds, 1 silver, 1 bronze, 1956-76) and Ludger Beerbaum (4 golds and a bronze, 1988 to 2016). GDR never won a medal in Equestrianism.

Rowing (64-31-29, 1st). Kathrin Boron won 4 golds (1992-2004) and a bronze (2008), three in quadruple sculls and two in double sculls. The other four women to have won this many golds are all Romanian. Germany have won medals at every Games since 1952, although they failed to win a gold in 2008 and 2021. Nine of their last 14 golds have been in quadruple sculls (both men and women).

Canoeing (54-37-38, 1st). Germany have won golds at every Games since 1956. The most successful canoeist from any country has been Birgit Fischer, who won 8 golds and 4 silvers between 1980 (when she was competing for GDR) and 2004. She was both the youngest and oldest Canoeing gold medallist (aged 18 and 42 respectively). Her medals came in the K1, K2 and K4 500m events.

Hockey (5-5-5, 3rd). Men's golds in 1972 (FRG), 1992, 2008 & 2012. Women's gold in 2004.

Beach Volleyball (2-0-1, 3rd). Men's gold in 2012 and women's gold in 2016. Men's bronze in 2000.

Cycling (26-32-28, 4th). Jens Fiedler won the men's sprint in 1992 & 1996, and the team sprint in 2004, making him Germany's only 3-time champion in Cycling. In 1988, Christa Rothenburger won a gold and silver for GDR in Speed Skating. She then won a silver in the women's sprint Cycling later that year, becoming the only person ever to win Summer and Winter medals in the same year (no longer possible, of course, due to staggering of the Games). Germany have medalled at every Games since 1952.

Swimming (56-62-73, 3rd). The German Swimming tally is considerably boosted by the extraordinary number of medals won by the GDR from 1976 onwards. Having never previously won a gold in women's Swimming, they won 11 out of 13 in 1976, followed by another 11 in 1980 and 10 in 1988. Widespread suspicion that their women were being drugged was proved years later; however, the medals have never been stripped, as it is impossible to prove in each individual case. Kristin Otto won six golds, all in 1988. The GDR men were less successful, though Roland Matthes won the backstroke double in both 1968 and 1972. Since reunification, Germany have won 38 medals, but only 4 of them have been gold. Franziska van Almsick (1992-2004) holds the all-time Olympic record for most medals without a gold (4 silvers and 6 bronzes).

Handball (2-3-2, 6th). Won the inaugural men's event in 1936, and GDR took men's gold in 1980. Two medals since reunification, both for men (2004 silver & 2016 bronze). Both women's medals went to the GDR.

Triathlon (1-1-0, 6th=). Jan Frodeno was the 2008 men's champion. Stephan Vuckovic took silver in 2000.

Athletics (73-97-97, 3rd). Of Germany's 73 golds, 38 of them were won by GDR between 1968 and 1988 (FRG won 12 in the same period). Barbel Wockel-Eckert won four of them (women's 200m and 4x100m in 1976 and 1980). Prior to 1936, Germany had only ever won one Athletics gold, but they won 5 in Berlin, all in throwing events, to please the authorities. They didn't win another gold after that until 1960, when the controversial Armin Hary won the men's 100 metres, and helped Germany to the 4x100m title too.

Fencing (15-19-12, 5th). A rare sport where the FRG (16 medals) vastly outperformed the GDR (1 medal). Two golds this century, both in 2008 (men's foil and women's épée). Future IOC President Thomas Bach was on the winning men's foil team for FRG in 1976. Helene Mayer won foil gold in 1928 and silver in 1936, where she was allowed onto the German team as a token Jew; her complicity or otherwise with Hitler is a matter of debate.

Diving (8-12-15, 4th). Ingrid Engel-Kramer is the star of German Diving, winning women's platform gold (1960) and silver (1964), and taking springboard gold in both of those years. Prior to that, no non-American woman had won a Diving gold since 1920. The last German Diving gold was in 1980; this century has seen 2 silvers and 6 bronzes.

Shooting (18-21-14, 4th). Only one German has won more than one gold – Ralf Schumann, who has won 3 in rapid-fire pistol (1992, 1996 & 2004), plus 2 silvers (1988 & 2008).

Tennis (4.5-6-3, 4th). Shared in men's doubles gold in 1896, and won the mixed doubles in 1912. Since Tennis's return in 1988, there have been singles golds for Steffi Graf (1988, FRG) and Alexander Zverev (2021), and doubles gold for Boris Becker and Michael Stich in 1992.

Football (2-2-6, 5th). The GDR won men's gold in 1976 and silver in 1980; unified Germany won silver in 2016, losing to Brazil on penalties. After three bronzes, the women won gold in 2016.

Gymnastics (21-26-34, 6th). In 1896, three gymnasts won 3 golds each (winning 2 team and 1 individual gold each). In 1936, Konrad Frey emulated them with golds in parallel bars, pommel horse and the team event. Just 3 golds since reunification – men's horizontal bar (1996 & 2016) and women's trampoline (2004).

Modern Pentathlon (2-0-1, 7th). The men won a bronze in 1928 and a gold (Gotthardt Handrick) in 1936. Lena Schoneborn won the women's event in 2008. The best by a man since reunification is 5th.

Boxing (11-14-23, 6th). The last two golds came in 1992. Just four bronzes this century.

Sailing (8-10-13, 10th). The same three men who won Soling gold for GDR in 1988 won for Germany in 1996. These remain the last 2 German golds in Sailing; this century has seen just three silvers and five bronzes. One of them, Jochen Schumann (Soling silver in 2000) had previously won three golds, the first of them back in 1976.

PWDS (1-0-0, 8th). Entered Tug of War once (1906), beating Austria and Greece to take gold. Entered Polo once (1936), coming 5th out of 5.

Weightlifting (9-13-21, 5th). Matthias Steiner (2008 super-heavyweight) is the only champion this century. Ronny Weller won men's heavyweight gold in 1992, and silvers in super-heavyweight in 1996 and 2000.

Judo (5-10-25, 7th). Medals have been won at every Games in which Judo has been contested. GDR (1980) and FRG (1984) won one gold each, with the unified team winning golds in 1996, 2004 & 2008.

Water Polo (1-2-1, 8th). Gold in 1928, silvers in 1932 & 1936, and a bronze for FRG in 1984. Their post-reunification best is 5th in 2004. The women have never entered.

Wrestling (9-25-20, 12th). In 2021, Aline Rotter-Focken (women's freestyle heavyweight) became the first German female medallist, and the first German champion since 1992. Heavyweight Wilfried Dietrich won Greco-Roman silver (1956) and bronzes (1960 & 1964), as well as freestyle gold (1960) and bronze (1968).

Table Tennis (0-4-5, 5th). Dimitrij Ovtcharov has six medals (2008-21), including two bronzes in men's singles.

Rugby (0-1-0, 7th). Lost their only match in 1900, 27-17 to France, and shared the silver medal (only 3 teams entered).

Volleyball (0-2-0, 12th). Both medals went to GDR – men in 1972 and women in 1980. The FRG's best was 6th, whilst the unified team have had three quarter-final defeats so far (women in 1996 & 2000, men in 2012).

Archery (0-2-2, 16th=). Lisa Unruh took women's individual silver in 2016; the other medals were all in women's team (1996, 2000 & 2021).

Taekwondo (0-1-1, 25th=). Men's silver in 2000, and women's bronze in 2012, both in welterweight.

Karate – Four entries in 2021, the highest finisher of which was Noah Bitsch (5th, men's <75kg).

Artistic Swimming – Gudrun Hanisch came 5th in women's solo in 1984 for FRG. No entries since 1992.

Basketball – The men came 7th in 1992 and 8th in 1984 (FRG) & 2021. The women have never entered.

Badminton – Two quarter-final defeats – Chinese-born Huaiwen Xu in the 2008 women's singles (7th) and the 2012 mixed doubles pair (8th).

Sport Climbing – Two entries in the 2021 men's event, finishing 9th and 12th.

Skateboarding – 9th in women's park in 2021, and 15th in men's park.

Golf – Martin Kaymer came joint 15th in the 2016 men's event, the highest finish so far.

Surfing – One entry in 2021, coming 17th in the men's event.

Baseball/Softball – never entered

WINTER

Luge (38-26-23, 1st). Including 13 golds for GDR and 1 for FRG, Germany have won 38 Luge golds, with the rest of the world managing just 14 between them. If anything, their domination has grown even further in recent years, having taken 13 of the 15 golds awarded since 2010. In 20 events over the years, the Germans have taken gold and silver, and in 10 of those they took the bronze as well. Tobias Arlt and Tobias Wendl have shared 6 golds (men's 2-seater and mixed relay in 2014, 2018 and 2022). Natalie Geisenberger also has 6 golds (the same 3 mixed relays, and the women's single-seat in the same 3 years).

Bobsleigh (22-17-12, 1st). Since 1994, Germany have taken 14 of the 25 gold medals awarded. Four people have won four golds in Olympic history – all of them German. They are Andre Lange and Kevin Kuske (2002-10), and Francesco Friedrich and Thorsten Margis (2018-22).

Nordic Combined (12-7-9, 2nd). Ulrich Wehling won the men's individual three times (1972-80) for GDR, and Eric Frenzel won 7 medals (3-2-2) between 2010 and 2022.

Biathlon (24-27-19, 1st). Having won 52 medals in 8 games from 1992 to 2018, Germany won just 2 in 2022. Ricco Gross (1992-2006) and Sven Fischer (1994-2006) won 4 golds each.

Ski Jumping (9-10-6, 3rd). Jens Weissflog won 3 golds and a silver in 1984 (for GDR) and 1994.

Skeleton (2-3-1, 3rd). The first medals came in 2010. Both golds came in 2022, to Christopher Grotheer (men's) and Hannah Neise (women's), adding Skeleton to their litany of domination in the sliding sports.

Speed Skating (25-28-19, 5th). GDR won 29 medals between 1976 and 1988; FRG didn't win any after 1972. The most decorated German speed skater is Claudia Pechstein with 9 medals (5-2-2) between 1992 and 2006.

Alpine Skiing (17-14-10, 4th). Maria Hofl-Riesch won 3 golds and a silver (2010-14). Katja Seizinger won 3 golds and 2 bronzes (1992-98). FRG won 9 medals, GDR didn't win any.

Figure Skating (8-7-9, 3rd). Katarina Witt won the women's title for GDR in 1984 & 1988. Only one gold since then – in the pairs event in 2018.

Nordic Skiing (5-11-5, 6th). GDR won 4 medals (2-1-1) in 1976 & 1980. The other medals have all come since 2002. Barbara Petzold won the women's 10km in 1980; the other golds all came in women's relay or team events.

Snowboarding (1-4-2, 8th). All 7 medals have gone to women, including gold for Nicola Thost (1998 halfpipe).

Ice Hockey (0-1-2, 8th). The medals all went to men – 1932 bronze, 1976 bronze (FRG) and 2018 silver. The women did not enter until 2002.

Freestyle Skiing (0-1-1, 17th). Women's moguls silver for Tatjana Mittermayer in 1998, and bronze (after a controversial finish and an appeal) for Daniela Maier in women's ski cross in 2022.

Curling – The women came 5th in 2002, the men came 6th in 2002 & 2010.

Short Track Speed Skating – Tyson Heung came 5th in the men's 500m in 2010, the best finish so far.

NETHERLANDS   **Olympic Rank 14th**

Population: 17,463,930 (rank 71st)
Olympic rank/ population differential: +57
Population per gold: 117,208 (rank 15th)
Population per medal: 36,844 (rank 16th)

Summer: 96 gold, 106 silver, 124 bronze (total 326) *(plus Neth Antilles: 1 silver)*
Winter: 53 gold, 49 silver, 45 bronze (total 147)
Total: 149 gold, 155 silver, 169 bronze (total 473) *(plus Neth Antilles: 1 silver)*

Best sports: Speed Skating (48 golds, 23.53%, 1st)
Hockey (6 golds, 17.14%, 2nd)
Cycling (23 golds, 8.52%, 5th)

The Netherlands have only missed the Summer Games of 1896 and 1904, and the Winter Games of 1924 and 1932. Their highest Summer medal table position in that time is 7th in 2021 (with a record 36 medals won in total), followed by 8th in 1928 (at home) and 2000. Those Sydney Games saw a record 12 golds won. They last failed to win a gold in 1976 and 1980; in 1956, for the only time, they failed to win a medal at all (although they boycotted the Melbourne Games protesting the Soviet invasion of Hungary, they had earlier entered one Equestrian event in Stockholm).

Their Winter success has been predicated almost entirely on Speed Skating. They won a total of 8 golds in 2014, 2018 and 2022, giving them top-six finishes each time (in 2014, they won a record 24 medals), but their highest finish is 4th in 1972. The 1984 Games were the most recent without a medal at all, whilst the 1994 Games were the most recent without a gold.

SUMMER

Hockey (6-6-6, 2nd). The Dutch women won their first medal in 1984, and have won medals at every Games since apart from 1992 (when they came 6th). They won golds in 1984, 2008, 2012 and 2021 (only losing the 2016 final on a penalty shoot-out). Eva de Goede and Lidewij Welten both won three golds (2008-21). The men won golds in 1996 and 2000, since when they have won silvers in 2004 and 2012.

Cycling (23-22-16, 5th). The Netherlands have produced a steady stream of world-class cyclists throughout the last century, but surely the most impressive is Leontien Zijlaard-Van Moorsel. In 2000, she won golds in three very contrasting disciplines – road race, road time trial, and 3000m individual pursuit. She also took points race silver, followed by another road time trial gold and pursuit bronze in 2004. Only Britain's Laura Kenny can beat her tally of four golds in women's Cycling.

Equestrianism (10-13-4, 6th). The Dutch won five golds in three-day eventing from 1924 to 1932, including four for Charles Pahud de Mortanges, the most for a three-day eventer from any country. They then waited 60 years for their next Equestrianism gold. Anky van Grunsven took the individual dressage title three Games running, 2000 to 2008.

Sailing (8-10-9, 11th). The only double gold medallist is Dorian van Rijsselberghe (men's windsurfer, 2012 & 2016). In 1988, the silver medallist in the same event was Jan Boersma, representing the Netherlands Antilles. His was the Antilles' only ever Olympic medal – the Antilles participated at all Summer Games from 1952 to 2008 apart from 1956 and 1980, and the Winter Games in 1988 and 1992. They were, though, dissolved in 2010, since when their athletes have largely represented the Netherlands (or, alternatively, Aruba).

Swimming (22-21-19, 7th). Inge de Bruijn is the most decorated Dutch swimmer, taking 8 medals (4-2-2) in 2000 & 2004. Rie Mastenbroek (1936), Pieter van den Hoogenband (2000 & 2004) and Ranomi Kromowidjojo (2008 & 2012) won three golds each. Only 13 of their 62 medals have been in men's events.

Volleyball (1-1-0, 8th). The men won silver in 1992 and gold in 1996. The women came 4th in 2016.

Water Polo (1-0-2, 11th=). The women won gold in 2008. The men took bronze in 1948 and 1976, and last entered in 2000.

Rowing (8-14-14, 11th). The Netherlands have won medals at every Games since 1984, but it is their first gold that is the most interesting. In the coxed pairs of 1900, the Dutch dropped their cox after the semi-final, fearing he was too heavy, and replaced him with a young Parisian boy. They won gold and were photographed with their replacement cox, but he then disappeared back to the streets of Paris and nobody has ever traced who he was – he is probably the youngest Olympic champion in history.

Judo (4-2-18, 11th). Anton Geesink won the men's open class in 1964, Wim Ruska won the same in 1972, plus the heavyweight gold. Mark Huizinga won the men's middleweight in 2000. The Netherlands have won medals at all Games since 1988.

Archery (1-1-1, 11th). They won a team gold in 1920, a bronze in 2000 and a mixed team silver in 2021.

Gymnastics (3-0-0, 21st=). The golds went to the women's team in 1928, Epke Zonderland (men's horizontal bar) in 2012 and Sanne Wevers (women's balance beam) in 2016.

Athletics (8-7-9, 23rd). Prior to 1984, the Netherlands had won just four Olympic golds – all of them going to the iconic housewife Fanny Blankers-Koen in 1948 (100m, 200m, 80m hurdles and sprint relay). Only 8 medals (none of them gold) have been won by Dutch men. The Dutch won six medals in 1948 and eight in 2021, but only six in all the years in between.

Boxing (1-2-5, 32nd). Bep van Klaveren won gold in 1928. Arnold Vanderlijde won three bronzes (1984-92), whilst Nouchka Fontijn won silver in 2016 and bronze in 2021.

Football (0-0-3, 31st). Bronzes in 1908, 1912 and 1920. The men have only entered once since 1952, finishing 7th in 2008. The women have only entered once, finishing 5th in 2021.

Beach Volleyball (0-0-1, 11th=). The four top-eight finishes have all been for the men, including 2016 bronze.

PWDS (0-1-0, 10th=). Lost the Tug of War final to Great Britain in 1920.

Fencing (0-1-7, 24th). All the medals were won between 1906 (when George van Rossem won silver in the three-cornered sabre) and 1924 (when Arie de Jong won the last of his five bronzes). Just one top-eight finish since 1960 – 8th in the men's épée in 2008.

Canoeing (0-3-5, 29th). The most recent silver was in 1972, and the most recent bronze was in 1988.

Tennis (0-1-1, 22nd). Mixed doubles bronze in 1924, and women's doubles silver (Kristie Boogert & Miriam Oremans) in 2000.

Badminton (0-1-0, 11th). Indonesian-born Mia Audina took women's singles silver in 2004.

Weightlifting (0-0-3, 60th). Two bronzes in 1928 and one in 1948. Only one top-eight finish since – 6th in 2021.

Shooting (0-1-1, 45th=). Team bronze in 1900, and skeet silver in 1976. Five top-eight finishes since then.

Triathlon – Two 4th places, both in 2021 involving Rachel Klamer (women's individual, and mixed relay).

Diving – 4th in women's platform in 1928, and 5th in women's springboard in 2021.

Handball – Just two entries, both for the women, who came 4th in 2016 and 5th in 2021.

Artistic Swimming – Marijke Engelen came 4th in 1984, the best of four top-eight finishes.

Taekwondo – Three top-eight finishes, including 4th place in women's featherweight in 2000.

Wrestling – 4th place in 1920 is their best finish. Their best since 1948 is an 8th place in 2000.

Baseball/Softball – Entered Baseball four times, with a best finish of 5th (1996 and 2000). Entered Softball twice, with a best finish of 7th (1996).

Skateboarding – Roos Zwetsloot came 5th in the 2021 women's street event.

Basketball – Never entered regular Basketball, but finished 5th in men's 3x3 in 2021.

Table Tennis – Five quarter-final defeats – two in 1988, one in 1992 and two in 2012.

Modern Pentathlon – Christiaan Tonnet came 8th in 1924 and equal 7th in 1928. They have only entered one Games since the war (1972), with a best finish that year of 18th.

Golf – Two entries, with a best finish of joint 27th (in 2016).

Karate, Rugby, Sport Climbing, Surfing – never entered

WINTER

Speed Skating (48-44-41, 1st). The Netherlands are, by some distance, the world's top nation at Speed Skating, and their dominance only seems to be growing; since 2002, they have won 75 medals in 74 events. Special mention should be made of Ireen Wust, who between 2006 and 2022 has accrued 13 medals (6-5-2); her six golds is matched only by Lidiya Skoblikova of the Soviet Union, and she comfortably holds the Dutch Olympic record for both golds and total medals across all sports.

Short Track Speed Skating (3-3-3, 6th). Suzanne Schulting won women's 1000 metres gold in 2018 and 2022, and was part of the relay gold in 2022 as well. She also has a silver and two bronzes.

Snowboarding (1-0-0, 14th). Nicolien Sauerbreij won the 2010 women's parallel giant slalom.

Figure Skating (1-2-0, 12th). Sjoukje Dijkstra won women's silver in 1960 and gold in 1964 (the only non-Speed Skating Winter gold the Dutch ever won prior to 2010). Dianne de Leeuw won silver in 1976. No further entries after that until 2022. No men have ever competed.

Skeleton (0-0-1, 12th=). Two entries, both for Kimberley Bos. She came 8th in 2018 and 3rd in 2022.

Bobsleigh – The two-woman bob came 6th in 2002, 8th in 2010 and 4th in 2014.

Ice Hockey – Came 9th in 1980 (men's event) in their only entry so far.

Alpine Skiing – Two top-30 finishes, 14th in 1936 and 18th in 2022.

Freestyle Skiing – Came 17th in 1994 in their only entry so far.

Biathlon, Curling, Luge, Nordic Combined, Nordic Skiing, Ski Jumping – never entered

SWITZERLAND　　　　　　　　　　**Olympic Rank 17th**

Population:	8,563,760 (rank 102nd)
Olympic rank/ population differential:	+85
Population per gold:	71,365 (rank 7th)
Population per medal:	22,318 (rank 8th)
Summer:	57 gold, 82 silver, 75 bronze (total 214)
Winter:	63 gold, 47 silver, 58 bronze (total 168)
Total:	120 gold, 129 silver, 133 bronze (total 382)
Best sports:	Bobsleigh (10 golds, 18.87%, 2nd)
	Alpine Skiing (27 golds, 16.36%, 2nd)
	Snowboarding (8 golds, 15.69%, 2nd)

Switzerland are one of only three nations (France and Great Britain are the others) that have competed in every Summer and Winter Olympics. They actually boycotted the 1956 Melbourne Games in protest at the Soviet invasion of Hungary, but had already competed in the Equestrian events, which had been held earlier in the year in Stockholm. Their highest finish in a Summer Games was in 1900 (5th place). Their record number of golds is seven (in 1924 & 1928), and their highest medal total is 25 (in 1924). Most of their success came in the Games up to 1952; their 2021 total of 13 medals was their highest since then.

Switzerland are one of the five nations that have won more Winter medals than Summer. They came 3rd in the medal tables of 1948, 1972 and 1988 – the latter saw a total of 15 medals, equalled in 2018 and 2022 but not yet bettered. The 2014 and 2022 Games saw their record of seven golds.

Gymnasts Eugen Mack (2-4-2) and Georges Miez (4-3-1) hold the Swiss record of 8 medals each. The Olympian with most Swiss golds is shooter Louis Richardet, with five.

SUMMER
Triathlon (2-1-2, 2nd). Women's golds for Brigitte McMahon (2000) and Nicola Spiring (by a tiny margin in 2012). Just one men's medal – a bronze in 2004.

Gymnastics (16-19-14, 7th). The golden era of Swiss Gymnastics was between 1924 and 1952, with 42 of their 49 medals won in that period. Georges Miez won 4 golds, 3 silvers and a bronze (1924-36). Only two medals since 1952 – men's pommel horse gold for naturalised Li Donghua in 1996, and a women's vault bronze in 2016.

Tennis (3-3-0, 6th). The men's singles gold went not to Roger Federer (he won doubles gold in 2008 and singles silver in 2012), but Marc Rosset (1992). The women's singles gold went not to Martina Hingis (she won doubles silver in 2016), but Belinda Bencic (2021; she also won doubles silver the same year).

Shooting (11-9-11, 10th). Switzerland won 9 of the 20 Shooting gold medals available in 1900 and 1906; Louis Richardet won 5 golds and a silver in that time. They have only added two more golds since then, though – Emil Grunig (men's free rifle, 3 positions) in 1948 and Nina Christen (women's small-bore rifle, 3 positions) in 2021.

Equestrianism (5-10-8, 10th). The most recent medal was gold in individual jumping for Steve Guerdat (2012). Henri Chammartin picked up five dressage medals (1952-68), including individual gold in 1964.

Rowing (7-8-9, 12th). 15 of the 24 medals came between 1920 and 1952. Only two medals this century, including one gold (men's lightweight four in 2016).

Cycling (6-11-8, 11th). Only 4 of their 25 medals have come on the track, including just one of the 20 won since 1984. Most have come in road or cross-country events. Fabian Cancellara won road time trial gold and road race silver in 2008, and road time trial gold again in 2016.

Wrestling (4-4-7, 21st). Only one medal since 1948 – a bronze in 1984, which was also the only Greco-Roman medal (the other 14 were in freestyle). The last gold was in 1928.

Judo (1-1-2, 25th). Jurg Rothlisberger won half-heavyweight bronze in 1976 and middleweight gold in 1980. The only medal since then was a bronze in 2008. All four medals have been won by men.

Sailing (1-2-1, 22nd). The gold was won in 1900, though there is considerable dispute as to whether the Sailing events that year should be considered as having full Olympic status. Only two medals since that year – a bronze in 1960 and silver in 1968, both in the 5½ metre class. Despite being a landlocked country, Switzerland won the America's Cup in 2003, but their best Olympic performances since 1968 have been 4th places in 2004 and 2021.

Fencing (1-4-3, 17th). All 8 medals came in épée. The most recent was the gold for Marcel Fischer in 2004.

Beach Volleyball (0-0-2, 10th). Bronze in the men's event in 2004, and in the women's event in 2021.

Handball (0-0-1, 17th=). Bronze in the first event in 1936; only three entries since then, most recently in 1996.

Football (0-1-0, 25th=). Men's silver in 1924; only two entries since then, 1928 and 2012, also both in men's.

Weightlifting (0-2-2, 45th). All four medals, and all 8 top-eight finishes, came in the 1920s, including two silvers for Fritz Hunenberger. Last entered in 1984.

Athletics (0-6-2, 67th). Only two medals since 1952 – silver for Markus Ryffel (1984 men's 5000 metres) and bronze for Werner Gunthor (1988 men's shot put). Their best this century is 4th in the 2021 women's 4x100m.

Swimming (0-0-3, 46th). One bronze in 1984 and another two in 2021 (in the men's 100m butterfly and 200m individual medley).

Canoeing (0-1-0, 34th). Silver for the women's K4 500m in 1996.

Boxing – Four quarter-final appearances (1924, 1948 and two in 1960). In 1948, Hans Muller finished 4th after withdrawing from the bronze medal match. This was the last Games before both losing semi-finalists were given bronze. Last entered in 1972.

Modern Pentathlon – Came 4th in the team event in 1984. Their only top-eight finishes in an individual event both came in 1948 (6th and 7th in the men's event).

Artistic Swimming – Three 5th places, all involving Karin Singer – duet in 1984 and 1988, and solo in 1988.

Hockey – The men came 7th in 1928 and 5th in 1948. They last entered in 1960. The women have never entered.

Karate – Their only entrant, Elena Quirici (2021 women's >61kg), came 5th.

Diving – Came 8th out of 8 in the women's synchronized springboard in 2000. Their best in an individual event is 11th (2021 women's springboard).

Archery – Lotti Tschanz came 8th in the 1980 women's event. They last entered in 2012.

Water Polo – Came 10th in 1920, and also entered in 1924, 1928, 1936 and 1948. Never entered the women's.

Table Tennis – Just two entries, in 1996, when Chinese-born Dai-Yong Tu reached the last 16 of the women's singles, and 2021.

Basketball – Took part in the men's competitions of 1936, 1948 and 1952. Came 14th in 1936, their best finish. Never entered the women's.

Sport Climbing – One entry in 2021 – came 16th in the women's.

Taekwondo – Just one entry – in the 2008 women's flyweight, when they lost in the first round without scoring a point.

Golf – The 1900 women's silver medallist, Polly Whittier, was living in Switzerland, and is sometimes listed as Swiss. However, she was US-born and was a US citizen. Switzerland's best finish is therefore joint 18th (2021 women's event).

Badminton – A total of five matches have been won, but never two in the same event. No top-16 finishes.

Baseball/Softball, Rugby, Skateboarding, Surfing, Volleyball, PWDS – never entered

WINTER

Bobsleigh (10-10-11, 2nd). All the medals so far have been won by men. Just one gold since 1994, won by Beat Hefti and Alex Baumann in the 2014 two-man event.

Alpine Skiing (27-23-25, 2nd). Pride of place goes to Vreni Schneider, who won three golds, a silver and a bronze across the slalom, giant slalom and Alpine combined events in 1988 and 1994.

Snowboarding (8-2-4, 2nd). Philipp Schoch won back-to-back men's parallel giant slalom titles in 2002 & 2006; Switzerland have won Snowboarding medals at every Games in which they have been contested.

Freestyle Skiing (6-3-4, 3rd). Mathilde Gremaud won three medals in 2018 and 2022, including gold in the women's slopestyle in 2022.

Ski Jumping (4-1-0, 7th). Walter Steiner won silver in 1972, before Simon Ammann took over, winning the normal hill/ large hill double in 2002, finishing way down in 2006, then winning the double again in 2010.

Skeleton (1-0-2, 6th). Bronzes in men's in 2002 & 2006 for Gregor Stahli, and a gold in the 2006 women's event for Maya Pedersen-Bieri.

Curling (1-3-3, 4th). The men won gold in 1998 and have won three bronzes since. The women won silver in 2002 and 2006, as did the Swiss mixed doubles pair in 2018.

Nordic Combined (1-2-1, 8th). Gold went to Hippolyt Kempf in 1988. The most recent medal was a team bronze in 1994.

Nordic Skiing (4-0-4, 8th). All four golds went to Dario Cologna (men's 15km in 2010, 2014 and 2018, and the 2014 skiathlon as well).

Biathlon (1-1-0, 10th). Military patrol gold in 1924, and just one medal since – Selina Gasparin in women's 15km individual in 2014.

Ice Hockey (0-0-3, 9th). Men's bronzes in 1928 and 1948, and women's bronze in 2014. The men have 10 top-eight finishes, and the women five.

Figure Skating (0-2-1, 19th). Medals in the men's event in 1924 (bronze), 1948 (silver) and 2006 (silver again).

Speed Skating – The best two finishes were both by Livio Wenger in the men's mass start – 4th in 2018 and 7th in 2022.

Luge – Martina Kocher came 7th in the women's singles in 2010 – the only top-eight finish.

Short Track Speed Skating – never entered

AUSTRIA   **Olympic Rank 18th**

Population: 8,940,860 (rank 99th)
Olympic rank/ population differential: +81
Population per gold: 95,116 (rank 11th)
Population per medal: 25,186 (rank 9th)

Summer: 23 gold, 38 silver, 44 bronze (total 105)
Winter: 71 gold, 88 silver, 91 bronze (total 250)
Total: 94 gold, 126 silver, 135 bronze (total 355)

Best sports: Alpine Skiing (40 golds, 24.24%, 1st)
Ski Jumping (7 golds, 12.96%, 4th)
Luge (6 golds, 11.54%, 3rd)

Austria have entered every Olympic Games, Summer and Winter, with one exception – the Summer Games of 1920, when they were barred as a result of their involvement with the Central Powers in the First World War. They won two golds in 1896 – one each in Cycling and Swimming – which makes it, proportionally, still Austria's best Summer Games.

Overall, Austria's Summer Games record is mediocre at best. They have not finished in the top 10 in any Games since 1906 (their best position of 7th coming in 1896 and 1904). Their best Games in terms of golds (4) and total medals won (13) were the Berlin Games of 1936. They have won only 10 Summer golds since the Second World War, and no medals at all in 1964 or 2012.

The Winter Games are a very different story. They are 6th in the all-time Winter table, and have only twice failed to win gold (1928 & 1984, the latter being the only time they have ever been out of the top 10). They are one of the five countries that have won more Winter golds than Summer golds. They were 2nd in 1956 & 1964, and 3rd in 1924 & 2006. In the last of those, they won 9 golds and 23 medals in total – both national records.

Austria's most successful Olympian is Felix Gottwald who, between 2002 and 2010, won 3 golds, 1 silver and 3 bronzes in Nordic Combined. Matthias Mayer, Toni Sailer and Thomas Morgenstern have also won 3 golds each. No Austrian has won more than 2 golds, or 3 medals, in Summer Games as yet.

SUMMER
Triathlon (1-0-0, 8th=). Australian-born Kate Allen switched nationalities to that of her husband, and took gold in 2004. In 2008, she finished 14th. The best finish by any other Austrian is 27th.

Weightlifting (4-5-2, 15th). Josef Steinbach (1906) and Hans Haas (1928 & 1932) each won a gold and a silver. No medals since 1936, when Robert Fein won gold. One top-eight finish this century (7th in 2004).

Sailing (3-4-1, 15th). Hans-Peter Steinacher and Roman Hagara took men's Tornado gold in 2000 and 2004. The other gold went to Christoph Sieber (men's windsurfing) in 2000.

Judo (2-3-2, 16th). Both golds went to Peter Seisenbacher (men's middleweight, 1984 & 1988).

Canoeing (3-5-6, 20th). All three golds came in 1936, including two for Gregor Hradetzky. Just one medal this century – a women's K1 slalom bronze in 2008. The last flatwater medal came in 1968.

Cycling (2-0-2, 18th=). In 1896, Adolf Schmal won the 12-hour race (a horrendously gruelling event with only two finishers), and took bronzes in the much more civilised 10km race and one-lap race. The only other Austrian Cycling medal came 125 years later – a gold for Anna Kiesenhofer in the 2021 women's road race. This was, in fact, Austria's first Summer gold in any sport since 2004.

Equestrianism (1-1-1, 17th). Two medals in individual dressage (bronze in 1936 and gold, for Elisabeth Theurer, in 1980). The most recent medal was a team jumping silver in 1992.

Fencing (1-1-5, 20th). Only three medals in the last 100 years, all for Ellen Preis in women's foil – a gold in 1932, and bronzes in 1936 & 1948. The last top-eight finish came in 1996 (4th in women's team foil).

Shooting (1-2-5, 26th). Hubert Hammerer won gold in men's free rifle, three positions in 1960. The most recent medal was a bronze in 2004, in men's small-bore rifle, three positions.

Swimming (2-6-6, 20th). Golds for Paul Neumann (men's 500m freestyle in 1896) and Otto Scheff (men's 400m freestyle in 1906). Markus Rogan's two silvers in 2004 were the first medals since 1912. A women's bronze followed in 2008 – the first women's medal since 1912.

Gymnastics (1-1-0, 31st=). The only Austrian Olympic Gymnastics champion, Julius Lenhart, represented an American club in 1904, and is therefore sometimes listed as American. He remained an Austrian citizen, though, and won the 1904 all-around title, as well as the 1904 team event (which is credited to the USA). He also took silver in the three-event combined competition. There have been no top-eight finishes since 1952.

Wrestling (1-2-3, 35th). Four medals came in 1906, including gold for Rudolf Watzl (Greco-Roman lightweight). The other two medals both came in 1932. One top-eight finish this century (8th in 2004).

Athletics (1-2-5, 51st). The only Austrian champion was Herma Bauma (women's javelin in 1948). In 2021, Lukas Weisshaidinger became the first Austrian man to win an Athletics medal (bronze in the discus).

Sport Climbing (0-0-1, 5th). Jakob Schubert took bronze in the 2021 men's; Austria came 7th in the women's.

Karate (0-0-1, 15th=). Bettina Plank was Austria's only entrant in 2021, and she took bronze in the <55kg.

Handball (0-1-0, 12th=). Silver in the first event in 1936. Only three entries since, all for women, in 1984, 1992 and 2000, finishing 5th in the latter two.

Football (0-1-0, 25th=). Men's silver in 1936. They have not competed since 1952.

Rowing (0-3-3, 30th). Two medals since 1960 – a men's double sculls silver (1992) and women's single sculls bronze (2021).

Tennis (0-1-0, 23rd=). Men's doubles silver in 1912. Four quarter-final defeats this century.

Diving (0-0-1, 18th). Otto Satzinger took the bronze in 1906. Three 4th places – in 1932, 1948 and 2000.

Water Polo – Finished 4th in 1912, 6th in 1936 and 13th in 1952. Those remain their only entries.

Table Tennis – A number of quarter-final exits in recent years, plus one top-four finish. The men's team beat Croatia and Japan in 2008 to compete for bronze, but lost out to South Korea.

Taekwondo – Only three entries, and none since 2004. Turkish-born Tuncay Caliskan came 4th in the men's featherweight in 2000 which, since 2008, would have been good enough for bronze.

PWDS – Entered Tug of War in 1906, but came last out of the four countries entered.

Hockey – Austria came 5th out of 6 in the boycott-wrecked women's competition of 1980; this was the only time the women have entered. The men have entered three times, but not since 1952, when they secured their best position of 7th.

Modern Pentathlon – Edmond Bernhardt came 8th in 1912, and Thomas Daniel came 6th exactly a century later. These are the only top-eight finishes for Austria so far.

Beach Volleyball – Stefanie and Doris Schwaiger were losing quarter-finalists in the women's 2008 and 2012 competitions, as were Florian Gosch and Alexander Horst in the men's event in 2008.

Boxing – Eduard Kerschbaumer (1948 featherweight) is Austria's only Boxing quarter-finalist, and he only needed to win one match in order to do it. Austria have not had an Olympic boxer since 1988.

Artistic Swimming – Greek-born sisters Anna-Maria and Eirini-Marina Alexandri came 7th in the 2021 duet event – Austria's first top-eight finish in the sport.

Golf – Josef Straka came 10th in the men's competition in 2021 – just one stroke off a potential bronze.

Skateboarding – An 18th-place finish in their one event in 2021 – women's street.

Archery – Only four entries, and only one since 1984. The best finish is 21st (1980 men's event).

Badminton – Nine entries, but only three wins between them. No last-16 finishes.

Baseball/Softball, Basketball, Rugby, Surfing, Volleyball – never entered

WINTER

Alpine Skiing (40-44-44, 1st). Two Austrians have won three golds each – Toni Sailer (who won the men's downhill, slalom and giant slalom in 1956), and Matthias Mayer (men's downhill in 2014, and super-G in 2018 & 2022). Austria are a long way clear of neighbours Switzerland at the top of the all-time Alpine Skiing medal table.

Ski Jumping (7-10-10, 4th). Thomas Morgenstern won large hill and team golds in 2006, and another team gold in 2010.

Luge (6-10-9, 3rd). Andreas and Wolfgang Linger won the two-man event in 2006 and 2010.

Snowboarding (5-2-4, 4th). Two of the five golds went to Anna Gasser (women's big air, 2018 & 2022).

Nordic Combined (3-2-11, 4th). Felix Gottwald won men's sprint gold in 2006, and contributed to both the other golds, in the 2006 & 2010 team events.

Figure Skating (7-9-4, 4th). At one time, Austria had huge success in Figure Skating, including back-to-back golds for Karl Schafer in the men's events of 1932 & 1936. But they have not won a medal since 1972.

Bobsleigh (1-2-0, 6th). Silvers in 1964 and 1968, and gold in 1992 – all in the four-man event.

Nordic Skiing (1-2-3, 12th). Christian Hoffmann won gold in the men's 30km in 2002.

Speed Skating (1-2-3, 14th=). Emese Hunyady won gold in the women's 1500 metres in 1994; she also won a silver and a bronze.

Skeleton (0-1-0, 10th=). Silver for Martin Rettl in the 2002 men's event. The best in the women's is 4th (2018).

Biathlon (0-3-3, 14th). All 6 medals came between 2002 and 2018, including three for Dominik Landertinger.

Freestyle Skiing (0-1-0, 18th). Silver for Andreas Matt in 2010. The best in a women's event is 4th (also 2010).

Ice Hockey – Regular participants in the men's competition, they have never entered the women's. They finished 6th on their first attempt in 1928, and have not finished as high since. Their last top-eight finish was in 1976.

Short Track Speed Skating – Their only entrant is Veronika Windisch, who entered five events across 2010 and 2014, finishing 11th in the women's 1500 metres in 2014.

Curling – never entered

BELGIUM   **Olympic Rank 27th**
Population: 11,913,633 (rank 82nd)
Olympic rank/ population differential: +55
Population per gold: 248,201 (rank 30th)
Population per medal: 68,865 (rank 27th)

Summer: 46 gold, 58 silver, 61 bronze (total 165)
Winter: 2 gold, 2 silver, 4 bronze (total 8)
Total: 48 gold, 60 silver, 65 bronze (total 173)

Best sports: Archery (11 golds, 15.49%, 3rd)
                Equestrianism (5 golds, 3.27%, 11th)
                Hockey (1 gold, 2.86%, 9th)

Belgium did not enter the inaugural modern Olympics of 1896, but they did travel to Paris in 1900, and took advantage of the proximity of the venue to finish 4th in the medal table with 18 medals, including six golds. They did not travel to St Louis in 1904, but have participated in all Summer Games since then. In 1920, they hosted the Games in Antwerp and, not surprisingly, had their best Games. They won 14 gold, 11 silver and 11 bronze, finishing 5th in the medal table. Another three golds saw them into 10th place in Paris in 1924, but thereafter they were overtaken by other countries, and would not win three golds in a Games again until 2021. The only time they have ever not won a medal in a Summer Games was 1932 in Los Angeles (they had a couple of 4th-place finishes in Fencing).

Of Belgium's 46 Summer golds, 28 of them were won in or before 1924, with just 18 won since then. Six of those have been in Cycling (including four in road race events). Overall, Cycling has provided 28 medals, the most of any sport. A further six golds have come in Athletics, beginning with Gaston Reiff (men's 5000 metres in 1948) and Gaston Roelants (men's 3000m steeplechase in 1964). Tia Hellebaut won the women's high jump in 2008, with Belgium also taking the women's sprint relay that year. Then, Nafi Thiam won back-to-back women's heptathlon titles in 2016 and 2021.

The other six golds in the modern era have included two in Judo. In Swimming, Fred Deburghgraeve won the men's 100m breaststroke in 1996, still Belgium's only Swimming gold. Justine Henin won the women's singles Tennis in 2004, whilst in Gymnastics Nina Derwael won the women's asymmetrical bars in 2021, Belgium's first medal in the sport for 81 years. Also in 2021, Belgium won the men's Hockey gold, having won silver in that event in 2016.

The most successful sport for Belgium is Archery, but this really is a rather misleading state of affairs. There were seven Archery events in 1900, with all the entrants either French or Belgian. Belgium won 3 golds, 3 silvers and a bronze. In 1920, there were 10 events, with Belgium taking 8 golds, 4 silvers and 2 bronzes. There was one Dutch entry, but otherwise all the competition was again French. On both occasions, all the events were ones that were never repeated at the Olympics. Indeed, in two of the 1920 events, the Belgian team was the only won that entered, and merely had to turn up to win gold.

Hubert van Innis competed both times, aged 34 and 54 respectively, winning six golds and four silvers, with Edmond von Moer and Emile Cloetens winning three golds each in 1920. Archery was discontinued after 1920, and returned in 1972. Since then, no man from any country has won more than two golds in the sport, and no Belgian archer has won a medal at all (although they have had a couple of 4th places).

Belgium have won five golds in Equestrianism, but none since 1920 (since then, they have won just three bronzes). They have also won five golds in Fencing, but none since 1924 (their last medal in the sport was in 1948). Fernand de Montigny won five medals (1-2-2) between 1906 and 1924, all in team Fencing events. Other sports where Belgium had much more success pre-war than post-war include Boxing, Football, Shooting, Water Polo, Weightlifting and Wrestling.

Belgium have contested every Winter Games except for 1960 and 1968. They started off fairly well, winning four medals in their first five Games, two in Bobsleigh and two in Figure Skating, including a gold in the pairs skating for Pierre Baugniet and Micheline Lannoy. However, they then had to wait 50 years for another medal (a bronze in Speed Skating in 1998), and another 20 years for a medal after that. In 2018, Bart Swings won a silver in Speed Skating's mass start event; he won gold in the same event in 2022 (Belgium's second ever Winter gold), and there was a bronze in Short Track Speed Skating that year too.

LIECHTENSTEIN Olympic Rank 81st

Population: 39,993 (rank 199th)
Olympic rank/ population differential: +118
Population per gold: 19,997 (rank 1st)
Population per medal: 3,999 (rank 1st)

Summer: *no medals (best finish: 7th)*
Winter: 2 gold, 2 silver, 6 bronze (total 10)
Total: 2 gold, 2 silver, 6 bronze (total 10)

Best sports: Alpine Skiing (2 golds, 1.21%, 12th)
Judo
Nordic Skiing

Liechtenstein have the most unique Olympic record of any of the 206 IOC nations. They are the only country to have won any Winter medals without ever winning any Summer medals. They are also ranked 1st in the world in terms of both the ratio of population per gold medal, and population per medal, beating Norway into 2nd place on both counts. For a population so small that it could entirely fit into most Olympic Athletics stadia twice over, their record of ten Olympic medals is impressive indeed.

Seven of those ten medals have, in truth, been won by the same family, and all ten have been won in the same sport – Alpine Skiing. Their first ever Olympic medal was won in 1976 in Innsbruck, just a couple of hours drive from the Liechtenstein border. It was a bronze, claimed in the women's slalom by Hanni Wenzel. But it was four years later that Wenzel really proved to be a star of the sport. She won gold in both the slalom and giant slalom, and nearly won the downhill as well – but was pipped by Annemarie Moser-Proll of Austria, and had to settle for silver. Nonetheless, her place at the top of Liechtensteiner sports legend was secure.

Hanni's brother Andreas, meanwhile, won silver in the giant slalom at Lake Placid, and then won bronze in the same event in Sarajevo in 1984. The 1980 Lake Placid games saw Liechtenstein claim two golds and two silvers (all won by the Wenzels); it was the only Games in which they won any medals other than bronzes, and saw them finish 6th in that year's medal table.

Another pair of siblings from Liechtenstein was also proving successful in the same era. Willy Frommelt took bronze in the slalom in 1976, and his brother Paul took bronze in the same event in 1988. Liechtenstein's other medal of that era was somebody who was unrelated to either the Wenzels or the Frommelts – Ursula Konzett took bronze in the women's slalom in 1984.

After their 1988 bronze, Liechtenstein fell away from medal contention. It took until 2006 for them even to claim another top-eight finish (this was for another Alpine skier, Marco Buchel, who finished 6th and 7th that year, and 8th in 2010). But in 2018, their 30-year medal drought ended with a bronze in the women's super-G for Tina Weirather, who also finished 4th in the downhill, and just happened to be Hanni Wenzel's daughter.

Liechtenstein have managed a total of 15 top-eight finishes in Winter Olympic events – all of them in Alpine Skiing. Their best performances in any other Winter sport are three 11th-place finishes, two in Nordic Skiing and one in Luge. They have competed in all Winter Games since 1936, with the exception of 1952.

They also made their Summer Games debut in 1936, and have since only missed out in 1956 and 1980. They have stuck to just a few sports in that time – Athletics and Shooting (most Games since 1936), Cycling (most Games from 1936 to 1992), Judo (1972-96, returning in 2021), Swimming (only since 2012), as well as rare appearances in Tennis, Artistic Swimming, Gymnastics and Equestrianism.

They have scored two top-eight finishes, both in Judo. Magnus Buchel came 7th in the 1984 men's middleweight, and Johannes Wohlwend came 8th in the 1988 men's lightweight. Both won one bout and lost two. Their best Swimming finish is 12th (Julia Hassler, women's 400m freestyle in 2021). Their best Athletics finish is 14th (Alois Buchel, men's decathlon in 1964). Their best in any other sport is 17th, both in Cycling and Artistic Swimming.

LUXEMBOURG   Olympic Rank 87th

Population:	660,924 (rank 167th)
Olympic rank/ population differential:	+80
Population per gold:	660,924 (rank 45th)
Population per medal:	165,231 (rank 47th)

Summer:	1 gold, 1 silver, 0 bronze (total 2)
Winter:	0 gold, 2 silver, 0 bronze (total 2)
Total:	1 gold, 3 silver, 0 bronze (total 4)
Best sports:	Athletics (1 gold, 0.10%, 63rd=)
	Alpine Skiing (2 silver, 16th=)
	Weightlifting (1 silver, 54th=)

Luxembourg's Olympic history began in 1900 in Paris, with one of the bigger historical controversies the Games have ever produced. The marathon that year was won by Michel Theato, who was feted as a hometown French winner, albeit he was apparently not awarded his medal until 1912, due to unsubstantiated claims by his opponents that he had taken several shortcuts through the Parisian backstreets (he allegedly used his local knowledge to his advantage). Nearly a century later, a historian discovered he had been born in Luxembourg and had never applied for French citizenship, and many people treat him as Luxembourg's first Olympic champion. The IOC, however, still recognise his victory as a French one. He has variously been described as a baker's delivery boy and a carpenter (he may have done both jobs in his time).

The country's first official Olympic entry came in 1912, when they managed 4th and 5th places in two separate Gymnastics team events. Since then, they have entered every Summer Games with the exception of the sparsely attended Los Angeles Games of 1932. They did, in fact, enter the 1932 Olympic Art competitions, but they didn't need to actually attend to do so – just one of the reasons why the Olympic Art competitions should not be considered too seriously when collating medal tables. In 1920, they won their first official Olympic medal. Joseph Alzin took silver in the men's heavyweight Weightlifting; he sadly died ten years later at the age of just 36. That same year, they reached the final of the men's 4x100m relay and finished 6th; still the second-highest finish they have ever managed in an Athletics event.

The 1924 Games saw Luxembourg's best ever Swimming performance – Laury Koster finished 6th in the women's 200m breaststroke. The best Swimming finish they have managed since the war is 13th in 1956. There were no top-eight finishes in 1932, but in 1936, they did manage some more including, for the first time, in Boxing and Canoeing. Between 1948 and 1960, Luxembourg accrued a further seven top-eight finishes, five of which came in Fencing, all in épée, a discipline in which they really made a name for themselves for a couple of decades before fading away again. But the main story of that period was Luxembourg's only ever official Olympic gold medal, won by the legendary Josy Barthel in the 1952 men's 1500 metres. That he won in one of the tightest finishes in the event's history just made his achievement all the more memorable. After his death in 1992, Luxembourg's national stadium was renamed the Stade Josy Barthel, and although it was superseded in 2021 by a new updated stadium, his name will never be forgotten.

Up to 1960, Luxembourg had managed 18 top-eight finishes. As the Games became more global, however, more populous nations began to prosper, and Luxembourg found it more difficult. The only top-eight finish they managed in the next 40 years was a 7th place for Daniele Kaber in the 1988 women's marathon. Cycling's men's road race then saw Kim Kirchen (6th in 2004) and Andy Schleck (4th in 2008) do well. Judoka Marie Muller then finished 5th in 2012 to add a ninth sport to Luxembourg's roster of top-eight finishes in Summer Games.

Luxembourg's Winter Olympic history, meanwhile, began in 1928, when they finished 20th in the Bobsleigh. They missed 1932, but entered Bobsleigh and Alpine Skiing in 1936 to no great success. They then didn't enter a Winter Games again until 1988. Their one entrant that year was Austrian-born Marc Girardelli, a world-class Alpine skier who had switched nationality after a dispute with the Austrian federation. His best finish in Calgary was 9th, but in 1992 in Albertville, again as Luxembourg's only entrant, he won silver medals in both the super G and the giant slalom. In 1994, yet again representing his adopted nation by himself, he finished 4th in super G and 5th in downhill. Thus all four of Luxembourg's top-eight finishes in Winter Olympic history have been achieved by him. Since then, the nation have entered figure skaters in 1998 and 2006, a Nordic skier in 2014, and Alpine skiers in 2018 and 2022. The highest finish any of them has managed has been 24th.

CHAPTER ELEVEN - Eastern Central Europe (Hungary, Czech Republic, Poland, Slovakia)

HUNGARY   **Olympic Rank 11th**
Population: 9,670,009 (rank 94th)
Olympic rank/ population differential: +83
Population per gold: 52,270 (rank 6th)
Population per medal: 18,211 (rank 6th)

Summer: 183 gold, 159 silver, 179 bronze (total 521)
Winter: 2 gold, 2 silver, 6 bronze (total 10)
Total: 185 gold, 161 silver, 185 bronze (total 531)

Best sports: Water Polo (9 golds, 26.47%, 1st)
Modern Pentathlon (9 golds, 21.43%, 1st)
Fencing (38 golds, 16.45%, 3rd)

At 11th in the all-time Olympic rankings, Hungary are the highest-ranked nation never to have hosted either the Summer or Winter Games (they have showed interest several times, most recently for the 2024 Games). They have participated in all Winter Games, and all but two Summer Games (they were barred in 1920 following the Great War, and boycotted in 1984). As with most Eastern Bloc nations, their best Olympic days are several decades ago now, but they have nonetheless continued to perform most impressively in a number of sports.

Their best Games of all were the final ones before the Soviet invasion of 1956 – they won 16 golds in 1952, 42 medals in total, and finished 3rd – all national records (although they also finished 3rd in 1936). They finished 4th in 1948, 1956 and 1968. As recently as 2012, however, they finished inside the top 10. They have only once finished outside the top 20 – in 2008, when they won just 3 golds. They have never failed to win a gold at any Summer Games. The Winter Games have proved much less successful. Up until 2018, their only medals had been 2 silvers and 4 bronzes in Figure Skating, but they have now won their first two golds, both in Short Track Speed Skating.

Four Hungarians have won more than 5 golds – three fencers (Aladar Gerevich with 7, and Pal Kovacs and Rudolf Karpati with 6), and canoeist Danuta Kozak, also with 6.

SUMMER
Water Polo (9-3-5, 1st). Hungary first won a Water Polo medal (a silver) in 1928; they then won medals at every Games up until 1980, including golds in 1932, 1936, 1952, 1956 (the year of the infamous "Blood in the Water" match against the Soviet Union, the nation that had recently invaded Hungary), 1964 and 1976. Two lean decades followed, before three further golds consecutively from 2000 to 2008. In 2021, both men and women won bronze – the first time the women had medalled since their event was introduced in 2000. The most decorated Water Polo player in history is Deszo Gyarmati, who won 3 golds, 1 silver and 1 bronze (1948-64), not to mention a gold (1976) and bronze (1980) as coach.

Modern Pentathlon (9-8-6, 1st). In the men's team event, Hungary won 4 golds, 2 silvers and 2 bronzes between 1952 and 1988, as well as taking men's individual gold in 1960, 1964, 1972 and 1988, and women's individual gold in 2004. They have, more recently, taken bronzes in both the men's (2004) and women's (2021) events. Andras Balczo, who won team gold in 1960 and 1968, and individual gold in 1972, is the only modern pentathlete ever to win 3 Olympic golds. He also took two silvers.

Fencing (38-24-29, 3rd). One of the longest streaks of domination any country has had in a single Olympic event is Hungary's seven consecutive golds in men's team sabre from 1928 to 1960. Aladar Gerevich contributed to six of those (1932 to 1960), as well as taking three individual medals (including gold in 1948), and even a team foil medal for good measure. Gerevich's seven golds is an all-time Fencing record. Hungary's last gold in the team event was in 1988, but they won bronze in 2021. Aron Szilagyi has continued the grand tradition, winning men's individual sabre gold in 2012, 2016 and 2021. Hungary have also won numerous épée medals, including recent women's individual golds for Timea Nagy (2000 & 2004) and Emese Szasz (2016). By contrast, their last foil medal was in 1988, and their last gold in 1976. All in all, Hungary have medalled in Fencing at every Games in which they have participated since 1906.

Canoeing (28-31-27, 3rd). Hungary have won 32 medals, including 18 golds, this century alone in Canoeing. Their biggest star is Danuta Kozak, with 6 golds, 1 silver and 1 bronze (2008-21); in 2016 alone she won golds in K1 500m, K2 500m and K4 500m. They have won medals in every Games since 1952 (other than the 1984 boycott), but have won all but five of their golds since 1988.

Football (3-1-1, 2nd). The world-famous "Mighty Magyars" stormed to the gold in 1952. Leading the communist domination of Olympic Football, Hungary took bronze in 1960 and golds in 1964 and 1968. Dezso Novak played in all three, and is the most-decorated male footballer in Olympic competition. A silver followed in 1972, but their only entry since then was in 1996, when they came last. The women have never competed.

Swimming (30-28-20, 4th). Hungary's great Swimming tradition dates stretches right through the history of the modern Games. Alfred Hajos won two golds in 1896 (100m and 1200m freestyle; the latter being a particularly arduous outdoors affair in the freezing sea – he feared for his life). Zoltan von Halmay won 9 medals, including 3 golds, from 1900 to 1908. They didn't win any golds between 1952 and 1980, but have produced a number of stars since then. Tamas Darnyi won both individual medley events in 1988, and repeated the feat in 1992. Krisztina Egerszegi won 5 golds, 1 silver and 1 bronze (1988-96), including three wins in a row in the women's 200m backstroke. Katinka Hosszu won 4 medals, including 3 golds, in 2016.

Wrestling (20-17-20, 7th). Since 1906, Hungary have won Wrestling medals in all Games they've entered apart from 1996 and 2016. All their golds since 1952 have been in Greco-Roman events.

Gymnastics (15-12-14, 8th). Over half of these medals (21 out of 41) came in the 1948-56 period. Agnes Keleti won 10 medals, including 5 golds, in 1952 & 1956 – she's the only Hungarian other than Aladar Gerevich to win 10 medals in any sport. The most recent medal is Krisztian Berki's pommel horse gold in 2012.

Boxing (10-2-8, 7th). The legendary Laszlo Papp won a historic three golds in a row (1948-56) in middleweight and light-middleweight. This feat has only been emulated by two boxers since – both Cuban. The last gold came in 1996, and the last medal in 2000.

Shooting (7-3-7, 13th). Karoly Takacs was a world-class pistol shooter until his right hand (his shooting hand) was badly injured by an army grenade. He duly switched to his left hand, and won golds in 1948 and 1952. Hungary's only two medals since 1988 have been won by Diana Igaly in skeet, including gold in 2004.

Athletics (11-15-19, 16th). Of the 19 medals won by Hungary since 1960, 16 of them have come in the throwing events. Just one gold this century – Krisztian Pars in the 2012 men's hammer. The last gold in a non-throwing event came in 1948 (women's long jump).

Weightlifting (2-9-9, 20th). Golds for Imre Foldi (1972) and Peter Baczako (1980). Two medals this century (2000 & 2004), both silvers in women's competition.

Judo (1-3-6, 22nd). Antal Kovacs won men's half-heavyweight gold in 1992.

Handball (0-1-2, 11th). The women won bronze in 1976 and 1996, and silver in 2000. The men have agonisingly come 4th five times, most recently in 2012, but never higher.

Karate (0-0-1, 15th=). Hungary's only entrant in 2021, Gabor Harspataki, took bronze in the men's <75kg.

Tennis (0-0-1, 26th=). One win was enough for Momcsillo Tapavicza to claim bronze in the 1896 men's singles. He was from Vojvodina, part of Hungary then, but Serbian now. The only quarter-final appearance since was in the women's doubles in 2000.

Rowing (0-1-2, 34th=). Bronzes in 1908 & 1948; silver in coxless fours in 1968. Two top-eights this century.

Sailing (0-1-1, 32nd=). Flying Dutchman bronze in 1980, and Finn silver in 2021.

Equestrianism (0-0-1, 29th=). Won bronze in individual jumping in 1936. All top-eight finishes have been in 1936 and the heavily boycotted events of 1980.

Volleyball – The men entered only in 1964, coming 6th. The women entered in 1972, 1976 and 1980, coming 5th, 4th and 4th again.

Cycling – Nine top-eight finishes, including 4th for the men's 2000m tandem in 1924, and Blanka Vas in women's cross-country in 2021.

Table Tennis – 4th in the 1988 men's singles (Tibor Klampar) and the 2000 women's doubles.

Diving – Jozsef Gerlach came 4th in men's platform in 1956. Three of their four top-eight finishes came that year, the other came in 1980.

Basketball – The women came 4th on their only entry in 1980. The men have entered four times (most recently in 1964), with a best of 9th in 1960.

PWDS – Entered polo in 1936, where they beat Germany but lost 16-2 to Mexico in the bronze play-off.

Archery – The only top-eight finish was in 1980 (5th in men's individual). 2021 saw their first entry since 1996.

Taekwondo – Only two entries, both in men's flyweight – Jozsef Salim in 2000, and his nephew Omar Salim in 2021. Both came 6th.

Triathlon – Bence Bicsak came 7th in the men's event in 2021, the best of their numerous entries.

Hockey – Finished 8th on their only entry (men's event in 1936).

Artistic Swimming – 23rd in the duet in 2000, and 21st in the duet in 2012.

Badminton – Eight entries (four of which were in 1992) – they have lost every match they've played.

Baseball/Softball, Beach Volleyball, Golf, Rugby, Skateboarding, Sport Climbing, Surfing – never entered

WINTER
Short Track Speed Skating (2-0-2, 8th). All four medals have involved Shaoang Liu, who was born to a Chinese father and Hungarian mother in Budapest. He won the men's 500 metres and took bronze in the 1000 metres in 2022, also winning a relay gold in 2018 and bronze in 2022.

Figure Skating (0-2-4, 18th). Hungary's first six Winter medals were all in Figure Skating – a silver and four bronzes in the pairs between 1932 and 1956, and ice dance silver in 1980. The last top-eight finish was in 2002.

Speed Skating – Kornel Pajor came 4th in 1948 (men's 10000m); still their only top-eight finish.

Alpine Skiing – One top-eight finish, 7th in the women's downhill in 2014.

Ice Hockey – Entered only in 1928, 1936 and 1964 – their best finish was 8th in 1936.

Nordic Skiing – Numerous entries; their best two performances both came in 1964 (8th in the women's relay and 19th in the women's 10km).

Bobsleigh – 13th in the two-woman event in 2002. Last entered in 2006.

Biathlon – Numerous entries, but no higher than 14th (men's relay in 1984). Their best finish in an individual event is 26th.

Snowboarding – Entered for the first time in 2022, coming 17th, 19th and 28th.

Ski Jumping – 19th in 1968; they have not entered since that year.

Freestyle Skiing – Came 24th and last on their only entry – women's halfpipe in 2018.

Nordic Combined – Entered six times between 1924 and 1936, but never managed to finish.

Curling, Luge, Skeleton – never entered

CZECH REPUBLIC   Olympic Rank 21st

Population: 10,706,242 (rank 87th)
Olympic rank/ population differential: +66
Population per gold: 133,828 (rank 18th)
Population per medal: 38,861 (rank 18th)

Summer: 19 gold, 22 silver, 26 bronze (total 67)
Winter: 10 gold, 11 silver, 13 bronze (total 34)
Total: 29 gold, 33 silver, 39 bronze (total 101)

plus Czechoslovakia: Summer (49-49-44 tot 142); Winter (2-8-16 tot 26); Total (51-57-60 tot 168)
plus Bohemia: Summer (0-1-5 tot 6);   Total (0-1-5 tot 6) (plus mixed team 0.5 bronze)

Combined totals: Summer: 68 gold, 72 silver, 75.5 bronze (total 215.5)
                 Winter: 12 gold, 19 silver, 29 bronze (total 60)
                 Total: 80 gold, 91 silver, 104.5 bronze (total 275.5)

Best sports: Snowboarding (3 golds, 5.88%, 6th)
                           Canoeing (12 golds, 4.96%, 5th)
                           Gymnastics (12 golds, 3.13%, 10th)

The Games of 1900, 1906, 1908 and 1912 saw participation by Bohemia, a state roughly equivalent to the modern-day Czech Republic. The European map was redrawn after World War I, and Czechoslovakia took part in every Summer and Winter Games from 1920 to 1992, with the exception of the 1984 Soviet-led boycott. The Czech Republic have taken part in every Games since then.

The most golds won in a Summer Games is 7 (1952 and 1968). The most medals won is 14 (1964 & 1980). The highest medal table position is 6th (1952), and the most recent top-10 finish came in 1968. Since independence, the Czech Republic's bests have been in 1996, 2012 and 2021; on each of these occasions, they won 4 golds and 11 medals in total. The last time they failed to win any golds was in 1920; the only time they have ever failed to win a medal was in 1912 (as Bohemia).

In the Winter Games, the only time since independence that the Czech Republic failed to win a gold was in 1994, when they ended without any medals at all. They won 9 medals in 2014, but have never won more than two golds in any one year.

The most medals by a single athlete is 11 for Vera Caslavska (Gymnastics), followed by 7 for Martina Sablikova (Speed Skating). The most golds is 7 for Caslavska, followed by 4 for Emil Zatopek (Athletics).

SUMMER
Canoeing (12-10-7, 5th). After a period of 10 medals, including 6 golds, from 1936 to 1952, the Czechs didn't win another Canoeing medal until 1992. Since then, they have won 19 medals, 13 of which have been in slalom events. Stepanka Hilgertova (slalom, 1996 & 2000) and Martin Doktor (flatwater, 1996) have won two golds each, as did Josef Holecek and Jan Brzak-Felix in the 1936-52 period.

Gymnastics (12-13-10, 10th). The wonderful Vera Caslavska won 7 golds and 4 silvers in the 1960s, and became a focus of anti-communist protest during the era. There has only been one Czech medal since then – a bronze in 1980.

Football (1-1-0, 17th). Won men's silver in 1964 and gold in 1980. No other top-eight finishes. The last entry came in 2000, and the women have never entered.

Tennis (2-4-9.5, 9th). Miloslav Mecir won men's singles gold on Tennis's Olympic return in 1988. Barbora Krejcikova & Katerina Siniakova won women's doubles gold in 2021.

Modern Pentathlon (1-1-2, 9th). David Svoboda won men's gold in 2012.

Shooting (7-7-6, 12th). Katerina Kurkova-Emmons is the most successful Czech shooter, winning a gold (in women's air rifle in 2008), a silver and a bronze.

Athletics (16-11-13, 14th). Four of the first five Athletics gold medals won by the Czechs went to the legendary Emil Zatopek (the men's 10000 metres in 1948, and an unfathomably impressive treble of 5000m, 10000m and marathon in 1952). The other went to his wife, Dana Zatopkova, in the 1952 women's javelin. The last seven golds (1992-2012) have all come in either javelin (Jan Zelezny three times and Barbora Spotakova twice), or decathlon (Robert Zmelik and Roman Sebrle).

Judo (2-0-1, 20th). Lukas Krpalek won back-to-back golds (2016 half-heavyweight & 2021 heavyweight). The only other medal came in 1980.

Weightlifting (3-2-3, 18th). Golds in 1932, 1964 & 1980. No medals since then. The best finish for the Czech Republic has been 6th.

Boxing (3-2-2, 22nd). Golds in 1948, 1952 & 1960. One medal since 1980 – a silver in 2000.

Cycling (3-3-2, 14th). Track golds in 1964 & 1976, and cross-country gold for Jaroslav Kulhavy in 2012.

Rowing (3-5-8, 16th). Golds for the men's coxed four (1952) and double sculls (1960), and for Miroslava Knapkova (women's single sculls) in 2012.

Diving (1-1-0, 11th). Milena Duchkova won women's platform gold in 1968 and silver in 1972. Czechoslovakia also had a 4th place in 1992. Only one entry for the Czech Republic since independence.

Equestrianism (1-0-0, 19th=). Jumping gold for Frantisek Ventura in 1928. No top-eight finishes since 1936.

Wrestling (1-7-8, 32nd). Vitezslav Macha won Greco-Roman welterweight gold in 1972. Just one Czech Republic medal – a bronze in 2008.

Triathlon (0-0-1, 14th=). Men's bronze in 2000 – the only top-eight finish so far.

Volleyball (0-1-1, 13th=). The men won silver in 1964 & bronze in 1968. The men last entered in 1980, and the women in 1972.

Handball (0-1-0, 12th=). The men won silver in 1972, and last entered in 1992. The women last entered in 1988.

Hockey (0-1-0, 13th=). The women won silver in 1980; still the only Czech entry ever in Olympic Hockey.

Fencing (0-0-3, 28th). Two bronzes in 1908 (for Bohemia), and one in 2021.

Sailing (0-1-0, 34th=). Silver in the women's Europe class in 2004. Two other top-eight finishes (2000 & 2008).

Table Tennis – Two 4th places – for Czechoslovakia in women's singles in 1988, and the Czech Republic in men's singles in 1996.

Swimming – The best finish was 4th in the men's 100m backstroke in 1980. Since independence, the Czech Republic's best is 5th in the men's 100m & 200m breaststroke in 2000.

Basketball – The women came 4th in 1976, and last entered in 2012. The men came 5th in 1960, and last entered in 2021.

Archery – The best three Czech finishes – 4th, 20th and 24th – all came in 1980.

Beach Volleyball – One top-eight finish so far – 5th in the women's event in 2012.

Water Polo – The only Czech top-eight finish was a 6th place in 1924. Only one post-war appearance – in 1992, when Czechoslovakia's men came last out of 12.

Sport Climbing – One entry in 2021 – Adam Ondra came 6th in the men's.

Artistic Swimming – The best finish is 14th (in the duet in both 2004 & 2012).

Golf – Equal 23rd (women's in 2021) is their best finish so far.

Badminton – Entered in 1992, 2008, 2012 & 2016, but have not managed a top-16 finish yet.

Baseball/Softball, Karate, Rugby, Skateboarding, Surfing, Taekwondo, PWDS – never entered

WINTER

Snowboarding (3-0-1, 6th). Ester Ledecka won the women's parallel giant slalom in 2018 & 2022. Eva Samkova took gold (2004) and bronze (2008) in the women's snowboard cross.

Ice Hockey (1-4-5, 5th). The Czech Republic took gold in 1998 and bronze in 2006. All other medals were for Czechoslovakia, and all medals have been won by the men.

Ski Jumping (1-2-4, 9th). Jiri Raska took a gold and silver in 1968. The last medal was a bronze in 1992. The Czech Republic's best finish since independence is 7th.

Freestyle Skiing (1-0-0, 14th=). Ales Valenta won men's aerials in 2002.

Speed Skating (3-2-3, 11th). All but one medal (a bronze) were won by Martina Sablikova (2010-2022).

Figure Skating (1-1-3, 13th). Ondrej Nepela won the men's title in 1972. The last medal was a bronze in 1992. The Czech Republic's best finish since independence is 6th.

Alpine Skiing (1-0-2, 13th). Remarkably, Ester Ledecka won women's super-G gold in 2018, the same year in which she won gold in the very different sport of Snowboarding. The bronzes came in 1984 & 2010.

Nordic Skiing (1-6-7, 11th). Katerina Neumannova won six medals (1998-2006), including gold in the women's 30km (2006). The most recent medals came in 2010.

Biathlon (0-4-4, 13th). All eight medals came in 2014 & 2018.

Nordic Combined – 4th place in 1968. Since independence, the Czechs have come 5th in 1994, 1998 & 2010.

Luge – Three 6th places (1964, 1968 & 1976). The Czech Republic's post-independence best is 9th.

Short Track Speed Skating – One top-eight finish – 6th place in the women's 500 metres in 2006.

Curling – Only one entry – the mixed doubles of 2022, in which they came 6th.

Skeleton – Two entries – 7th in the 2022 women's, and 24th in the 2002 men's.

Bobsleigh – A best finish of 8th, in the two-man bobs of both 1994 & 1998.

POLAND   Olympic Rank 22nd

Population: 37,991,766 (rank 39th)
Olympic rank/ population differential: +17
Population per gold: 480,908 (rank 40th)
Population per medal: 118,354 (rank 42nd)

Summer: 72 gold, 89 silver, 137 bronze (total 298)
Winter: 7 gold, 7 silver, 9 bronze (total 23)
Total: 79 gold, 96 silver, 146 bronze (total 321)

Best sports: Ski Jumping (4 golds, 7.41%, 6th)
                Modern Pentathlon (3 golds, 7.14%, 5th)
                Volleyball (1 gold, 3.33%, 9th)

Poland made their Olympic debut in 1924, when they won just a silver and a bronze. In 1928, Halina Konopacka became their first Olympic champion (in women's discus). They have entered every Summer Games since then, other than the 1984 boycott, and they have never missed a Winter Games.

Their best gold medal tally at a Games is 7, which they have achieved four times (1964, 1972, 1976 & 1996). But their best overall medal total came in 1980, when they won 32, of which just 3 were gold. Their next best tally was 26 in 1976, when they achieved their highest medal table position of 6th. They left three of their first five Games (1924, 1936 & 1948) without a gold, but have not done so since. In every Summer Games this century, they have won between 10 and 14 medals.

All but four of their Winter medals have come this century. Ski jumper Wojciech Fortuna took a gold in 1972, but that was the only gold for Poland in a Winter Games until 2010. Four of their seven golds came in 2014.

Robert Korzeniowski (Athletics) is the only Pole to have won four Olympic golds. Irena Szewinska (Athletics), Anita Wlodarczyk (Athletics) and Kamil Stoch (Ski Jumping) have each won three. Szewinska's tally of seven medals in total is a Polish record.

SUMMER
Modern Pentathlon (3-0-1, 5th). Poland won the last ever men's team gold, in 1992, with one of that team, Arkadiusz Skrzypaszek, taking individual gold too. Poland took the women's bronze in 2016.

Volleyball (1-0-2, 9th). Women's bronzes in 1964 & 1968, and men's gold in 1976. The men have competed at the last five Games, whilst the women have only competed once since the 1960s (in 2008).

Boxing (8-9-26, 8th). Five of the eight golds came in the 1960s, including two for Jerzy Kulej in light-welterweight. The last gold came in 1976, and the last medal in 1992.

Football (1-2-0, 14th). Gold in 1972, and silver in 1976 & 1992. Have not competed since then, and the women have never competed.

Athletics (29-20-17, 7th). Poland have produced a long line of impressive Olympic champions. Irena Szewinska won three golds (women's sprint relay 1964, 200 metres 1968 and 400 metres 1976), as well as two silvers and two bronzes. Robert Korzeniowski won the men's 50km walk in 1996, 2000 and 2004, as well as the 20km walk in 2000. Anita Wlodarczyk took three women's hammer titles in a row (2012-21). But perhaps the most widely recalled is Stanislawa Walasiewicz (also known as Stella Walsh), who won the women's 100 metres in 1932. After her death in 1980, she was found to have had male bodily characteristics (ironically, a Polish reporter had once forced her American rival to undergo a sex test, which had proved she was a woman).

Weightlifting (6-6-22, 10th). Waldemar Baszanowski took lightweight gold in 1964 & 1968. Two golds since 1972 – in 2008 (Szymon Kolecki) and 2012 (Adrian Zielinski).

Judo (3-3-2, 12th). Waldemar Legien won golds in 1988 & 1992, and Pawel Nastula in 1996. No medals this century.

Fencing (4-9-9, 11th). The last golds came in 1972, Witold Woyda winning men's individual foil, and leading the team to victory too. The last medal was men's team épée in 2008 (silver).

Rowing (4-4-11, 14th). Robert Sycz and Tomasz Kucharski won lightweight double sculls gold in 2000 and 2004. Further Polish golds followed in 2008 and 2016.

Shooting (4-3-5, 19th). Two golds each for Jozef Zapedzki (men's rapid-fire pistol 1968 & 1972), and Renata Mauer (women's air rifle 1996 and small-bore rifle, 3 positions 2000). The last medal was a silver in 2012.

Wrestling (5-9-13, 15th). The last three golds all came in 1996, including one for Andrzej Wronski in men's Greco-Roman heavyweight; he'd also won gold in 1992. Four medals this century, all bronze.

Equestrianism (1-3-2, 15th). Four pre-war medals, plus two in the boycott-ravaged 1980 Games (both in jumping – individual gold for Jan Kowalczyk, and team silver). Poland came 8th in team dressage in 2012.

Sailing (1-1-3, 24th). Mateusz Kusznierewicz won the men's Finn in 1996 and took bronze in 2004. The other three medals came in 2012 (twice) and 2021.

Gymnastics (1-1-2, 29th). Two medals in the 1950s, followed by a bronze (2000) and gold (2008) for Leszek Blanik in the men's long horse vault.

Swimming (1-3-2, 26th). Three medals this century, all for Otylia Jedrzejczak in 2004 (women's 200m butterfly gold, and silvers in 100m butterfly and 400m freestyle). The last men's medal was in 1992.

Canoeing (0-8-14, 28th). 22 medals without a gold is a record for any country in any sport. Medals have been won at every Games since 1988.

Cycling (0-7-4, 29th). The last track medal came in 1972. Since then, there have been three road race medals, two team road time trial medals, and two cross-country medals (silvers for Maja Wloszczowska, 2008 & 2016).

Handball (0-0-1, 17th=). 1976 bronze for the men, who last entered in 2016. The women have never entered.

Archery (0-1-1, 20th). Silver for Irena Szydlowska in 1972, and women's team bronze in 1996. The men's team came 5th in 2008.

Basketball – 4th place in 1936 remains their best effort. The men last entered in 1980. The women have entered once – finishing 8th in 2000.

Hockey – Both top-eight finishes came thanks to boycotts in 1980 (the men were 4th and the women 6th). Just one entry since then – the men in 2000.

Sport Climbing – One entry in 2021; Aleksandra Miroslaw finished 4th in the women's competition.

Badminton – Four quarter-final defeats, all featuring Robert Mateusiak (men's doubles 2008, and mixed doubles 2008, 2012 & 2016).

Table Tennis – Two quarter-final defeats, both in men's doubles (1988 and 2004).

Tennis – Two quarter-final defeats, men's doubles in 2008 and mixed doubles in 2021.

Taekwondo – 5th in 2021 (women's heavyweight) and 6th in 2016 (men's welterweight).

Diving – Finishes of 5th in 1968 and 8th in 1972, both in women's events. No entries since 1992.

Beach Volleyball – The only top-eight finish is 5th in the men's event in 2012.

Skateboarding – One entry in 2021; a 17th-place finish in women's park.

Triathlon – A best finish of 22nd (women's event in 2016). The best men's finish is 47th.

Golf – The only Polish Olympic golfer came equal 51st in 2021.

Artistic Swimming, Baseball/Softball, Karate, Rugby, Surfing, Water Polo, PWDS – never entered

WINTER

Ski Jumping (4-3-3, 6th). Kamil Stoch took two golds in 2014, and another gold and bronze in 2018. Adam Malysz won four medals (2002-10), but none of them gold.

Nordic Skiing (2-1-2, 9th). All five medals went to Justyna Kowalczyk (2006-2014). The next best effort was a women's team 4th place in 1960.

Speed Skating (1-2-3, 14th=). The last three medals came in 2014, including gold for Zbigniew Brodka (men's 1500 metres).

Nordic Combined (0-0-1, 11th=). Bronze for Franciszek Gasienica Gron in 1956. The last top-eight finish was in 1992.

Biathlon (0-1-0, 17th=). Silver for Tomasz Sikora in 2006 (men's 15km mass start).

Luge – 4th in 1964 (women) and 1968 (men & women). A total of 19 top-eight finishes (1964-2022).

Ice Hockey – The men came 4th in 1932. The last top-eight finish was in 1984, and the last entry in 1992. The women have never entered.

Snowboarding – 4th in 2002. The other two top-eight finishes (7th and 8th) were both in 2022.

Alpine Skiing – Four top-eight finishes; the best was 5th in 1998, the most recent was 8th in 2022.

Figure Skating – 5th place in 1988 (men's) and 7th in 2002 (pairs).

Short Track Speed Skating – 6th in the women's relay in 2022; their only top-eight finish so far.

Bobsleigh – 13th in the four-man in 2018 is their best finish.

Freestyle Skiing – Two entries, finishing 16th in 2010 and 15th in 2014.

Skeleton – One entry, 15th in the women's in 2006.

Curling – never entered

SLOVAKIA   Olympic Rank 43rd

Population: 5,425,319 (rank 121st)
Olympic rank/ population differential: +78
Population per gold: 387,523 (rank 34th)
Population per medal: 129,174 (rank 44th)

Summer: 10 gold, 14 silver, 8 bronze (total 32)
Winter: 4 gold, 4 silver, 2 bronze (total 10)
Total: 14 gold, 18 silver, 10 bronze (total 42)

Best sports: Canoeing (8 golds, 3.31%, 9th)
                                               Biathlon (3 golds, 3.13%, 7th)
                                               Alpine Skiing (1 gold, 0.61%, 15th)

Following the "Velvet Revolution", the old Czechoslovakia split up, and Slovakia became an independent country in 1993. They have entered every Summer and Winter Olympics since, starting with 1994.

By far their most successful Summer sport since then has been Canoeing, and the vast majority of that success has come in the slalom events. Four people have been particularly prominent in Slovakian success in the discipline. Elena Kaliska won gold in the women's K1 slalom in 2004 and 2008 (at the time, this was the only slalom event open to women). Michal Martikan won C1 slalom medals in five successive Games – gold, silver, silver, gold and bronze, in that order, from 1996 to 2012. Martikan's five medals are the most for any slalom canoeist; he is a controversial national hero, having been spared prison by a presidential pardon following a 1997 drink-driving charge in which a pedestrian was killed.

Slovakia's most successful and feted Summer Olympians, however, are the Hochschorner twins, Pavol and Peter, who won C2 slalom gold in 2000, 2004 and 2008, and bronze in 2012. In 2016, the same event was won by Slovakian cousins Ladislav and Peter Skantar (Slovakia's eighth Olympic slalom gold), but sadly for the country, the event was then removed from the Olympic programme. Slovakia have won 15 slalom medals in total. By contrast, flatwater Canoeing, despite having many more events overall, has produced just three silvers and two bronzes for Slovakia, mostly in the K4 events. The three Canoeing golds won in 2008 make those Games the most successful for Slovakia, finishing 26th in the medal table. Their total of six medals that year equals their record set in 2004. They have won medals at every Summer Games they have entered, and won golds in all of them except 2012.

Slovakia have only ever won two Summer golds outside of slalom Canoeing. These were won by Matej Toth in the 2016 men's 50km walk and Zuzana Rehak-Stefecekova in the 2021 women's trap Shooting. Rehak-Stefecekova is Slovakia's most successful Summer Olympian outside of Canoeing, having previously taken silvers in the same event in 2008 and 2012 (she missed the 2016 Games due to maternity leave). Other Slovakian shooters have taken three medals between them, all bronze. Toth's medal remains the only one Slovakia have won in Athletics – the next highest position they have managed is 5th.

The five other Summer medals Slovakia have won have come in Golf (won by a naturalised South African), Wrestling (won by a naturalised Russian), Judo and two in Swimming, both of which were won by Martina Moravcova. Her medals came in 2000, in the women's 100m butterfly and 200m freestyle; she has been responsible for all six of Slovakia's top-eight finishes in Swimming.

Slovakia did not win a medal in their first three Winter Games – their duck was broken with a Snowboarding silver for Radoslav Zidek in 2006. They have won one gold at each Games since then, with a national record three medals being won in both 2010 and 2018. Their most successful Olympian, Summer or Winter, is Russian-born Anastasiya Kuzmina. Competing in Biathlon, she won gold in the sprint in 2010 and 2014, silver in the pursuit in 2010 and 2018, silver in the 15km individual in 2018 and gold in the mass start in 2018. Her six medals account for more than half of Slovakia's Winter total of ten. The others were Zidek's silver, a men's biathlon bronze in 2010, and two medals in 2022 – a gold for Petra Vlhova in the women's Alpine Skiing slalom, and a bronze for the men's Ice Hockey team. A national obsession in Slovakia, they had competed in the men's Ice Hockey at every Games since 1994, and finally, 28 years on, secured their first medal with a 4-0 win over Sweden.

CHAPTER TWELVE – Balkans (Romania, Bulgaria, Greece, Serbia, Croatia, Slovenia, Kosovo, North Macedonia, Montenegro, Albania, Bosnia & Herzegovina)

ROMANIA   **Olympic Rank 19th**

Population:	18,326,327 (rank 68th)
Olympic rank/ population differential:	+49
Population per gold:	203,626 (rank 24th)
Population per medal:	59,309 (rank 25th)
Summer:	90 gold, 97 silver, 121 bronze (total 308)
Winter:	0 gold, 0 silver, 1 bronze (total 1)
Total:	90 gold, 97 silver, 122 bronze (total 309)
Best sports:	Rowing (20 golds, 7.30%, 4th)
	Gymnastics (25 golds, 6.51%, 5th)
	Canoeing (10 golds, 4.13%, 6th)

Only Hungary have a better Olympic record without ever having hosted the Games at least once. Romania's first Olympian was shooter Gheorghe Plagino, the sole Romanian in the 1900 Games. They next entered the Games in 1924, and since then have missed only the 1932 and 1948 Games. Notably, they were the only Eastern Bloc country to compete in 1984. They have entered every Winter Games except 1924 and 1960.

Only two medals were won prior to the war; a Rugby bronze (by default, having lost both games in a three-team tournament) in 1924, and an Equestrian silver for Henri Rang in 1936. The 1952 Games saw their first gold – Iosif Sirbu in men's small-bore rifle (prone). They won at least two golds at every Games from 1956 to 2012, but just one each in 2016 and 2021 (in Fencing and Rowing respectively).

Romania's best Games by far were those of 1984, when they were one of the very few Eastern European nations not to join the Soviet-led boycott. They won 20 golds and 53 medals in total that year, finishing 2nd in the medal table behind the USA (who won a huge 83 golds), and dominated Rowing and Gymnastics in particular. The other Games in which they reached double figures in golds was 2000 (11 golds), whilst their second-best Games in terms of medals won was 1976 (with 27). They have been top-10 finishers in 1956, 1976, 1980, 1984 and 1988; their second-best position was 7th in 1980. They have been in decline since then.

SUMMER
Rowing (20-12-9, 4th). Romania's first Rowing gold came in 1980 (Sanda Toma in women's single sculls); their first medal having come eight years earlier. Of their 41 medals, 31 have come in women's events, including all but two of their golds. Four of the five most successful female rowers of all time have been Romanian. Top of the list is Elisabeta Lipa, whose record of 5 gold, 2 silver and 1 bronze makes her the most decorated Olympic rower ever, male or female. Incredibly, she won golds 20 years apart, in 1984 and 2004 (aged 19 and 39 respectively). Georgeta Damian also won five golds (and a bronze), between 2000 and 2008. Doina Ignat (1992-2004) won four golds and a silver, and Viorica Susanu also won four golds (2000-2008).

Gymnastics (25-21-26, 5th). Romania's greatest Olympian of all time is Nadia Comaneci – she has won the most medals of any Romanian (nine), and her five golds has been equalled only by rowers Lipa and Damian. As a 14-year-old in 1976, she won the all-around, asymmetrical bars and balance beam golds, and then won balance beam (again) and floor golds in 1980. Those five were the first five Gymnastics medals her country won – she really was a trailblazer. She also won 3 silvers and a bronze across those two Games. But she is not the only Romanian Gymnastics star. Ekaterina Szabo won 4 golds and a silver (all in 1984), whilst Daniela Silivas (1988), Simona Amanar (1996-2000) and Catalina Ponor (2004) have all won 3 golds. Only 9 of their 72 medals have been won by men, including just one gold – Marius Urzica in pommel horse in 2000. Medals were won at all Games from 1976 to 2012, but none since. Despite this, it is by far the sport in which Romania have won the most medals. In the 1996 women's all-around, the silver medallist and both bronze medallists were Romanian.

Canoeing (10-10-14, 6th). Between 1956 and 1984, Romania picked up a huge stash of medals in Canoeing, but since then, there have been only a handful in 1996 and 2000. Ivan Patzaichin was the standout performer, competing in ten events between 1968 and 1984, and winning medals in seven of them – 4 gold, 3 silver.

Shooting (6-4-5, 15th). All 15 of their medals have been won by men, evenly spread between 1952 and 2012.

Fencing (4-6-7, 12th). Romania have won two golds in foil, and one each in sabre and épée (the latter was in 2021). Medals have been won at seven of the last eight Games.

Wrestling (7-8-19, 13th). Medals were won at every Games from 1956 to 1992, but only two since (bronzes in 2008 and 2016). Nobody has yet won two golds, but Stefan Rusu won three medals in total (silver in 1976, gold in 1980 and bronze in 1984).

Athletics (11-14-10, 18th). Just two of these 35 medals (one silver and one bronze) have been won by men. Iolanda Balas won the women's high jump in 1960 and 1964, and is the only Romanian two-time gold medallist in Athletics. Medals were won in every Games from 1960 to 2008, with the exception, surprisingly, of 1980. However, no medals have been won since 2008, when Constantina Tomescu took gold in the women's marathon.

Weightlifting (2-6-3, 21st). Eight of their 11 medals came in 1984, including both golds (Petre Becheru and Nicu Vlad). Vlad also won silver in 1988 and bronze in 1996; the other medal was in 1992.

Judo (1-2-3, 23rd). Alina Dumitru (2008) won the gold. She also won silver in 2012.

Swimming (3-2-4, 17th). No medals since 2004. Diana Mocanu (women's 100m and 200m backstroke in 2000) won two of the three golds. Razvan Florea (bronze in 200m backstroke in 2004) is the only male medallist.

Boxing (1-9-15, 28th). The only one of their 25 medals to be gold was that of Nicolae Linca in men's welterweight in 1956, beating Ireland's Fred Tiedt on a 3-2 split decision. Romania won Boxing medals at every Games from 1952 to 2004 except for 1964, but have not won a single Boxing medal since 2004.

Handball (0-1-3, 10th). Silver in 1976, and bronze in 1972, 1980 and 1984, all for the men, who last competed in 1992. The women came 4th in 1976, and last competed in 2016, but have yet to win a medal.

Rugby (0-0-1, 8th=). Only entered once, in 1924. They lost 61-3 to France and 37-0 to the USA, but as only three countries entered, they won bronze.

Volleyball (0-0-1, 17th=). Five entries – the men and women both came 4th in 1964, the men came 5th in 1972, and in 1980 the men claimed bronze with a win over Poland, whilst the women came 8th.

Equestrianism (0-1-1, 23rd). A jumping silver in 1936, and a team dressage bronze in 1980. However, the latter event had just four entries – it was the only Olympic event since 1960 with fewer than six entries, and every remotely prominent country boycotted. Romania have only had one entry since 1980 (in 2004).

Tennis (0-1-0, 23rd=). Romania are regular participants, but their only medal so far went to Florin Mergea and Horia Tecau (silver in men's doubles in 2016).

Water Polo – Last entered in 2012, their best so far is 4th in 1976. All their entries have been male.

Table Tennis – Seven quarter-final appearances since 1992, but no medal yet.

Cycling – A 5th-place in the men's road race in 1960 remains their best. A 7th-place finish in the 2021 men's cross-country was their first top-eight finish since 1960.

Football – Came 5th in 1964, after which they did not compete again until 2021, when they came 11th. They have yet to compete in the women's event.

Modern Pentathlon – 6th in 1956 (men's team); last entered in 2000.

Diving – A best finish of 9th in the 1992 women's platform; no entries since 2008.

Sailing – Only entered in 1980 (three events) and 1996 (two events); their best finish is 11th.

Archery – Their best 4 finishes were all in 1980 (13th being their best). Besides that year, they have only entered in 2008 and 2021, finishing outside the top 30 both times.

Basketball – Just one entry in regular Basketball (men's in 1952) – they came 23rd out of 23. They came 7th in the inaugural women's 3x3 event in 2021.

Badminton – Just one entry (in 1992) – it was a first-round defeat.

Triathlon – Entered for the first time in 2021 (men's), and came 36th.

Artistic Swimming, Baseball/Softball, Beach Volleyball, Golf, Hockey, Karate, Skateboarding, Sport Climbing, Surfing, Taekwondo, PWDS – never entered

WINTER
Bobsleigh (0-0-1, 12th=). Ion Panturu and Nicolae Neagoe won bronze in the two-man in 1968, finishing ahead of Austria. This remains Romania's only ever Winter Olympic medal. The pair were also part of the four-man team that same year that missed out on bronze to Switzerland by 0.1 seconds. Nine of Romania's 19 top-eight finishes in Winter events have come in Bobsleigh, but none since 1980.

Luge – A best of 4th (two-man in 1992). Raluca Stramaturaru came 7th in the women's singles in 2018; this is Romania's only top-eight finish in any Winter Olympic event since 1994.

Biathlon – Vilmos Gheorghe came 5th in the men's 20km in 1964. Best this century is 9th in the women's relay in 2010.

Speed Skating – The best 9 finishes all came in 1992 and 1994; the best four were all by Mihaela Dascalu, whose best was 6th in the women's 1000 metres in 1992.

Ice Hockey – 7th in 1976 and 8th in 1980; they have not entered since, and never entered the women's.

Nordic Skiing – 10th in the 1952 men's relay; their best this century is 15th in the 2018 men's team sprint.

Figure Skating – 13th in 1936 (mixed pairs), and 14th in 1994 and 2006 (both in men's singles).

Short Track Speed Skating – Katalin Kristo entered 7 events (2002-10), with a best finish of 17th; nobody else has ever entered.

Skeleton – Best finish of 18th (women's in 2018).

Nordic Combined – Only one entry – 19th place in the men's event in 1952.

Alpine Skiing – Finished 20th in both 1972 and 1994.

Ski Jumping – Finished 25th equal in 2018, and 25th in 2022; their only top-40 finishes.

Freestyle Skiing – Just one entry – 33rd place in 2010 (women's ski cross).

Curling, Snowboarding – never entered

BULGARIA   Olympic Rank 23rd

Population:	6,827,736 (rank 107th)
Olympic rank/ population differential:	+84
Population per gold:	124,141 (rank 16th)
Population per medal:	29,686 (rank 12th)
Summer:	54 gold, 88 silver, 82 bronze (total 224)
Winter:	1 gold, 2 silver, 3 bronze (total 6)
Total:	55 gold, 90 silver, 85 bronze (total 230)
Best sports:	Karate (1 gold, 12.50%, 5th=)
	Weightlifting (12 golds, 5.22%, 4th)
	Wrestling (16 golds, 3.70%, 8th)

Bulgaria arguably entered the first modern Olympics in 1896. Their one competitor was Charles Champaud, a gymnast who was a Swiss national, but lived in Sofia at the time of the Games, and represented his Bulgarian Gymnastics club in Athens. As competitors did not enter as part of official national delegations, it is debatable as to whether he should be seen as Bulgarian or Swiss.

Thereafter, Bulgaria next entered in 1924. Since then, they have competed in all Summer Games except 1932, 1948 and 1984. They have finished in the top 10 of the medal table four times, all in consecutive appearances during their golden era, supported by the communist regime of the time. They finished ninth in 1972, seventh in 1976, third in 1980 (helped by the Western boycott) and seventh again in 1988. Their highest medal count was 41 (in 1980, of which eight were gold). Their highest number of golds was ten, in 1988. Then, the communist era ended, and so did Bulgaria's status as an Olympic heavyweight.

Bulgaria did not manage their first gold medal until 1956. Their first seven golds were all in Wrestling, which remains their most lucrative sport (16 golds, 71 medals in total). They have been successful in both Greco-Roman and freestyle, and have won medals in the sport in every Games since 1956. They have won 12 golds (37 medals total) in Weightlifting, which is the sport in which they are highest in the medal table – fourth, behind Russia, China and the United States. They won multiple Weightlifting medals in all Games from 1972 (the first year they won medals in the event) to 2004, but have won just one since (a silver in the 2012 women's middleweight).

They have won five golds in Athletics; the most recent was Tereza Marinova in the triple jump in 2000, and the only male was Khristo Markov in the same event in 1988. They have also won five golds in Boxing, and four in Canoeing and Shooting. Other golds have come in Rowing, Gymnastics, Karate and just the one in Swimming – Tania Dangalakova in the 100m breaststroke in 1988 (Bulgaria won all three of their Olympic Swimming medals in that year).

Other medals have come in Basketball, Equestrianism, Football, Judo, Tennis and Volleyball. Other top-eight finishes have come in Badminton, Cycling and Fencing.

Six Bulgarians have won two gold medals each. They are Boyan Radov (Wrestling, 1964-68), Petar Kirov (Wrestling, 1968-72), Norair Nurikyan (Weightlifting, 1972-76), Nikolay Bukhalov (Canoeing, 1992), Tanyu Kiryakov (Shooting, 1988 & 2000) and Maria Grozdeva (Shooting, 2000-04). The most successful Bulgarian Olympian of all is Grozdeva; her two golds both came in sport pistol, but she also won three bronzes in air pistol (1992, 1996 and 2004).

Bulgaria have entered all Winter Games since their debut in 1936. Their first medal finally arrived in 1980, a bronze in Nordic Skiing for Ivan Lebanov. Their next medal was a gold in 1998, for Ekaterina Dafovska in Biathlon (15km individual event). This remains their only Winter gold. Their only other Winter medals came in 2002 and 2006, in Biathlon (one) and Short Track Speed Skating (three). They have also managed top-eight finishes in Alpine Skiing, Figure Skating and Snowboarding.

GREECE   Olympic Rank 28th

Population: 10,497,595 (rank 89th)
Olympic rank/ population differential: +61
Population per gold: 244,130 (rank 29th)
Population per medal: 67,683 (rank 26th)

Summer: 43 gold, 58 silver, 54 bronze (total 155)
Winter: *no medals (best finish: 13th)*
Total: 43 gold, 58 silver, 54 bronze (total 155)
           (plus mixed team: 0 gold, 0.1 silver, 0 bronze (total 0.1))

Best sports: Weightlifting (7 golds, 3.04%, 9th)
                     Taekwondo (1 gold, 2.08%, 13th)
                     Shooting (6 golds, 2.01%, 14th)

Greece are by no means the most successful country in the Olympic Games, but they are undoubtedly the most important. As the inspiration for the Olympic movement, the founders of the Olympic ideal, and the hosts of the first modern Games (as well as all ancient Games), their place in Olympic history is unique. As recognition for this fact, they always enter the stadium first during the opening ceremony, and have their flag displayed and their national anthem played at the closing ceremony.

Inevitably, their most successful Games have been the three held in Athens. In 1896, they won 47 medals, including 10 golds. In 1906, they won 34 medals, including 8 golds. And in welcoming the world back to their country in 2004, they won 16 medals, including 6 golds. They finished 2nd, 3rd and 15th respectively in those medal tables. At overseas Games, the most golds they have won is 4 (in 1996 and 2000), the most medals they have won is 13 (in 2000), and the highest medal table position they have gained is 10th (in 1904, but with only two medals won, in that least internationally representative of Games). In fact, for most of the modern Olympic era, they had been conspicuously unsuccessful, despite having attended every Summer Games. They didn't win a medal at all between 1924 and 1952, and only two golds between 1920 and 1988 (Sailing in 1960 and Wrestling in 1980). But they have won at least one medal at every Games since 1980.

In terms of numbers, their most successful Olympic sport is Athletics (37 medals, including 9 golds). Six of those golds have come since 1992, but the most famous was won by water carrier turned national icon Spyridon Louis in the most high-profile event of the 1896 Games – the men's marathon. The only sport in which Greece rank in the top 10 is Weightlifting. All 16 of their medals in that sport came in the periods 1896-1906 and 1992-2004. Pyrros Dimas won gold in the men's light heavyweight in 1992, 1996 and 2000, followed by a bronze in 2004, to make him Greece's only 3-time gold medallist of the modern era. The only other Greek to win four Olympic medals overall is Konstantinos Tsiklitiras, who won a gold, two silvers and a bronze in the long-defunct standing high jump and standing long jump events in 1908 and 1912. The only other Greek to win two golds in any event was another weightlifter – Akakios Kakhiashvili, who won gold in the first heavyweight category in 1996 and middle-heavyweight in 2000. He had also won gold in 1992, representing the Unified (former Soviet) team (his father was Georgian and his mother was Greek).

A mention should be made, however, of Leonidas of Rhodes, whose record of 12 gold medals between 164BC and 152BC stood for over 2000 years until broken by US swimmer Michael Phelps. Those golds consisted of four each in the stadion (c.200m), diaulos (c.400m) and hoplitodromos (also c.400m, but run in full armour).

Back to the modern Games – they have won 21 medals in Shooting (all but two were won over 100 years ago), 14 in Gymnastics and 11 in Wrestling. They have won four medals in the relatively brief history of Olympic Taekwondo, and also picked up medals in Sailing, Rowing, Judo, Swimming, Water Polo, Tennis (1896 and 1906 only), Fencing (ditto), Cycling (1896), Tug of War (1906), Football (1906) and Diving (just one, but it was a stunning gold in Athens in 2004). Six of their seven Swimming medals came in 1896, with the other coming 120 years later – a silver for Spyridon Gianniotis in the 2016 men's marathon event.

Despite entering a wide variety of Winter events since their debut in 1936 (they have since missed only the 1960 Games), they have never fared better than 13th (and last) in the women's Skeleton in 2002. Their highest position in any event where they were not the slowest finisher is 23rd. They entered Alpine Skiing and Nordic Skiing in 1936, and have since added Biathlon (1992), Luge and Bobsleigh (1994), Snowboarding (1998), Skeleton (2002) and Ski Jumping (2014). Of all the nations to have entered the Winter Olympics without ever winning a medal, none has won more Summer medals than Greece.

SERBIA   Olympic Rank 33rd

Population:	6,693,375 (rank 108th)
Olympic rank/ population differential:	+75
Population per gold:	196,864 (rank 23rd)
Population per medal:	54,418 (rank 23rd)

Summer:	6 gold, 7 silver, 11 bronze (total 24) *(plus Yugoslavia: 28g 34s 33b (tot 95))*
Winter:	*no medals (best finish: 14th)* *(plus Yugoslavia: 0g 3s 1b (tot 4))*
Total:	6 gold, 7 silver, 11 bronze (total 24) *(plus Yugoslavia: 28g 37s 34b (tot 99))*

Best sports: Water Polo (5 golds, 14.72%, 2nd)
Karate (1 gold, 12.50%, 5th=)
Handball (3 golds, 11.54%, 4th)

Of the constituent countries of the former Yugoslavia, Serbia are the biggest and most populous, and also have the old Yugoslav capital, Belgrade. For those reasons, they inherit the old Yugoslavia's Olympic record, despite the fact that, in Olympic terms, Serbia are less successful than either Croatia or Slovenia.

Yugoslavia first entered the Olympics in 1920, when they entered only men's Football. In 1924, gymnast Leon Stukelj won his first two golds; he won another in 1928 to become the nation's only 3-time Olympic champion. Yugoslavia entered all Olympics from then until the Winter Games of 1992, except for the Winter Games of 1932 and 1960. For the Summer Games of 1992, they competed as Independent Olympic Athletes (although for the purposes of this book, these medals are still counted under Yugoslavia's total). In 1994, they were banned from competing due to the war. From 1996 to 2002, they competed again as Yugoslavia, although in reality they consisted only of Serbia and Montenegro. In 2004 and 2006, they were named as Serbia and Montenegro, and from 2008 onwards, Serbia have competed as an independent nation.

The only time the nation won more than 3 golds in one Games was in Los Angeles in 1984, when they won seven. Their total of 18 medals that year was also a national record, as is their position of 9th in the medal table. They have won medals at all Games since 1924, other than 1932, when they sent only one athlete. The last time they failed to win gold was 2008. In 2021, they won 3 golds and 9 medals in total – the best since the dissolution of Yugoslavia.

Yugoslavia/ Serbia have won five golds in men's Water Polo – 1968, 1984, 1988, 2016 and 2021, and have won medals in the event at every Games this century. Only Hungary have a better record in the sport. Other team sports have also proved successful. Golds were won in Handball (1972 men, 1984 both men and women), and numerous medals were won in Basketball, including a gold in 1980, taking advantage of the Americans' absence. They have the third best record in Basketball, behind the Americans and Russians. They have a good record in Volleyball, too, including a gold for the men in 2000.

Only three medals have ever been won in Athletics – silvers in men's hammer (1948) and marathon (1956), and a bronze in women's long jump (2016). Swimming has also produced just three medals. The first two were both for Djurdica Bjedov (gold in the women's 100m breaststroke in 1968, and a silver in the 200m of the same year). The other was a silver for Milorad Cavic in the men's 100m butterfly; he looked to have won gold, but was pipped on the line by Michael Phelps, who went on to complete his haul of 8 golds in one Games.

The sport in which the country has won most medals in Wrestling (18, including 5 golds). Of those 18, 14 were in Greco-Roman. They have won 14 in Shooting, including a gold, three silvers and a bronze (1988-2004) for pistol shooter Jasna Sekaric. Uniquely, she won two medals for Yugoslavia (pre-breakup), one as an independent Olympic athlete, one for Yugoslavia (post-breakup) and one for Serbia & Montenegro. Since Serbia became independent, the only Serbian two-time champion outside of Water Polo is Milica Mandic in women's heavyweight Taekwondo (2012 and 2021).

Yugoslavia were appointed as hosts of the 1984 Winter Games, despite never having won a Winter medal in any of the 11 Games they had entered up to that point. Slovenian Jure Franko won a historic silver in the men's giant slalom Alpine Skiing in Sarajevo, before a further two silvers and a bronze were claimed in 1988 (one in Alpine Skiing and two in Ski Jumping – Matjaz Debelek was involved in both of the latter, a silver and a bronze). Neither Yugoslavia or Serbia have come anywhere near a Winter medal since then.

CROATIA   **Olympic Rank 40th**

Population:	4,169,239 (rank 130th)
Olympic rank/ population differential:	+90
Population per gold:	231,624 (rank 27th)
Population per medal:	80,178 (rank 34th)
Summer:	14 gold, 13 silver, 14 bronze (total 41)
Winter:	4 gold, 6 silver, 1 bronze (total 11)
Total:	18 gold, 19 silver, 15 bronze (total 52)
Best sports:	Handball (2 golds, 7.69%, 8th)
	Water Polo (1 gold, 2.94%, 9th)
	Alpine Skiing (4 golds, 2.42%, 9th)

Croatia have competed in every Summer and Winter Games since 1992. They have won medals at every Summer Games in which they have competed. In Barcelona in 1992, their three medals were all notable – bronzes in both men's singles and doubles for prominent Tennis player Goran Ivanisevic, and a silver behind the legendary USA "Dream Team" in the men's Basketball. In 1996, a silver in the men's Water Polo was followed by the nation's first gold – beating Sweden 27-26 in a dramatic men's Handball final. Both of those sports have been reliably successful for Croatia – they won a second Handball gold in 2004, and a first Water Polo gold in 2012, though they have not won any Basketball medals since 1992.

The only Summer sport to have provided three golds is Athletics – two for Sandra Perkovic (women's discus in 2012 and 2016), and one for Sara Kolak in women's javelin in 2016. Not content with two Olympic golds, Perkovic also has two world titles and no fewer than six European titles in discus. Croatia have won two other Olympic medals in Athletics, one silver and one bronze – both for Blanka Vlasic in women's high jump. Surprisingly, no Croatian man has ever finished higher than 10th in an Athletics event.

The sport with most Summer medals overall for Croatia is Rowing, with 2 gold, 3 silver and 2 bronze. Both golds were won by brothers Valent and Martin Sinkovic (double sculls 2016, coxless pairs 2021). They were also both in the quadruple sculls crew which took silver in 2012, which makes them Croatia's most successful Summer Olympians. The only other three-time medallists are fellow rower Damir Martin (two silvers and a bronze, 2012-21) and Venio Losert (Handball golds 1996 and 2004, and silver 2012). As well as the Sinkovic brothers, Losert and Perkovic, there are two other two-time gold medallists, both also in Handball.

Tennis has continued to be successful, with the 2021 men's doubles producing an all-Croatian final (Pavic and Mektic beat Dodig and Cilic); this is the only time Croatia have won two medals in the same event. They have won five Tennis medals in all, and five also in Taekwondo – a gold for Matea Jelic in 2021, and four bronzes. Swimming has been less successful. Croatia's best three finishes were all achieved in 2004, and all by Duje Draganja (a silver in the men's 50m freestyle, as well as 6th in the 100m freestyle and 7th in the 100m butterfly).

The Rio games of 2016 were Croatia's best (on all counts – golds, total medals and medal table position), with 5 golds, 3 silvers and 2 bronzes placing them 17th in the medal table. Prior to 2012, they had never won more than one gold in a Games, but they have won at least three at all Summer Games since. The only Games with no golds have been 1992 and 2008.

Croatia have won 11 Winter medals, and have had a total of 15 top-eight finishes. No fewer than 14 of these 15 have been achieved by just two people – Janica Kostelic and her elder brother Ivica. Shortly after her 16th birthday, Janica competed in Alpine Skiing at the 1998 Games, before breaking several records with three golds and a silver in 2002. She added a further gold and silver in 2006, making her the greatest Croatian Olympian of all time. Meanwhile, Ivica won four silvers between 2006 and 2014. Croatia's Winter bronze was won by Jakov Fak in Biathlon in 2010 – he switched allegiance to Slovenia a few months later.

SLOVENIA **Olympic Rank 46th**

Population: 2,099,790 (rank 148th)
Olympic rank/ population differential: +102
Population per gold: 174,983 (rank 21st)
Population per medal: 40,381 (rank 19th)

Summer: 8 gold, 9 silver, 11 bronze (total 28)
Winter: 4 gold, 8 silver, 12 bronze (total 24)
Total: 12 gold, 17 silver, 23 bronze (total 52)

Best sports: Sport Climbing (1 gold, 50.00%, 1st=)
Ski Jumping (2 golds, 3.70%, 8th)
Judo (2 golds, 1.32%, 19th)

Relative to their size, Slovenia are one of the most impressively-performing countries in this book, and quite possibly the most underrated. Prior to the Second World War, Yugoslavia won a total of eight medals – three gold, two silver and three bronze. All of these were won in Gymnastics; seven in individual events, all won by Slovenians, and one by a team consisting of one Croatian and seven Slovenians. The legendary Leon Stukelj won most of these – three golds, a silver and two bronzes – and is still the most-decorated Slovenian Olympian. He appeared at the opening ceremony of the 1996 Games, aged 97, and lived to 100. Yugoslavia also won four Winter Olympic medals, comprising a total of six different medallists, all of them Slovenian.

As an independent nation, Slovenia have competed at all Summer and Winter Games since 1992. They have won medals at all their Summer Games – their worst return was at their first Games in 1992 (just two bronzes), and their best was at their most recent Games in 2021 (three gold, one silver, one bronze). That total of five equalled their Summer best set in 2008, but does not match their hauls in the 2014 or 2022 Winter Olympics, of 8 and 7 respectively (although only two golds each time). They have won medals at all Winter Games since 2010 (as well as 1994 and 2002).

The first two golds they won both came on the same day in 2000 – Iztok Cop and Luka Spik in the men's double sculls Rowing, and Rajmond Debevec in the men's 50m rifle (3 positions). Cop had, in fact, won a bronze in the coxless pair in 1992, which was Slovenia's first medal of any colour as an independent nation. Cop and Spik went on to win silver in the double sculls in 2004, and bronze in 2012, making Cop the only Slovenian with four Summer medals.

Two Slovenians, however, have won four Winter medals. The first was Alpine skier Tina Maze, who won silvers in the giant slalom and super-G in 2010, and golds in the giant slalom and downhill in 2014, making her the most decorated Slovenian in Olympic competition since independence. The other was ski jumper Peter Prevc, who won individual silver and bronze in 2014 (in normal hill and large hill respectively), and returned in 2022 to win men's team silver and mixed team gold. One of his teammates in the latter event was Ursa Bogataj, who also won individual gold in women's normal hill, making her only the second Slovenian, after Maze, to win two Olympic golds. No Slovenian has yet managed that in the Summer Games.

The Summer sport with the most Slovenian medals is Judo with six (2-1-3). All six have been won by women, with Urska Zolnir (2012) and Tina Trstenjak (2016) taking the golds. Their other four gold medallists have been Primos Kozmus (men's hammer throw in 2008), and three in 2021 – Benjamin Savsek in slalom Canoeing, Primos Roglic in road Cycling, and Janja Garnbret, who took the inaugural women's Sport Climbing gold. It means that Slovenia's eight Summer golds have come in seven different sports. They have also won three medals in Sailing and one in Swimming (Sara Isakovic in the women's 200m freestyle in 2008). Besides Kozmus's gold, Slovenia have also won two silvers (including Kozmus himself in 2012) and a bronze in Athletics.

Their top Winter sports have been Alpine Skiing (8 medals) and Ski Jumping (7 medals), with medals having also been won in Snowboarding, Biathlon and Nordic Skiing.

KOSOVO   **Olympic Rank 74th**

Population: 1,964,327 (rank 150th)
Olympic rank/ population differential: +76
Population per gold: 654,776 (rank 44th)
Population per medal: 654,776 (rank 71st)

Summer: 3 gold, 0 silver, 0 bronze (total 3)
Winter: *no medals (best finish: 15th)*
Total: 3 gold, 0 silver, 0 bronze (total 3)

Best sports: Judo (3 golds, 1.97%, 14th)
Wrestling
Alpine Skiing

The issue of whether or not Kosovo is an independent state and should thus be eligible to compete in the Olympics is a thorny one. They declared independence from Serbia in 2008, and this independence has been recognised by just over half of the UN's 193 member states, including most of NATO and most of the EU. However, many nations, obviously including Serbia, refuse to recognise their independence. Nonetheless, in recent years they have been increasingly recognised by international organisations, and in 2014 they got the go-ahead from the IOC to compete as an independent team in the Olympics. Prior to that, three Kosovans had taken part in Yugoslavia's gold medal-winning men's Football team of 1960, and another had won bronze for Yugoslavia in Boxing in 1984.

Making their official debut in 2016, Kosovo sent eight competitors to Rio – two each in Athletics, Judo and Swimming, and one each in Cycling and Shooting. In Athletics, both Kosovans finished 7th in their first-round heats and failed to advance. In Swimming, they finished 34th and 57th. In Shooting they finished 48th, and in Cycling they failed to finish.

In Judo, however, they were much more successful. On the second day of competition, Majlinda Kelmendi competed in the women's half-lightweight. A Kosovo Albanian, she represented Albania at the 2012 Games, losing to Christianne Legentil of Mauritius in the last 16. In 2016, now able to represent the country of her birth, she had a tough draw. She had to meet Legentil again, this time in the quarter-finals, sneaking through this time after a tight contest. Further wins over Misato Nakamura (Japan) and Odette Giuffrida (Italy) gave her a historic gold medal. The following day, compatriot Nora Gjakova (another Kosovo Albanian) reached the last 16 of the women's lightweight.

In 2021, Kosovo entered 11 people in six different sports – five in Judo, two in Swimming, and one each in Athletics, Boxing, Shooting and Wrestling. In Athletics, they finished 8th in their first-round heat and failed to advance. In Swimming, they finished 24th (in the women's 400m freestyle) and 65th. They finished 46th in Shooting, and lost in the first round in Boxing. In Wrestling, Egzon Shala beat an Algerian in the first round (last 16) of the men's super-heavyweight freestyle, thus reaching the quarter-finals. He was eventually ranked 7th – Kosovo's only top-eight finish so far outside of Judo.

Once again, Judo was the sport where Kosovo excelled. Nora Gjakova returned, taking gold this time after victories over the Japanese favourite in the semi-finals and a Frenchwoman in the final. Anybody wanting to win a Judo gold is likely to have to beat a Japanese opponent at some point, and this was also true of Distria Krasniqi, who took gold in the women's extra-lightweight, beating Funa Tonaki in the final. So three Olympic medals so far for Kosovo, all in Judo, all for women, and all gold. Gjakova's brother, Akil, also reached the quarter-finals of the men's lightweight.

Kosovo have entered the Winter Olympics in both 2018 and 2022. Albin Tahiri was born in Slovenia, to a Kosovo Albanian father and Slovenian mother. He initially represented Slovenia, before switching allegiance in 2009. He entered all five men's Alpine Skiing events in 2018, and a further four in 2022. His best finish so far is 15th in the men's combined in 2022. Kosovo's only other Winter Olympian is Kiana Kryeziu, another Alpine skier; she came 49th in the women's giant slalom in 2022, aged just 17.

NORTH MACEDONIA **Olympic Rank 115th**
Population: 2,133,410 (rank 147th)
Olympic rank/ population differential: +32
Population per gold: n/a
Population per medal: 1,066,705 (rank 82nd)

Summer: 0 gold, 1 silver, 1 bronze (total 2)
Winter: *no medals (best finish: 29th)*
Total: 0 gold, 1 silver, 1 bronze (total 2)

Best sports: Taekwondo (1 silver, 29th=)
Wrestling (1 bronze, 52nd=)
Karate

North Macedonia (known as Macedonia until 2019) have competed at all Olympic Games (both Summer and Winter) since 1996, shortly after the break-up of the former Yugoslavia. Prior to that, Macedonians had competed for Yugoslavia. Several had won medals, but seemingly the only individual gold medallist was freestyle wrestler Shaban Trstena in 1984. And it is Wrestling that has dominated the country's success since independence. Four of their five top-eight finishes have come in Wrestling (all in men's freestyle), including a bronze in 2000 for middleweight Magomed Ibragimov.

However, their only top-two finish so far came in Taekwondo – Dejan Georgievski taking silver in men's heavyweight in 2021. This was, in fact, their first and only entry in Taekwondo. The other Summer sports in which they have participated have been Canoeing, Shooting, Swimming and Wrestling (all debuting in 1996), Athletics (from 2000), Judo (from 2016) and Karate (2021). Besides Wrestling and Taekwondo, their only other top-ten finish was in their only Karate entry (finishing 9th). In Athletics, the nation has never progressed beyond round one of any event. In Swimming, their best finish is 17th (courtesy of Mirjana Bosevska, who is responsible for each of their best five Olympic Swimming results). In the Winter Games, they have only ever entered Alpine Skiing and Nordic Skiing. Their best finish so far is 29th (Alpine Skiing, 2014).

MONTENEGRO **Olympic Rank 120th**
Population: 602,445 (rank 170th)
Olympic rank/ population differential: +50
Population per gold: n/a
Population per medal: 602,445 (rank 67th)

Summer: 0 gold, 1 silver, 0 bronze (total 1)
Winter: *no medals (best finish: 38th)*
Total: 0 gold, 1 silver, 0 bronze (total 1)

Best sports: Handball (1 silver, 12th=)
Water Polo
Athletics

Another former Yugoslav republic, Montenegro did not become independent until breaking away from Serbia in 2006. They have entered all Summer and Winter Games since 2008. On their Summer debut, they competed in Athletics, Swimming, Water Polo, Boxing, Judo and Shooting. They added Handball and Sailing in 2012, and Tennis in 2016.

All of their top-eight finishes have come in the two team events, Water Polo and Handball. In the former, their men have agonisingly finished fourth three times in succession, losing the bronze medal matches to Serbia in 2008 and 2012, and Italy in 2016. They also finished 8th in 2021. In Handball, conversely, it's the women who have entered the Olympics. They won silver in 2012, beating France 23-22 in the quarter-finals and Spain 27-26 in the semi-finals before losing 26-23 to Norway in the final. It remains Montenegro's only Olympic medal, but they finished 6th in the same event in 2021. In Athletics, their best finish is 9th by Marija Vukovic in the 2021 women's high jump. In Swimming, they have never managed better than 31st. In the Winter Olympics, all of their entries have been in Alpine Skiing and Nordic Skiing – their best finish is 38th (Alpine Skiing, 2014).

ALBANIA   Olympic Rank 139th

Population: 3,101,621 (rank 137th)
Olympic rank/ population differential: -2

Summer: *no medals (best finish: 4th)*
Winter: *no medals (best finish: 28th)*

Best sports: Weightlifting
Wrestling
Gymnastics

Albania made their Olympic debut in 1972, sending four shooters and a weightlifter, but then didn't enter again until 1992. Their first top-eight finish came from weightlifter Ilirian Suli (5th place in 2000). Indeed, six of their seven top-eight finishes in Olympic history have come in Weightlifting. Their best finish of all was Briken Calja's 4th place in the 2021 men's middleweight – finishing agonisingly, 2kg short of his nation's first ever Olympic medal. Their other top-eight finish came in Greco-Roman Wrestling in 2008 (7th place).

Nationally-renowned steeplechaser Luiza Gega finished 13th in the 2021 Games – Albania's best Athletics finish. The best the nation has managed in Swimming is 37th (men's 100m freestyle, 2012). Their best finish outside of Weightlifting and Wrestling was a 10th place in their first (and, so far, only) Gymnastics entry (men's pommel horse in 2021). The only other Summer sports they have entered are Shooting, Judo and, in 1996 only, road Cycling. Albania have entered all Winter Games since their debut in 2006, but have only sent three different people in that time – all of them in Alpine Skiing; their best finish is 28th in 2022 (men's slalom).

Although Albania have never won an Olympic medal, a number of athletes with Albanian heritage have done so whilst representing other countries. These include javelin thrower Mirela Maniani, who finished 24th for Albania in 1996, before marrying a man from Greece, switching national allegiance, and winning silver in 2000, and bronze in 2004, in the same event.

BOSNIA & HERZEGOVINA   Olympic Rank 150th

Population: 3,807,7644 (rank 132nd)
Olympic rank/ population differential: -18

Summer: *no medals (best finish: 6th)*
Winter: *no medals (best finish: 21st)*

Best sports: Shooting
Athletics
Taekwondo

Bosnia & Herzegovina made their Olympic debut, in the midst of devastating war, in 1992, and have entered every Summer and Winter Games since. On that first appearance, Mirjana Horvat finished 8th in women's air rifle, but the nation have only managed three more top-eight finishes since. All of them finished 6th, and thus tie for the honour of being Bosnia's highest ever Olympic finisher. They were Nedzad Fazlija (men's air rifle, 2000), Nedzad Husic (men's featherweight Taekwondo, 2021) and Amel Tuka (men's 800 metres, 2021). Tuka finished only 0.6 seconds off the podium, whilst Fazlija scored 692.7 points, which was just 1.1 points off bronze.

Bosnia's best Swimming finish is 19th (women's 100m butterfly, 2021). The other Summer sports they have entered are Judo, Canoeing, Tennis, Table Tennis and, once each, Weightlifting and Wrestling. In the Winter Olympics, they have entered Alpine Skiing, Nordic Skiing, Biathlon, Luge and Bobsleigh. Their best finish is 21st (men's downhill Alpine Skiing, 1998). Bosnia and Albania are the only two European countries with populations over one million which have never won an Olympic medal. However, there have been some Bosnian-born Olympians who won medals for Yugoslavia prior to independence, mostly as part of Football, Basketball and Handball teams. The one Bosnian-born athlete who won a medal for Yugoslavia in an individual sport was Anton Josipovic, who won gold in 1984 light-heavyweight Boxing, following the controversial disqualification of future professional Boxing legend Evander Holyfield in the semi-finals.

CHAPTER THIRTEEN - Former USSR, European (Russia, Ukraine, Belarus, Estonia, Georgia, Azerbaijan, Lithuania, Latvia, Armenia, Moldova)

RUSSIA **Olympic Rank 2nd**
Population: 141,698,923 (rank 9th)
Olympic rank/ population differential: +7
Population per gold: 189,184 (rank 22nd)
Population per medal: 70,497 (rank 30th)

Summer: 167 gold, 158 silver, 176 bronze (total 501) *plus USSR (440-357-325 tot 1122)*
Winter: 55 gold, 57 silver, 58 bronze (total 170)   *plus USSR (87-63-67 tot 217)*
Total: 222 gold, 215 silver, 234 bronze (total 671) *plus USSR (527-420-392 tot 1339)*

Combined totals: Summer: 607 gold, 515 silver, 501 bronze (total 1623)
                 Winter: 142 gold, 120 silver, 125 bronze (total 387)
                 Total: 749 gold, 635 silver, 626 bronze (total 2010)

Best sports: Artistic Swimming (12 golds, 60.00%, 1st)
             Figure Skating (31 golds, 32.29%, 1st)
             Ice Hockey (9 golds, 28.13%, 2nd)

The first Russian involvement in the Olympics came in 1900, when the Russian Empire participated in Fencing and Equestrianism without winning a medal. They sat out the 1904 and 1906 Games, but returned in 1908, winning two silvers in Wrestling and a gold (Nikolay Panin) in Figure Skating. Five more medals followed in 1912 (2 silver, 3 bronze), but then came the Russian Revolution in 1917, and the nation would not return to Olympic competition until the debut of the USSR as late as 1952.

Quickly making up for lost time, the Soviets entered nine Summer Games between 1952 and 1988 (they boycotted in 1984), and finished 1st or 2nd every time. Their weakest Games were 1952 (22 golds, 71 medals) whilst their strongest were 1980 in Moscow (80 golds, 195 medals). Those Games were of course heavily affected by a large-scale boycott, but 80 golds in a Games has been beaten only once (the USA won 83 in 1984), and 195 medals in a Games also only once (the USA won 234 in 1904). In Seoul in 1988, the USSR won 55 golds and 132 medals; both of these were the highest ever totals by any non-hosting nation at any Olympics.

The Soviet Union was then dissolved in the early 1990s. In the 1992 Games, a Unified Team took part, consisting of the entire ex-Soviet Union apart from Estonia, Latvia and Lithuania. They topped the table with 45 golds. An independent Russia then took part in all Games from 1996 onwards. They finished 2nd in 1996 and 2000, then 3rd in the next two Games, 4th in the next two Games, and 5th in 2021. In the latter Games, Russians were not able to compete under their own flag due to widespread doping outrages over previous Games, which have seen many of their medallists from those Games being stripped of their medals.

The Soviets made their Winter debut in 1956, competing in all Games thereafter until 1988. Again, a Unified Team took part in 1992, with Russia taking over since then, albeit as independent participants in 2018 and 2022 due to the doping scandal. In the Soviet era, they never finished lower than 2nd. Russia then topped the medal table at their first attempt in 1994, but have fallen away slightly since then. They did win 10 golds in Sochi in 2014 to finish 2nd, but failed to reach the top 10 in either 2010 (3 golds) or 2018 (2 golds). In 2022, they finished 9th, but with a total of 32 medals (their highest ever). Their best gold haul is 13, achieved by the Soviets in 1976.

SUMMER
Artistic Swimming (12-0-0, 1st). Prior to 2000, the Russians had come close to medals, but never won one. Since then, they have won every single gold medal available, and established complete domination. Svetlana Romashina leads the way with 7 golds (team 2008-21 and duet 2012-21).

Gymnastics (107-97-74, 1st). The Russians' total of 107 golds in Gymnastics is bettered, in terms of one country in one sport, only by the US in Athletics and Swimming. Their nearest rivals in Gymnastics are also the US, who have won only 38. The Russians won 11 golds in 1956, 10 in 1960 and 1992, and 12 in 1988. However, they have won only 12 in the last five games (2004-21) put together. Their highest overall haul of medals was 26 in 1960; they won just four in 2008. All of their most decorated Olympians have been gymnasts. Viktor Chukarin (1952-56), Borys Shakhlin (1956-64) and Nikolai Andrianov (1972-80) won 7 golds each.

Andrianov won 15 medals in total, the second highest of any male in Olympic history. Vitaly Scherbo (1992) won 6 golds in one Games. Larysa Latinina won 9 golds, and 18 medals in total; records that were not beaten in any Olympic sport until Michael Phelps came along.

Handball (7-3-3, 1st). The Russians won medals in both men's and women's in 1976, 1980, 1988 and 1992, although medals have been more sporadic since. Andrey Lavrov won 3 golds and a bronze (1988-2004).

Volleyball (8-9-3, 1st). Since the sport's introduction in 1964, the only times the Russian men have failed to reach the podium have been 1992, 1996 and 2016. The men and women have won four golds each.

Wrestling (103-50-46, 1st). Russia have won at least 3 Wrestling golds in every Games they've entered since 1952. Their biggest haul of gold is 12, in 1976 and 1980. In 1976, they won a record 18 Wrestling medals in total. They have been evenly split between Greco-Roman medals (97) and Freestyle (102). Aleksandr Karelin won Greco-Roman super-heavyweight gold three times (1988-96) before taking silver in 2000. Also taking 3 golds each are Aleksandr Medved (1964-72 in freestyle light heavyweight, heavyweight and super-heavyweight) and Buvaysa Saytiev (freestyle welterweight, 1996, 2004 & 2008).

Modern Pentathlon (9-7-6, 2nd). Andrey Moiseev won the men's title in 2004 and 2008, becoming only the second man to defend the title. Pavel Lednev won seven medals in all (2-2-3) from 1968 to 1980, including three team medals and four individual.

Weightlifting (48-32-8, 1st). The Russians won numerous golds every year from 1952 to 1996 (except the 1984 boycott), culminating in 7 golds in 1976 alone, but have added just two golds this century. Perhaps the most famous champion is Vasily Alekseyev, the gargantuan super-heavyweight champion of 1972 and 1976.

Fencing (35-26-27, 4th). Numerous medals have been won at every Games they have entered since 1956. Yelena Belova-Novikova (women's foil, 1968-76), Viktor Krovopuskov (men's sabre, 1976-80) and Stanislav Pozdniakov (men's sabre, 1992-2000) have won four golds each.

Basketball (5-6-7, 2nd). The first Soviet gold came in 1972, in one of the most enduring controversies in Olympic history, when they managed to beat the US with a basket scored in a twice-played final second. The men's only other gold came in 1988, whilst the women won in 1976, 1980 and 1992. The most recent regular Basketball medal was a men's bronze in 2012; however, both men and women secured silvers in 3x3 in 2021.

Canoeing (32-18-16, 2nd). Russia failed to win a Canoeing medal in 2021 for the first time ever. Vladimir Morozov won four successive golds (1964-76), three in K4 1000m and one in K2 1000m.

Shooting (31-35-32, 2nd). Russia have never failed to win a Shooting medal, though they came close in 2012 (just a single bronze). Marina Logvinenko-Dobrancheva won five medals in total (1988-96) in pistol events.

Boxing (25-26-38, 3rd). The last time Russia failed to win a Boxing gold was 1992; they have never failed to win a medal. Boris Lagutin (light middleweight, 1960-68) and Oleg Saitov (welterweight, 1996-2004) hold the Russian record of 2 golds and 1 bronze each.

Athletics (90-88-96, 2nd). Up until 2008, Russia had won at least 10 Athletics medals at every Games they'd entered. Then in 2012, they won only 6, in 2016 they won none at all, and in 2021 they won 2. Of the 50 medals won this century, 35 of them have been won by women. Their top performers have been Tamara Press (women's shot and discus, 1960-64) and Viktor Saneyev (men's triple jump, 1968-80) with 3 golds and a silver each. Tamara Press and her sister Irina both retired from Athletics shortly before gender verification became mandatory, further fuelling existing rumours on the subject.

Judo (12-9-25, 3rd). Only five of the 46 medals (and none of the golds) have gone to women. Three of the golds came in 2012, after they had failed to win a medal at all in 2008.

Diving (8-14-14, 3rd). Dmitry Sautin won platform gold in 1996 and synchro platform gold in 2000. There have been Russian medals at all Games since 1960, apart from 1984 (due to boycott), 1988 and 2016.

Cycling (16-9-20, 7th). Russia's last 3 golds all came in 2004; the Soviets won 4 golds in 1988. Vyacheslav Yekimov won team pursuit gold in 1988, and road time trial gold in 2000 and 2004.

Water Polo (2-3-7, 6th). The Soviets won men's gold in 1972 and 1980. The most recent medals for men (2004) and women (2016) were both bronzes.

Football (2-0-3, 7th). Soviet golds in 1956 and 1988. But they have not entered since 1988, and have never entered the women's since its inception in 1996.

Tennis (4-5-4, 5th). Golds in men's singles (Yevgeny Kafelnikov, 2000), women's singles (Elena Dementieva, 2008), women's doubles (Ekaterina Makarova & Elena Vesnina, 2016) and mixed doubles (Anastasia Pavlyuchenkova & Aslan Karatsev, 2021).

Rowing (13-22-14, 7th). Won golds every year from 1952 to 1980, but only 1 gold since 1980 (the men's quadruple sculls of 2004). Vyacheslav Ivanov won men's single sculls 3 times (1956-64).

Taekwondo (2-3-3, 5th). Both golds came in 2021, for Vladislav Larin and Maksim Khramtsov.

Swimming (25-35-37, 5th). Vladimir Salnikov won 4 freestyle golds (1980-88), whilst Aleksandr Popov took 4 golds (50m and 100m freestyle in both 1992 & 1996) and 5 silvers between 1992 and 2000. Evgeny Rylov's 2 backstroke golds in 2021 were Russia's first in the pool since 1996 (they did win a marathon gold in 2008). Having won only 28 medals prior to 1980, they won 22 in Moscow alone.

Equestrianism (6-5-4, 8th). Prior to 1980, the Soviets had won seven medals, all in dressage. In 1980, they ripped through a depleted field, winning all three team golds, and taking medals in all three individual events too. They have not won a medal since then (the highest finish for post-Soviet Russia has been 6th).

Sailing (4-6-5, 13th). No golds since 1980. Only two post-Soviet medals for Russia (1996 silver & 2016 bronze).

Archery (1-6-6, 7th). Women's gold for USSR's Keto Losaberidze in 1980. Won two silvers in 2021.

Beach Volleyball (0-1-0, 7th=). Men's silver in 2021, having finished 4th in 2016.

Hockey (0-0-2, 17th=). The Soviets won both men's and women's bronze as hosts in 1980. Only two other entries – the men came 7th in 1988 and 10th in 1992.

Badminton (0-0-1, 12th). Women's doubles bronze in 2012, and top-eight finishes in men's doubles in 1996 & 2016.

Table Tennis – Six quarter-final defeats, and one 4th place – in men's doubles in 2004.

Triathlon – 7th place in the men's in 2012. The women's best is 12th in 2000.

Rugby – The women beat Kenya in 2021, helping them to 8th place, in Russia's only Rugby entry to date.

Sport Climbing – In 2021, Russia came 9th and 17th in women's, and 13th in men's.

Golf – Came equal 16th in women's in 2016

Baseball/Softball, Karate, Skateboarding, Surfing, PWDS – never entered

WINTER
Figure Skating (31-24-10, 1st). The Russians won pairs gold every year from 1964 to 2006, and ice dance gold every year from 1976 to 1998, with the exception of 1984 (when they won silver and bronze behind Torvill & Dean). They also won the men's title five times in a row from 1992 to 2006, and two golds and a silver in the three team events thus far. Irina Rodnina won the pairs event three times in a row (1972-80).

Ice Hockey (9-3-2, 2nd). The Soviets won their first gold in 1956, then dominated from 1964 to 1992, winning every year except for the famed 1980 "Miracle on Ice", when they had to settle for silver. Russia won gold in 2018. The women have never finished better than 5th.

Nordic Skiing (46-41-42, 2nd). The 22 medals won in the 1990s all came in women's events. Lyubov Yegorova won 6 golds and 3 silvers (1992-94), and Larissa Lasutina won 5 golds, a silver and a bronze (1992-98).

Biathlon (20-13-18, 3rd). Aleksandr Tikhonov was part of the gold-medal relay teams of 1968, 1972, 1976 & 1980; he also won an individual silver in 1968. The Soviets won that event every year from 1968 to 1988.

Speed Skating (27-23-26, 4th). Lidiya Skoblikova won two golds in 1960, and all four women's golds in 1964; she jointly holds the all-time record of 6 golds with Ireen Wust of the Netherlands. Yevgeny Grishin won four golds and a silver (1956-64). The last gold came in 2006; since 2010, there have been 3 silvers and 5 bronzes.

Skeleton (1-1-2, 5th). Alexander Tretiakov, having won men's bronze in 2010, took gold in 2014. Elena Nikitina took the only women's medal so far (bronze in 2014).

Short Track Speed Skating (3-2-4, 7th). Having won three golds and a bronze for South Korea in 2006, Ahn Hyun-soo fell out with the South Korean authorities, moved to Russia, gained naturalisation within a few months, changed his name to Viktor Ahn, and won another three golds (two individual and one relay) and a bronze in 2014.

Snowboarding (2-2-2, 7th). US-born Vic Wild switched to his wife's nationality in 2011, and won two golds in 2014, as well as a bronze in 2022.

Luge (1-5-4, 4th). Vera Zozula won gold in the women's single-seat in 1980. Post-Soviet Russia have won three silvers and a bronze so far.

Bobsleigh (1-1-3, 7th=). The USSR won the two-man bob in 1988. Post-Soviet Russia have won a silver and a bronze. All five medals have come in men's events.

Ski Jumping (1-1-0, 10th). Vladimir Belousov won men's large hill gold in 1968, which remained the only medal until a mixed team silver in 2022.

Freestyle Skiing (0-2-8, 16th). The silvers came in 1992 & 1994; bronzes have arrived regularly since then.

Nordic Combined (0-1-3, 9th). A silver in 1964, and bronzes in 1960, 1988 & 1998, all in men's individual.

Alpine Skiing (0-1-1, 18th). A bronze in women's slalom in 1956, and a silver in women's super-G in 1994.

Curling – The best finishes are 6th (2006 women's) and 7th (2014 men's).

UKRAINE   **Olympic Rank 30th**

Population: 43,306,477 (rank 35th)
Olympic rank/ population differential: +5
Population per gold: 1,139,644 (rank 49th)
Population per medal: 292,611 (rank 54th)

Summer: 35 gold, 36 silver, 68 bronze (total 139)
Winter: 3 gold, 2 silver, 4 bronze (total 9)
Total: 38 gold, 38 silver, 72 bronze (total 148)

Best sports: Gymnastics (7 golds, 1.82%, 12th)
                                Freestyle Skiing (1 gold, 1.75%, 11th)
                                Boxing (4 golds, 1.51%, 15th=)

Ukraine have entered every Summer and Winter Games since their debut at the Winter Games of 1994. Their first Summer Games, in 1996, is still their best, winning 9 golds and 23 medals in total, providing their only top-10 finish (they finished 9th). The total of 23 was emulated in 2000, and they won 22 at each of the two Games after that. In contrast, the last two Games have been their weakest, winning just two golds in 2016 and one in 2021 (Zhan Beleniuk in Wrestling). The 2016 Games saw just 11 medals won in total.

Their most successful Summer sport has been Gymnastics, providing 7 golds (no other sport has provided more than 4) and 19 medals in total (again, the most of any sport). Lilia Popkopayeva won two golds (all-around and floor) and one silver (balance beam) in 1996, making her Ukraine's most successful gymnast.

Popkopayeva was, in fact, continuing an extraordinary rich seam of Ukrainian Gymnastics success; two of the most successful four male gymnasts of all time were Ukrainians representing the USSR (Borys Shakhlin and Viktor Chukarin, with 7 golds each), whilst their compatriot Larysa Latinina won 9 golds, and 18 medals in total, both all-time Olympic records for many years until beaten by US swimmer Michael Phelps.

There are four sports which have provided four golds each – Boxing, Shooting, Wrestling and Swimming. The four in Boxing have gone to Wladimir Klitschko (1996), Vasyl Lomachenko (2008 and 2012) and Oleksandr Usyk (2012). All three went on to become professional world champions. Pistol shooter Olena Kostevych has won a gold and three bronzes.

In Swimming, meanwhile, all four golds went to Yana Klochkova, who did the 200m/400m individual medley double in both 2000 and 2004 – and won silver in the 800m freestyle in 2000 as well. She is Ukraine's most decorated Olympian, both in terms of golds and overall medals, of all time (since independence).

In Athletics, Ukraine have won 18 medals, though 13 of those were bronze and only 2 were gold. The two golds went to Inessa Kravets (1996 women's triple jump) and Nataliia Dobrynska (2008 women's heptathlon); no Ukrainian has yet won more than one medal in Athletics. Other golds have been won in Archery, Canoeing, Weightlifting, Fencing, Sailing and Rowing, with further medals in Karate, Artistic Swimming, Handball, Modern Pentathlon, Judo, Diving, Cycling and Tennis.

Ukraine have won nine medals in eight appearances at the Winter Games, winning two each in 1994, 2006 and 2014, and none in 2002 and 2010 (having a best finish of 5th both times). They have won their three golds in three different sports. Their first Olympic gold (Winter or Summer) was one of the most famous – the 1994 women's Figure Skating was dominated by the extraordinary saga between Americans Tonya Harding and Nancy Kerrigan, but it was Oksana Baiul who rose above it all to take gold. Ukraine took the women's Biathlon relay gold in 2014, and Oleksandr Abramenko took gold in the men's aerials (Freestyle Skiing) in 2018. He then took silver in 2022 to become Ukraine's top Winter performer. All of their other Winter medals have come in the same three sports.

BELARUS   **Olympic Rank 38th**

Population:	9,383,853 (rank 96th)
Olympic rank/ population differential:	+58
Population per gold:	446,850 (rank 37th)
Population per medal:	89,370 (rank 35th)
Summer:	13 gold, 30 silver, 42 bronze (total 85)
Winter:	8 gold, 7 silver, 5 bronze (total 20)
Total:	21 gold, 37 silver, 47 bronze (total 105)
Best sports:	Freestyle Skiing (4 golds, 7.02%, 7th)
	Biathlon (4 golds, 4.17%, 6th)
	Tennis (1 gold, 1.33%, 14th=)

Belarus first entered the Olympics at the 1994 Winter Games, and have entered all Summer and Winter Games since then. Their first gold medal was won by Ekaterina Khadatovich in the women's single sculls Rowing in 1996, and she went on to become Belarus's most successful Summer Olympian of all time, retaining her title in 2000 (now known as Ekaterina Karsten), and winning silver in 2004 and bronze in 2008, all in the same event. She had previously won bronze in the quadruple sculls in 1992, representing the Unified Team. Besides her medals, Belarus have won just three bronzes in Rowing.

The sports with most medals have been Athletics (15), Wrestling (14) and Gymnastics (13). Of the 15 Athletics medals, ten have come in the throwing events, with a further three in decathlon/heptathlon. Elya Zvereva (bronze in 1996 and gold in 2000 in women's discus) has been the most successful. The 14 medals in Wrestling have been 7 silver and 7 bronze, but no golds yet. The Gymnastics medals began with four bronzes in 1996 for Vitaly Scherbo, who had sensationally won six golds in 1992, representing the Unified Team. Incidentally, sportspeople from Belarus won numerous medals as part of the Soviet Union, perhaps none more prominent than gymnast Olga Korbut, who won 4 golds and 2 silvers between 1972 and 1976.

Other Belarusians with multiple medals include canoeists Raman Piatrushenka and Vadzim Makhneu, who won gold in the K4 1000m in 2008, as well as a silver and two bronzes in K2 events between 2004 and 2012. Apart from Athletics (3), no Summer sport has produced more than 2 golds. Two medals have been won in Tennis – Australian Open champion Victoria Azarenka took bronze in the women's singles in 2012, and also teamed up with Max Mirnyi to win the mixed doubles, beating home favourites Andy Murray and Laura Robson in the final. All three of Belarus's Swimming medals have been won by Aliaksandra Herasimenia – silver in the women's 50m and 100m freestyle in 2012, and bronze in the former event in 2016.

Belarus have won at least one gold at every Summer Games they have entered so far; they won three in both 2000 and 2008. The Sydney 2000 Games were their best overall, with a total of 17 medals (including 11 bronze).

In Winter competition, Belarus's success has been less widespread, but notable all the same. They have won medals at every Games, although all of their golds came between 2010 and 2018. Their first Winter medal was won in 1994 by Igor Zhelezovsky – a silver in Speed Skating. They have added 19 further Winter medals since then, all of them in two sports – Biathlon (11) and Freestyle Skiing (8). They have won 4 golds in each, which is more than they have managed in any Summer sports.

Biathlon has produced the greatest Olympian of Belarus's independent era. Darya Domracheva won bronze in the women's 15km individual in 2010, before dominating the 2014 Games with golds in 10km pursuit, 12.5km mass start and 15km individual. After some time off to have a baby, she returned in 2018 to win a fourth gold as part of the relay team, and a silver in the 12.5km mass start. Her success made the 2014 Games the best for Belarus, with five golds in total.

In Freestyle Skiing, Belarus have won medals at every Games since 1998, all in aerials events. Alexei Grishin (gold and bronze), Dmitri Dashinski (silver and bronze) and Hanna Huskova (gold and silver) have won two each.

ESTONIA **Olympic Rank 44th**

Population:	1,202,762 (rank 159th)
Olympic rank/ population differential:	+115
Population per gold:	85,912 (rank 9th)
Population per medal:	27,336 (rank 10th)

Summer:	10 gold, 9 silver, 17 bronze (total 36)
Winter:	4 gold, 2 silver, 2 bronze (total 8)
Total:	14 gold, 11 silver, 19 bronze (total 44)
Best sports:	Nordic Skiing (4 golds, 2.20%, 7th)
	Wrestling (5 golds, 1.16%, 17th)
	Weightlifting (1 gold, 0.43%, 31st)

Estonia made their Olympic debut in Antwerp in 1920. They continued to participate until World War Two, appearing in the Winter Games in 1928 and 1936, but were then subsumed into the Soviet Union. They re-entered in 1992, and have entered every Games since.

Proportionately speaking, Estonia have had slightly more success in the Winter Olympics than the Summer, although it took them until 2002 to win any medals at all. Seven of their eight Winter medals have come in Nordic Skiing (all between 2002 and 2010), and in fact six of them have been won by just two people. Andrus Veerpalu won gold in the 15km event in both 2002 and 2006, as well as a silver in 50km in 2002. Kristina Smigun-Vahi matched Veerpalu's record of two golds and a silver, winning gold in both 10km and the combined pursuit in 2006, and winning silver in the 10km in 2010. She later became an MP. No Estonian athlete, Summer or Winter, can match the record of those two. In 2022, Kelly Sildaru won Estonia's only non-Nordic Skiing winter medal, a bronze in Freestyle Skiing (slopestyle).

In the Summer Games, they have only twice entered without winning at least one medal. These were 1932 (when only two people entered, and only one of those finished an event, finishing 10th), and 1996 (their best finish that year was 5th). Their most successful Games was 1936, when they won two golds, two silvers and three bronzes, finishing equal 13th in the medal table. Both of the golds were won by Kristjan Palusalu, who won the heavyweight Wrestling golds in both the Freestyle and Greco-Roman categories (one of only two people to win Greco-Roman and freestyle golds in the same year). He remains the only Estonian to win more than one Summer gold.

Since returning to the Olympics in 1992, Estonia's best finishing position in a Summer medal table is equal 34th (1992; one gold and one bronze). Their most medals won is three (2000 and 2004). Five of their ten Summer golds have come in Wrestling, but they have won only one medal in the sport since 1936 (a silver in 2012).

Their other golds have come in Weightlifting (1920), Cycling (1992), Athletics (2000 – Erki Nool in decathlon and 2008 – Gerd Kanter in discus) and Fencing (2021). Their best sports by total medals won are Wrestling (11), Weightlifting (seven), and Athletics (six). The six Athletics medals have all come in men's events – marathon (1920), decathlon (1924, 2000) and discus (2004, 2008, 2012).

Their other medalling sports have been Boxing (1936), Sailing (1928 and 1992), Judo (2000 and 2004) and Rowing (2004, 2008, 2016). The only other sports with top eight finishes for Estonia have been Modern Pentathlon, Shooting, Nordic Combined and Speed Skating.

GEORGIA   Olympic Rank 49th

Population:	4,936,390 (rank 127th)
Olympic rank/ population differential:	+78
Population per gold:	493,639 (rank 42nd)
Population per medal:	123,410 (rank 43rd)

Summer:	10 gold, 12 silver, 18 bronze (total 40)
Winter:	*no medals (best finish: 6th)*
Total:	10 gold, 12 silver, 18 bronze (total 40)
Best sports:	Judo (4 golds, 2.63%, 8th)
	Weightlifting (3 golds, 1.30%, 19th)
	Wrestling (3 golds, 0.69%, 24th)

Georgia have won 40 Olympic medals, but these have been spread across just five different sports – the three listed above, plus Boxing (a single bronze) and Shooting (a single bronze). They have won 19 medals in Wrestling, 12 in Judo and seven in Weightlifting.

They made their Olympic debuts in 1994 (Winter) and 1996 (Summer). The first two Summer games in which they participated saw them win eight medals, but all of them were bronze. Athens 2004 saw their first golds – won in Judo by Zurab Zviadauri and Weightlifting by Giorgi Asanidze.

In 2021, Lasha Talakhadze retained his super-heavyweight Weightlifting title, becoming the first Georgian ever to win two Olympic golds. He has won numerous golds in World Championships and European Championships, and is widely considered as the greatest weightlifter of all time (even though he was handed a two-year ban early in his career for doping).

Also in 2021, another Lasha – Lasha Shavdatuashvili – became the first Georgian ever to win three Olympic medals. In winning silver in Judo's lightweight division, he added to his gold from 2012 and bronze from 2016.

Other Georgians to have won two medals are Giorgi Asanidze (a gold and bronze in Weightlifting), Vladimer Khinchegashvili (a gold and silver in Wrestling), Giorgi Godshelidze (a silver and bronze in Wrestling), Geno Petriashvili (also a silver and bronze in Wrestling), and Eldari Kurtanidze (two bronzes in Wrestling)

The nation's record in Athletics is remarkably poor. Shot putter Elvira Urusova has the honour of being their highest ever finisher in a track & field event – she came 17th in 1996. No Georgian has reached even the semi-finals of a track event. Similarly, in Swimming the best ever finish by a Georgian is 28th.

Besides their five medalling sports, the closest they have come to a medal in any other sport is in Beach Volleyball (a fourth place in the 2008 men's event) and Fencing (a fourth place in men's sabre in 2021). They have also had five top eight finishes in Gymnastics (of which four were in women's trampolining), and one in Karate.

Their best Summer Games were Beijing 2008 (three golds, ranking 28th in the medal table). They won seven medals in all that year; their best games in terms of total medal count was Tokyo 2021 (eight medals).

The best Georgian display in a Winter Olympic event is 6th place in the mixed team Figure Skating event in 2022. In fact, 11 of their best 14 ever finishes in Winter Olympics events have come in Figure Skating, as well as all four of their top-ten finishes (the others came in Alpine Skiing (twice) and Luge).

AZERBAIJAN   **Olympic Rank 55th**

Population:	10,420,515 (rank 90th)
Olympic rank/ population differential:	+35
Population per gold:	1,448,645 (rank 52nd)
Population per medal:	212,664 (rank 50th)
Summer:	7 gold, 14 silver, 28 bronze (total 49)
Winter:	*no medals (best finish: 12th)*
Total:	7 gold, 14 silver, 28 bronze (total 49)
Best sports:	Taekwondo (1 gold, 2.08%, 19th=)
	Wrestling (4 golds, 0.93%, 18th)
	Judo (1 gold, 0.66%, 24th)

Azerbaijan first entered the Olympics at the 1996 Summer Games, and have entered every Games, Summer and Winter, since. At those first Summer Games, they won just a single medal – a silver for Namik Abdullayev in Wrestling (freestyle flyweight). They then increased their medal total in each of the next five games – to three, five, six, nine and 18, before falling back to seven in 2021. The only other country ever to have increased its overall medal haul in five consecutive Summer Games is Great Britain (who coincidentally achieved it in the same years).

Their seven gold medals (two each in Sydney and London, one each in Athens, Beijing and Rio) have come in four sports. Four of the seven have come in Wrestling; the others in Shooting (2000), Judo (2008) and Taekwondo (2016). The Shooting gold medallist was Zemfira Meftakhetdinova in the skeet – the only woman to have won gold for Azerbaijan. She followed that up with a bronze in 2004, to become one of the country's few multi-medallists. The others are all wrestlers, including a couple who have won three medals each: Khetag Gazyumov in freestyle heavyweight (bronze in 2008 & 2012, silver in 2016), and Mariya Stadnik in freestyle flyweight (silver in 2012 & 2016, bronze in 2021).

Azerbaijan's other medals have come in Boxing (one silver and eight bronzes), Karate (two silvers) and Canoeing (a silver and a bronze). They have managed top eight finishes in Weightlifting (best finish of 4th), Gymnastics (4th), Rowing (5th) and Fencing (7th).

As for the two biggest sports, Azerbaijan have been much less successful. In Swimming, they have never finished higher than 26th in any event. In Athletics, they have only once finished in the top 12 of any event – Hayle Ibrahimov (born and raised in Ethiopia) finished ninth in the 5000m in 2012.

Although Azerbaijan have competed in all Winter Games since 1998, they have only ever entered two sports – Figure Skating, where their best ever finish is 12th, and Alpine Skiing, where their best ever finish is 53rd.

LITHUANIA   **Olympic Rank 58th**

Population:	2,655,755 (rank 142nd)
Olympic rank/ population differential:	+84
Population per gold:	442,626 (rank 36th)
Population per medal:	102,144 (rank 37th)
Summer:	6 gold, 7 silver, 13 bronze (total 26)
Winter:	*no medals (best finish: 5th)*
Total:	6 gold, 7 silver, 13 bronze (total 26)
Best sports:	Modern Pentathlon (1 gold, 2.38%, 8th)
	Shooting (1 gold, 0.33%, 40th=)
	Athletics (3 golds, 0.29%, 39th)

Having re-declared independence in 1918 at the end of World War I, Lithuania entered the Summer Olympics of 1924, and both the Summer and Winter Games in 1928. After that, however, they declined to enter in 1932 or 1936, and then lost independence during the Second World War. They did not enter the Olympics as an independent nation again until 1992, at the end of the Cold War. Since then, they have entered every Summer and Winter Games.

Unlike their fellow Baltic states Estonia and Latvia, Lithuania did not win any medals in their pre-WWII entries into the Olympics. The closest they came was a boxer who, in 1928, reached the quarter-finals – their only pre-war top-eight finish.

Lithuania's best Games in terms of golds won are 2000 and 2012 (two each). In terms of total medals, both of those Games garnered five medals, as did 2008. Their best finishing position was achieved in 2000; they came 33rd.

Arguably Lithuania's two most enduringly promising Olympic events have been the men's discus and the men's Basketball. Since 1992, they have only once failed to record a top-eight finish in the former (2016), and have won gold three times (Romas Ubartas in 1992, and Virgilijus Alekna in 2000 and 2004; the latter also won bronze in 2008). In men's Basketball, Lithuania won three successive bronzes in 1992, 1996 and 2000. They have been on a downward spiral since; in the subsequent Games, they finished 4th, 4th, 8th and 7th before, in 2021, they failed to qualify for the first time. The only player who played in all three bronze-medal-winning teams was Gintaras Einikis, making him the only Lithuanian besides Alekna to have won three Olympic medals. Alekna, meanwhile, is the only Lithuanian to have won two golds.

Besides the men's discus, Lithuania's only other medals in Athletics have both come in women's heptathlon, and both for Austra Skujyte (silver in 2004, bronze in 2012). And other than their three men's discus golds, the three other golds Lithuania have won have come in three different sports, and all won by women. In 2000, Daina Gudzineviciute won the trap Shooting event, still Lithuania's only Shooting medal. The other two both came in 2012. Laura Asadauskaite won the Modern Pentathlon (she also won silver in 2021, and has continued another Lithuanian tradition – five of their 26 Olympic medals have come either in men's or women's Modern Pentathlon). Meanwhile, 15-year old Plymouth-based schoolgirl Ruta Meilutyte won a famous gold in the 2012 women's 100m breaststroke Swimming. The nation have never finished higher than 7th in any other Olympic Swimming event.

Lithuania have also won silvers in Sailing, Rowing and Greco-Roman Wrestling, whilst they have peaked at bronze in Cycling, Boxing, Canoeing and Weightlifting. So, for a country that has only won 26 Olympic medals, they have come in an impressively varied array of sports.

Lithuania are still awaiting their first Winter Olympic medal. They have secured three top-eight finishes, all achieved by the Figure Skating duo of Margarita Drobiazko and Povilas Vanagas (8th, 5th and 7th respectively, between 1998 and 2006). They have also achieved top-16 finishes in Nordic Skiing, Biathlon and Short Track Speed Skating.

LATVIA	**Olympic Rank 59th**
Population:	1,821,750 (rank 151st)
Olympic rank/ population differential:	+92
Population per gold:	364,350 (rank 33rd)
Population per medal:	58,766 (rank 24th)
Summer:	4 gold, 11 silver, 6 bronze (total 21)
Winter:	1 gold, 3 silver, 6 bronze (total 10)
Total:	5 gold, 14 silver, 12 bronze (total 31)
Best sports:	Basketball (1 gold, 2.94%, 5th)
	Bobsleigh (1 gold, 1.89%, 9th)
	Cycling (2 golds, 0.74%, 20th)

Latvia participated in both the Summer and Winter Games from 1924 to 1936, only missing the 1932 Winter Games. They were then subsumed into the Soviet Union, and did not regain independence until 1991. They re-entered both the Winter and Summer Games in 1992, and have been ever-present since. They managed a 5th place in 1924 and 4th in 1928, but their first medal came in Los Angeles in 1932. They only sent two competitors to those Games, but one of them, Janis Dalins, won silver in the men's 50km walk. Adalberts Bubenko won bronze in the same event in 1936, and there was a Wrestling silver too (they have not won a Wrestling medal since). There were no medals in the Winter Games in that pre-war period.

Latvia's four Summer golds have come in four different Games. Their best record in an individual Games is 1 gold, 1 silver and 1 bronze, achieved in both 2000 and 2008. The most medals they have won at a single Games, however, is four in 2004 (all silver). The 2014 Winter Games, however, beats both of those records, as Latvia won a gold (its only Winter gold), a silver, and 3 bronzes. They have won medals at all Winter Games since winning their first Winter medal in 2006. They have missed out on medals at just one Summer Games since reclaiming independence – that was in 2016, when they came 4th in both Weightlifting and Athletics (heptathlon).

In 1992 and 1996, Latvia won three silvers and a bronze (two of the silvers went to canoeist Ivans Klementjevs). Their first Olympic champion was Igors Vihrovs, who took gold in the men's Gymnastics floor exercises in 2000, pushing the favourite, Aleksey Nemov of Russia, into silver. Latvia's greatest Olympian is Maris Strombergs, who took gold in men's BMX cycling in both 2008 and 2012; he was also a two-time world champion in the discipline.

Latvia have won two further golds since then – both in team events. In 2014, they looked to have won silver in the four-man Bobsleigh, but Russia were eventually stripped of their gold due to doping, and Latvia promoted in their place. Then, in 2021, Latvia claimed the inaugural Olympic men's 3x3 Basketball title, with an exciting 21-18 win over Russia in the final.

Only two Latvian women have ever won Olympic medals. Jelena Rublevska took Modern Pentathlon silver in 2004, and Eliza Turima was the one woman on the mixed Luge relay team that took bronze in 2014, and again in 2022.

Besides Klementjevs, Strombergs and Turima, various other Latvians have won more than one Olympic medal. Oskars Melbardis won bronze in the two-man Bobsleigh in both 2014 (alongside Daumants Dreiskens) and 2018 (partnering Janis Strenga this time). All three of those men were in the gold-medal winning four-man crew in 2014 as well. Brothers Andris and Juris Sics won two-man Luge silver in 2010 and bronze in 2014, and both were involved alongside Turima in winning mixed bronze in 2014. Thus Melbardis and the two Sics brothers have won a Latvian record three Olympic medals each. The fourth member of that 2014 team was Martins Rubenis, who had won single-seat Luge bronze in 2006. Martins Dukurs won silver in men's Skeleton in both 2010 and 2014 whilst, back in the Summer Games, Viktors Scerbatihs won silver in the men's super-heavyweight Weightlifting in 2004, and bronze in the same event in 2008.

Latvia's three post-war medals in Athletics have all been silvers – one in the 50km walk, and two in javelin. Other medals have come in Beach Volleyball, Judo, Shooting and Weightlifting. Their best finish in Swimming is 13th (men's 200m breaststroke in 1996).

ARMENIA   **Olympic Rank 76th**
Population: 2,989,091 (rank 139th)
Olympic rank/ population differential: +63
Population per gold: 1,494,546 (rank 53rd)
Population per medal: 166,061 (rank 48th)

Summer: 2 gold, 8 silver, 8 bronze (total 18)
Winter: *no medals (best finish: 18th)*
Total: 2 gold, 8 silver, 8 bronze (total 18)

Best sports: Wrestling (2 golds, 0.46%, 29th)
                                     Weightlifting (4 silvers, 2 bronzes, 44th)
                                     Boxing (2 bronzes, 58th=)

Armenia have entered all Winter and Summer Games since 1994. In that time they have won 18 medals, of which nine have come in Wrestling, six in Weightlifting, two in Boxing, and one in the rather different discipline of Artistic Gymnastics.

On their Summer debut in 1996, Armenia went away with two medals, both in Wrestling. On the very first full day of action, Armen Nazaryan got the country off to a flying start, winning gold in the Greco-Roman flyweight. Later in the Games, Armen Mkrtchyan won silver in the Freestyle light-flyweight (the only one of Armenia's nine Wrestling medals that has come in Freestyle, as opposed to Greco-Roman). Nazaryan later switched allegiance to Bulgaria, for whom he won a further Olympic gold in 2000, followed by a bronze in 2004.

In 2000, Armenia won only a single bronze – Arsen Melikyan in middleweight Weightlifting. In 2004, they won no medals at all for the first, and so far only, time in a Summer Games (the best they managed was a couple of 4th places in Weightlifting and Shooting). In 2008, Tigran Varban Martirosyan won a silver in light-heavyweight Weightlifting, and there were four bronzes as well. These five medals mark Armenia's best ever medal total in a single Games.

In 2012, Armenia settled for just a silver and a bronze, both in Greco-Roman Wrestling. In 2016, however, they enjoyed their best Games yet, winning one gold and three silvers, and finishing 42nd in the medal table. The gold was won by Artur Aleksanyan in men's heavyweight Greco-Roman Wrestling, whilst there was a silver in Wrestling and two in Weightlifting too.

Aleksanyan is Armenia's greatest Olympian. As well as his gold in 2016, he won bronze in 2012 and silver in 2021, all in the same event. He is a four-time world champion and five-time European champion. The only other Armenian multi-medallist is Simon Martirosyan, who won silvers in heavyweight Weightlifting in 2016 and 2021. In the delayed Games of 2021, two more silvers came; the ones previously mentioned for Aleksanyan and Martirosyan, as well as a bronze in Boxing, and one in Gymnastics (Artur Davtyan in the men's vault).

All 18 of Armenia's medals have been won by men. The best performance so far by an Armenian woman came from Nazik Avdalyan, who came 5th in the light-heavyweight Weightlifting in 2016. Overall, Weightlifting and Wrestling have accounted for 45 of Armenia's 57 top-eight finishes in Olympic competition. Five more have come in Boxing, with the other seven coming in Gymnastics (two), Shooting (two), Athletics, Judo and Taekwondo. In Athletics, Armen Martirosyan finished 5th in the men's triple jump back in 1996, and Armenia's next best performance in Athletics is a 21st-placed finish, also in the men's triple jump, 25 years later. In Swimming, they have never managed better than 38th (men's 100m freestyle in 2021).

In the Winter Games, their best finish is a mere 18th, achieved in Figure Skating's Ice Dance competition in 2022 by Tina Garabedian and Simon Proulx-Senecal, both of whom were born in Canada. They have entered two sports in all Winter Games since 1994 – Nordic Skiing (best finish 23rd) and Alpine Skiing (best finish 27th). They have also entered Bobsleigh twice (a best of 33rd) and Freestyle Skiing once (19th).

Although Armenia have only competed as an independent nation since 1994, Armenians have been winning Olympic medals for thousands of years. King Varazdat, for example became bare-knuckle Boxing champion at the ancient Games in the fourth century AD. More recently, Albert Azaryan won three golds for the Soviet Union in Gymnastics (1956-60), and numerous others with Armenian heritage have won medals for other countries, most prominently the American Andre Agassi (men's singles Tennis gold, 1996).

MOLDOVA   **Olympic Rank 106th**
Population: 3,250,532 (rank 135th)
Olympic rank/ population differential: +29
Population per gold: n/a
Population per medal: 541,755 (rank 65th)

Summer: 0 gold, 2 silver, 4 bronze (total 6)
Winter: *no medals (best finish: 8th)*
Total: 0 gold, 2 silver, 4 bronze (total 6)

Best sports: Canoeing (1 silver, 1 bronze, 31st=)
                Shooting (1 silver, 49th=)
                Boxing (2 bronzes, 58th=)

Moldova have entered all Summer and Winter Olympics since independence, beginning with the Winter Games of 1994. The general pattern in that time is one of decline; they managed 16 top-eight finishes in their first two Summer Games (1996 & 2000), then only six in their next four, before a mini-revival at Tokyo 2021 produced a further seven.

The first Moldovan Olympic medallist was Sergei Mureiko in the Greco-Roman super-heavyweight Wrestling in 1996. A silver in Canoeing's C2 500m event for men soon followed (they were pipped on the line by Hungary). Four years later, they earned another silver (Oleg Moldovan in Shooting's running game target) and another bronze (in Boxing), before more bronzes followed in Boxing (2008) and Canoeing (2021).

All in all, Moldova have had 30 top-eight finishes; these have included 9 in Weightlifting, 8 in Wrestling (5 freestyle and 3 Greco-Roman) and 4 in Canoeing. There have also been two each in Boxing, Shooting and Athletics (their best in Athletics is 5th for Zalina Marghieva in the 2016 women's hammer). Finally, there have been one top-eight finish each in Judo, Swimming (Serghei Mariniuc was 8th in the 1996 men's 400m individual medley) and Biathlon (their best Winter performance – Natalia Levcencova was 8th in the women's 15km event in 2006).

CHAPTER FOURTEEN - Middle East, northern (Turkey, Iran, Israel, Syria, Jordan, Kuwait, Lebanon, Cyprus, Iraq, Palestine)

TURKEY   **Olympic Rank 29th**
Population: 83,593,483 (rank 19th)
Olympic rank/ population differential: -10
Population per gold: 2,038,865 (rank 59th)
Population per medal: 810,800 (rank 77th)

Summer: 41 gold, 26 silver, 36 bronze (total 103)
Winter: *no medals (best finish: 6th)*
Total: 41 gold, 26 silver, 36 bronze (total 103)
                   (plus mixed team: 0 gold, 0.1 silver, 0 bronze (total 0.1))

Best sports: Wrestling (29 golds, 6.71%, 4th)
                                           Weightlifting (8 golds, 3.48%, 8th)
                                           Taekwondo (1 gold, 2.08%, 12th)

Turkey first entered the Olympics in 1908, when a single gymnast took part, finishing 67th equal. Since then, they have missed only the 1920, 1932 and 1980 Summer Games. In 1908 and 1912, the Turkish team represented the entire Ottoman Empire, which was then broken up following World War I. In fact, one Ottoman citizen, from modern-day Armenia, won a silver as part of the "Smyrna" Football team in the 1906 Intercalated Games (hence the 0.1 referred to above). In their first four Games, they failed to win a medal; their best finish in that time was 4th, in Wrestling in 1928. Thereafter, they won at least one gold in every Games up until 1968 (starting with Yasar Erkan in 1936). They then hit a bad patch; just a single silver in 1972 (Wrestling again), no medals at all in 1976 (but a 4th place in Wrestling), and three bronzes in 1984 (two in Boxing, one in Wrestling). They returned to the top of an Olympic podium in 1988, and have won golds at all Games since.

Their best Games in terms of golds has been 1960, with 7 golds and 2 silvers, all in Wrestling (they dominated the programme that year, winning 7 of the 16 events). It put Turkey 6th overall in 1960, their best finish in any year's medal table. Their record of 12 medals in a single Games, set in 1948, was finally broken in 2021, with 13 (2 gold, 2 silver and 9 bronze), with four medals in the new Olympic sport of Karate. Wrestling has utterly dominated Turkish Olympic history, being responsible for 29 of their 41 golds, and 66 of their 103 total medals. They have been fairly split between Freestyle (41 medals) and Greco-Roman (25 medals). However, Wrestling's dominance has waned in recent years. Prior to their 20-year gap between golds (1968 to 1988), all 23 of their golds had come in the sport. Since then, however, they have added 18 further golds, of which only 6 have been in Wrestling, with 8 in Weightlifting, and one each in Judo (2000), Taekwondo (2012), Archery (Mete Gazoz in the men's individual in 2021) and Boxing (Busenaz Surmeneli in women's welterweight in 2021; Turkey's second ever female gold medallist, following flyweight weightlifter Nurcan Taylan in 2004).

Two Turkish wrestlers have become repeat Olympic champions – Mustafa Dagistanli (freestyle bantamweight 1956 and featherweight 1960), and Greco-Roman middleweight Hamza Yerlikaya in 1996 and 2000. But Turkey's two greatest Olympians of all (three gold medals each) have both been weightlifters. First of all, the world-renowned Naim Suleymanoglu, who was only 4ft 10, but a giant of his sport. Born to an ethnic Turkish family in Bulgaria, he covertly defected from communist Bulgaria in the mid-1980s, and won the featherweight Olympic title in 1988, 1992 and 1996 (he almost certainly would have won for Bulgaria in 1984 too, had they not boycotted the Games). Another sub-five-footer, Halil Mutlu, then followed suit, defecting from Bulgaria a few years after Suleymanoglu, and winning flyweight gold in 1996, and bantamweight golds in 2000 and 2004.

The only other sports to have seen Turkish medals have been Gymastics (a parallel bars bronze in 2021) and Athletics (bronzes in the 1948 men's triple jump and the 2016 men's 400m hurdles). They also won four medals in women's middle-distance events in 2008 and 2012, but had them all later rescinded for doping offences. Their best Swimming finish is 9th (women's 200m breaststroke in 2016).

Turkey have entered all Winter Games since 1936, other than 1952, 1972 and 1980. Their finish of 15th and last in a Nordic Skiing relay in 1968 remained their best, until Furkan Akar finished 6th in Short Track Speed Skating (men's 1000m) in 2022.

IRAN Olympic Rank 36th

Population:	87,590,873 (rank 17th)
Olympic rank/ population differential:	-19
Population per gold:	3,649,620 (rank 70th)
Population per medal:	1,152,511 (rank 83rd)

Summer:	24 gold, 23 silver, 29 bronze (total 76)
Winter:	*no medals (best finish: 30th)*
Total:	24 gold, 23 silver, 29 bronze (total 76)

Best sports: Karate (1 gold, 12.50%, 5th=)
Taekwondo (2 golds, 4.17%, 8th)
Weightlifting (9 golds, 3,91%, 6th)

In 1900, the men's Fencing épée competition included an entry from Freydoun Malkom Khan, the British-based son of a prominent Persian diplomat. He is listed as Iran's first Olympian. However, no other Iranians entered until their first official delegation competed in 1948. Since then, Iran have entered every Games except those of 1980 and 1984 – they were one of the few countries that boycotted both Games, due to their antipathy against both Cold War superpowers.

Impressively, Iran have won medals at every Games they have entered since 1948. By far their most successful Games was London 2012. They won seven golds (the most they have won in any other Games is three – in 2000, 2016 and 2021). They won 13 medals in total in London (their next best is 8, in 2016), and they finished 12th in the medal table.

As can be seen above, there are three sports in which Iran are currently in the all-time Olympic top eight. When Karate made its debut in 2021, the heaviest men's weight category was won by Sajjad Ganjzadeh. Iran also managed top-eight finishes in two of the women's weight categories. In Taekwondo, Iran have had eight top-eight finishes, all in featherweight and welterweight. They include two golds, a silver and three bronzes. Both of the golds and one of the bronzes were won by Hadi Saei (featherweight bronze 2000 and gold 2004, welterweight gold 2008). Saei is one of two Iranians with two golds, and one of three Iranians with three medals. He also has the joint best medal record of anybody from any country in Olympic Taekwondo. One of Iran's other Taekwondo bronzes was won by featherweight Kimia Alizadeh in 2016; it is the only one of Iran's 76 Olympic medals to be won by a woman. She defected in early 2020 in protest at the treatment of women in Iran, and competed at the 2021 Games as a member of the Refugee Team.

Weightlifting has provided 20 medals for Iran (9 gold, 6 silver and 5 bronze). Unlike in Taekwondo, medals have come from right across the weight spectrum. Perhaps the best-known Iranian Olympian of all is Hossein Rezazadeh, gold medallist in the men's super-heavyweight in 2000 and 2004. He became such a star that his wedding was broadcast on state TV in 2003. Iran's other great Weightlifting star was Mohammad Nassiri, who won bantamweight gold in 1968 and silver in 1972, then flyweight bronze in 1976.

For all their success in those three sports, though, the sport that has brought by far the most medals to Iran is Wrestling. Ninth in the all-time medal table in the sport, Iran have won 11 gold, 15 silver and 21 bronze medals – a total of 47, which is well over half of all their Olympic medals. Of those 47, 38 have come in Freestyle, with just 9 in Greco-Roman, and no golds in the latter until 2012. They have won at least one Wrestling medal at every Olympics in which they have competed. Their most decorated Olympic wrestler was Gholamreza Takhti, who won a gold in 1956, with silvers in 1952 and 1960. He died aged 37 in 1968, seemingly suicide.

Iran have won just two medals in other sports. They were a silver for Ehsan Haddadi in men's discus in 2012 (this is the only time Iran have finished in the top ten of an Athletics event), and a gold for Javad Foroughi in men's 10m air pistol in 2021. There have also been top-eight finishes in Boxing, Fencing and Judo, as well as Football in 1976 and Volleyball in 2016. The best they have managed in Swimming is 33rd (achieved twice).

Iran have competed at the Winter Games a surprising number of times. First entering in 1956, they also entered all Games from 1964 to 1976, and from 1998 onwards. They have entered two sports in that time – Alpine Skiing (every time) and Nordic Skiing (every time from 2002 onwards). Their best finishes have all been in Alpine Skiing's men's slalom event – their best being 30th (in both 1998 and 2014).

ISRAEL **Olympic Rank 72nd**

Population:	9,043,387 (rank 98th)
Olympic rank/ population differential:	+26
Population per gold:	3,014,462 (rank 65th)
Population per medal:	695,645 (rank 73rd)

Summer:	3 gold, 1 silver, 9 bronze (total 13)
Winter:	*no medals (best finish: 6th)*
Total:	3 gold, 1 silver, 9 bronze (total 13)
Best sports:	Gymnastics (2 golds, 0.52%, 27th)
	Sailing (1 gold, 0.52%, 25th)
	Judo (1 silver, 5 bronzes, 34th)

Israel declared independence in 1948, and first entered the Olympics in 1952. They have entered all Summer Games since then, other than the 1980 boycott. In that time, they have entered the vast majority of sports, though they have had the most entries in Swimming, Athletics, Sailing, Gymnastics and Judo.

They had a slow start as an Olympic nation. Not until 1968 did they manage a top-eight finish (only losing their men's Football quarter-final to Bulgaria on a coin toss, penalty shoot-outs having not yet been invented). Their 1972 participation was completely overshadowed by the horrific murders of 11 of their team by Palestinian terrorists. In 1976, they had top-eight finishes in Football, Weightlifting, Athletics and Wrestling. In 1988, their 4th place in Sailing's Flying Dutchman class was their best finish yet.

Then in 1992, 40 years after their debut, they finally won their first medals. They both came in Judo, a silver for Yael Arad followed by a bronze for Oren Smadja. Since that breakthrough, Israel have medalled at every Summer Games except one – London 2012, when their best finish was 5th (Erlich and Ram in men's Tennis doubles). The Athens 2004 Games saw Israel's first ever gold, claimed by Gal Fridman in men's windsurfing. Having won a bronze in the same event eight years earlier in Atlanta, Fridman is one of two Israelis to have won multiple medals at the Olympics. The other is judoka Or Sasson with two bronzes, individually in 2016 and as part of the inaugural mixed team event in 2021.

After Fridman's 2004 gold, it took 17 years for Israel to add to that tally, but they did so with two golds in 2021, both in Gymnastics, albeit very different events; Ukrainian-born Artem Dolgopyat took the men's floor title, before Linoy Ashram won the women's rhythmic all-around event. With Israel also taking bronzes in Judo and Taekwondo that year, it made 2021 their most successful Games in terms of golds (2), overall medals (4) and medal table position (39th equal).

Overall, six of Israel's 13 medals have come in Judo. Sailing has provided three, Gymnastics two, and Canoeing (in 2000) and Taekwondo (in 2021) one each. Their best performance in Athletics is 5th, achieved by Konstantin Matusevich (men's high jump in 2000) and Hanna Knyazyeva-Minenko (women's triple jump in 2016). Both were born in Kyiv. Russian-born Yakov Toumarkin holds Israel's best finish in an Olympic Swimming event – 7th in the 2012 men's 200m backstroke. Israel have also achieved top-eight finishes in Wrestling, Weightlifting, Football, Tennis, Baseball, Boxing and Shooting.

Israel have entered all Winter Games since first participating in 1994. In their first two Games, they entered only Figure Skating. They have since added Short Track Speed Skating (2002), Alpine Skiing (2006) and Skeleton (2018). Their only Skeleton entry came 28th (ahead of entries from Jamaica and Ghana), and in Short Track Speed Skating their best position is 12th. In Alpine Skiing, their best five performances were all achieved by the same man (Barnabas Szollos) in the same year (2022), which included a 6th-place finish in the combined event. Figure Skating, though, has been Israel's most consistent Winter sport. Their ice dance pair of Galit Chait and Sergey Sakhnovsky finished 6th in 2002 and 8th in 2006. The other one of Israel's four top-eight finishes in Winter Games was an 8th place in the Figure Skating team event in 2018.

SYRIA   **Olympic Rank 92nd**

Population: 22,933,531 (rank 59th)
Olympic rank/ population differential: -33
Population per gold: 22,933,531 (rank 93rd)
Population per medal: 5,733,383 (rank 112th)

Summer: 1 gold, 1 silver, 2 bronze (total 4)
Winter: *never participated*
Total: 1 gold, 1 silver, 2 bronze (total 4)

Best sports: Athletics (1 gold, 0.10%, 63rd=)
Wrestling (1 silver, 44th=)
Weightlifting (1 bronze, 61st=)

Syria made their Olympic debut in London in 1948, just a couple of years after they gained independence from France. Their one entrant that year was a platform diver who came 10th. They weren't represented at the next two Olympics. In 1958, Syria formed a political union with Egypt called the United Arab Republic, which competed at the 1960 Games, although it appears all members of the team were Egyptian. The following year, Syria broke away from the union, and didn't compete at the Games again until 1968, when they sent two wrestlers. In 1972, they sent a small delegation competing in Athletics, Shooting and Wrestling, and in 1976 they didn't enter at all.

They have entered every Summer Games since 1980, but have yet to make their Winter Olympic debut. Their first Olympic medal came in 1984. Joseph Atiyeh was born in Syria, but moved to Pennsylvania as a toddler and was raised in the US. Representing the land of his birth, he reached the final of the men's heavyweight freestyle Wrestling, but was easily beaten by his old adversary Lou Banach of the US, and settled for silver.

In 1996 Syria won their only Olympic gold medal. Ghada Shouaa had won the women's heptathlon at the 1995 world championships and, with double Olympic champion Jackie Joyner-Kersee struggling with injury, she was fancied in the Atlanta Olympics. She lived up to the expectations, winning gold pretty easily. It was a superb achievement, when you bear in mind that she was the only female who had even competed at the Olympics for Syria (in any sport) since 1980. She was later, not surprisingly, declared the best Syrian athlete of the 20th century.

Since then, Syria have never entered more than ten events in any one Games, and have only added two bronzes to their medal tally. The first came in 2004, for Nasser Al Shami in men's heavyweight Boxing, and the other came in 2021, for Man Assad in men's super-heavyweight Weightlifting.

Syria have had a total of 16 top-eight finishes in Olympic competition. Eight of these have come in Wrestling (six in 1980 and 1984, plus one each in 1988 and 1996). A further four have come in Weightlifting, all in men's heavyweight or super-heavyweight. Ahed Joughili came 4th in heavyweight in 2012, Syria's only 4th-place finish in Olympic history.

Of Syria's other four top-eight finishes, two of them were the aforementioned medals for Al Shami in Boxing and Shouaa in Athletics. The others were in Judo (men's extra-lightweight) in 1980, and in the men's high jump in 2016, where Majed Ghazal came equal 7th. Their best finish in Swimming was equal 18th, in the men's 50m freestyle in 2004.

JORDAN **Olympic Rank 94th**

Population: 11,086,716 (rank 84th)
Olympic rank/ population differential: -10
Population per gold: 11,086,716 (rank 89th)
Population per medal: 3,695,572 (rank 107th)

Summer: 1 gold, 1 silver, 1 bronze (total 3)
Winter: *never participated*
Total: 1 gold, 1 silver, 1 bronze (total 3)

Best sports: Taekwondo (1 gold, 2.08%, 16th=)
Karate (1 bronze, 15th=)
Boxing

Jordan first entered the Olympics in 1980; they have entered every Summer Games since. That year, they stuck to Shooting. They have since made Olympic debuts in Athletics and Fencing (1984), Archery, Boxing, Table Tennis and Archery (1988), Swimming (1996), Equestrianism and Taekwondo (2000), Judo and Triathlon (2016) and Karate (2021).

In their first five Olympics, they never came close even to a top-16 finish. But the advent of Taekwondo as an Olympic sport in 2000 changed much for them. In fact, they had already achieved some podium finishes in Taekwondo when it acted as a demonstration sport in 1988 and 1992. But on its full debut in 2000, welterweight Mohamed Al-Farajeh gained his country's first top-eight finish, albeit without winning a match (he finished 7th equal as a result of reaching the repechage, which he only did as a result of the person who beat him in the first round reaching the final). But, to be fair, he did make a decent fist of his repechage match, only losing 5-4. In 2004, two heavyweights did better. Ibrahim Kamal in the men's event, and Nadin Dawani in the women's, both reached the semi-finals, but lost out in the repechage, finishing 4th and 5th respectively.

The following two Games were less successful, albeit with Taekwondo still looking the most likely sport for them. Sure enough, in 2016, featherweight Ahmad Abughaush became a national hero, with victories over opponents from Egypt, South Korea, Spain and Russia to make Jordan's first ever Olympic medal a gold one. That same year, Jordan also achieved its first top-eight finish in a different sport when Hussein Iashaish reached the quarter-finals of the super-heavyweight Boxing.

In 2021, Jordan earned their second and third Olympic medals. Saleh El-Sharabaty gained a silver in welterweight Taekwondo, whilst Abdel Rahman Al-Masatfa won a bronze in Karate. Iashaish also reached another quarter-final in Boxing.

Jordan's best two Athletics performances have both been achieved by the same woman – shot putter Nada Kawar finished 24th in 1996 and 25th in 2000. Their best Swimming performance is 26th (men's 200m breaststroke in 2021). Jordan have never entered the Winter Olympics.

KUWAIT   Olympic Rank 97th

Population: 3,103,580 (rank 136th)
Olympic rank/ population differential: +39
Population per gold: 3,103,580 (rank 66th)
Population per medal: 620,716 (rank 69th)

Summer: 1 gold, 0 silver, 4 bronze (total 5)
Winter: *never participated*
Total: 1 gold, 0 silver, 4 bronze (total 5)

Best sports: Shooting (1 gold, 0.33%, 36th)
                                            Football
                                            Taekwondo

Kuwait's Olympic Rank is listed in this book as 97th; however, the IOC would argue that it should be at least 30 places lower than that, given that in their eyes Kuwait have never won an Olympic gold medal. More on that later. The nation's first foray into Olympic competition came in Mexico City in 1968, where they sent two athletes, both of whom were entered in the men's marathon, which neither managed to finish. They have not missed a Summer Games since. In 1972, the delegation consisted of only two athletes and two swimmers, but their teams have been much bigger since then.

Their biggest team was the one that was sent to the 1980 Moscow Games. Many of them competed for the men's Football team, who achieved Kuwait's first Olympic top-eight finish; they finished the group stage with a win over Nigeria and two draws, but lost 2-1 to the hosts in the quarter-finals. It would be 20 years before they managed another top-eight finish, but in Sydney they managed three. Khaled Al-Mudhaf finished 4th in the men's trap Shooting, but Fehaid Al-Deehani went one better in the men's double trap, taking bronze. It was his third Olympics, having first entered in 1992. Meanwhile, Kuwait also managed an 8th place in men's flyweight Taekwondo, courtesy of a first-round win over Swaziland.

In 2004, Al-Deehani was back, finishing 8th this time, with Al-Mudhaf finishing 6th. One further top-eight followed in 2008, again in Shooting. In 2012, Al-Deehani, now in his fifth Olympics at the age of 45 (he had not competed in 2008), came 4th in the double trap and took bronze in the trap – Kuwait's second Olympic medal, both won by himself.

Al-Deehani had been lucky to be able to participate under the Kuwaiti flag in 2012. The Kuwaiti Olympic Committee had been suspended by the IOC in 2010 due to undue government interference, and the suspension was only lifted two weeks before the start of the Games. However, the same issue re-arose, and Kuwait were suspended again in 2015. This time, the suspension remained in place for the 2016 Games, and meant that the nine Kuwaitis that travelled to Rio had to compete as "Independent Olympic Athletes", under the IOC flag. They won two medals, both in Shooting. Abdullah Al-Rashidi took bronze in the men's skeet, and Al-Deehani (now 49 and in his sixth Games) took gold in the double trap. But Kuwait's one and only Olympic gold was not achieved under their own flag, they did not have their own national anthem played, and as far as the IOC are concerned, it doesn't count for Kuwait. But, as far as I am concerned, it was won by a Kuwaiti (indeed, he already had two Olympic medals as a Kuwaiti), so I am crediting his country with his achievement. Ironically, 2016 was the only Games so far with Kuwait winning two medals.

The second suspension was lifted in 2019, meaning that when Al-Rashidi won his second successive skeet bronze, this time he did it in Kuwaiti colours. So Kuwait's five Olympic medals have been won by just two men. They have had 15 top-eight finishes in all, 13 in Shooting (all in men's trap, double trap and skeet), and one each in Football and Taekwondo.

Kuwait's best Athletics achievement is a 14th place finish for Mohamed Al-Zinkawi in the 1980 men's shot put. His son finished 16th in the hammer in 2012. Their highest Swimming finish was also in 1980 – 25th (and last) in the men's 200m butterfly (their highest position that wasn't last is 31st). Women didn't compete for Kuwait in the Olympics until 2004; their best position so far is 28th (in the 10m air rifle in 2012). Kuwait have never yet taken part in the Winter Olympics, either officially or unofficially.

LEBANON   **Olympic Rank 109th**
Population: 5,331,203 (rank 122nd)
Olympic rank/ population differential: +13
Population per gold: n/a
Population per medal: 1,332,801 (rank 89th)

Summer: 0 gold, 2 silver, 2 bronze (total 4)
Winter: *no medals (best finish: 19th)*
Total: 0 gold, 2 silver, 2 bronze (total 4)

Best sports: Wrestling (1 silver, 2 bronzes, 41st=)
                           Weightlifting (1 silver, 54th=)
                           Judo

Lebanon made both their Summer and Winter Olympic debuts in 1948, and have only missed three Games since then – the Summer Games of 1956, and the Winter Games of 1994 and 1998. By far their most successful sport in that time has been Greco-Roman Wrestling. It has provided three of their four medals, and eight of their ten top-eight finishes (the other two both came in Weightlifting). The 1952 Games remain the only one to provide two medals – a bronze in welterweight and a silver for bantamweight Zakaria Chibab. The other Lebanese medals were a silver for middleweight weightlifter Mohamed Traboulsi in 1972, and another Greco-Roman bronze in 1980. Since July 2020, none of their four medallists are now living.

Lebanon's best finish outside of these two sports is ninth in Judo in 1992, merely by virtue of finding himself in the repechage and taking over four minutes to lose once there. Their best finish in Athletics is 22nd (men's javelin, 1976; he finished nearly 18 metres behind the next shortest valid distance), and their best in Swimming is 19th (women's 800m freestyle, 2012). They have not come close to a medal since 1980; indeed, they have not even entered their one-time strongest sport of Wrestling since 1988. Almost all of their Winter entries have been in Alpine Skiing; their best finish is 19th. They entered Skeleton once, coming last, whilst the only other Winter sport they have entered (Nordic Skiing) has never garnered a better finish than 87th.

CYPRUS   **Olympic Rank 122nd**
Population: 1,308,120 (rank 158th)
Olympic rank/ population differential: +36
Population per gold: n/a
Population per medal: 1,308,120 (rank 86th)

Summer: 0 gold, 1 silver, 0 bronze (total 1)
Winter: *no medals (best finish: 21st)*
Total: 0 gold, 1 silver, 0 bronze (total 1)

Best sports: Sailing (1 silver, 34th=)
                           Shooting
                           Athletics

The first Cypriot Olympian was Limassol-born 110m hurdler Anastasios Andreou, who competed in 1896 when Cyprus was a British colony; however, he is now listed as representing Greece. It took until 1980 for Cyprus to send an official Olympic team – they have entered all Summer and Winter Games since that year. Despite entering a variety of events, they failed to register any top-eight finishes in their first five Summer Games. Since 2000, though, they have totalled 10 top-eight finishes. Five of those have come in skeet Shooting, including their first ever top-eight finish (Antonis Andreou in 2000), and two in the same event in 2008 (finishing 4th and 5th in the men's skeet; 4th-placed Antonis Nikolaidis having agonisingly lost a shoot-off for bronze).

Two of the other five top-eight finishes have come in Athletics, both in 2016 (7th in the men's 100m hurdles, and 8th in the men's discus). The remaining three were all achieved by Pavlos Kontides in Sailing's laser class. He comfortably gained Cyprus's first (and only) Olympic medal with a silver in 2012, before finishing 7th and 4th in the same event in 2016 and 2021 respectively. He is also a double world champion. Meanwhile, in Swimming, Cyprus's best finish is 20th (men's 50m freestyle, 1992). The nation has had a surprisingly large number of Winter Olympic entries, but every single one has come in Alpine Skiing. Their best finish is 21st (women's slalom, 1984).

IRAQ — Olympic Rank 133rd

Population:	41,266,109 (rank 36th)
Olympic rank/ population differential:	-97
Population per gold:	n/a
Population per medal:	41,266,109 (rank 137th)

Summer:	0 gold, 0 silver, 1 bronze (total 1)
Winter:	*never participated*
Total:	0 gold, 0 silver, 1 bronze (total 1)

Best sports:	Weightlifting (1 bronze, 61st=)
	Football
	Wrestling

Iraq made their Olympic debut in London in 1948, when they entered Athletics and Basketball. There was then a 12-year absence before they made a medal-winning return, with Abdul Wahid Aziz taking a bronze in the men's lightweight Weightlifting. He had also won a bronze the previous year at the World Championships, but in later life got in trouble for his opposition to the Iraqi government. Nonetheless, he remains Iraq's only ever Olympic medallist. Of current nations, only Haiti (1928) have waited longer since their last medal.

Since 1960, Iraq have entered all Summer Games except 1972 and 1976. The closest they have come to a medal since then has been the remarkable run of their men's Football team in 2004. A year after the US-led invasion of Iraq, they knocked Portugal out in the group stage and reached the semi-finals, but had to settle for 4th place. They have had 11 top-eight finishes overall, finishing between 5th and 8th nine times (four in Wrestling, two in Weightlifting, and one each in Boxing, Football and Taekwondo). They have had none since 2004, though.

In Athletics, their best finish is 14th (men's 4x100m relay in 1960 and triple jump in 1980). In Swimming, it is 42nd (men's 100m butterfly in 2012). Besides the sports already mentioned, Iraq have also participated in Shooting, Rowing, Cycling, Table Tennis, Archery and Judo. They have never entered the Winter Olympics.

PALESTINE — Olympic Rank 193rd

Population:	5,088,504 (rank 126th)
Olympic rank/ population differential:	-67

Summer:	*no medals (best finish: 13th)*
Winter:	*never participated*

Best sports:	Weightlifting
	Swimming
	Judo

Following the Oslo Accords in the mid-'90s, Palestine first participated in the Olympics in its own right in 1996. They have entered every Summer Games since, but never as yet the Winter Games. Their only Olympian in 1996, Majed Abu Maraheel, finished the men's 10000 metres heat more than a minute slower than any other finisher. Since 2000, Palestine have entered Athletics and Swimming in every Games. They have never progressed beyond round one of any Athletics event. Their best swimmer, Ahmed Gebrel, finished 27th out of 28 in the men's 400m freestyle in London 2012.

It was also in 2012 that they first entered another sport, namely Judo. They have entered Judo a total of three times, and been knocked out in their first bout every time (although two of those were good enough for 29th-place finishes). They also finished 57th in the Equestrianism dressage event in 2016, and 13th in the men's middle-heavyweight Weightlifting in 2021. The latter, achieved by Mohammed Hamada, is Palestine's highest ever Olympic finish – there were 15 entrants in total, of whom two failed to achieve a valid lift in the clean & jerk section.

CHAPTER FIFTEEN Middle East, southern (Qatar, Bahrain, United Arab Emirates, Saudi Arabia, Oman, Yemen)

QATAR   **Olympic Rank 82nd**
Population: 2,532,104 (rank 143rd)
Olympic rank/ population differential: +61
Population per gold: 1,266,052 (rank 50th)
Population per medal: 316,513 (rank 58th)

Summer: 2 gold, 2 silver, 4 bronze (total 8)
Winter: *never participated*
Total: 2 gold, 2 silver, 4 bronze (total 8)

Best sports: Weightlifting (1 gold, 0.43%, 40th=)
                                        Athletics (1 gold, 0.10%, 52nd=)
                                        Beach Volleyball (1 bronze, 11th=)

Qatar gained independence from the UK in 1971, and first entered the Olympics in 1984. They have entered every Summer Games since, but never the Winter Games as yet. In their first two Games, they entered Athletics, Football, Sailing and Shooting, with no success whatsoever, but they have had top-eight finishes at every Games since.

Their first medal came in 1992, and was won by Mohamed Suleiman in the men's 1500 metres (a bronze). Their next was also a bronze, won in 2000 by Said Saif Asaad in men's heavyweight Weightlifting. Asaad was born Angel Popov in Bulgaria (who are the fourth most successful Weightlifting nation in Olympic history), and was recruited by Qatar to compete for them. After two medal-less Games in 2004 and 2008, a third bronze came in 2012 for Nasser Al-Attiya in men's skeet Shooting (he was also a world-class rally driver).

A few days later, Mutaz Essa Barshim won a bronze in the men's high jump, leaving Qatar with a record of four medals – all bronzes. Just one medal followed in 2016 – again won by Barshim in the high jump, it was silver this time, behind Canadian Derek Drouin.

Having not won an Olympic gold so far, Qatar duly won two in 2021. The first was won in men's middle heavyweight Weightlifting by Fares Ibrahim, who had been born in Egypt as Fares El-Bakh (his father had been an Egyptian Olympic weightlifter), but he had been competing for Qatar for many years. The very next day, Barshim won his third Olympic medal in the men's high jump (no other Qatari has won more than one), this time famously being allowed to share gold with Italian Gianmarco Tamberi – the first shared gold in any Athletics event since 1908. More good news followed for Barshim later that year when his 2012 bronze was finally upgraded to silver, following the disqualification of the original Russian gold medallist for a doping violation. It meant that Barshim has now won three of Qatar's four gold or silver medals at the Olympics.

By the end of the 2021 Games, Qatar had added a third medal, ensuring it became their most successful Games by number of golds (2), number of total medals (3) and final medal table position (41st). That medal came in men's Beach Volleyball, won by the pair of Cherif Younousse (born in Senegal) and Ahmed Tijan (born in Gambia), who outclassed the Latvian pair in the bronze medal match. It was only Qatar's second entry into Olympic Beach Volleyball, Younousse having lost in the last 16 in 2016 alongside a Brazilian-born partner.

Qatar's four medal sports of Athletics, Weightlifting, Shooting and Beach Volleyball have accounted for 22 of their 25 top-eight finishes. The others have come in three different sports. In 1992, they reached the quarter-finals of the men's Football thanks to a win over Egypt (they lost 2-0 to Poland). In 2016, they took part in Olympic Handball for the only time, where a win over Argentina saw them into the quarter-finals in which they lost to Germany. Finally, in 2021, Sheikh Ali Al-Thani came 6th in the individual Equestrian show jumping event.

Qatar had never entered a woman into the Olympics up to 2008, but finally bowed to IOC pressure in 2012. Qatari women have competed in various sports since then, and their best finish is 17th out of 56 in the 10m air rifle Shooting in 2012. Qatar have only finished in the top 40 of a Swimming event three times, and on all three occasions they came last out of those who finished. The "best" is 36th in the men's 400m individual medley in 2012. The best finish they have had in a Swimming event where they didn't come last is 43rd.

BAHRAIN   **Olympic Rank 83rd**

Population: 1,553,886 (rank 153rd)
Olympic rank/ population differential: +70
Population per gold: 776,943 (rank 47th)
Population per medal: 388,472 (rank 62nd)

Summer: 2 gold, 2 silver, 0 bronze (total 4)
Winter: *never participated*
Total: 2 gold, 2 silver, 0 bronze (total 4)

Best sports: Athletics (2 golds, 0.19%, 46th)
                Handball
                Modern Pentathlon

Bahrain, who have never entered the Winter Olympics, have contested every Summer Games since debuting in 1984. They have won four medals in that time, but attracted considerable controversy in doing so, as all four have been won by naturalised East African women, all in events traditionally dominated by East African women.

In their first six Olympic appearances, Bahrain never came close to a medal – their best finish in that period was 13th, in the men's team Modern Pentathlon event in 1984. Starting in 2008, however, their rate of success has increased hugely – almost entirely thanks to imported talent on the Athletics track. In 2008, they achieved their first three top-eight finishes – Youssef Saad Kamel (5th in the men's 800m), Belal Mansoor Ali (7th in the men's 1500m) and Maryam Jamal (5th in the women's 800m). All three had recently changed nationality – Kamel and Ali from Kenya, and Jamal from Ethiopia.

In 2012, Jamal secured Bahrain's first ever medal, finishing 3rd in the women's 1500 metres. The race was later found to have been the "dirtiest" Athletics event in Olympic history. Numerous competitors were found to have committed doping offences, including both of the Turkish runners who finished ahead of Jamal, who was thus retrospectively promoted to the gold medal.

In 2016, Bahrain added two more medals – gold for Ruth Jebet (Kenyan-born) in the 3000m steeplechase, and silver for Eunice Kirwa (also Kenyan-born) in the marathon. One further medal arrived in 2021 – a silver for Kalkidan Gezahegne (Ethiopian-born) in the 10000 metres. Overall, Bahrain have had 15 top-eight finishes in Olympic history. Fourteen of these have been in Athletics events, spread between 400m, 800m, 1500m, 3000m steeplechase, 5000m, 10000m and the marathon. The best performance by any Olympian born in Bahrain was 6th place in the 2016 men's 400 metres by Ali Khamis.

Bahrain's other top-eight finish occurred in the men's Handball in 2021, where a single group-stage victory over Japan was enough to take them to the quarter-finals, in which they lost to eventual champions France. In all, Bahrain have competed in nine Olympic sports – Athletics (every time), Handball (2021 only), Swimming (1984, and every time since 2000), Shooting (1984, and every time since 2004), Modern Pentathlon (1984 and 1988), Fencing (1988), Cycling (1992), Sailing (1996 and 2004), and Boxing (2021).

In Swimming, they have never competed in a race longer than 100 metres, and never finished higher than 43rd. Their best in other sports have been 24th in Shooting, 13th in Modern Pentathlon, 16th in Fencing, 22nd in Cycling, 22nd in Sailing, and 16th in Boxing.

UNITED ARAB EMIRATES   **Olympic Rank 101st**

Population:	9,973,449 (rank 92nd)
Olympic rank/ population differential:	-9
Population per gold:	9,973,449 (rank 85th)
Population per medal:	4,986,725 (rank 109th)
Summer:	1 gold, 0 silver, 1 bronze (total 2)
Winter:	*never participated*
Total:	1 gold, 0 silver, 1 bronze (total 2)
Best sports:	Shooting (1 gold, 0.33%, 40th=)
	Judo (1 bronze, 46th=)
	Taekwondo

Having established full independence in 1971, the United Arab Emirates entered the Olympics for the first time in 1984. They have competed in all Summer Games since, although they have never yet ventured into the Winter Olympics.

On their debut, they competed only in Athletics, although they did not progress beyond the first round of any of the events in which they participated. In 1988, they did not compete in Athletics, but instead had numerous entries in two sports – Swimming and road Cycling. Their best finish that year was 14th in the men's 4x200m freestyle relay. This remains their highest ever finish in a Swimming event (their best in an individual Swimming event is 37th, in the men's 100m backstroke in 2016).

In 1992, the UAE stuck to the same three sports they had previously entered, and in 1996 they had their first entry into what would become their most successful sport – Shooting. No joy on that first occasion, though – the best they could manage was 43rd. In 2000, Sheikh Saeed Al-Maktoum was one of ten people tied on 122 out of 125 in the men's skeet Shooting, but he finished equal 9th following a shoot-off, and failed to reach the final. Al-Maktoum, who entered five Olympics, although this was his highest finish, was the son of the prime minister of the UAE.

In 2004, the UAE tasted Olympic glory for the first time. Not surprisingly, it came at the Shooting range. First, Ahmed Al-Maktoum finished 4th in the men's trap, one point behind the Australian bronze medallist; it was his nation's first ever top-eight finish in any Olympic event. A couple of days later, though, the same man won the gold medal in the double trap, winning the title by a huge margin – he scored 189, with the other five finalists all scoring between 175 and 179. Al-Maktoum was, like Sheikh Saeed, a member of the ruling Al-Maktoum family, albeit a more junior one. He later coached Peter Wilson, who won gold in the same event for Great Britain in 2012. Al-Maktoum himself finished 7th in the same event in 2008, meaning that he was responsible for all of the UAE's first three top-eight finishes.

In their first six Olympic appearances, the UAE only entered four sports – Athletics, Swimming, road Cycling and, of course, Shooting. In 2008, however, they added four new sports – Equestrianism, Judo, Sailing and Taekwondo. This was their only ever Taekwondo appearance to date, and although the UAE's representative (in the women's welterweight) lost both of her matches, she nonetheless finished 7th due to the unusual Taekwondo ranking system. This was the fourth of the UAE's five top-eight finishes to date. Unlike the previous three, it was not in Shooting; however, like the previous three, it was achieved by a member of the same family – in this case, Maitha Al-Maktoum, a cousin of Sheikh Saeed and, like him, she would become the child of a prime minister.

In 2012, the UAE made their Olympic debuts in Football and Weightlifting – their 9th place in women's heavyweight Weightlifting was the best they could manage in any event that year. No new sports were entered in 2016 or 2021, but they made some headlines in Judo. They entered three judokas in 2016, all of whom were born in Moldova (two of them had, in fact, competed in previous Olympics for their country of origin). One of them, Sergiu Toma, beat an Italian to claim bronze in the men's half-middleweight. It was the UAE's second Olympic medal and fifth top-eight finish – and the only one not to have been earned by an Al-Maktoum. The best the UAE have ever managed in Athletics is 23rd (a position they have achieved three times in all).

SAUDI ARABIA   **Olympic Rank 108th**

Population: 35,939,806 (rank 42nd)
Olympic rank/ population differential: -66
Population per gold: n/a
Population per medal: 8,984,952 (rank 124th)

Summer: 0 gold, 2 silver, 2 bronze (total 4)
Winter: *no medals (best finish: 44th)*
Total: 0 gold, 2 silver, 2 bronze (total 4)

Best sports: Karate (1 silver, 13th)
Athletics (1 silver, 78th=)
Equestrianism (2 bronzes, 28th)

Saudi Arabia attended an Olympics for the first time in 1972, participating only in Athletics on that occasion. They have taken part in all Summer Games since then, except for 1980, and began taking part in other sports from 1984 onwards. Famously, they refused to allow women to compete on their team until 2012 (although they had competed in some mixed-gender events, notably Equestrianism).

Prior to 2000, they had never finished in the top eight of any event. However, they have done so on eight occasions since, including four medals. Their first two medals both came in Sydney in that year. Hadi Soua'an Al-Somaily narrowly missed out on gold in the 400m hurdles, finishing just behind Angelo Taylor (USA), and Khaled Al Eid claimed bronze in the show jumping. They also had a 4th place in Taekwondo in 2000, but no more success was to come in either 2004 or 2008.

In 2012, Kamal Bahamdan came 4th in the show jumping, but he did help the Saudis claim bronze in the team event. Saudi Arabia also managed a 7th place in Weightlifting that year, and a 5th place in 2021. Their most recent success was a silver in the new Karate +75kg event for men, won by Tareg Hamedi. Hamedi had in fact been on course for gold in the final, when a kick he unleashed on his Iranian opponent was controversially deemed worthy of immediate disqualification. Saudi Arabia's wait for a first Olympic gold therefore goes on. Meanwhile, Fayik Abdi became Saudi Arabia's first ever Winter Olympian in 2022, finishing 44th in the men's giant slalom in Alpine Skiing.

OMAN   **Olympic Rank 167th**

Population: 3,833,465 (rank 131st)
Olympic rank/ population differential: -36

Summer: *no medals (best finish: 8th)*
Winter: *never participated*

Best sports: Athletics
Weightlifting
Shooting

Oman have been competing at the Summer Olympics (though never the Winter Olympics) since 1984, and are still waiting for their first medal. They have entered seven sports in that time. They have entered Sailing once, coming 37th in windsurfing in 1984. They have entered Boxing once (1988), losing their only bout. They have entered Cycling once (the 1996 road race), but failed to finish. They have entered four Swimming events across four different Olympics (1996, 2000, 2008, 2021), with a best finish of 34th.

More successfully, they have entered Weightlifting once (2021), with Amur Al-Kanjari finishing 10th out of 14 in the men's light-heavyweight. They have entered Shooting in every Olympics they have participated in, entering a range of different events. Their best finishes have been 17th equal in the 1988 men's 10m air rifle, and 19th in the 2012 men's double trap. Finally, they have also entered Athletics in every Olympics they have participated in. They have only ever entered running events, and have only ever got beyond the first round of heats once. That was in 1988, when Mohamed Al-Malky got all the way to the final of the men's 400 metres, finishing in 8th place. He participated in five Olympic events across three Games, but never got close to repeating that feat.

YEMEN **Olympic Rank 178th**
Population: 31,565,602 (rank 47th)
Olympic rank/ population differential: -131

Summer: *no medals (best finish: 10th)*
Winter: *never participated*

Best sports: Taekwondo
Gymnastics
Wrestling

North Yemen took part in the Summer Games of 1984 and 1988, with South Yemen also participating in 1988. The two countries united in 1990, and have competed in all Summer Games since, though never the Winter Games. The North competed in Athletics in 1984, and Athletics, Judo and Wrestling in 1988. The South competed in Athletics and Boxing in 1988. The unified Yemen have competed in Athletics every time, and Judo and Swimming five times each, as well as Taekwondo (2004 and 2012), Wrestling (1996), Gymnastics (2004) and Shooting (2021).

Their highest two finishes have both come in men's Flyweight Taekwondo. In 2004, Akram Al-Noor came 14th out of 16 after losing 7-5 in the first round. In 2012, Tameem Al-Kubati finished 10th out of 16 (he actually won a match against an opponent from the Dominican Republic, but lost in the quarter-finals and didn't reach the repechage). In the 2008 men's Gymnastics, Nashwan Al Harazi entered a number of events, finishing 16th (and last) in the vault. His next best was 74th (out of 76) in the pommel horse. Their only Wrestler came last out of 19 in 1996. Yemen's best finish in Swimming is 36th. In Athletics, apart from a single marathon appearance in 1996, their entries have all been in track events; they have never progressed beyond the first round.

CHAPTER SIXTEEN - Northern Africa (Egypt, Morocco, Algeria, Tunisia, Libya)

EGYPT Olympic Rank 53rd

Population: 109,546,720 (rank 15th)
Olympic rank/ population differential: -38
Population per gold: 13,693,340 (rank 92nd)
Population per medal: 2,882,808 (rank 105th)

Summer: 8 gold, 11 silver, 19 bronze (total 38)
Winter: *no medals (best finish: 46th)*
Total: 8 gold, 11 silver, 19 bronze (total 38)

Best sports: Karate (1 gold, 12.50%, 3rd=)
Weightlifting (5 golds, 2.17%, 13th)
Wrestling (2 golds, 0.46%, 30th)

Egypt first entered the Olympics in 1912. Since then, they have only missed the two Los Angeles Games of 1932 and 1980. In 1960 and 1964, they competed as the United Arab Republic; it was a political union with Syria, though in practice all competing athletes appear to have been Egyptian.

Their first medals came in 1928 (two golds, a silver and a bronze). The golds came for Sayed Nosseir in Weightlifting and Ibrahim Moustafa in Wrestling. They matched that two-gold haul in their next two appearances, in 1936 and 1948, but have only won two golds in total since then, one in 2004 and one in 2021. The 2021 Games saw Egypt secure a record six medals in total (one gold, one silver and four bronzes). In fact, 14 of their 38 medals came between 1928 and 1948, and 20 of them since 2004. The other four were won in the generally fallow period from 1952 to 2000.

Of their 38 medals, 14 have come in Weightlifting and eight in Wrestling. Four Egyptians have won two medals each, but only one of those four has won a gold. That man was Ibrahim Shams, who won Weightlifting bronze in 1936 and gold (in lightweight) in 1948. That was their most recent Weightlifting gold; they did not win another medal in the sport for 60 years, but have won two silvers and four bronzes since 2008.

In 2004, Karam Ibrahim (in Greco-Roman heavyweight) became Egypt's first Wrestling gold medallist since 1928. Their other gold came in Karate. Making its Olympic debut in 2021, it produced Egyptian medals – a gold and a bronze – in two of its eight categories.

Egypt have won four medals each in Boxing (one in 1960 and three in 2004) and Taekwondo (2004-2021). They have won two in Diving (both for Farid Simaika in 1928), two in Judo (1984 and 2008), one in Fencing (2012) and one in Modern Pentathlon (2021).

Remarkably, it took until 2021, in which an Egyptian finished eighth in men's shot put, for any top eight finish in Athletics. Swimming has only ever had two, both in 1948 (7th in the men's 200m breaststroke, and 8th in the men's 100m freestyle). Other sports with top eight finishes have been Artistic Swimming, Equestrianism, Football, Handball, Rowing, Shooting, Table Tennis and Water Polo.

Egypt's sole participation in the Winter Olympics was thanks to alpine skier Jamil El-Reedy. Born in Cairo, but raised in upstate New York, he entered three events; his best result was a 46th-place finish in the slalom.

MOROCCO   Olympic Rank 57th

Population: 37,067,420 (rank 40th)
Olympic rank/ population differential: -17
Population per gold: 5,295,346 (rank 76th)
Population per medal: 1,544,476 (rank 94th)

Summer: 7 gold, 5 silver, 12 bronze (total 24)
Winter: *no medals (best finish: 38th)*
Total: 7 gold, 5 silver, 12 bronze (total 24)

Best sports: Athletics (7 golds, 0.67%, 26th)
                Boxing (4 bronzes, 56th)
                Taekwondo

Morocco first entered the Olympic Games in 1960, four years after independence from France, and have competed in all Olympics since, other than the 1980 boycott. They also boycotted in 1976, but not before they had competed in Boxing.

They won a silver medal on their debut, with Rhadi Ben Abdesselam finishing 2nd in the men's marathon. But it would be 24 years before they won another medal. Their best Olympic era started in 1984 and lasted a couple of decades. That year, they won two medals, but both were notable golds, and put them 18th in the medal table. Said Aouita won a famous victory in the men's 5000 metres, and Nawal El-Moutawakel became the first woman from an Islamic country ever to win Olympic gold, taking the title in the 400m hurdles.

The only other time that Morocco have won two golds in a Games was 2004. On that occasion, both were won by the legendary Hicham El Guerrouj. In winning both the 1500 and 5000 metres, he emulated the achievement of the "Flying Finn" Paavo Nurmi 80 years earlier. Having also won a silver in the 1500 four years earlier, he is the only Moroccan to have won three Olympic medals. Two others have won two; they are Said Aouita who, four years after winning the 5000 metres gold, won a bronze in the very different event of 800 metres; and Hasna Benhassi, who won silver in the women's 800 metres in 2004 and a bronze in the same event in 2008.

The only Games in which Morocco won more than three medals was Sydney, when they claimed El Guerrouj's aforementioned silver as well as four bronzes – three in Athletics and one in Boxing. They have won at least one medal in every Games since 1984, although they have won only a single medal in each of the last three.

All seven of Morocco's golds, all five of their silvers, and eight of their 12 bronzes, have come in Athletics. The other four bronzes have come in Boxing. Of their 64 top-eight finishes, 39 of them come in Athletics, all in running events of 400 metres or further. Boxing has produced 12, and Taekwondo nine. The others have been in Judo (twice, both in 1972), Football (quarter-finalists in 1972) and Tennis (Karim Alami reached the last eight of men's singles in 2000 before losing to a young Roger Federer). Morocco's three top-20 finishes in Swimming have all been achieved by Sara El-Bekri; her best is 11th in the 200m breaststroke in 2012.

Morocco's Winter Olympic history began in Alpine Skiing in 1968, 1984 and 1988. In 1992, they competed in both Alpine and Nordic Skiing. They then didn't compete again until 2010. They have entered all Winter Games since, but have not entered any other sports in that time. Their best finish is 38th, achieved in Alpine Skiing in 1984.

ALGERIA   **Olympic Rank 62nd**

Population:	44,758,398 (rank 34th)
Olympic rank/ population differential:	-28
Population per gold:	8,951,680 (rank 81st)
Population per medal:	2,632,847 (rank 104th)

Summer:	5 gold, 4 silver, 8 bronze (total 17)
Winter:	*no medals (best finish: 40th)*
Total:	5 gold, 4 silver, 8 bronze (total 17)
Best sports:	Athletics (4 golds, 0.38%, 32nd)
	Boxing (1 gold, 0.38%, 38th)
	Judo (1 silver, 1 bronze, 37th=)

Algeria secured their independence from France in 1962, and entered the Summer Olympics at the first opportunity, two years later. Since then, they have only missed one Games, joining the large-scale African boycott of 1976.

Most of their Olympic success has come in Athletics and Boxing. Their first two Olympic medals came in Los Angeles in 1984 – bronzes in Boxing for Mustapha Moussa and Mohamed Zaoui. After a fruitless trip to Seoul in 1988, Algeria won another two medals in 1992. One was a bronze in Boxing for Hocine Soltani, but the other was perhaps the most celebrated of all Algeria's 17 Olympic medals. Hassiba Boulmerka arrived in Barcelona as the world champion in the women's 1500 metres, and she would add the Olympic title too, despite having to contend with death threats from Islamist fundamentalists who disapproved of her legs not being sufficiently covered whilst running. The fact that, as a Muslim woman, she was able to win Olympic gold was a big global statement.

In 1996, Noureddine Morceli won his own 1500m Olympic title. With Hocine Soltani's gold in Boxing, it marked Atlanta as being the only Games in which Algeria have won more than one gold (they ranked 34th equal in the medal table). They also claimed another Boxing bronze. In Sydney in 2000, Algeria won their record total medal haul of five. For the third Games in a row, they won a 1500m gold – this time Nouria Merah-Benida in the women's event. They added a silver in the men's 5000 metres, and bronzes in the men's 800 metres and high jump, and yet another Boxing bronze as well.

Since then, Algerian performance has slipped, and they have won only five more medals in the five Games since. They included a silver and bronze in Judo (both in 2008), as well as three more Athletics medals. All three have been won by Taoufik Makhloufi – a gold in the men's 1500 metres in 2012, and silvers in both the 800 and 1500 metres in 2016. However, the 2012 gold was achieved amidst much controversy. Having been entered in the 800 metres too, he wanted to withdraw but failed to do so in time. He was forced to run the 800 against his wishes, jogged for a bit then dropped out. He was thrown out of the Olympics for "lack of effort", but then produced an apparently independent medical certificate showing that his performance had been hampered by a medical ailment. He was then reinstated, his "ailment" resolved itself remarkably quickly, and just a day after dropping out of the 800 metres, he won the 1500. Controversy notwithstanding, he is the only Algerian to have won three Olympic medals. The only other one to have won two is Hocine Soltani, who died in mysterious circumstances near Marseille in 2002.

Besides the three sports in which they have medalled, Algeria have also achieved top-eight finishes in Weightlifting, Wrestling, Football (a quarter-final defeat in 1980) and Swimming – two top-eight finishes, both achieved in 2004 by freestyle swimmer Salim Iles, who came 8th in the 50 metres and 7th equal in the 100 metres.

In the Winter Olympics, Algeria entered Alpine Skiing in 1992 and 2006, and Nordic Skiing in 2006 and 2010. Their best finish is 40th (Alpine Skiing, 2006).

TUNISIA **Olympic Rank 63rd**

Population: 11,976,182 (rank 81st)
Olympic rank/ population differential: +18
Population per gold: 2,395,236 (rank 63rd)
Population per medal: 798,412 (rank 75th)

Summer: 5 gold, 3 silver, 7 bronze (total 15)
Winter: *never participated*
Total: 5 gold, 3 silver, 7 bronze (total 15)

Best sports: Swimming (3 golds, 0.50%, 18th=)
Athletics (2 golds, 0.19%, 45th)
Taekwondo (1 silver, 1 bronze, 25th=)

Tunisia achieved independence from France in March 1956. The Olympics that year came too soon for them to compete, but they made their debut in Rome in 1960, and have competed in every Summer Games since, other than when they participated in the widespread boycott of 1980. They have never yet entered the Winter Games.

They did not manage any top-eight finishes in 1960, but won their first two medals in 1964. Their first medallist was Mohamed Gammoudi. A military man by occupation, he was relatively unknown when he took part in the men's 10000 metres. The favourite was Ron Clarke of Australia, but Gammoudi held Clarke off in the closing stages, only for the even more unknown Billy Mills of the USA to overtake them both just before the finish. Having taken that silver, Gammoudi then easily qualified for the final of the 5000 metres, but pulled out of the final for reasons unknown.

Gammoudi then caused another shock four years later, beating Kenyan Kip Keino to take gold in the 5000 metres – Tunisia's first ever gold medal. He also took the 10000 metres bronze that year, and went on to win the silver in the 5000 metres in 1972. His final Olympic tally of a gold, two silvers and a bronze meant that he had claimed four of Tunisia's first five Olympic medals. The only other medallist in that time was Habib Galhia (bronze in men's light-welterweight Boxing in 1964), and it would take until 1996 before anybody else won a medal for Tunisia. Gammoudi is still the only Tunisian to win four.

The only other Tunisian to win more than one Olympic medal is Oussama Mellouli. He had been to the Olympics in 2000 and 2004 without winning a medal. He was then given a ban in 2007 for failing a drugs test – he had seemingly taken a pill to treat ADHD in order to help him complete an academic assignment. Luckily, his ban expired shortly before the qualification period for the 2008 Games ended – he duly qualified, and took a surprise gold in the men's 1500m freestyle. He became the first male swimmer from Africa ever to win an individual Olympic gold. In 2012, he took a bronze in the same event, but this time took gold in the 10km open water event. It made him the only Tunisian to win two golds.

Tunisia have won two other Olympic golds. Habiba Ghribi originally came second in the 2012 women's 3000m steeplechase, but was upgraded to gold in 2016 following the disqualification of the Russian winner for doping offences. She was Tunisia's first female medallist, and still its only female gold medallist. In the 2021 men's 400m freestyle Swimming, there was a sensation. Ahmed Hafnaoui sneaked into the final as the eighth-fastest qualifier, and was accordingly placed in lane eight. But he took the lead in the last 50 metres and took the win.

Athletics and Swimming, then, have accounted for nine of Tunisia's 15 medals, including all five of their golds. There has only been one silver in another sport. In the men's flyweight Taekwondo in 2021, Mohamed Khalil Jendoubi beat the tournament favourite (from South Korea) in the semi-finals, but was beaten by his Italian opponent in the final. There were also two bronzes in men's light-welterweight Boxing (1964 and 1996), one in men's welterweight Taekwondo (2016), one in women's foil Fencing (2016) and one in women's freestyle welterweight Wrestling (2016). There have also been numerous top-eight finishes in Judo and Weightlifting, as well as an 8th-place finish in men's Handball in 2012.

The 2012 Games are the only ones in which Tunisia won two golds. They won three medals in all that year, a record they equalled in 2016 (with three bronzes). Their highest medal table position is 28th (in 1968, with one gold and one bronze). The last time they failed to win a medal was 2004; the last time they failed to finish in the top eight of any event was 1992.

LIBYA   Olympic Rank 166th

Population: 7,252,573 (rank 106th)
Olympic rank/ population differential: -60

Summer: *no medals (best finish: 8th)*
Winter: *never participated*

Best sports: Taekwondo
                   Volleyball
                   Cycling

Libya first entered the Olympics in 1964, though their only entrant – a male marathon runner – failed to start the race. They returned in 1968, again with one athlete, who this time did manage to compete. They did not take part in 1972, 1976 or 1984, but did compete in 1980, and at all Summer Games since 1988. They have never entered the Winter Olympics. They have competed in ten sports in all.

By far the biggest delegation they have sent to an Olympics was in 1980. Their best finish in Athletics – 19th in the men's 4x400m relay, came in that year, as did their best finish in Swimming – 19th in the women's 400m freestyle. Also in that year, they replaced the boycotting Tunisia team in the men's Volleyball, and lost all of their matches to finish 10th out of 10 – still their second-best finish in any Olympic event. Their best was also achieved entirely by default. In the men's flyweight Taekwondo in 2004, Ezedin Belgasem was outclassed in the first round, but due to his opponent reaching the final, he moved into the repechage, with a guaranteed top-eight finish. He duly withdrew and finished 8th. He became a civilian casualty of the Libyan Civil War in 2011.

Libya's best in Cycling is 14th, and in Weightlifting 15th. They have also entered Judo, Archery, Table Tennis and Rowing.

CHAPTER SEVENTEEN Western Africa, west coast (Senegal, Sierra Leone, Liberia, Guinea-Bissau, Mauritania, Gambia, Guinea, Cape Verde)

SENEGAL	**Olympic Rank 121st**
Population:	18,384,660 (rank 67th)
Olympic rank/ population differential:	-54
Population per gold:	n/a
Population per medal:	18,384,660 (rank 130th)
Summer:	0 gold, 1 silver, 0 bronze (total 1)
Winter:	*no medals (best finish: 45th)*
Total:	0 gold, 1 silver, 0 bronze (total 1)
Best sports:	Athletics (1 silver, 78th=)
	Wrestling
	Football

Sierra Leone have entered all Summer Olympics since 1964. That first year, they entered only Athletics; they have returned to Athletics every time since, and the sport has been responsible for seven of Senegal's 18 top-eight finishes, including all three of their top four finishes. The first of these was achieved by Amadou Gakou, who finished fourth in the 1968 men's 400 metres (behind three Americans). Twenty years later, in 1988, Amadou Dia Ba, who had finished 5th in the men's 400m hurdles in 1984, claimed silver in the same event, behind Andre Phillips of the US, and pushing the legendary American Ed Moses down into bronze. It is still Senegal's only Olympic medal. Senegal then finished 4th in the men's 4x400m relay in 1996.

Senegal's other top-eight finishes have come in Wrestling (five, all in freestyle events, including two by women), Judo (five, but none since 1984) and Football (the men's event in 2012). Both Wrestling and Judo have been part of Senegal's Olympic programme in all Games since 1972. They have been entering Swimming since 1988, and have a best finish of 29th (and last) in the women's 800m freestyle in 2004. Their best finish that wasn't last was equal 37th. They have entered eight other Summer sports, but with little success. Three Senegalese men – all Alpine skiers – have taken part in the Winter Olympics, across the 1984, 1992, 1994, 2006 and 2010 Games. Their best finish so far went to Lamine Gueye (45th in the 1992 downhill event).

SIERRA LEONE	**Olympic Rank 146th**
Population:	8,908,040 (rank 100th)
Olympic rank/ population differential:	-46
Summer:	*no medals (best finish: 5th)*
Winter:	*never participated*
Best sports:	Athletics
	Boxing
	Weightlifting

Sierra Leone made their Olympic debut in 1968, before returning in 1980, and for all Summer Games since then. They have never entered the Winter Olympics. They have entered Athletics in all the Games in which they have taken part, and their best performance was Eunice Barber's 5th place in the 1996 women's heptathlon. Soon after, she switched allegiance to France (where she had been based for many years); she won five world championship medals for her new country, including two golds. Since then, Sierra Leone have not finished higher than 19th in any Athletics event. In all their Boxing entries, Sierra Leone have only ever won two matches, both of them by Israel Cole on his way to the 1984 light-middleweight quarter-finals; he finished 8th.

In Swimming, Sierra Leone have competed in only three Games, each time sticking to the 50m freestyle – their best finish is 63rd (men's event in 1996). They have entered Weightlifting twice (with a best finish of 16th) and Cycling once (but did not finish). They also (sort of) entered Judo once – Frederick Harris went to Tokyo in 2021, and carried the flag, but was then disqualified for being overweight.

LIBERIA   Olympic Rank 149th

Population:	5,506,280 (rank 120th)
Olympic rank/ population differential:	-29
Summer:	*no medals (best finish: 5th)*
Winter:	*never participated*
Best sports:	Athletics
	Boxing
	(Judo)

Liberia, Africa's oldest republic, has been competing in the Summer Olympics (although never the Winter Olympics) since 1956. They have missed four editions in that time – 1968, 1976, 1980 and 1992. And yet, they have only ever competed in two sports. It seems remarkable that they are one of the only countries in the world never even to have entered Swimming. One of those two sports is Boxing – they entered four boxers in 1988, who won just one match between them – but have never entered in any other year.

Liberia have entered Athletics in all the Games in which they have participated. It took until 2021 for them to manage a top-16 finish, and then they managed two. First Ebony Morrison reached the semi-finals of the women's 100m hurdles, finishing 12th overall. Then, Joseph Fahnbulleh achieved his country's best ever Olympic finish, coming 5th in the final of the men's 200 metres. Both Morrison and Fahnbulleh learnt their trade in the United States – in fact, Fahnbulleh was born there to Liberian parents. He had never been to Liberia, and indeed he had never left the US at all until going to Tokyo for the Games.

Liberia did also enter Judo in London 2012, but embarrassingly their representative – Levi Saryee – had apparently got accreditation under false pretences, and knew nothing about Judo. He confessed just before the match, and forfeited.

GUINEA-BISSAU   Olympic Rank 158th

Population:	2,078,820 (rank 149th)
Olympic rank/ population differential:	-9
Summer:	*no medals (best finish: 7th)*
Winter:	*never participated*
Best sports:	Wrestling
	Judo
	Athletics

Despite independence being recognised in the mid-1970s, Guinea-Bissau took until 1996 to enter the Olympic Games. They have entered every Summer Games since then, but have never yet entered the Winter Games. Their participation in each of those Games, though, has been limited, and has only taken in three sports.

The sport to have given them the greatest success is Wrestling. Their greatest Olympian is freestyle middleweight Augusto Midana – he debuted in 2008 and is now a four-time Olympian. He is a six-time African champion, and is the only wrestler from Guinea-Bissau ever to win a match at the Olympics – winning in the first round against a Venezuelan opponent in 2012. This was enough to rank him 7th in the final classification. His 11th-place finish in 2021 is his nation's second-best Olympic Wrestling ranking.

They have entered Athletics every time, but never more than two events in any year. They have stuck to flat track events between 100 and 1500 metres, with the exception of one female shot putter in 2016. They have never progressed past round one in any of their 13 events so far.

Guinea-Bissau's third sport is Judo, in which they have competed in 2016 and 2021. In the first of those, Taciana Lima, in the women's extra-lightweight, was given a bye in the first round, and lost in the second. But by taking her opponent to a golden score period, she ended up 9th.

MAURITANIA   **Olympic Rank 175th**
Population: 4,244,878 (rank 129th)
Olympic rank/ population differential: -46

Summer: *no medals (best finish: 10th)*
Winter: *never participated*

Best sports: Wrestling
                              Athletics

Mauritania remains, to the western world at least, one of the most impenetrable nations on the planet, and unsurprisingly that is reflected in its Olympic record. It has entered the Summer Games ever since 1984, but never entered the Winter Games, and has only competed in two different sports in that time.

On their debut, they sent two competitors to Los Angeles, both in men's freestyle Wrestling, and both failed to win a match. Mamadou Diallo was 13th best out of 16 in the light-heavyweight, and Oumar Samba Sy withdrew prematurely from the heavyweight event, to finish 11th out of 11. They had a further five Wrestling entries in 1988, of which two did win matches. Oumar Samba Sy won one match in the men's Greco-Roman heavyweight, and Babacar Sar won two matches in the freestyle equivalent. Both finished their competitions in 10th place (out of 18 and 22 respectively). Despite this modest success, though, the nation have never entered Wrestling since.

Since then, they have stuck solely to Athletics. First competing in 1988, they have entered all eight of the flat running distances in their time, but have never progressed past the first round of any of them. Up to 1996, they only had men entering, but in all Games since 2000, their team has consisted of one man and one woman.

GAMBIA   **Olympic Rank 181st**
Population: 1,468,569 (rank 155th)
Olympic rank/ population differential: -26

Summer: *no medals (best finish: 11th)*
Winter: *never participated*

Best sports: Athletics
                              Wrestling
                              Judo

The Gambia have entered every Summer Olympics since their debut in 1984, but have never entered the Winter Games. They have entered Athletics every time (all in track events up to 1500 metres, with the single exception of a 1996 long jump entry). They have also entered Wrestling (1988), Boxing (2008), and Swimming and Judo (both in 2016 and 2021).

Their two Swimming entries have both been in the men's 50m freestyle – their best finish so far is 66th. In Judo, their record is played two, lost two; in Boxing, it is played one, lost one. Two of their three wrestlers in 1988 failed to win a match, but a single win for Adama Damballey in the men's freestyle welterweight saw him finish 13th.

But it is Athletics that has produced most of their higher finishes. The Gambia finished last in the women's 4x100m relay, but only 11 countries entered – therefore, this is their highest Olympic finish. By far the most successful Gambian individual, though, has been Gina Bass, who in 2021 reached the semi-finals of both the women's 100 metres (finishing 15th) and 200 metres (finishing 14th). These three Athletics events, plus Damballey in the Wrestling, make up the Gambia's four top-16 finishes.

GUINEA   Olympic Rank 189th

Population: 13,607,249 (rank 75th)
Olympic rank/ population differential: -114

Summer: *no medals (best finish: 12th)*
Winter: *never participated*

Best sports: Wrestling
                            Football
                            Judo

Guinea made their Olympic debut in 1968, when the only event they entered was the men's Football. Although they finished bottom of their group, they did win a match – 3-2 over Colombia – ensuring they finished 13th out of 16. They have never entered Football since, and in fact didn't enter the Olympics at all for 12 years thereafter, but have entered every Summer Games since 1980 (they have never entered the Winter Games as yet). They have entered six sports in that time – Athletics, Swimming, Wrestling, Judo, Boxing and Taekwondo – but have only ever bettered that 13th-placed finish once – and that was not until 2021.

Since 1968, they have achieved three top-16 finishes. In Taekwondo, they have entered only once (2008) and finished 16th out of 16. In Judo, they once (1980) finished 15th out of 29. But the best was Fatoumata Yarie Camara, an African Championship bronze medallist, who finished 12th out of 16 in the women's lightweight freestyle Wrestling in Tokyo (she lost both fights she took part in, but got enough points to finish 12th). This was in fact Guinea's first Olympic Wrestling appearance since a couple of entrants took part in 1988.

As for their other sports, their best finish in Boxing is 18th (in 1980) and in Swimming 46th (women's 200m breaststroke in 2012). In Athletics, only once has an athlete ever progressed beyond the first round. This was Joseph Loua in the 200m in 1996, who finished 34th in the end.

CAPE VERDE   Olympic Rank 195th

Population: 603,901 (rank 169th)
Olympic rank/ population differential: -26

Summer: *no medals (best finish: 14th)*
Winter: *never participated*

Best sports: Judo
                            Boxing
                            Athletics

The Cape Verde islands were uninhabited prior to the arrival of Portuguese explorers in the 15th century. They established a community there, which eventually gained independence from Portugal in 1975. The country first entered the Olympics in 1996 – they have entered every Summer Games since, but have yet to venture into the Winter equivalent. In 1996 and 2000, they stuck to Athletics (which they have entered in every Games since), but have now also branched into Boxing (2004, 2016, 2021), Judo (2012, 2021), Taekwondo (2016), Swimming (2021) and, perhaps surprisingly, Rhythmic Gymnastics (2004, 2008, 2016, 2021).

Their best finish in any event is 14th, achieved by Adysangela Moniz in women's heavyweight Judo in 2012. Unfortunate to be drawn against eventual champion Idalys Ortiz of Cuba in the first round, she lasted two minutes before losing, which was longer than two of her fellow last-16 losers. Cape Verde also finished 16th on their other Judo appearance (2021). Two of their three boxers have finished 15th in their events. Their one entrant in Taekwondo finished 16th out of 16. More impressively, Jordin Andrade (USA born and raised) finished 16th for Cape Verde in the men's 400m hurdles in 2016. Their best finish in rhythmic Gymnastics is 24th, and their best in Swimming is 40th.

CHAPTER EIGHTEEN - Western Africa, central & south (Nigeria, Ivory Coast, Ghana, Niger, Burkina Faso, Togo, Mali, Benin)

NIGERIA   **Olympic Rank 65th**
Population: 230,842,743 (rank 6th)
Olympic rank/ population differential: -59
Population per gold: 76,947,581 (rank 98th)
Population per medal: 8,549,731 (rank 122nd)

Summer: 3 gold, 11 silver, 13 bronze (total 27)
Winter: *no medals (best finish: 19th)*
Total: 3 gold, 11 silver, 13 bronze (total 27)

Best sports: Football (1 gold, 2.86%, 16th)
                                             Athletics (2 golds, 0.19%, 41st)
                                             Boxing (3 silvers, 3 bronzes, 42nd)

Nigeria made their Olympic debut in 1952. They have entered every Summer Games since, with the exception of the 1976 African boycott, despite the first three of those being contested as a British colony. The first two Games saw them enter only Athletics; they added Boxing in 1960 and Football in 1968, before branching out into other sports in the 1980s.

The first Olympic medal came Nigeria's way in 1964, a bronze in Boxing for Nojim Maiyegun. Another Boxing bronze followed in 1972, before they won two medals in a Games for the first time in 1984. This time, it was a silver in Boxing, and a first Athletics medal – a bronze in the men's 4x400m relay. In 1988, they failed to win any medals, but since then they have won at least one medal in every Summer Games except 2012.

In 1992, they won two more Boxing silvers, and medals in both 4x100m relays (silver for the men, bronze for the women). Nigeria's best Olympics arrived in Atlanta in 1996. Two of their three golds came in that year, and they also got their highest number of overall medals too, with six (2 gold, 1 silver, 3 bronze). It put them 32nd in the medal table (they had finished equal 30th in 1984 with their one silver and one bronze). Their first Olympic gold was surprisingly won by Chioma Ajunwa in the women's long jump; she had only recently returned from a four-year suspension for a doping offence (and, before that, had represented Nigeria in the 1991 Women's World Cup in Football).

Meanwhile, the men's Football team were going well. They beat Mexico 2-0 in the quarter-finals, and beat Brazil in a legendary semi-final (3-1 down with 15 minutes left, they got a last-minute equaliser from Nwankwo Kanu, who then scored a golden goal winner in extra-time). In the final against Argentina, they twice came from a goal down, before Emmanuel Amunike scored an 89th-minute winner.

Having won those two golds in 1996, only one more has followed since, and even then only by default. The Nigerian men's 4x400m relay team did well to finish 2nd behind the all-conquering Americans in 2000, but were promoted to gold eight years later when it emerged that the American Antonio Pettigrew had used drugs. In all, Nigeria won 20 medals in five Games during their glory years of 1992 to 2008, but have won only three medals in the three Games since. Of their 27 medals overall, 14 have come in Athletics (including eight in relays, and three for three different women in the long jump). Six have come in Boxing, and three in men's Football (1996 gold, 2008 silver, 2016 bronze). Weightlifting (twice), Taekwondo and Wrestling make up the other four.

Of their 86 top-eight finishes, 48 have been in Athletics, all in track events up to 400 metres, long jump or triple jump. There have been 18 in Boxing, 8 in Weightlifting and 6 in Football (3 each for men and women). Finally, there have been 3 in freestyle Wrestling, and one each in women's Handball (1992), men's Taekwondo (2008) and men's singles Table Tennis (2016). They have entered Olympic Swimming since 1992, all in 50 and 100-metre races, but have never finished better than 39th.

Nigeria's first entry into Winter Olympics came in 2018, when they came last in both events they entered – 19th in the two-woman Bobsleigh competition, and 20th in the women's Skeleton. In 2022, they entered another two events – both in Nordic Skiing, coming 73rd out of 88 in one and failing to finish in the other.

IVORY COAST — Olympic Rank 90th

Population:	29,344,847 (rank 52nd)
Olympic rank/ population differential:	-38
Population per gold:	29,344,847 (rank 94th)
Population per medal:	7,336,212 (rank 117th)

Summer: 1 gold, 1 silver, 2 bronze (total 4)
Winter: *never participated*
Total: 1 gold, 1 silver, 2 bronze (total 4)

Best sports: Taekwondo (1 gold, 2.08%, 19th=)
Athletics (1 silver, 78th=)
Boxing

The Ivory Coast gained independence from France in 1960. The Summer Games of that year came too soon for them (they started just a couple of weeks later), but they did send a team for the first time at the 1964 Games, and they have returned at every Summer Games since, with the exception of the 1980 boycott. They have, however, never yet competed at the Winter Games.

In 1964, they made an impact straight away when Gaoussou Kone finished equal 6th in the men's 100 metres final. This would remain the nation's only top-eight finish for 20 years. Prior to the 1980 boycott, they had only entered Athletics, Boxing and Canoeing, but they began entering more sports thereafter.

In 1984, they won their first medal, when the men's 400 metres silver medal went to Gabriel Tiacoh, who tragically died in 1992, aged 29, from TB meningitis. This would remain Ivory Coast's only Olympic medal for 32 years. Then, in Rio in 2016, they won two more, including what is so far their only ever gold. Both 2016 medals came in Taekwondo. Having waited so long for another medal, two came on the same day. Ruth Gbagbi took bronze in the women's welterweight, before Cheick Sallah Cisse took gold in the men's welterweight around an hour later. Cisse's gold was won in hugely dramatic circumstances, scoring a 3-point head-shot with 0.1 seconds left to beat Britain's Lutalo Muhammad 8-6 in the final. The Ivory Coast's fourth Olympic medal was also a second for Gbagbi – another bronze in Tokyo in 2021.

As well as providing the Ivory Coast with three of their four medals, Taekwondo has also provided 9 of their 23 top-eight finishes. Athletics, however, has provided 10. These include five appearances in 100-metre finals; Kone as mentioned in 1964, plus Ben Youssef Meite finishing 6th in 2016, and three on the women's side (Murielle Ahoure finished 7th in 2012, and Marie-Josee Ta Lou finished 4th in both 2016 and 2021). There has been real agony for Ta Lou, who missed a medal in 2016 by 7/1000ths of a second; she also came 4th in the 200 metres that year, and 5th in the 200 metres in 2021, but has yet to win that elusive medal. Ahoure also finished 6th in the 200 metres in 2012. As well as Tiacoh's medal, the Ivory Coast also finished 8th in the men's sprint relay in 1992, so all 10 of their top-eight finishes have been in track distances of 400 metres and lower.

Their other four top-eight finishes comprise quarter-final appearances in men's Boxing in 1984, and men's Football in 2008 and 2021, as well as an appearance in women's Handball in 1988, when they lost heavily in all five of their matches to finish 8th.

The Ivory Coast have, over the years, also appeared in Canoeing, Judo, Tennis, Swimming, Wrestling, Archery, Fencing and Rowing. The best finish they have had in any of those is 11th (in Judo). In Swimming, the best they have managed is 25th, in the women's 400m freestyle in 2021.

GHANA   **Olympic Rank 112th**
Population: 33,846,114 (rank 44th)
Olympic rank/ population differential: -68
Population per gold: n/a
Population per medal: 6,769,223 (rank 116th)

Summer: 0 gold, 1 silver, 4 bronze (total 5)
Winter: *no medals (best finish: 30th)*
Total: 0 gold, 1 silver, 4 bronze (total 5)

Best sports: Boxing (1 silver, 3 bronzes, 50th=)
Football (1 bronze, 32nd=)
Athletics

When Ghana first entered the Olympics, in 1952, they were still known as the Gold Coast. They didn't enter in 1956, and achieved independence under their new name the following year. They returned to the Olympics in 1960, when Ike Quartey progressed through four ties to earn a silver medal in the men's light welterweight Boxing. More than sixty year later, it remains Ghana's best Olympic performance ever.

Since then, they have entered all Summer Olympics apart from 1976 and 1980. Three of their four bronzes have also come in Boxing – in 1964, 1972 and 2021. Their five medals have all come in different games; their only non-Boxing medal was another bronze – in the men's Football in 1992, when they beat Australia in the bronze medal play-off. They also reached the quarter-finals in Football in 1964 and 1996.

The only other sport in which they have managed top-eight finishes is Athletics. They have had nine in all; six in the sprint events, and three in the men's long jump. The only Ghanaian ever to finish fourth in an Olympic event was Joshua Owusu, in the 1972 long jump. Swimming is, by contrast, not Ghana's forte. They never entered it until 2016, and their best finish to date in a Swimming event is 42nd.

Only three Ghanaians have entered the Winter Olympics – they were in Alpine Skiing in 2010 and 2022 (they failed to finish in the latter), and in Skeleton in 2018, in which Akwasi Frimpong achieved their best Winter finish of 30th (out of 30).

NIGER   **Olympic Rank 116th**
Population: 25,396,840 (rank 56th)
Olympic rank/ population differential: -60
Population per gold: n/a
Population per medal: 12,698,420 (rank 127th)

Summer: 0 gold, 1 silver, 1 bronze (total 2)
Winter: *never participated*
Total: 0 gold, 1 silver, 1 bronze (total 2)

Best sports: Taekwondo (1 silver, 29th=)
Boxing (1 bronze, 61st=)
Athletics

Niger became an Olympic nation in 1964, when their only competitor was welterweight boxer Issaka Dabore, who reached the quarter-finals. Dabore entered again in 1968, before winning a bronze – Niger's first Olympic medal – in 1972. Niger boycotted the Games in 1976 and 1980, but have competed in every Olympics since. They have, though, only added one further medal in that time – a silver for Razak Alfaga in the 2016 heavyweight Taekwondo (he lost the final 6-2 to Azerbaijan's Radik Isayev). Their fourth and, to date, final top eight finish came in women's featherweight Taekwondo in 2021 – a quarter-final defeat.

Besides Boxing and Taekwondo, they have only once finished even in the top 16 of an event. This was achieved by the hyperandrogenic Aminatou Seyni, who recorded the 10th-fastest time in the semi-finals of the 2021 women's 200m. In Swimming, Niger's best finish is 41st, achieved in their Olympic debut in the sport in 2000 (this was the slowest time of all those who finished). In fact, prior to 2000, they had never competed in any sports besides Boxing and Athletics. The nation have yet to make their Winter Olympic debut.

BURKINA FASO   **Olympic Rank 137th**
Population: 22,489,126 (rank 60th)
Olympic rank/ population differential: -77
Population per gold: n/a
Population per medal: 22,489,126 (rank 133rd)

Summer: 0 gold, 0 silver, 1 bronze (total 1)
Winter: *never participated*
Total: 0 gold, 0 silver, 1 bronze (total 1)

Best sports: Athletics (1 bronze, 88th=)
                                     Taekwondo
                                     Boxing

In 1960, Upper Volta gained independence from France. It took 12 years for them to send anybody to the Olympics – a single athlete who failed to advance from the first round of the 100 metres. They were due to compete in 1976, only to join the African boycott. By the time they turned up again, in 1988, they had changed their name to Burkina Faso. They have entered every Summer Games since then, although they have not competed in the Winter Games as yet. As well as Athletics (every time), Burkina Faso have competed in Judo (1992, and 2000 onwards), Boxing (1988, 1996 and 2000), Swimming (2004 onwards), Fencing (2008), and Taekwondo and Cycling (both in 2021).

Prior to 2021, Burkina Faso's best every Olympic finish was 10th, achieved in the women's 400 metres hurdles of 2008 by Aissata Soulama (who was fifth in her semi-final). But that was beaten twice in Tokyo. First, Faysal Sawadogo finished 8th in the men's welterweight Taekwondo by default (he lost in the first round, but qualified for the repechage due to his opponent reaching the final – he then lost in the first round of the repechage). But then triple jumper Hugues Fabrice Zango, who was born in Ouagadougou, and in 2019 won Burkina Faso's first ever medal in the World Athletics Championship (a bronze), emulated that feat in the Olympics. In contrast, their best finish in a Swimming event is 42nd.

TOGO   **Olympic Rank 138th**
Population: 8,703,961 (rank 101st)
Olympic rank/ population differential: -37
Population per gold: n/a
Population per medal: 8,703,961 (rank 123rd)

Summer: 0 gold, 0 silver, 1 bronze (total 1)
Winter: *no medals (best finish: 55th)*
Total: 0 gold, 0 silver, 1 bronze (total 1)

Best sports: Canoeing (1 bronze, 35th=)
                                     Boxing
                                     Athletics

Like Burkina Faso, Togo gained independence in 1960, and first entered the Olympics in 1972. Since then, they have only missed the boycotted Games of 1976 and 1980. They have competed in Athletics every time, with their best finish being 13th in the men's sprint relay of 1992. They have only entered Swimming since 2012, and have a best finish of 57th, having never entered any event longer than 50 metres.

They've entered Judo in 2000, 2008 and 2012, finishing 14th in 2008. In Boxing, they entered in 1972, 1984 and 1988, finishing 12th in 1988. They've also entered Cycling (1972 & 1992), Tennis (2008), Table Tennis (both Komi-Mawussi Agbetoglo and Dodji Fanny lost in the first round, in 2012 and 2021 respectively) and Rowing (2016 & 2021). But their best success has come from their one Olympic canoeist. Benjamin Boukpeti was born and raised in France, but chose to represent Togo, his father's country, despite having only visited once (during childhood). In the men's K1 slalom, he finished 18th in 2004, won bronze in 2008, and finished 10th in 2012.

Two Togolese competitors have participated in the Winter Olympics. Italian-born Alessia Afi Dipol contested the women's slalom and giant slalom (Alpine Skiing) in 2014, finishing 55th in the latter, whilst Mathilde-Amivi Petitjean, born in Togo, competed in Nordic Skiing in 2014 and 2018, with a best finish of 59th.

MALI   Olympic Rank 145th

Population: 21,359,722 (rank 61st)
Olympic rank/ population differential: -84

Summer: *no medals (best finish: 5th)*
Winter: *never participated*

Best sports: Football
Taekwondo
Judo

Mali made their Olympic debut in 1964, four years after independence. Since then, they have missed only the 1976 Summer Games, though have never competed in the Winter Games. They have competed in just seven sports so far. One of those is Football, for which they have qualified only once (2004, men's event), but finished 5th – their best Olympic finish ever. They finished top of their group with two draws and one win (2-0 against hosts Greece), and took Italy to extra-time in their quarter-final.

Their other two top-eight finishes were both achieved by Daba Modibo Keita in men's heavyweight Taekwondo. He finished 8th in 2008 after winning through round one; then, in 2012, he reached the bronze medal play-off but was forced to withdraw due to injury and finished 6th.

Prior to 2000, Mali had only ever competed in Athletics, Boxing and Judo. Their best three Athletics finishes have all been achieved by Namakoro Niare in the men's discus (15th twice, and 13th in 1972). Despite entering Judo in most Games since 1972, they have never won a match. In Boxing, they have reached the last 16 once (in 1988). In Swimming, their best finish is 40th (women's 100m breaststroke in 2000, the first year they entered Swimming). Finally, they competed in women's Basketball in 2008, but lost all five group matches.

BENIN   Olympic Rank 190th

Population: 14,219,908 (rank 74th)
Olympic rank/ population differential: -116

Summer: *no medals (best finish: 13th)*
Winter: *never participated*

Best sports: Athletics
Taekwondo
Judo

Benin, who have never competed in the Winter Games, first entered the Summer Games in 1972, boycotted in 1976, and have entered every time after that. Their best Olympic finish is 13th, which they have achieved three times, in three different sports. Noelie Yarigo was 13th fastest in the semi-finals of the women's 800 metres in 2016. The country are, in fact, improving in Athletics – heptathlete Odile Ahouanwanou finished 15th in 2021.

In Taekwondo, they have only entered twice, losing in the first round both times – but Stanislas Ogoudjobi finished 13th out of 14 in the men's Featherweight in 2000. Judoka Celtus Dossou Yovo finished 13th in men's middleweight in 2016 having got through one round – the only time Benin have ever got through a Judo round in four attempts.

Benin's best Swimming performance is 50th (women's 100m freestyle in 2004). Benin have also competed in Boxing in four different Games, reaching the last 16 once, and competed once each in Cycling (in which both of the road race entrants failed to finish), Tennis (beaten 6-1 6-1 in the first round by French Open champion Gustavo Kuerten of Brazil), Fencing (lost 15-9 in the first round) and Rowing (finished 27th out of 31).

CHAPTER NINETEEN - Middle Africa (Cameroon, Gabon, Congo, Angola, Central African Republic, Chad, Congo DR, Sao Tome & Principe, Equatorial Guinea)

CAMEROON	**Olympic Rank 73rd**
Population:	30,135,732 (rank 51st)
Olympic rank/ population differential:	-22
Population per gold:	10,045,244 (rank 87th)
Population per medal:	5,022,622 (rank 110th)
Summer:	3 gold, 1 silver, 2 bronze (total 6)
Winter:	*no medals (best finish: 65th)*
Total:	3 gold, 1 silver, 2 bronze (total 6)
Best sports:	Football (1 gold, 2.86%, 22nd)
	Athletics (2 golds, 0.19%, 49th)
	Boxing (1 silver, 1 bronze, 53rd)

Cameroon first entered the Olympics in 1964. They have entered all Summer Games since (they joined the African boycott in 1976, but not before they had competed in one event). They did not threaten the medals on their debut, but had welterweight boxer Joseph Bessala to thank for their first Olympic medal four years later.

The six Olympic medals they have won have all come in different Games. All three of their golds have been memorable. Prior to 2000, the only two medals they had won had both come in Boxing, neither of them gold. But their men's football team caused a sensation in Sydney. Having struggled in the group stage, they faced hot favourites Brazil in the quarter-finals and, despite being down to nine men won the game with an extra-time golden goal. They went on to beat Chile in the semi-finals, and Spain on penalties in the final.

Four years later, Francoise Mbango Etone took gold in the women's triple jump. It was perhaps particularly surprising, as no other Cameroonian, before or since, has finished higher than 12th in any Athletics event. But more impressively, she retained her title four years later in Beijing, despite having barely competed in the interim due to giving birth and raising her child.

Besides Football, Athletics and Boxing, Cameroon's other medal came in Weightlifting – Madias Nzesso claiming bronze in the women's heavyweight in 2012. They have also managed top eight finishes in Judo (twice) and Wrestling (three times). Those sports aside, perhaps their most prominent achievement was finishing 11th in women's Volleyball in 2016.

In 2002, Isaac Menyoli became Cameroon's first, and so far only, Winter Olympian. An architect by day, Menyoli competed in Nordic Skiing in order to draw attention to the problem of AIDS in his own country. He finished 80th out of 83 in the 10km pursuit (the other three were disqualified), but went faster than four other finishers in the sprint event to finish 65th.

GABON   **Olympic Rank 129th**
Population: 2,397,368 (rank 145th)
Olympic rank/ population differential: +16
Population per gold: n/a
Population per medal: 2,397,368 (rank 102nd)

Summer: 0 gold, 1 silver, 0 bronze (total 1)
Winter: *never participated*
Total: 0 gold, 1 silver, 0 bronze (total 1)

Best sports: Taekwondo (1 silver, 19th=)
                                            Judo
                                            Boxing

Gabon entered the Olympic stage with a single boxer in 1972. They then returned in 1984, and have entered the Summer Games ever since. They have not, however, competed in the Winter Games as yet. They entered Athletics for the first time in 1984, Judo in 1992, Taekwondo in 2008, Football in 2012, and Swimming in 2016. They have only ever finished in the top eight of an event once, but on that occasion Anthony Obame beat his Turkish opponent in the semi-finals to guarantee Gabon's first Olympic medal, and led Carlo Molfetta in the final until the Italian levelled the score late, and won on the judges' decision of superiority.

Boxing, Judo and Football have both produced top-16 finishes over the years, as has Athletics (albeit only once – Odette Mistoul coming 13th in the women's shot put in 1984). In Swimming, Gabonese competitors have only ever entered the 50 metres freestyle, and their best finish is 68th.

CONGO   **Olympic Rank 142nd**
Population: 5,677,493 (rank 116th)
Olympic rank/ population differential: -26

Summer: *no medals (best finish: 4th)*
Winter: *never participated*

Best sports: Athletics
                                            Handball
                                            Boxing

Having gained independence from France in 1960, Congo have entered the Summer Games of 1964 and 1972, and have subsequently entered every Games since 1980. Like many of their sub-Saharan counterparts, though, they have never entered the Winter Games. Having stuck to Athletics at their first two appearances, they have since branched out into Handball and Boxing (1980), Judo (1984), Swimming (1992), Fencing (2004) and Table Tennis (2008).

Congo are one of six countries to have finished fourth in an Olympic event but never won a medal. In the 2016 men's shot put final, Franck Elemba's lifetime best distance of 21.20m put him in a medal position until the fifth of six rounds, when overtaken by Tom Walsh of New Zealand. In 1980, Congo were one of the six countries in the women's Handball competition (they were knocked out of qualifying by South Korea, only to be reinstated when the Koreans boycotted the Games). They lost all five matches at the Olympics heavily, finished sixth, and have never competed in Olympic Handball again. These are their only two top-eight finishes.

Other than Elemba, Congo's best Athletics finish is 12th, in the men's sprint relay in 1980. Their best Swimming finish is 43rd.

ANGOLA Olympic Rank 157th

Population: 35,981,281 (rank 41st)
Olympic rank/ population differential: -116

Summer: *no medals (best finish: 7th)*
Winter: *never participated*

Best sports: Handball
Judo
Basketball

Angola are ranked as the fourth most populous country in the world never to have won an Olympic medal. They first entered the Olympics in 1980, missed 1984, but have been ever-presents since 1988. On their debut, they entered numerous competitors in Athletics, Boxing and Swimming. They added Judo in 1988, Basketball and Sailing in 1992, Handball and Shooting in 1996, Beach Volleyball and Canoeing in 2008, and Rowing in 2016. They have yet to enter the Winter Olympics.

Their best achievements have all come in Handball. Although they have never entered the men's event, they have been ever presents in the women's event since 1996. That year, they lost all three group games, but beat the United States 24-23 in the 7th-place play-off to secure what is still the nation's best ever Olympic finish. Their only other top-eight finish came in the same event 20 years later, when group wins over Romania and Montenegro helped them to 8th place. They have also managed 9th twice and 10th twice in the same event.

Outside of women's Handball, their best achievement is a 9th-place finish in men's lightweight Judo in 1988. Their men's Basketball team competed in every Games from 1992 to 2012, achieving a best finish of 10th in 1992. In Swimming, they finished 11th out of 13 in the 1980 men's 4x100m medley relay (the other two teams were disqualified). Their next best Swimming finish is 23rd. They have never progressed from the first round of heats in any Athletics event, though they did finish 17th in the men's marathon in 2000.

CENTRAL AFRICAN REPUBLIC Olympic Rank 165th

Population: 5,552,228 (rank 119th)
Olympic rank/ population differential: -46

Summer: *no medals (best finish: 8th)*
Winter: *never participated*

Best sports: Taekwondo
Basketball
Boxing

Gabriel M'Boa was the Central African Republic's Olympic trailblazer, finishing 35th out of 39 in the men's 5000m at the 1968 Mexico City Games. It would be 16 years before they entered another Olympic event – entering Athletics (again) and Boxing. They have since made debuts in Basketball (1988), Judo and Cycling (1992), Archery (2000), Taekwondo (2004), and Wrestling and Swimming (2012). They have, unsurprisingly for a republic in the centre of Africa, never entered the Winter Olympics.

They have achieved top-16 finishes on six occasions. Four of these were in Taekwondo. Three of those came 16th out of 16. The other, Patrick Boui in the men's featherweight in 2012, achieved the nation's best ever finish of 8th, albeit by default. The Taekwondo format allows for anybody losing to one of the eventual finalists to enter a repechage, which automatically guarantees them a top-eight finish, no matter how outclassed they may be. So Boui lost in the first round, and lost again in the first round of repechage, and finished eighth.

The other two top-16 finishes were achieved by boxer Judith Mbougnade, who finished 12th out of 12 in the 2016 women's flyweight event, and the 1988 men's Basketball team, who actually merited their position – wins over South Korea and Egypt saw them finish 10th out of 12.

In Swimming, they have restricted their entries so far to the 50m freestyle (men's and women's) – their best finish is 55th. In Athletics, they have never progressed past the first round of heats, though the best finish by a athlete from the country is 24th, achieved in the 1992 men's discus.

CHAD   Olympic Rank 174th

Population: 18,523,165 (rank 66th)
Olympic rank/ population differential: -108

Summer: *no medals (best finish: 9th)*
Winter: *never participated*

Best sports: Athletics
Judo
Boxing

The nation of Chad achieved independence in 1960, and entered the Olympics for the first time four years later. They have entered all Summer Games since, with the exception of boycotts in 1976 and 1980, but have never competed in the Winter Games. Most unusually for a nation that has competed for almost sixty years, they have only ever competed in four different sports – and two of those only once.

The vast majority of Chad's Olympic entries have come in Athletics – a sport they have entered in every Games in which they have competed. They have managed four top-16 finishes in all, three of which came in their first two Games. On their Olympic debut in 1964, Mahamat Idriss finished 9th in the men's high jump. Chadian-born, he had finished 12th four years earlier whilst competing for France. He went on to finish 21st in 1968, in a competition in which teammate Ahmed Senoussi finished 12th. Idriss died in 1987, but his Chadian national record has still never been beaten (although it has been equalled). Also in 1968, Ahmed Issa finished 15th in the men's 1500 metres. Chad's best Olympic performance this century came from Kaltouma Nadjina, who was 16th fastest in the semi-finals of the women's 400 metres in 2004.

Meanwhile, in both Boxing (1972) and Archery (2021), Chad lost in the first round. They have also never won a match in Olympic Judo in four attempts (1992 twice, and 2012 and 2021).

CONGO DR   Olympic Rank 176th

Population: 111,859,928 (rank 14th)
Olympic rank/ population differential: -162

Summer: *no medals (best finish: 10th)*
Winter: *never participated*

Best sports: Boxing
Athletics
Basketball

Of countries that have never won an Olympic medal, only Bangladesh have a larger population than the Democratic Republic of Congo. They first entered the Olympics in 1968 (known as Congo-Kinshasa). There was then a 16-year break before they returned (now known as Zaire). They have entered every Summer Games since (reverting to the name Congo DR in 1997), and have yet to make their Winter Olympic debut.

In 1968, they only entered Cycling, finishing 30th in the team time trial and entering four men into the road race, none of whom finished. Since then, they have entered Athletics, Boxing and Judo (and Cycling again) in multiple Games, Taekwondo twice, and Basketball, Table Tennis and Swimming once each.

Their only Swimming event was the men's 50m freestyle in 2008, in which they came 97th and – by some distance – last. The Zaire women's Basketball team lost all seven of their matches in 1996, thus finishing 12th. In Table Tennis in 2004, they had three entries, but lost first round matches by 4 games to 0 in each. Congo DR's best Cycling finish is 28th. They have only ever won one match in their 10 Judo entries. In Taekwondo, Rosa Keleku Lukusa lost in the first round of the women's flyweight in 2016, finishing 13th out of 16. Their other Taekwondo entry (in the 2021 women's welterweight) failed the weigh-in.

In Boxing, their best performance was a narrow last-16 defeat for Kitenge Kitengewa in the 1984 men's Welterweight – he finished 10th, the nation's best ever finish in an Olympic event. Athlete Gary Kikaya has had his country's best two Athletics finishes – reaching the men's 400m semi-finals twice, finishing 14th in 2004 and 11th in 2008. In 2006, he set a new record for the fastest 400 metres ever by a non-American.

SAO TOME & PRINCIPE — Olympic Rank 196th

Population: 220,372 (rank 179th)
Olympic rank/ population differential: -17

Summer: *no medals (best finish: 14th)*
Winter: *never participated*

Best sports: Canoeing
Athletics

Sao Tome & Principe have competed in all Summer Games since 1996, though they have never yet appeared at the Winter Games. In 1996, they competed only in the men's and women's 100m. Gradually, they branched out in terms of Athletics events – they have now competed in the 400m, 800m, 1500m, 5000m, sprint hurdles, and 20km walk. Their best finish in any of these events is 29th (which was, by some distance, last place) by Celma Bonfim in the 2008 women's 5000m.

They have only ever entered one other sport – sprint Canoeing. A total of three different canoeists have participated. Alcino Silva came 26th in both the K1 500m and K1 1000m events in 2008 and Buly Triste came 16th out of 19 in the 2016 C1 1000m. Then, in 2021, Triste and Roque Ramos came 30th and 32nd respectively (out of 32) in the same event, but teamed up to finish 14th (and, again, last) in the C2 1000m. The other 13 pairs all clocked times between 3 mins 24 secs and 3 mins 34 secs, whilst the Sao Tome pair came in at 4 mins 12 secs. Nonetheless, it remains their best ever finish in any Olympic event.

EQUATORIAL GUINEA — Olympic Rank 204th

Population: 1,737,695 (rank 152nd)
Olympic rank/ population differential: -52

Summer: *no medals (best finish: 32nd)*
Winter: *never participated*

Best sports: Athletics
Judo
Swimming

Equatorial Guinea made their Olympic debut in 1984 and, predictably enough, have never participated in the Winter Games. Of their 42 Olympic entries, 38 have come in Athletics. The others came in Swimming (three) and Judo (one).

Their one judo performance is, by default, their joint best Olympic performance ever. Jose Mba Nchama, participating in the 2008 men's half-middleweight, was beaten in 1 min 46 secs in the last 32, to finish 32nd overall. However, three judokas had gone out in a preliminary round (Nchama had not had to compete in that), so technically he did finish ahead of those three fellow competitors.

Their two best Athletics finishes have been 32nd (the men's 4x100m relay team in 1996, who had the slowest time of any finishers, but there were five teams that failed to finish), and 36th (Roberto Mandje in the men's 1500m in 2004; he finished ahead of two of his rivals). Despite competing in Athletics in every Games since 1984, they have never managed better than this.

But the final word must go to Equatorial Guinea's most famous Olympian. In 2000, the nation competed in Swimming for the first time. Eric "the Eel" Moussambani was selected to compete in the 100m freestyle. He won his heat by default as both his rivals false started, but his time of 1 min 52 secs was 50 seconds slower than the next slowest, and would only have placed him 27th in the 200m, let alone the 100m. He had never seen an Olympic-sized swimming pool before. A few days later, supermarket cashier Paula Barila Bolopa took part in the women's 50m freestyle, and finished in a time more than double that of the second-to-last finisher. Equatorial Guinea returned to Olympic Swimming in 2021, when Diosdado Miko took part in the men's 50m freestyle. Again, he finished last, but this time he was only three seconds behind his nearest rival.

CHAPTER TWENTY - Eastern Africa, north (Kenya, Ethiopia, Uganda, Sudan, Eritrea, Djibouti, Seychelles, Somalia, South Sudan)

KENYA **Olympic Rank 32nd**
Population: 57,052,004 (rank 27th)
Olympic rank/ population differential: -5
Population per gold: 1,630,057 (rank 57th)
Population per medal: 504,885 (rank 64th)

Summer: 35 gold, 42 silver, 36 bronze (total 113)
Winter: *no medals (best finish: 38th)*
Total: 35 gold, 42 silver, 36 bronze (total 113)

Best sports: Athletics (34 golds, 3.24%, 6th)
Boxing (1 gold, 0.38%, 35th)
Swimming

Kenya are well clear of South Africa and Ethiopia as the most successful African nation in Olympic history. They have won 113 Olympic medals, of which 106 have come in Athletics. The other seven (1 gold, 1 silver and 5 bronzes) have all come in Boxing. Their first Summer Olympics were in 1956 (seven years before independence), and they have entered all Games since, apart from the boycotts of 1976 and 1980. They failed to win a medal in their first two appearances (although Nyandika Maiyoro came close in the 5000 metres both times), but won their first medal – a bronze – in 1964, courtesy of Wilson Kiprugut in the 800 metres. The Mexico City Games of 1968 saw their first three gold medals – in the 1500 metres (Kip Keino), 3000 metre steeplechase (Amos Biwott) and 10000 metres (Naftali Temu). Since then, they have won at least one gold in every Summer Games. Their best Games by medals won is Beijing 2008 (16 medals – 6 gold, 4 silver, 6 bronze), which saw them finish 13th, equalling their best finishing position, which they also achieved in Seoul 1988. The six golds they won in Beijing has also been equalled just once, in 2016 in Rio de Janeiro.

Kenya's signature event has been the men's 3000 metres steeplechase. Since winning it in 1968, they have won gold in the event every single time except for their two boycott years, and 2021 (when they had to settle for bronze). In total, they have won 27 medals at the distance (men and women). As is well known, the vast majority of their Athletics success has come in the middle-distance events. They have won 2 medals at 400 metres, 1 in the 400 metres hurdles, 2 in the 4x400m relay, 18 in the 800 metres (they have won the last four men's titles at this distance), 12 in the 1500 metres, 16 in the 5000 metres, 12 in the 10000 metres and 15 in the marathon. They have also won a single medal in a field event – Julius Yego (silver) in javelin in 2016. Initially, their medal success was confined to men's events, but they won their first women's medal in 1996, and their first women's gold in 2008, and they are now represented more or less equally by both sexes on the podiums. Kenya have had five two-time gold medallists in their Olympic history. They are Kip Keino (1500 metres in 1968 and steeplechase in 1972), Ezekiel Kemboi (3000m steeplechase, 2004 & 2012), David Rudisha (800m, 2012 & 2016), Eliud Kipchoge (marathon, 2016 & 2021), and Faith Kipyegon (1500m, 2016 & 2021). Kipchoge became the third man in history to win the Olympic marathon twice – after Abebe Bikila (Ethiopia, 1960 & 1964) and Waldemar Cierpinski (East Germany, 1976 & 1980). Keino and Kipchoge have each won four Olympic medals in all, as has one-time gold medallist Vivian Cheruiyot (5000m & 10000m, 2012 & 2016).

Kenya's one Olympic Boxing champion was Robert Wangila in the 1988 welterweight. However, Kenya have not won a Boxing medal since that year. Wangila turned professional the following year, but tragically died following a match in 1994. They have managed top-eight finishes in three other sports. They are Hockey (men's quarter-finalists three times in a row from 1960 to 1968), Taekwondo (2008 and 2021) and Swimming (just the one top-eight finish – achieved by Jason Dunford, coming 5th in the 2008 men's 100 metres butterfly). Jason Dunford and his brother David are responsible for all six of Kenya's best Olympic Swimming performances. Both were born in Kenya but largely educated overseas.

Only two Kenyans have ever entered Winter Olympic events. Philip Boit entered a total of four Nordic Skiing events in 1998, 2002 and 2006, never finishing higher than 64th. Then Sabrina Simader entered two women's Alpine Skiing events in 2018, finishing 38th in the Super G. Born to a Kenyan mother, the family moved to Austria with her Austrian stepfather when she was young.

ETHIOPIA Olympic Rank 37th

Population:	116,462,712 (rank 12th)
Olympic rank/ population differential:	-25
Population per gold:	5,063,596 (rank 73rd)
Population per medal:	2,007,978 (rank 100th)
Summer:	23 gold, 12 silver, 23 bronze (total 58)
Winter:	*no medals (best finish: 83rd)*
Total:	23 gold, 12 silver, 23 bronze (total 58)
Best sports:	Athletics (23 golds, 2.19%, 10th)
	Boxing
	Taekwondo

Ethiopia are, by some distance, the most successful one-trick pony in this book. They have won no fewer than 58 Olympic medals, and every single one of them has come in Athletics. Not only that, but all their medals have come in just a small number of athletic events. They are the 1500m (1 silver, 1 bronze), 3000m steeplechase (2 silver, 1 bronze), 5000m (6 gold, 3 silver, 7 bronze), 10000m (11 gold, 5 silver, 10 bronze) and marathon (6 gold, 1 silver, 4 bronze).

They first entered the Olympics in 1956, and have since missed out on three Games – joining the boycotts of 1976 and 1984, and strangely failing to turn up in 1988 either. Their most successful Games in terms of golds were 2000 and 2008 (4 golds each); in terms of medals it was 2000, 2012 and 2016 (8 medals each), and in terms of position in the medal table it was 2008 (17th).

They did not threaten the medals in 1956, but in 1960 the marathon was won by Abebe Bikila, famously running barefoot. He defended the title in 1964, this time wearing shoes. Ethiopia has produced six other multiple gold medallists – Miruts Yifter (2 golds and a bronze 1972-80), Haile Gebrselassie (2 golds 1996-2000), Derartu Tulu (2 golds and a silver 1992-2004), Meseret Defar (2 golds and a silver 2004-12), Tirunesh Dibaba (3 golds and 3 bronzes 2004-16) and Kenenisa Bekele (3 golds and a silver 2004-08). Every one of those medals was won in the 5000 or 10000 metres. As a nation, they have won medals in every Games in which they have competed apart from 1956, and won at least one gold in all of those apart from 1972.

Prior to 2012, they had only ever competed in three sports – Athletics, Boxing and road Cycling. Since then, they have added only Swimming (since 2012) and Taekwondo (2021 only). In total, Ethiopia have managed 117 top eight finishes, of which 115 have come in Athletics. The others were quarter-final appearances in the 1972 light-flyweight Boxing and the 2021 men's flyweight Taekwondo (their only appearance in that sport). In Swimming, they have never finished higher than 57th. In Cycling, they have never bettered the 9th place they managed on their debut in 1956, in the men's team road race.

Robel Teklemariam holds the distinction of being the only person ever to represent Ethiopia in the Winter Olympics. Born in Addis Ababa, but living in the United States from the age of nine, he came 83rd in the Nordic Skiing 15km event in 2006, and 93rd in the same event four years later.

UGANDA   **Olympic Rank 64th**

Population:	47,729,952 (rank 31st)
Olympic rank/ population differential:	-33
Population per gold:	11,932,488 (rank 90th)
Population per medal:	4,339,087 (rank 138th)
Summer:	4 gold, 4 silver, 3 bronze (total 11)
Winter:	*never participated*
Total:	4 gold, 4 silver, 3 bronze (total 11)
Best sports:	Athletics (4 golds, 0.38%, 34th)
	Boxing (3 silvers, 1 bronze, 43rd)
	Weightlifting

Uganda first competed at the Olympics in 1956, a full six years before they gained independence. They have competed at every Summer Games since then, with the exception of the African boycott of 1976. They have never yet appeared at the Winter Games.

Their 30 top-eight finishes have all come in just two sports – Boxing and Athletics. Up to the end of the 1980s, they had 16 top-eight finishes, of which 13 were in Boxing and just three in Athletics, albeit Athletics provided their only gold up to that point. The roles were then reversed, with Athletics having provided 13 of their 14 top-eight finishes since then.

Athletics has provided all four of Uganda's gold medals. The first came in 1972, when John Akii-Bua won an astonishing victory in the men's 400m hurdles. Reigning champion David Hemery of Great Britain was favourite, and led for much of the race, but Akii-Bua showed great strength to streak to a new world record. He was unable to defend his title in 1976 due to the boycott, and then found his family life disrupted by the murderous regime of Idi Amin. He returned to Uganda in later life, but died after a long illness in 1997, aged 47, and was given a state funeral.

It would be 40 years before Uganda won their second gold. It went to Stephen Kiprotich, who won the prestigious men's marathon title in London 2012 – it was the final medal of the Games to be awarded, and the only one to go to Uganda. It was also Uganda's only Olympic medal between 2000 and 2016. Then, in 2021, Uganda won two golds – Peruth Chemutai in the women's 3000m steeplechase and Joshua Cheptegei in the men's 5000 metres. Cheptegei had gone into the Games as the world record holder in both the 5000 and 10000 metres. He had to settle for silver in the 10000 metres behind Selemon Barega of Ethiopia. Jacob Kiplimo won bronze, making it the only time that two Ugandans have won medals in the same event. Cheptegei, with his gold and silver, is however the most decorated Ugandan Olympian. Chemutai, meanwhile, is currently the only Ugandan woman ever to win an Olympic medal.

With those four medals in Tokyo (two for Cheptegei, one each for Chemutai and Kiplimo), it made 2021 Uganda's best Games in terms of both golds and overall medals. They finished equal 36th in the medal table – their best finishing position remains 24th in 1972 (with Akii-Bua's gold plus a Boxing silver).

The only Ugandan Athletics medal not mentioned so far was a bronze in the men's 400 metres in 1996 for Davis Kamoga. As previously mentioned, Uganda were strong in Boxing from the 1960s to the 1980s, but have only had one quarter-final since then (in 2004). They won a silver and bronze in 1968, and further silvers in 1972 and 1980. The silvers were won by Eridadi Mukwanga, Leo Rwabwogo and John Mugabi respectively, with flyweight Rwabwogo also winning the bronze – he was Uganda's only multi-medallist until Cheptegei in 2021, but saw out his later life as a peasant farmer.

The vast majority of Uganda's Olympic entries have been (and still are) in these two sports. Of the other sports they have entered, the one in which they have achieved the highest position is Weightlifting – they finished 9th in the women's light-heavyweight in 2004. They have entered Hockey once, finishing 15th out of 16 in the men's event in 1972. In Swimming, they entered first in 1984, then in every Games since 2000, but have not done any better than 40th (in the women's 100m breaststroke in 2016). They have also entered Table Tennis three times, Badminton twice, and Cycling, Archery and Rowing once each.

SUDAN   Olympic Rank 124th

Population:	49,197,555 (rank 30th)
Olympic rank/ population differential:	-94
Population per gold:	n/a
Population per medal:	49,197,555 (rank 138th)
Summer:	0 gold, 1 silver, 0 bronze (total 1)
Winter:	*never participated*
Total:	0 gold, 1 silver, 0 bronze (total 1)
Best sports:	Athletics (1 silver, 78th=)
	Football
	Boxing

Sudan gained independence in 1956 and entered the Olympics for the first time four years later. They subsequently participated in 1968, 1972, and in every Summer Games from 1984 onwards. They have never entered the Winter Games. They have competed in Athletics in every Games they have entered, and all their best performances have come in that sport, including all five of their top-eight finishes in Olympic competition. These have been Omar Khalifa's 8th place in the 1984 men's 1500 metres, Yamile Aldama's 5th place in the 2004 women's triple jump, and three appearances in a men's 800-metre final. Ismail Ahmed Ismail finished last in the 2004 final, but four years later he won a surprise silver behind Kenya's Wilfred Bungei – this is still Sudan's only ever Olympic medal. Abubaker Kaki Khamis then finished 7th in 2012.

Sudan have entered Olympic Football once – their men's team finished 15th out of 16 in 1972 after three narrow defeats in the group stage. Their only other top-16 finish was by a boxer, Mohamed Hammad, who threw in the towel shortly before his first bout as a protest against a decision in a different match, thus finishing 16th without actually competing. Sudan have also entered events in Swimming, Shooting, Weightlifting, Judo, Table Tennis and Rowing without making any waves. Their best Swimming finish is 45th (men's 100m breaststroke in 2021).

ERITREA   Olympic Rank 132nd

Population:	6,274,796 (rank 111th)
Olympic rank/ population differential:	-21
Population per gold:	n/a
Population per medal:	6,274,796 (rank 114th)
Summer:	0 gold, 0 silver, 1 bronze (total 1)
Winter:	*no medals (best finish: 39th)*
Total:	0 gold, 0 silver, 1 bronze (total 1)
Best sports:	Athletics (1 bronze, 88th=)
	Cycling
	Alpine Skiing

Eritrea gained independence from Ethiopia in 1993, and debuted at the 2000 Summer Olympics. They have competed in all Summer Games since. They have participated in Athletics every time, plus Cycling (road events only) since 2012, and Swimming in 2021 only.

Being an East African nation, Eritrea's strength is in middle to long-distance Athletics. The only Athletics events they have entered are the 1500, 5000 and 10000 metres, as well as the 3000m steeplechase and the marathon. They have enjoyed nine top-eight finishes, all in Athletics. Five of these nine have been achieved by national icon Zersenay Tadese, in the only five Olympic events he entered. They were 7th in the 2004 5000 metres, and 3rd, 5th, 6th and 8th in the 10000 metres from 2004 to 2016. The first of those, finishing behind two Ethiopians, is the only Olympic medal his nation have won. The next best is Ghirmay Ghebreslassie's 4th place in the 2016 marathon. The best finish by any Eritrean woman is 15th in the 2021 10000 metres.

Eritrea's only swimmer finished 46th out of 73 in the men's 50m freestyle. Their best Cycling finish is 33rd. Remarkably, Eritrea have produced a Winter Olympian, and not a bad one either. Shannon-Ogbnai Abeda entered the Alpine Skiing slalom and giant slalom in 2018, and then the giant slalom again in 2022, finishing 39th out of 87. Unsurprisingly, he was born and raised in Canada, to Eritrean immigrant parents.

DJIBOUTI   **Olympic Rank 134th**

Population:	976,143 (rank 161st)
Olympic rank/ population differential:	+27
Population per gold:	n/a
Population per medal:	976,143 (rank 81st)
Summer:	0 gold, 0 silver, 1 bronze (total 1)
Winter:	*never participated*
Total:	0 gold, 0 silver, 1 bronze (total 1)
Best sports:	Athletics (1 bronze, 88th=)
	Judo
	Sailing

Djibouti, who have never competed at the Winter Games, made their Summer debut in 1984 (seven years after independence from France), when all three of their entrants were there for the men's marathon. One of them, Djama Robleh, finished 8th. Another, Hussain Ahmed Salah, finished 20th, but returned four years later to claim the bronze medal – still his nation's only Olympic medal.

Djibouti have returned to compete in Athletics at all but one Games since then (mostly in middle- and long-distance races). The only other top-eight finish they have managed in Olympic competition came in the men's 1500 metres in 2016, when Ayanleh Souleiman, who wasn't born when Salah won bronze, finished 4th, just 0.05 seconds off a medal. The one year that Djibouti failed to compete in Athletics, or anything else at the Olympics, was 2004. They participated in the opening ceremony that year, but for some reason subsequently failed to appear in any of the events – they were the only country in the world not to compete at those Games.

They have only competed in four other sports so far. They are Swimming (2012-2021, all in the men's 50m freestyle, with a best finish of 49th in 2012); Sailing (1988-1996, with a best finish of 39th); Judo (1992, 2016 and 2021, with just one win from four entries); and Table Tennis (once, in 2012, losing in the first round by an aggregate score of 44 points to 8).

SEYCHELLES   **Olympic Rank 147th**

Population:	97,617 (rank 191st)
Olympic rank/ population differential:	+44
Summer:	*no medals (best finish: 5th)*
Winter:	*never participated*
Best sports:	Boxing
	Badminton
	Weightlifting

The Seychelles became an independent nation in 1976, and made their Olympic debut four years later. They have never entered the Winter Olympics, but have entered all Summer Olympics since then, with the exception of 1988. Their most successful sport has been Boxing, in which they have reached the quarter-finals twice. In 1992, light-heavyweight Roland Raforme came 7th after convincing wins over boxers from Australia and France in the first two rounds. In 1996, light-middleweight Rival Cadeau came 5th after two convincing wins of his own over boxers from Brazil and Ghana. These remain the country's only two top-eight finishes in Olympic competition. Both boxers have won Commonwealth Games medals in their time.

The Seychelles have entered Athletics in all their Games, but have never progressed beyond the first round. They've entered Swimming in all Olympics since 1992, with a best finish of 26th (women's 200m backstroke in 2021). They've also had multiple entries in Weightlifting (best finish of 12th), Judo (best finish of 14th), Sailing (best finish of 20th), and Canoeing (best finish of 23rd). Finally, their one Badminton entry, in the 2008 mixed doubles, saw them lose in the first round, but make a game of it, finishing 11th out of 16.

SOMALIA Olympic Rank 154th

Population: 12,693,796 (rank 78th)
Olympic rank/ population differential: -76

Summer: *no medals (best finish: 6th)*
Winter: *never participated*

Best sports: Athletics
Boxing

Somalia's first Olympic participation came in Munich in 1972 with a team of three, all competing in Athletics. After missing the next two Games due to joining large-scale boycotts, they returned in 1984, again only in Athletics. Since then, they have competed in all Summer Games except 1992 (when they gave it a miss due to an ongoing famine at home). They have not entered the Winter Olympics as of yet.

Only one Somali has ever competed in the Olympics in anything other than Athletics – Ramla Ali took part in the women's featherweight Boxing in 2021 and finished 15th. This finishing position has been equalled once (by Ibrahim Okash in the men's 800 metres in 1988), but only ever bettered once. The man who did it was Abdi Bile. Bile had taken part in 1984 as a 19-year-old; he had become the 1500-metre world champion in 1987, and having missed the next two Olympics, he finished 6th in the same event in 1996.

The most successful Somali-born athlete in Olympic history is of course four-time gold medallist Mo Farah, who represented Great Britain during his career.

SOUTH SUDAN Olympic Rank 205th

Population: 12,118,379 (rank 80th)
Olympic rank/ population differential: -125

Summer: *no medals (best finish: 32nd)*
Winter: *never participated*

Best sports: Athletics

South Sudan gained internationally-recognised independence from Sudan in 2011, making it currently the youngest independent country in the world. The London 2012 Games came too quickly for them to enter an official team. However, South Sudanese marathon runner Guor Marial was allowed to compete as an independent athlete in London, after refusing to represent Sudan. He came 47th.

Four years later, the new country did send a team to Rio. Marial returned in the marathon, finishing 81st this time, and he was joined by Santino Kenyi in the men's 1500 metres and Margaret Hassan in the women's 200 metres. In Tokyo in 2021, their team consisted of just two – again in the men's 1500 metres (Abraham Guem this time) and the women's 200 metres (Lucia Moris this time). None of the four mentioned got past the first round. Kenyi and Guem did best, both finishing 32nd in their 1500 metres events. South Sudan have never yet entered any sport other than Athletics, and have of course yet to make their Winter Olympic debut.

CHAPTER TWENTY-ONE - Eastern Africa, south (Zimbabwe, Burundi, Mozambique, Tanzania, Zambia, Mauritius, Madagascar, Malawi, Rwanda, Comoros)

ZIMBABWE   **Olympic Rank 69th**

Population: 15,418,674 (rank 73rd)
Olympic rank/ population differential: +4
Population per gold: 5,139,558 (rank 74th)
Population per medal: 1,927,334 (rank 97th)

Summer: 3 gold, 4 silver, 1 bronze (total 8)
Winter: *no medals (best finish: 57th)*
Total: 3 gold, 4 silver, 1 bronze (total 8)

Best sports: Hockey (1 gold, 2.86%, 10th=)
Swimming (2 golds, 0.33%, 22nd)
Athletics

Zimbabwe, in their former guise of Rhodesia, entered the Olympics for the first time in 1928. Just two people entered that year, both boxers, one of whom (Cecil Bissett) beat a Mexican in his first match to reach the quarter-finals, where he lost to eventual champion Carlo Orlandi of Italy. They subsequently did not enter the Olympics again until 1960 in Rome. They entered a number of sports that year, achieving another Boxing quarter-final, as well as 4th place in Sailing's Flying Dutchman class. Rhodesia had less success in 1964, and then didn't enter in 1968. In 1972, they did enter a number of Swimming events, but the IOC withdrew their invitation a few days before the start of the Games, having come under political pressure from numerous African countries, unhappy at the racially divisive governance of Rhodesia. They missed out again in 1976, but in April 1980 full independence was granted to the newly-named Zimbabwe by the UK, and the new country participated in the Moscow Games later that year.

They contributed a large team that year, and participated in a number of sports, only managing one top-eight finish – but what a story that was! Women's Hockey was making its debut that year, and six teams had qualified to take part. However, all five of those that qualified alongside the Soviet hosts then pulled out due to the US-led boycott, and organisers scrabbled around for replacement teams. Eventually, five other countries accepted invitations to form a tournament and, incredibly, Zimbabwe took the gold medal. In their five games of the round-robin tournament, they drew with Czechoslovakia and India, and beat Poland, the Soviet Union and, in their final game, Austria by 4 goals to 1, thus securing the title, making them one of 25 countries to win a gold in Moscow. It is still the only time Zimbabwe have ever competed in women's Hockey (the only time they competed in men's Hockey was 1964).

In 1984, Zimbabwe managed top-eight finishes in Boxing and Diving, and subsequently failed to reach the top eight in any event in 1988, 1992, 1996 or 2000. So up to this point, they had still just won the one medal – but a further seven were to be won in 2004 and 2008, all of them by the record-breaking swimmer Kirsty Coventry. She only entered seven events in those years, but medalled in all of them – two golds in the 200m backstroke, two silvers in the 100m backstroke, a bronze and silver in the 200m individual medley, and a silver in the 2008 400m individual medley as well. She came back in 2012 and 2016, reaching three more finals, and finishing 6th in all of them. No other Zimbabwean swimmer has ever finished higher than 11th – she did it ten times! Having won seven of the eight Olympic medals Zimbabwe have ever won, she later became a cabinet minister.

There have been four other top-eight finishes. Wayne Black and Kevin Ullyett reached the quarter-finals of men's doubles Tennis in 2004, whilst there has been a marked improvement in Zimbabwean Athletics in recent times. Ngoni Makusha finished just 1cm outside the medals in the men's long jump in 2008, and Brian Dzingai also finished 4th in the men's 200 metres in the same year. In 2012, Cuthbert Nyasango finished 7th in the men's marathon. But that first Athletics medal remains, for now, elusive. Makusha did win a bronze in the world championships in 2011 – Zimbabwe's only Athletics world championship medal so far.

Only one Zimbabwean has so far gone to the Winter Olympics – Luke Steyn came 57th in Alpine Skiing's men's giant slalom in 2014, and failed to finish in the slalom.

BURUNDI   Olympic Rank 96th

Population:	13,162,952 (rank 77th)
Olympic rank/ population differential:	-19
Population per gold:	13,162,952 (rank 91st)
Population per medal:	6,581,476 (rank 115th)
Summer:	1 gold, 1 silver, 0 bronze (total 2)
Winter:	*never participated*
Total:	1 gold, 1 silver, 0 bronze (total 2)
Best sports:	Athletics (1 gold, 0.10%, 57th=)
	Boxing
	Judo

Despite gaining independence back in 1962, Burundi's Olympic story did not begin until 1996 in Atlanta. They entered seven competitors, six men and one woman, all in Athletics, and all in running distances between 800 metres and marathon (to this date, these remain the only Athletics events Burundi have entered). For a country debuting in the Games, they did very well. Arthemon Hatungimana finished 9th in the 800 metres, narrowly missing a place in the final; Aloys Nizigama finished 4th in the 10,000 metres (the top eight were all African). But in the 5000 metres, Venuste Niyongabo won a four-man sprint finish to claim his nation's first ever Olympic gold medal. He had previously won a 1500 metres bronze in the 1995 World Championships, but never reached the same heights after the Olympics. He has been involved in various sport-related humanitarian projects since retiring, and remains Burundi's only Olympic champion.

Again sticking to Athletics in 2000, Nizigama was Burundi's highest finisher, claiming 9th place in the 10,000 metres. In 2004, nobody managed better than 12th. In that year, they also ventured away from Athletics for the first time, entering two competitors in Swimming. Burundi have entered Swimming in every Games since; their highest finish is 49th, achieved in 2004 in the women's 100m freestyle (they have still never entered any Swimming event other than the 50m and 100m freestyle events).

Burundi's worst Games was 2008; they only entered three competitors (they have entered at least six in each of their other Games), the best of whom came 28th (in an event where only 29 finished). Things were better in London in 2012. They added a third sport to their Olympic roster – Judo – although their representative only managed to last 38 seconds. But in the women's 800 metres, Francine Niyonsaba finished 5th. This was their third top-eight finish, and the first for 16 years. Another followed four years later, for the same person in the same event, and this time Burundi had a second medal to celebrate, 20 years after their first. Niyonsaba won silver, albeit some distance behind South African Caster Semenya.

But, like Semenya, Niyonsaba was subject to a controversial gender-recognition decision in 2019 when, due to high testosterone levels, she was banned by World Athletics from entering any events between 400 metres and one mile. That left her having to find a new event for Tokyo 2021. She entered the 10,000 metres (12½ times longer than she was used to) and impressively finished 5th. It meant that Burundi currently has managed five top-eight finishes, and Niyonsaba is responsible for three of them. The 2021 Games also saw Burundi enter a fourth Olympic sport – Boxing – but, as with Judo, they have yet to win a match.

Burundi have never entered the Winter Olympics.

MOZAMBIQUE **Olympic Rank 100th**

Population:	32,513,805 (rank 45th)
Olympic rank/ population differential:	-55
Population per gold:	32,513,805 (rank 96th)
Population per medal:	16,256,903 (rank 128th)

Summer:	1 gold, 0 silver, 1 bronze (total 2)
Winter:	*never participated*
Total:	1 gold, 0 silver, 1 bronze (total 2)

Best sports:	Athletics (1 gold, 0.10%, 61st=)
	Boxing
	Canoeing

The story of Mozambique in the Olympics is basically the story of Maria Mutola. Born into poverty, she would become a legend of the 800 metres. She never took up Athletics until 1988, aged 15, yet by the end of that year, she had competed in her first Olympics, albeit she went out in the first round. By 1992, she had improved enormously, and was looking good to win Mozambique's first ever Olympic medal, but faded in the closing stages and finished fifth. Four years later, in Atlanta, she did indeed win her nation's first Olympic medal, but the bronze was actually a bit of a disappointment, as she had been tipped for better. In Sydney 2000, she finally fulfilled that destiny and won a glorious gold. She went on to win the World Championships in 2001 and 2003, so was strongly fancied to retain her title in 2004. But in an unbearably tight finish, she came in just 0.13 seconds behind the winner, but still only came fourth. Finally, in 2008, aged 35 and competing in her sixth Olympics, she came fifth. But her run of 5th, 3rd, 1st, 4th and 5th constituted all five of her country's top Olympic performances prior to 2021. After retiring from Athletics, she played international football for Mozambique.

In 2021, Mozambique finally produced their only two people besides Mutola to finish in the top eight of an Olympic event. They were both boxers. Women's middleweight Rady Gramane lost her quarter-final on a 4-1 decision; with the other quarter-finals all decided by unanimous decision, she ranked fifth. That same year, another boxer from Mozambique – Alcinda Panguana in the women's welterweight – finished eighth.

Mozambique first entered the Olympics in 1980, and have entered every Summer Games since. They have never competed in the Winter Games. They stuck to Athletics and Swimming in 1980 and 1984, adding Boxing in 1988, Judo in 2008, Canoeing in 2016 and Sailing in 2021.

Their best finish in Canoeing is 11th and in Sailing 21st. In Judo, they have never won a bout in four attempts. In Swimming, they have never bettered the 24th place achieved in men's 200m butterfly on their Olympic debut (this was out of 25, beating only a swimmer from Kuwait).

TANZANIA   **Olympic Rank 110th**

Population:	65,642,582 (rank 23rd)
Olympic rank/ population differential:	-87
Population per gold:	n/a
Population per medal:	32,821,291 (rank 135th)
Summer:	0 gold, 2 silver, 0 bronze (total 2)
Winter:	*never participated*
Total:	0 gold, 2 silver, 0 bronze (total 2)
Best sports:	Athletics (2 silvers, 72nd=)
	Boxing
	Hockey

Tanzania first entered the Olympics in 1964, and have entered every Summer Games since, with the exception of the 1976 African boycott. They have never entered the Winter Games. The two medals they have won both came on the Athletics track in 1980. First, Filbert Bayi won a silver medal behind Poland's Bronislaw Malinowski in the men's 3000m steeplechase, helped inordinately by the Kenyan boycott that year. Then, the following day Suleiman Nyambui was pipped on the line by famed Ethiopian Miruts Yifter in the 5000 metres.

Their next best finish in an Olympic event is 5th. In Athletics, Tanzania have had four other top-eight finishes, besides their two medals, and all four have come in the men's marathon (Juma Ikangaa came 6th in 1984 and 7th in 1988; Alphonce Simbu came 5th in 2016 and 7th in 2021). Tanzania have reached six Boxing quarter-finals (all in men's events), but never got further. Meanwhile, in 1980 the men's Hockey tournament was destroyed when nine of the original 12 qualifiers boycotted the Games. Tanzania were one of three teams invited to help form a six-team tournament. They lost all five games, scoring three goals and conceding 54, and have never competed in Olympic Hockey before or since. Apart from Athletics and Boxing (and Hockey in 1980), Tanzania did not enter another sport until 2008 (Swimming). They added Judo in 2016, but that's it. Their best Swimming finish is 45th. In women's events, Tanzania have never finished higher than 18th.

ZAMBIA   **Olympic Rank 118th**

Population:	20,216,029 (rank 63rd)
Olympic rank/ population differential:	-55
Population per gold:	n/a
Population per medal:	10,108,015 (rank 125th)
Summer:	0 gold, 1 silver, 1 bronze (total 2)
Winter:	*never participated*
Total:	0 gold, 1 silver, 1 bronze (total 2)
Best sports:	Athletics (1 silver, 78th=)
	Boxing (1 bronze, 61st=)
	Football

Zambia made their Olympic debut in 1964 as Northern Rhodesia. They then gained independence later that year, and have competed as Zambia in all Summer Games since, other than 1976. They have never entered the Winter Games. They have entered Athletics and Boxing every time, as well as Swimming (1964, and 2000 onwards), Judo (1980, 1984, 1992, and 2012 onwards), Football (1980, 1988 and 2021), Fencing (1964), Wrestling (1964) and Badminton (2008).

Samuel Matete got their one silver medal, in the men's 400m hurdles in 1996. His 10th place in the same event in 2000 is Zambia's next best finish in Athletics. They have one other Olympic medal – that was won by Keith Mwila in light-flyweight Boxing in 1984 after victories in the last 16 and quarter-finals. They have had six other top-eight finishes, five of which have been in men's Boxing (all in the 1980s), and one in men's Football in 1988 (when they won their group ahead of Italy, whom they notably beat 4-0). Their best performance in a women's event is 9th by the women's Football team in 2021, earned largely through a 4-4 draw with China. Their best Swimming finish is 24th, by Alan Durrett in the 1964 men's 1500m freestyle.

MAURITIUS   Olympic Rank 135th

Population:	1,309,448 (rank 157th)
Olympic rank/ population differential:	+22
Population per gold:	n/a
Population per medal:	1,309,448 (rank 87th)
Summer:	0 gold, 0 silver, 1 bronze (total 1)
Winter:	*never participated*
Total:	0 gold, 0 silver, 1 bronze (total 1)
Best sports:	Boxing (1 bronze, 61st=)
	Athletics
	Judo

Mauritius made their Olympic debut in 1984. They have competed in every Summer Games since and, although they have never ventured into the Winter Games, they have spread their net far and wide in Summer competition, entering 13 different sports. They have only managed top-eight finishes in three of them – Boxing (three times), Judo (twice) and Athletics (once). The latter was achieved by Stephane Buckland, who reached the men's 200 metres semi-finals three times, and finished 6th in the final in 2004. Both of the Judo top finishes were achieved by Christianne Legentil, a quarter-finalist in the women's half-middleweight in 2012 and 2016.

Of Mauritius's three quarter-final appearances in Boxing, the one that resulted in the nation's Olympic medal came in the 2008 men's bantamweight. Bruno Julie beat boxers from Lesotho, Uzbekistan and Venezuela before losing his semi-final to the Cuban representative. He also won Commonwealth medals in 2006 and 2010. All of Mauritius's best Swimming performances came in 1992. They finished 13th and last in the women's 4x100m freestyle relay; their next best was 28th in the men's 1500m freestyle.

MADAGASCAR   Olympic Rank 161st

Population:	28,812,195 (rank 53rd)
Olympic rank/ population differential:	-108
Summer:	*no medals (best finish: 8th)*
Winter:	*no medals (best finish: 39th)*
Best sports:	Athletics
	Boxing
	Judo

Madagascar have missed two Summer Games since their first one in 1964. These were in 1976 and, surprisingly, 1988. They have entered eight sports in that time, the most common ones being Athletics, Swimming and Judo. They have entered Boxing on most occasions too, though not since 2008, and also had the occasional appearance in Tennis, Weightlifting, Cycling and Wrestling. Their best finish in any of the latter four is 11th (Weightlifting in 2021).

They have achieved just one top-eight finish in an Olympic event to date. That was back in 1968, in the men's 100 metres no less, when Jean-Louis Ravelomanantsoa (long surnames are a feature of Madagascar) reached the final and finished 8th. His 11th place in the same event in 1972 is his country's second-best Athletics finish. The next best in Athletics is 12th (Nicole Ramalalanirina, women's 100m hurdles, 1996).

In Swimming, Madagascar's best is 23rd (women's 100m butterfly, 1980 and women's 400m freestyle, 2021). In Boxing, they have had three last 16 appearances, including a 9th place for Anicet Rasoanaivo in the 1996 men's light-flyweight. In Judo, their best is also 9th (Justin Andriamanantena in the 1972 men's half-middleweight). They have also competed in the Winter Olympics of 2006, 2018 and 2022, all in Alpine Skiing, with a best finish of 39th in the men's giant slalom of 2006.

MALAWI   Olympic Rank 168th
Population: 21,279,597 (rank 62nd)
Olympic rank/ population differential: -106

Summer: *no medals (best finish: 8th)*
Winter: *never participated*

Best sports: Boxing
                         Athletics
                         Cycling

Malawi first entered the Olympics in 1972, in Boxing, Athletics and Cycling (road). They missed the next two Games, but have competed every time since 1984. The only new sports they have added to their repertoire are Swimming (from 2004), Archery (from 2016) and Judo (2021). They have never got past the first round in either Archery or Judo. In Cycling (which they have not entered since 1988), their best finish is 26th and last (men's 100km team time trial in 1984). In Swimming, they have only ever entered the 50m freestyle races, and their best finish is 46th in 2012.

Malawi have entered a variety of Athletics events, ranging from 100 metres to the marathon, as well as high jump, triple jump and decathlon. They have only ever progressed from a heat once (and that was a preliminary round in the 100 metres of 2021). Decathlete Wilfred Mwalawanda, though, was their highest finisher in Olympic Athletics history, finishing 22nd in 1972 (33 athletes competed, but only 22 finished).

By far Malawi's best success, though, has come in Boxing, which makes it all the more surprising that, having entered numerous boxers in their first three Olympic appearances (mostly in the lighter weight categories), they have not competed in the sport since 1988. Peter Ayesu is their best performer, winning through two rounds in the 1984 flyweight, but losing in the quarter-finals. Malawi have never competed in the Winter Olympics.

RWANDA   Olympic Rank 169th
Population: 13,400,541 (rank 76th)
Olympic rank/ population differential: -93

Summer: *no medals (best finish: 8th)*
Winter: *never participated*

Best sports: Athletics
                         Judo
                         Cycling

Rwanda made their Olympic debut in 1984, and have competed in all Summer Games since, though never yet the Winter Games. In that time, they have competed in four different sports: Athletics (every time), Swimming (2000 onwards), Cycling (1992, and 2012 onwards) and Judo (2012 only). Their one judoka lost in the first round, for a 30th-place finish. Their best finish in Swimming is 43rd (women's 100m butterfly in 2016). Their best in Cycling is 39th (men's cross-country in 2012).

All of their best performances, though, have come in Athletics. Unlike most underdog countries, Rwanda's Athletics history has not mainly been in the shorter distances. Most unusually, they have never entered a 100-metre or 200-metre race. They have not entered a race shorter than 5000 metres since 2000. They have, on the other hand, entered a marathon in every Games since 1988. Besides marathons, their other entries have all been in track events. Their best finishes have been 8th (Mathias Ntawulikura, men's 10000m in 1996), 14th (Robert Kajuga, men's 10000m in 2012) and 15th (Ntawulikura again, in the men's marathon in 2000). Ntawulikura entered five Olympics in all, and was 40 by the time of his last one in 2004.

COMOROS   **Olympic Rank 201st**
Population: 888,378 (rank 163rd)
Olympic rank/ population differential: -38

Summer: *no medals (best finish: 21st)*
Winter: *never participated*

Best sports: Weightlifting
                                        Athletics
                                        Judo

Although Comoros gained independence from France in 1975, it would be another two decades before they took their Olympic bow. They have competed in all Summer Games since 1996, but never in the Winter Games. Other than Athletics, they have competed in Swimming (2008 to 2016), Weightlifting (2004) and Judo (2021).

Their one Weightlifting entry ended in disappointment. In the men's light-heavyweight in 2004, Chaehoi Fatihou made his opening attempt at 80kg. He failed three times to lift in, and was eliminated with no valid lift. No other weightlifter even entered the competition until 115kg. Nonetheless, with only 21 entrants, it put him in 21st place, which is his nation's highest ever Olympic finish.

Their next best is in Athletics. In the women's 400m hurdles in 2004, Salhate Djamalidine finished 32nd out of 33, beating an athlete from Albania. In Swimming, their best finish is 48th out of 48 in the women's 100m freestyle in 2012. Their best finish which saw them beat somebody else was 76th out of 85 in the men's 50m freestyle in 2016. Their one Judo entry saw their entrant lose inside 42 seconds in the first round to finish 34th and last.

CHAPTER TWENTY-TWO - Southern Africa (South Africa, Namibia, Botswana, Lesotho, Eswatini)

SOUTH AFRICA   Olympic Rank 34th

Population: 58,048,332 (rank 25th)
Olympic rank/ population differential: -9
Population per gold: 2,149,938 (rank 61st)
Population per medal: 652,228 (rank 70th)

Summer: 27 gold, 33 silver, 29 bronze (total 89)
Winter: *no medals (best finish: 13th)*
Total: 27 gold, 33 silver, 29 bronze (total 89)

Best sports: Tennis (3 golds, 4.00%, 7th)
Boxing (6 golds, 2.26%, 12th)
Swimming (7 golds, 1.16%, 13th)

The first Olympic event ever to feature South Africans was the infamous 1904 men's marathon. Two Tswana tribesmen, in St Louis as part of an exhibit at the World's Fair, finished 9th and 12th, despite one of them having been chased a mile off course by a pack of wild dogs. South Africa also entered Tug of War that year, but lost in the first round. They didn't enter the Intercalated Games of 1906, but returned in London in 1908. Their first Olympic medal was gold in the men's 100 metres, no less, won by Reggie Walker, who was coached by the legendary Sam Mussabini (who later coached Great Britain's Harold Abrahams to the same title in 1924). South Africa also took silver in the men's marathon in 1908.

South Africa then entered every Summer Olympics up to 1960, after which they were excluded for three decades due to international condemnation of their racist national policy of apartheid. They returned as a fully integrated nation in 1992, and have entered all Games since. They have won medals at all their Games since 1908. They have broken into the top 10 of the medal table just once; this was in 1912, when they won 4 golds and 2 silvers, finishing 7th. Their total of 4 golds has been emulated once – exactly 100 years later at the London Games, but has never been beaten. The most medals they have won in a single Games is 10, achieved three times – 1920 (3-4-3), 1952 (2-4-4) and 2016 (2-6-2). They have only failed to win gold on six occasions; their worst Games were in 1936 and 2008 (just one silver on each occasion), whilst 1956 was the only time they failed to win gold or silver (they won four bronzes that year).

Four sports – Athletics, Swimming, Boxing and Tennis – have accounted for 25 of South Africa's 27 golds, and 73 of their 89 medals (although they haven't won a Boxing medal since 1960). Their most decorated Olympian in terms of total medals won is swimmer Chad le Clos. In 2012, he made a name for himself by beating Michael Phelps to gold in the 200m butterfly; he then won silver behind Phelps in the 100m butterfly. Four years later, he won 100m butterfly silver again, this time tying with Phelps, as well as silver in the 200m freestyle behind Chinese swimmer Sun Yang, who has twice been banned for doping.

Three South Africans have won two golds each. The first was Tennis player Charles Winslow. Taking advantage of the fact that most top players were playing at Wimbledon instead, he beat compatriot Harry Kitson to win the men's singles in 1912 (South Africa also finished 1st and 2nd in the men's marathon that year). Winslow and Kitson also teamed up to win the doubles. In 1920, the top players were again missing (this time competing in the US Championships), and Winslow took bronze in the singles. Penny Heyns won the women's 100m and 200m breaststroke titles in 1996, and took bronze in the 100 in 2000. Caster Semenya, meanwhile, overcame fierce controversy regarding her gender to take victory in the women's 800 metres in both 2012 and 2016 (she had finished 2nd in 2012, later upgraded to gold after the Russian winner was found guilty of doping).

South Africa's other two golds came in Cycling (1912) and Rowing (2012). They have also won one medal each in Shooting (1920), Canoeing (2012), Rugby Sevens and Triathlon (both 2016) and Surfing (2021). They didn't enter the Winter Olympics until 1960. Entering only Figure Skating that year, they finished 13th in the pairs event, which is still their best ever Winter Olympic finish, albeit there were only 13 entries in the competition. They didn't compete at a Winter Games after that until 1994. They then competed at all Games until 2010, but since then they have entered only once (2018), with just one Alpine skier, who failed to finish either of his events. Their best finish since re-admission is 21st in the men's Skeleton in 2006.

NAMIBIA   **Olympic Rank 104th**

Population:	2,777,232 (rank 141st)
Olympic rank/ population differential:	+37
Population per gold:	n/a
Population per medal:	555,446 (rank 66th)
Summer:	0 gold, 5 silver, 0 bronze (total 5)
Winter:	*never participated*
Total:	0 gold, 5 silver, 0 bronze (total 5)
Best sports:	Athletics (5 silvers, 68th)
	Boxing
	Shooting

Namibia gained independence from South Africa in 1990, and have entered all Summer Olympics since. They made a splash on their 1992 debut, thanks to sprinter Frankie Fredericks, who won silver medals in the men's 100 metres (behind Linford Christie) and 200 metres (behind Mike Marsh). Four years later, he again won silvers in the same events, behind Donovan Bailey and Michael Johnson this time. He became world champion in the 200 metres in 1993. He returned in 2004, aged 36, when he came 4th in the 200 metres. Namibia's other Olympic medallist, Christine Mboma, took silver in the women's 200 metres in 2021, aged 18, and finishing behind Elaine Thompson-Herah. Another Namibian, Beatrice Masilingi, finished 6th in the same event. Due to gender-recognition controversy, Mboma had not been allowed to compete in events longer than 200 metres.

Outside of Athletics, Namibia's best showings have been two quarter-final defeats in Boxing, both in 2004, and an 8th place in the men's air pistol Shooting in 1996. Their best finish in Cycling is 21st. In Swimming, they competed in 1992, 1996 and 2000, with a best finish of 32nd. They have not returned to the pool since, but they did finish 16th in the men's marathon (open-water) Swimming event in 2021. Namibia have also competed in Wrestling (twice), and Gymnastics and Rowing (once each), not finishing higher than 15th in any of them. Namibia have never competed in the Winter Olympics.

BOTSWANA   **Olympic Rank 114th**

Population:	2,417,596 (rank 144th)
Olympic rank/ population differential:	+30
Population per gold:	n/a
Population per medal:	1,208,798 (rank 85th)
Summer:	0 gold, 1 silver, 1 bronze (total 2)
Winter:	*never participated*
Total:	0 gold, 1 silver, 1 bronze (total 2)
Best sports:	Athletics (1 silver, 1 bronze, 75th=)
	Boxing
	Weightlifting

Botswana have never competed in the Winter Olympics, but have competed in all Summer Games since their debut in 1980. They have competed in six sports in that time, although three of them only once. By far their most successful Olympic displays have come in Athletics. They have taken part in it in all of their Olympic appearances, and have secured 11 top-eight finishes, including two medals. Their top-ranked Olympian of all time is Nijel Amos, born in the small village of Marobela. In the 800 metres of 2012, he ran the third fastest time ever, only to be beaten by David Rudisha's world record time; he had to settle for silver. He finished 8th in the same event in 2021. The men's 4x400m relay team finished 8th in 2004, 5th in 2016 and won bronze in 2021. Amantle Montsho came 6th in the 2008 women's 400 metres, and 4th in 2012 (she won gold in the 2011 world championships and silver in 2013, Botswana's only world championship medals). All of their top-eight finishes came over 400 or 800 metres, or the 4x400m relay, apart from an 8th place in the men's long jump in 2008.

Botswana have only ever had one non-Athletics top-eight finish, a quarter-final appearance for Khumiso Ikgopoleng in the men's bantamweight Boxing in 2008. They have competed in Boxing in every Games but one since 1988. They only made their Swimming debut on 2008, and their best finish so far is 35th (men's 100m backstroke in 2016 and men's 400m freestyle in 2021). They have also competed (once each) in Sailing, Judo and Weightlifting.

LESOTHO   Olympic Rank 159th

Population: 2,210,646 (rank 146th)
Olympic rank/ population differential: -13

Summer: *no medals (best finish: 7th)*
Winter: *never participated*

Best sports: Taekwondo
Boxing
Athletics

Lesotho, a small nation entirely surrounded by South Africa, gained independence from the UK in 1966, and first entered the Olympics in 1972. They had just one entrant that year – a sprinter called Motsapi Moorosi who did not progress far, either in the men's 100 or 200 metres. After missing out in 1976, they returned in Moscow in 1980, and have competed in all Summer Games since. They have never entered the Winter Games.

They have entered Athletics on every occasion. Their best two finishes (16th in 2000 and 20th in 2021) have both come in the marathon (men's and women's respectively). By contrast, they have only ever had a single Swimming entry, finishing 73rd in the women's 50m freestyle in 2012 (out of 73; the 72nd-place finisher was a full five seconds ahead).

Lesotho have only ever entered three other sports. They have had three Taekwondo entries (two in 2000, one in 2004). Their overall match record is 1 win and 4 defeats. However, Likeleli Alinah Thamae finished 7th despite losing two out of two, due to the fact she lost to an eventual finalist. This, by default, remains Lesotho's only top-eight finish in Olympic history. They have entered Boxing numerous times, reaching the last 16 twice (but only once by virtue of actually winning a match). And they have entered Cycling's mountain bike event once, but failed to finish.

ESWATINI   Olympic Rank 183rd

Population: 1,130,043 (rank 160th)
Olympic rank/ population differential: -23

Summer: *no medals (best finish: 11th)*
Winter: *no medals (best finish: 63rd)*

Best sports: Athletics
Taekwondo
Boxing

Eswatini were known as Swaziland prior to 2018, and first competed in the Olympics under that name in 1972. They sent one athlete (Richard Mabuza, who finished 17th out of 62 finishers in the marathon) and one shooter. They boycotted both the 1976 and 1980 Games, but have competed in every Summer Games since. They have only ever finished in the top 16 in three events.

Their best finish was in 2021, when Sibusiso Matsenjwa, a man who has come close to 10 seconds in the 100m and close to 20 seconds in the 200m, finished fifth in his semi-final, and 11th in the final ranking of the 200 metres. Their other best performances both came in Sydney 2000. Mfanukhona Dlamini came 14th (and last) in the flyweight Taekwondo event (he failed to go the distance in his first – and only – fight). And, in Boxing's featherweight category, Musa Simelane had a bye in the first round before being stopped midway through his second-round bout, so he finished 16th (which was the lowest he could have finished, having had that first-round bye).

Dlamini's entry was Eswatini's only ever entry in Taekwondo, whilst the aforementioned 1972 Shooting entry was their only one in that sport too. Athletics and Boxing have provided more entries. The only other Summer sports they have entered have been Weightlifting (but not since 1988) and Swimming (28th being their best finish in that sport, in the women's 800m freestyle in 1996).

Eswatini have also ventured into the Winter Olympics, albeit only once. Keith Fraser, born in Scotland but a naturalised Swazi, competed in 1992 in three Alpine Skiing events – the giant slalom (finished 63rd), super-G (79th) and slalom (failed to finish).

CHAPTER TWENTY-THREE - Former USSR, Asian (Kazakhstan, Uzbekistan, Tajikistan, Kyrgyzstan, Turkmenistan)

KAZAKHSTAN   **Olympic Rank 42nd**
Population: 19,543,464 (rank 64th)
Olympic rank/ population differential: +22
Population per gold: 1,302,898 (rank 51st)
Population per medal: 247,386 (rank 52nd)

Summer: 14 gold, 21 silver, 36 bronze (total 71)
Winter: 1 gold, 3 silver, 4 bronze (total 8)
Total: 15 gold, 24 silver, 40 bronze (total 79)

Best sports: Boxing (7 golds, 2.64%, 9th=)
Modern Pentathlon (1 gold, 2.38%, 10th=)
Nordic Skiing (1 gold, 0.55%, 13th=)

As with most other ex-Soviet republics, Kazakhstan entered the Olympics in their own right for the first time in 1994. Their most successful Olympian is Vladimir Smirnov, who won a gold and two silvers in Nordic Skiing in 1994, and a further bronze in 1998. In fact, those 1994 medals meant he single-handedly saw his country into 12th place in the medal table that year – the highest position they have ever finished. It also made him his nation's first ever Olympic champion.

Their best Summer Games is more debatable. Their highest medal haul came in Rio in 2016 (17 medals in total, although only two were gold); their best medal performance came in Atlanta in 1996 (3 gold, 4 silver, 4 bronze), whilst their best position in the medal table came four years later in Sydney (22nd, with 3 gold, 4 silver and 0 bronze).

Boxing has been, by some distance, their best sport, with a total of 7 golds, 7 silvers and 10 bronzes (24 medals in total). They have also won 17 medals in Wrestling (but only one gold) and 11 in Weightlifting (again, 1 gold). Other than Boxing, the only sport in which they have won more than one gold is Athletics. Their two Athletics golds have been won by Olga Shishigina (100m hurdles in 2000) and Olga Rybakova (triple jump in 2012).

Perhaps their most famous gold medallist is Alexander Vinokourov. Having finished third in the 2003 Tour de France, and won the 2006 Vuelta a Espana, he had also won silver in the 2000 Olympic road race, but went one better when achieving a shock win in the same event in London twelve years later.

They have only won one medal in Modern Pentathlon, but it is enough to place them 10th equal in that medal table. The medal was a memorable gold for Alexander Parygin, narrowly winning the men's event in 1996.

Other sports in which Kazakhstan have won medals are Swimming (just one – a gold for Dmitriy Balandin in the men's 200m breaststroke in 2016), Judo, Karate, Shooting, Taekwondo, Biathlon, Figure Skating, Freestyle Skiing and Speed Skating.

A 2021 study found that Kazakhstan were fourth in terms of most Olympic medals having been stripped due to doping. They have had nine medallists from Weightlifting and Wrestling retrospectively stripped of their medals; only Russia, Ukraine and Belarus have had more.

UZBEKISTAN   Olympic Rank 48th

Population: 31,360,836 (rank 48th)
Olympic rank/ population differential: 0
Population per gold: 2,850,985 (rank 64th)
Population per medal: 847,590 (rank 78th)

Summer: 10 gold, 6 silver, 20 bronze (total 36)
Winter: 1 gold, 0 silver, 0 bronze (total 1)
Total: 11 gold, 6 silver, 20 bronze (total 37)

Best sports: Taekwondo (1 gold, 2.08%, 21st=)
                Boxing (5 golds, 1.89%, 14th)
                Freestyle Skiing (1 gold, 1.75%, 14th=)

Uzbekistan have entered all Summer and Winter Olympics since their debut at Lillehammer in 1994. On that first appearance, Lina Cheryasova secured their first medal – a gold in the women's Freestyle Skiing aerials. Surprisingly, though, they have never won another Winter medal ever since, and have in fact only managed further top-eight finish – 8th place in women's Figure Skating in 1998. The only other Winter sport in which they have competed is Alpine Skiing.

In the Summer Games, they have been much more successful. In all, they have won 36 Summer medals, of which 31 have come in combat sports – 15 in Boxing (5 golds), 8 in Wrestling (2 golds), 7 in Judo (no golds) and 1 in Taekwondo (gold). They have also won 3 medals (2 golds) in Weightlifting, and a couple of Gymnastics bronzes for good measure.

Uzbekistan's most successful Games, whether you look at it in terms of medal table position, total golds or total medals, was Rio in 2016. They won 4 golds, 2 silvers and 7 bronzes to finish 21st in the medal table. They have won at least one medal at every Summer Games they have entered. Having had to settle for just a silver and a bronze first time out, they won their first gold at Sydney in 2000, thanks to boxer Muhammad Abdullaev. They only won three golds in their first five Summer Games, but have won seven in the two summer Games since.

Uzbekistan have secured 106 top-eight finishes in all. The four combat sports of Boxing, Wrestling, Judo and Taekwondo have been responsible for 79 of those, and Weightlifting for a further 11. Others have come in Athletics, Canoeing, Cycling, Fencing, Gymnastics, Shooting, and the two Winter sports previously mentioned. Their two best performances in Athletics have both come in women's high jump – Svetlana Radzivil was sixth in 2012, and Safina Sadullayeva was seventh in 2021. In Swimming, they have never bettered the 12th place of their men's 4x200m freestyle relay team in 1996.

Two Uzbeks have won more than one Olympic medal. The first was Artur Taymazov, who won silver in 2000 and gold in 2004 in the super heavyweight freestyle Wrestling. He went on to retain the title in 2008 and again in 2012, but both those golds were later stripped due to drug violations being found after the samples were re-tested many years later. The samples from his earlier medal successes were not able to be tested, so there is undoubtedly a huge cloud of suspicion over them. He later represented Vladimir Putin's governing party in the Russian parliament.

The other multi-medallist is Rishod Sobirov who, uniquely, has won three medals. All three were bronzes in men's Judo – in 2008 and 2012 as an extra lightweight, and in 2016 as a half lightweight. A quick glance at the records may indicate that there was another multi-medallist; the men's freestyle heavyweight Wrestling saw a silver in 2004 and a bronze in 2016 both being won for Uzbekistan by Magomed Ibragimov; however, they were two different people. Remarkably, a third different wrestler called Magomed Ibragimov won a bronze for Macedonia in 2000.

TAJIKISTAN | **Olympic Rank 93rd**

Population: 9,245,937 (rank 97th)
Olympic rank/ population differential: +4
Population per gold: 9,245,937 (rank 82nd)
Population per medal: 2,311,484 (rank 101st)

Summer: 1 gold, 1 silver, 2 bronze (total 4)
Winter: *no medals (best finish: 44th)*
Total: 1 gold, 1 silver, 2 bronze (total 4)

Best sports: Athletics (1 gold, 0.10%, 63rd=)
Wrestling (1 silver, 44th=)
Judo (1 bronze, 46th=)

Like the other ex-Soviet republics, Tajikistan first entered the Summer Olympics in 1996. They have entered all Games since. Their best finish in 1996 was 9th, and in 2000 they managed only 41st. In 2004, they achieved their first two top-eight finishes, both in Wrestling – 7th for Lidiya Karamchakova and 8th for Shamil Aliyev.

In 2008, Tajikistan won their first ever Olympic medal, courtesy of Rasul Boqiev winning a bronze in the men's lightweight Judo, to go with the World Championship bronze he won the previous year. Later in the same Games, Russian-born Yusup Abdusalomov reached the final of the men's freestyle light heavyweight Wrestling, but had to settle for silver after losing to his Georgian opponent. Like Boqiev, he won the same colour of medal that he had done in the World Championships the previous year. Also in 2008, Anvar Yunusov and Jahon Qurbanov reached quarter-finals in Boxing. The 2008 Games are still the only ones in which Tajikistan won two medals.

In 2012, Mavzuna Chorieva took bronze in the women's lightweight Boxing. Rasul Boqiev returned in the lightweight Judo, finishing 7th this time. Alisher Gulov also claimed a top-eight finish in men's heavyweight Taekwondo – doing so by default after losing both matches but reaching the repechage due to his first-round victor reaching the final.

So by this point, Tajikistan had accrued nine top-eight finishes, all in combat sports – three in Boxing, three in Wrestling, two in Judo and one in Taekwondo. The two Games since then have both been disappointing by and large. They have only added one further top-eight finish, but at least it was a glorious one. Dilshod Nazarov was entering his fourth Olympics in the men's hammer throw. He had failed to land a valid throw in 2004, and finished 11th in 2008 and 10th in 2012. He then won silver at the 2015 World Championships. A year later, he became Tajikistan's first and only Olympic champion, winning gold comfortably ahead of Belarus's Ivan Tsikhan. In 2021, all of Nazarov's results from 2011 to 2013 (including his 10th place from 2012) were annulled after re-tests found him guilty of doping; however, subsequent results, including his gold medal, were allowed to stand. Tsikhan, for his part, has also been found guilty of numerous doping violations, but again his silver medal still stands. Nobody besides Nazarov has ever finished even in the top 40 of any Athletics event for Tajikistan.

Besides these five sports, Tajikistan have competed in a further five sports in Olympic competition. In Swimming, their best finish is 54th (women's 100m freestyle in 2000). They entered Diving in 1996 only, finishing 29th and 39th. They have entered Archery twice, finishing outside the top 40 both times. They have had one person entering Shooting – Sergey Babikov entered three Games, with a best finish of 10th in the men's air pistol in 2004. Finally, their one weightlifter finished 22nd in 2008.

Tajikistan's Winter Olympic participation has been extremely limited. Alpine skier Andrey Drygin competed in a total of nine events across three Games in 2002, 2006 and 2010. His best finish was 44th in the 2010 men's super G. The only other Tajikistani Winter Olympian is Alisher Qudratov, who entered the men's slalom in 2014 but failed to finish. Tajikistan have not entered the Winter Olympics in either 2018 or 2022.

KYRGYZSTAN   **Olympic Rank 105th**

Population:	6,122,781 (rank 112th)
Olympic rank/ population differential:	+7
Population per gold:	n/a
Population per medal:	874,683 (rank 79th)
Summer:	0 gold, 3 silver, 4 bronze (total 7)
Winter:	*no medals (best finish: 36th)*
Total:	0 gold, 3 silver, 4 bronze (total 7)
Best sports:	Wrestling (3 silvers, 3 bronzes, 38th)
	Judo (1 bronze, 46th=)
	Weightlifting

Kyrgyzstan have entered all Summer and Winter Games since 1994. Their success has been dominated by Wrestling. The sport has produced six of their seven medals, and 19 of their 24 top-eight finishes, including at least one at every Summer Games since 1996. Their success is fairly evenly split between Freestyle (11 top-eights and 3 medals) and Greco-Roman (8 and 3 respectively). Their six Wrestling medals came in just two Games – a silver and two bronzes in 2008 (equal 64th in the medal table), and two silvers and a bronze in 2021 (70th in the medal table). The silvers have been won by Kanatbek Begaliev (men's Greco-Roman lightweight, 2008), Akzhol Makhmudov (men's Greco-Roman middleweight, 2021) and Aisuluu Tynybekova (women's freestyle middleweight, 2021).

Kyrgyzstan's other Olympic medallist – indeed, their first – was Aidyn Smagulov, who won bronze in men's extra-lightweight Judo in 2000. There have been two top-eight finishes in Judo, two in Weightlifting and one in Boxing. Their best in Swimming was 14th in the women's 4x200m freestyle relay in 2000, although that was much the slowest of any of the finishers – the next best is 16th in the men's 200m breaststroke, also in 2000. Their best in Athletics was also achieved in 2000, in the women's marathon (14th place).

Kyrgyzstan have also sent a delegation to every Winter Games since 1994, though their team has only ever consisted of one or two competitors. Their best finish is 36th (men's 20km Biathlon in 1998), and they have also competed in Ski Jumping (best of equal 39th), Alpine Skiing (best of 40th) and Nordic Skiing (best of 54th).

TURKMENISTAN   **Olympic Rank 123rd**

Population:	5,690,818 (rank 115th)
Olympic rank/ population differential:	-8
Population per gold:	n/a
Population per medal:	5,690,818 (rank 111th)
Summer:	0 gold, 1 silver, 0 bronze (total 1)
Winter:	*never participated*
Total:	0 gold, 1 silver, 0 bronze (total 1)
Best sports:	Weightlifting (1 silver, 54th=)
	Shooting
	Wrestling

Turkmenistan have competed at all Summer Games since 1996, but have never competed at the Winter Games, and they are the most northerly country in the world never to have done so. In the Summer Games, they have competed in eight sports – Athletics and Judo every time, Weightlifting six times, Swimming and Boxing five times, and Shooting, Wrestling and Table Tennis.

Their best finish in Athletics is 13th, achieved by Viktoriya Brigadnaya in women's triple jump in 2000 (nobody else has managed better than 30th). Their best in Swimming is 29th (men's 200m backstroke in 2021). However, their best success has come in Weightlifting, which has provided six of their seven top-eight finishes, as well as their only medal. Polina Guryeva was the woman who got it, in lightweight in 2021. She was given an apartment and a car in recognition of her achievement. The 4th place achieved, also in 2021, by Hojamuhammet Toycyyew is Turkmenistan's second-best finish in an Olympic event. Their only other top-eight finish was in men's small-bore rifle (prone) Shooting in 2000 (7th).

CHAPTER TWENTY-FOUR - Southern Asia (India, Pakistan, Sri Lanka, Afghanistan, Nepal, Bangladesh, Bhutan, Maldives)

INDIA **Olympic Rank 50th**
Population: 1,399,179,585 (rank 2nd)
Olympic rank/ population differential: -48
Population per gold: 139,917,959 (rank 102nd)
Population per medal: 39,976,560 (rank 136th)

Summer: 10 gold, 9 silver, 16 bronze (total 35)
Winter: *no medals (best finish: 25th)*
Total: 10 gold, 9 silver, 16 bronze (total 35)

Best sports: Hockey (8 golds, 22.86%, 1st)
Shooting (1 gold, 0.33%, 30th=)
Athletics (1 gold, 0.10%, 54th)

Of the 102 countries to have won Olympic gold medals, the vast nation of India have by far the worst ratio of gold medals to population. It would be even worse too, were it not for their complete domination of men's Hockey for three decades either side of World War II. In the 21st Century, however, their medal performances have improved massively. Despite not gaining independence from Britain until 1947, India competed as a separate Olympic nation right from their debut in 1900. That year, they sent one participant – Norman Pritchard – who won two silvers in the 200 metres and the 200m hurdles. Indian-born, he left for Britain in 1905, before moving to California and becoming a silent movie star. India returned to the Olympics in 1920, and have competed in all Games since.

They first entered the Hockey event in 1928, and won gold straight away. They retained their title in 1932, 1936, 1948, 1952 and 1956. In 1960, they reached the final yet again, although by this time their wins were getting narrower, and in the final they lost 1-0 to fierce rivals Pakistan, ending a run of 30 successive wins in Olympic matches. They went on to regain gold in 1964, before bronzes in 1968 and 1972. In 1976, they missed out on the medals entirely after losing what was effectively a quarter-final to Australia on penalties. In 1980, they won gold yet again. Their dominance fell away completely after that, although in 2021 they won their first hockey medal for 41 years (a bronze). In women's Hockey, their best finish so far is 4th (in both 1980 and 2021).

Between Pritchard's medals in 1900, and Leander Paes winning bronze in the men's singles Tennis in 1996, India only ever won one non-Hockey medal. That went to Khashaba Jadav in freestyle Wrestling in 1952. So in the 20th Century, India won 15 medals, of which 11 were in Hockey. In the 21st Century, India have won 20 medals, across a wide range of sports. Two of them have been golds – their first ever non-Hockey golds. Abhinav Bindra won the men's air rifle Shooting in 2008, and Neeraj Chopra won the men's javelin in 2021 – India's first Athletics medal of any colour for 121 years.

There have also been six further Wrestling medals, all in freestyle, three further Shooting medals, three medals each in Badminton and Boxing, and two in Weightlifting, as well as that Hockey bronze. They have come close to medals in Football (4th in 1956, men), Golf (4th in 2021, women) and Gymnastics (4th in the women's vault in 2016). India's best Swimming finish is 15th (both in the 1932 men's 1500m freestyle, when only 15 competed, and the 1956 men's 200m breaststroke).

India's best Olympics by medals won have been 2021 (1 gold, 2 silver and 4 bronze) and 2012 (2 silver and 4 bronze). They have never won more than one gold in a Games, and their highest finish is 18th in 1900. Two Hockey players have won 3 golds and a silver each – Leslie Claudius (1948-60) and Udham Singh (1952-64). Three non-Hockey players have won two medals each (but none of them gold) – Norman Pritchard, Sushil Kumar (Wrestling, 2008-12) and P.V. Sindhu (Badminton, 2016-21).

India's first Winter Olympian was the Polish-born Jeremy Bujakowski, who entered in 1964 and 1968 with no great success. The nation then returned in 1988, and have entered all Winter Games since, other than 1994. Six of their seven top-40 finishes have been achieved by Shiva Keshavan in the men's singles Luge; his (and India's) best finish is 25th.

PAKISTAN   **Olympic Rank 70th**

Population:	247,653,551 (rank 5th)
Olympic rank/ population differential:	-65
Population per gold:	82,551,184 (rank 99th)
Population per medal:	24,765,355 (rank 134th)
Summer:	3 gold, 3 silver, 4 bronze (total 10)
Winter:	*no medals (best finish: 71st)*
Total:	3 gold, 3 silver, 4 bronze (total 10)
Best sports:	Hockey (3 golds, 8.57%, 6th)
	Wrestling (1 bronze, 52nd=)
	Boxing (1 bronze, 61st=)

Like their bigger neighbours India, Pakistan's main sporting obsession is Cricket, whose absence from the Olympics does Pakistan no favours. Their national sport, however, is Hockey, and it is this sport which has provided the vast majority of Pakistan's rather meagre medal haul – all three golds, all three silvers, and two of their four bronzes. In fact, even their Hockey success is some time ago now.

Pakistan gained independence in 1947, and made their Olympic debut the very next year. They have entered all Summer Games since, with the exception of the 1980 boycott. The men's Hockey team finished 4th in their first two Olympics, but then won silver in 1956 and gold in 1960 (inflicting a famous defeat on India), followed by silver, gold, silver and bronze in the next four Games. After their 1980 absence, they won gold for the third time in 1984. Between 1988 and 2012, they managed top-eight finishes every time, but only one further medal (a bronze in 1992). In 2016, however, they failed to qualify for the first time ever, and the same happened again in 2021. The women's team have never qualified for the Olympics. Hockey has, of course, provided numerous multi-medallists for Pakistan, though nobody played in more than one gold medal-winning squad. The best individual records are held by six players – Anwar Khan, Manzoor Hussain Atif, Motiullah Khan, Muhammad Asad Malik, Munir Dar and Saeed Anwar – all of whom have one gold and two silvers in their collection.

There have been only two medals – both bronzes – ever won by Pakistan in any other sport. They were won by Muhammad Bashir in the men's freestyle welterweight Wrestling in 1960, and Hussain Shah in the men's middleweight Boxing in 1988. It means 1960 is the only time that Pakistan have ever won two medals at the same Games, giving them their best finishing position of 20th in that year. Other than their 16 top-eight finishes in Hockey, Pakistan have had 18 other top-eight finishes – 10 in Wrestling (nine between 1956 and 1964, and the other in 1984), three in Boxing (none since 1988), four in Athletics and one in Weightlifting.

In Tokyo in 2021, Arshad Nadeem finished 5th place in the men's javelin. In doing so, he created history by becoming the first Pakistani to compete in an Athletics final. The nation had managed three previous top-eight finishes; they were in the men's 100 metres and 200 metres in 1956, and the men's 110m hurdles in 1960 – but in those days, only six competed in the final. Also in 2021, Pakistan managed their first top-eight finish in Weightlifting – 5th place in the men's lightweight. It meant those two top-eights in 2021 were Pakistan's first outside of Hockey since 1988.

Pakistan's best finish in Swimming is 13th in the men's 4x200m freestyle relay in 1948, with by far the slowest time of any finishers. The next best is 16th in the men's 200m butterfly in 1956. The best finish by any Pakistani female in the Olympics is 28th, in the 10m air rifle Shooting in 2016.

Meanwhile, Pakistan have sent three men to the Winter Olympics. Muhammad Karim is the most prolific, entering Alpine Skiing events in 2014, 2018 and 2022, and he has the nation's best Winter finish (71st in the giant slalom in 2014). The others were an alpine skier in 2010 and a cross-country skier in 2018.

SRI LANKA   **Olympic Rank 111th**

Population:	23,326,272 (rank 58th)
Olympic rank/ population differential:	-53
Population per gold:	n/a
Population per medal:	11,663,136 (rank 126th)
Summer:	0 gold, 2 silver, 0 bronze (total 2)
Winter:	*never participated*
Total:	0 gold, 2 silver, 0 bronze (total 2)
Best sports:	Athletics (2 silvers, 72nd=)
	Boxing
	Badminton

The independence of Ceylon from Britain was secured in 1948, and they first entered the Olympics later that same year. They have since competed in every Summer Games, with the exception of 1976, having changed their name to Sri Lanka in 1972. They have never competed in the Winter Games.

On their first appearance, Duncan White, born and raised in British Ceylon, won a silver medal in the men's 400m hurdles. That same year, Albert Perera reached the quarter-finals in the bantamweight Boxing. The nation wouldn't get close to a medal again until light-flyweight boxer Hatha Karunaratne lost in the 1968 quarter-finals, and not again after that until 2000. That year in Sydney, Susanthika Jayasinghe won a bronze in the women's 200 metres, her nation's first medal for over 50 years. But rather than being celebrated, she was used as a political pawn and she didn't receive the kudos she had earned. Years later, her bronze was upgraded to silver when Marion Jones's gold was rescinded for extensive drug use.

Sri Lanka have not managed another top-eight finish since, despite competing in numerous sports over the years. Their best performance outside of Athletics and Boxing has been Niluka Karunaratne's narrow defeat in the last 16 of the 2012 men's singles Badminton. Sri Lanka's most successful swimmer has been Julian Bolling, who in 1984 finished 21st in the 400m individual medley, and 27th in the 1500m freestyle.

AFGHANISTAN   **Olympic Rank 130th**

Population:	39,232,003 (rank 37th)
Olympic rank/ population differential:	-93
Population per gold:	n/a
Population per medal:	19,616,002 (rank 131st)
Summer:	0 gold, 0 silver, 2 bronze (total 2)
Winter:	*never participated*
Total:	0 gold, 0 silver, 2 bronze (total 2)
Best sports:	Taekwondo (2 bronzes, 34th=)
	Hockey
	Wrestling

Afghanistan's involvement in the Summer Olympics has been more sporadic than most. They first entered in 1936. Since then, they have missed 1952, 1976, 1984, 1992 and 2000. They have participated over the years in Athletics, Hockey (most recently in 1956), Football (1948 only), Wrestling (most recently in 2004), Boxing, Judo, Taekwondo, Swimming (2021 only) and Shooting (also 2021 only). They have never entered the Winter Olympics. They first included women on their team in 2004.

Both of their medals have been won by the same man – Taekwondo's Rohullah Nikpai, who took bronzes in flyweight in 2008 and featherweight in 2012. On both occasions, he lost in the quarter-finals, but got a reprieve in the repechage, winning two matches each time to earn his medals. Another Taekwondo competitor, Nesar Ahmad Bahawi, has also managed two top-eight finishes. Of Afghanistan's seven top-eight finishes in Olympic competition, three have come outside of Taekwondo – two in men's Hockey (6th in 1936 and 8th in 1948) and one in freestyle Wrestling (5th in 1964). Their only Olympic swimmer thus far finished 69th in the men's 50m freestyle in 2021.

NEPAL Olympic Rank 156th

Population: 30,899,443 (rank 49th)
Olympic rank/ population differential: -107

Summer: *no medals (best finish: 7th)*
Winter: *no medals (best finish: 69th)*

Best sports: Taekwondo
Weightlifting
Boxing

Nepal have entered all Summer Olympics since 1964, with the exception of 1968. They have competed in Athletics, Swimming, Shooting, Boxing, Weightlifting, Judo, Taekwondo and Archery in that time. Only three times have they managed a top-eight finish, and all three of those were by default. All three were in Taekwondo and, in each case, the Nepalese competitor lost in the first round but entered into the repechage due to their conqueror reaching the final, only to lose in the first round of the repechage too. The way that Taekwondo rankings work, though, means that automatically earns a top-eight finish. Two of them, Sangina Baidya (2004 women's flyweight) and Nisha Rawal (2016 women's heavyweight) finished 7th; the other finished 8th. Bidhan Lama was a semi-finalist in 1988, but Taekwondo was only a demonstration sport at that time.

Nepal have finished as high as 14th in Weightlifting and 15th in Boxing. They first entered Swimming in 1996, and have a best finish of 31st (2016 women's 100m backstroke). In Athletics, they have never progressed beyond a first-round heat. Two Nepalese athletes have competed in the Winter Games – Jay Khadka (2002 and 2006) and Dachhiri Sherpa (2006 to 2014). Both were in Nordic Skiing; the best finish is Khadka's 69th in 2002. In 1924, gold medals were awarded by Baron de Coubertin to members of the 1922 British Mount Everest expedition. Among them was Nepalese national Tejbir Bura, but these medals are not officially recognised today.

BANGLADESH Olympic Rank 197th

Population: 167,184,465 (rank 8th)
Olympic rank/ population differential: -189

Summer: *no medals (best finish: 16th)*
Winter: *never participated*

Best sports: Archery
Athletics
Shooting

Of all the countries who have never won an Olympic medal, Bangladesh have by far the largest population, almost double that of the next country on the list, DR Congo. And, to be honest, they've never even come close to a medal. They have entered all Summer Games since 1984, though never the Winter Olympics. In that time they've entered Athletics (every time), Swimming (every time since 1988), Shooting (every time since 1992), Archery (since 2012), Gymnastics (2012 only) and Golf (2016 only).

In Golf, Siddikur Rahman became, in 2016, the only Bangladeshi in any sport ever to qualify by right for the Olympics (all others relied on wildcards). He finished 58th. In Swimming, Bangladesh's best is 39th (men's 50m freestyle in 2012). In Gymnastics, Bangladesh finished 27th out of 71 in the men's parallel bars. In Shooting, Abdullah Hel Baki finished 25th out of 50 in the men's air rifle in 2016.

In Archery, they finished 16th out of 29 in the ranking round of the inaugural mixed team event in 2021, which allowed them to sneak into the knockout stages – they lost to South Korea in the last 16. The male member of their team, Ruman Shana, that year also became the first Bangladeshi to win a round in an individual event, beating his British opponent in the first round. In Athletics, they've only ever entered the 100, 200, 400 and 800 metres, the 4x100m relay and the long jump. They've never progressed beyond the first round of any of them. Their best finishes have been in their two relay entries, 25th in 1988 and 22nd in 1992, both in the men's events. In 1988 they were faster than the Maldives, but in 1992 they were the slowest of all those who finished.

BHUTAN   **Olympic Rank 198th**
Population: 876,181 (rank 164th)
Olympic rank/ population differential: -34

Summer: *no medals (best finish: 17th)*
Winter: *never participated*

Best sports: Archery
                                                    Judo
                                                    Shooting

Bhutan first entered the Olympics in 1984, and their Olympic history is somewhat unusual. Up to and including 2008, the only sport they ever entered was Archery. Bhutan is, indeed, the only country in the world to have declared Archery as its national sport. They have entered Archery every time since then as well, but have now added Shooting, Judo and Swimming. Remarkably, however, they have never entered Athletics. It is also notable that, despite its proximity to the Himalayas, Bhutan have never entered the Winter Olympics.

What is also surprising about Bhutan is that, despite their obsession with Archery, they are not particularly good at it. In individual events, they have only twice reached the last 32 (Tashi Peljor in the men's, and Tshering Choden in the women's, both in 2004; both failed to progress further than that). The highest three positions that Bhutan have ever achieved in Olympic competition have all been in the Archery team competitions (17th by the women in 1992, 20th by the men in 1992 and 22nd by the men in 1988). In each case, Bhutan came last.

Bhutan have entered Shooting in 2012, 2016 and 2021, in each case in the women's 10m air rifle; their best position so far is 43rd. Their only Olympic swimmer so far is Sangay Tenzin, who came 68th in the men's 100m freestyle in 2021. Their only judoka is Ngawang Namgyel in the men's extra-lightweight in 2021; he came 23rd and last.

MALDIVES   **Olympic Rank 203rd**
Population: 389,568 (rank 174th)
Olympic rank/ population differential: -29

Summer: *no medals (best finish: 26th)*
Winter: *never participated*

Best sports: Athletics
                                                    Badminton
                                                    Swimming

The Maldives made their Olympic bow in 1988, and have entered every Summer Games since, though understandably never the Winter Games. They have only entered three different sports in that time – Athletics (every time), Swimming (every time since 1992), and Badminton (2012 and 2021 only).

In Swimming, all but one of their entries have been 50m or 100m freestyle. The one exception, the women's 100m breaststroke in 2021, produced their highest finish of 43rd, though the highest finish of any Maldivian swimmer who actually finished faster than somebody else was 53rd. The two Maldivian Badminton players both went out in the group stage after losing two out of two, and finished 39th and 40th in the final rankings.

Athletics, meanwhile, has provided the best finishing positions for the Islands, though none of their athletes have ever progressed past the first round of their competitions (albeit on two occasions they have had a 100-metre runner progressing from the preliminary round). Their highest finish of all is 26th in the men's sprint relay in 1988 – 30 teams entered, and four were either disqualified or failed to finish. In 1996, the men's 4x400m team finished 32nd, but again, that was the slowest out of those who finished. The highest finish by an individual athlete is 33rd, by Yaznee Nasheeda in the women's 800 metres in 1996 – once again, the slowest of those who finished.

CHAPTER TWENTY-FIVE - Eastern Asia (China, Japan, South Korea, North Korea, Chinese Taipei, Mongolia, Hong Kong)

CHINA   **Olympic Rank 5th**

Population:	1,413,142,846 (rank 1st)
Olympic rank/ population differential:	-4
Population per gold:	4,958,396 (rank 72nd)
Population per medal:	1,981,968 (rank 98th)
Summer:	263 gold, 199 silver, 174 bronze (total 636)
Winter:	22 gold, 32 silver, 23 bronze (total 77)
Total:	285 gold, 231 silver, 197 bronze (total 713)
Best sports:	Table Tennis (32 golds, 86.49%, 1st)
	Badminton (20 golds, 51.28%, 1st)
	Diving (47 golds, 36.15%, 2nd)

The Republic of China took part in the Summer Olympics of 1932 to 1948, without winning any medals. In 1949, the government relocated to Taiwan, and political difficulties between Taiwan and the mainland then meant that China did not appear at the Games after 1952 until the Winter Games of 1980. They boycotted the Summer Games that year, but have participated in every Games since 1984, going from strength to strength.

In 1984, they won 15 golds and finished 4th in the medal table. The 1988 Games were a disappointment, with just 5 golds putting them 11th, but since then they have won at least 16 golds every time, finishing 4th in 1992 and 1996, and in the top three every time since 2000. They have topped the medal table once – in Beijing in 2008, with a record 48 golds and 100 medals in total. But, surprisingly, they slipped back after that, winning 38 golds in 2012 and "only" 26 in 2016, before recovering to 38 golds in 2021. Four Chinese Olympians have won five golds each – Wu Minxia and Chen Ruolin (Diving), Zou Kai (Gymnastics) and Ma Long (Table Tennis).

They failed to win a medal in any of the three 1980s Winter Games, and failed to win a gold in any of the three 1990s Games. Their first gold came in 2002. By far their best Winter showing also came in Beijing, in 2022, with nine golds, 15 medals in total, and 3rd place in the medal table (their only other top-10 finish was in 2010).

SUMMER
Table Tennis (32-20-8, 1st). No country has ever dominated any Olympic sport as much as China have dominated Table Tennis. They have won all but five of the 37 golds ever awarded, and 27 of the 29 since 1996. There have been 17 events with all-Chinese finals. The most decorated of China's production line of Table Tennis stars is Ma Long with five golds (men's team 2012-21 and singles 2016-21).

Badminton (20-12-15, 1st). China have won 20 of the 39 Badminton events since its introduction in 1992, and only failed to medal in eight of them. Six of the events have had all-Chinese finals. There are ten people who have two Olympic Badminton golds – nine of those are Chinese.

Diving (47-24-10, 2nd). China have won 47 out of 64 available golds since 1984, and won seven out of eight in three of the last four Games (2008, 2016 & 2021). They have medalled in 62 of those most recent 64 events. Chen Ruolin won five golds in women's platform (2008-16), whilst Wu Minxia won five golds, a silver and a bronze in women's springboard (2004-16). They are the most successful divers of all time.

Weightlifting (38-16-8, 2nd). China have taken 17 of the 42 golds available in women's Weightlifting. But they have won at least one men's gold at each Games since 1996 too.

Taekwondo (7-1-3, 2nd). Won only a bronze in 2021, the first time they failed to win gold. Six of the seven golds have gone to women, including two each for Chen Zhong (2000 & 2004) and Wu Jingyu (2008 & 2012).

Volleyball (3-1-2, 5th). All six medals were for the women, including golds in 1984, 2004 & 2016. The men entered only in 1984 & 2008.

Shooting (26-16-25, 3rd). China have won golds at every Games since 1984 except for 1988.

Gymnastics (33-26-25, 4th). Zou Kai is the most decorated gymnast, with five golds and a bronze in 2008 & 2012. Li Xiaoshuang (1996) and Yang Wei (2008) won the men's all-around. The men won team gold in 2000, 2008 and 2012, and the women in 2008.

Judo (8-3-11, 5th). Just a single men's medal – a bronze in 2016. No medals in 2021, for the first time since 1988. Xian Dongmei won women's half-lightweight in 2004 & 2008.

Swimming (16-21-12, 9th). 38 of the 49 medals came in women's events, including all 21 won prior to 2008. Sun Yang took 3 golds, 2 silvers and a bronze in men's freestyle events in 2012 and 2016.

Fencing (5-7-3, 6th). China have won golds in five events – women's individual foil (1984), men's individual sabre (2008), men's individual foil and women's team épée (2012), and women's individual épée (2021).

Sailing (3-3-2, 16th). Yin Jian (2008) and Lu Yunxiu (2021) won windsurfing; Xu Lijia (2012) won laser radial. Six of the eight medals came in windsurfing; the other two in laser radial. Only one men's medal so far.

Archery (1-6-2, 8th). Zhang Juanjuan won the women's title in Beijing. The most recent medals came in 2012.

Tennis (1-0-1, 14th=). Both medals came in women's doubles (gold in 2004, bronze in 2008). All four top-eight finishes came in women's events.

Canoeing (3-2-0, 22nd). Won the men's C2 500m in 2004 & 2008, and the women's equivalent in 2021.

Boxing (3-5-6, 20th). Zou Shiming won China's first Boxing medal – a light-flyweight bronze in 2004. He went on to win gold in the event in 2008 & 2012. Zhang Xiaoping (2008) was the other gold winner.

Athletics (10-12-15, 19th). Half of China's 10 golds have come in walking events. Just nine medals for men; the only man to win a gold other than in walking is Liu Xiang, taking the 110m hurdles in 2004.

Cycling (2-3-3, 16th). The two golds were both in women's team sprint (2016 & 2021). Zhong Tianshi rode in both. All the medals have come since 2000, and all have gone to women.

Rowing (2-4-6, 19th). The two golds were both in women's quadruple sculls (2008 & 2021). All but one medal (a bronze in 2021) have gone to women.

Wrestling (2-5-8, 27th). The two golds were both in women's freestyle heavyweight (2004 & 2008). Nine of the 15 medals have gone to women.

Artistic Swimming (0-5-2, 4th). Have won silver in 5 of the 6 events since 2012 (losing to Russia each time).

Karate (0-1-1, 11th=). Two entries in 2021, both for women, and both won medals.

Beach Volleyball (0-1-1, 6th). Both medals came in the same event – the 2008 women's event.

Golf (0-0-1, 9th=). Feng Shanshan won women's bronze in 2016, and came 8th in 2021.

Baseball/Softball (0-1-0, 6th=). Won Softball silver in 1996, and came 4th in 2000 and 2004. Entered Baseball just once – as hosts in 2008.

Basketball (0-1-2, 11th). The women took bronze in 1984 and silver in 1992. The men's best is 8th (four times). China also took bronze in the 2021 women's 3x3 competition.

Handball (0-0-1, 17th=). Women's bronze in 1984. Their best this century is 6th (in 2008). The men also made their only entry that year (as hosts), losing every game.

Football (0-1-0, 25th=). Women's silver in 1996. Three other top-eight finishes, all for women. The men entered in 1936, 1948, 1988 and 2008.

Hockey (0-1-0, 13th=). Women's silver in 2008. Three other top-eight finishes, all for women. The men entered only in 2008 (as hosts).

Modern Pentathlon (0-1-0, 15th=). Cao Zhongrong took men's silver in 2012. China came 4th in both men's and women's events in 2008.

Skateboarding – Entered both women's events in 2021. Zeng Wenhui came 6th in the street event.

Rugby – Made their debut in the 2021 women's competition. Wins over Japan and Russia saw them into 7th.

Equestrianism – Never entered until the Beijing 2008 Games, but have entered a number of competitors since then. Hua Tian came 8th in the individual three-day eventing in 2016.

Water Polo – Made their debut in 1984, when the men finished 9th – still the best finish for the men. The women finished 5th in both 2008 and 2012.

Sport Climbing – Came 12th in the inaugural women's event in 2021, and 14th in the men's.

Triathlon – Have entered every Olympics since 2000, but never finished higher than 32nd.

Surfing, PWDS – never entered

WINTER
Short Track Speed Skating (12-16-9, 2nd). Medals in all Games since 1992, and golds in all Games since their first in 2002. Wang Meng is the most successful female ever in Short Track, winning a gold, silver and bronze in 2006, and three golds in 2010.

Freestyle Skiing (5-8-4, 4th). Two golds and a silver for Eileen Gu in 2022.

Figure Skating (2-3-4, 11th). Two women's bronzes in 1994 & 1998, since when all seven medals have been in the pairs event, including golds in 2010 & 2022.

Snowboarding (1-2-0, 12th). Su Yiming picked up a gold and a silver in 2022.

Speed Skating (2-3-4, 12th). Golds for Zhang Hong (2014) and Gao Tingyu (2022).

Skeleton (0-0-1, 12th=). Yan Wengang took women's bronze in 2022.

Curling (0-0-1, 12th=). Women's bronze in 2010. 4th places for the men in 2014 and mixed doubles in 2018.

Ice Hockey – The women finished 4th on their debut in 1998, which is still their best finish. The men made their debut in 2022, and lost every game.

Biathlon – Regular competitors. China's best finish is 5th by Yu Shumei in the women's 7.5km sprint in 1998.

Bobsleigh – Never entered until 2018, and only managed 26th place on that occasion. But in 2022, they had eight entries all doing better than that, including 6th place for Huai Mingming in the women's monobob.

Nordic Skiing – Regular entrants since 1980, but their best two performances both came in 2022 (10th in the women's relay, and 11th in the women's team sprint). Their best in an individual event is 18th.

Ski Jumping – Have competed in 2006, 2018 and 2022. Their best finish is 10th (and last) in the mixed team event in 2022. Their best finish that wasn't last was 20th (women's normal hill in 2018).

Nordic Combined – First entered in 2022, when they entered all three events, finishing 10th (and last) in the team event, and 43rd and 47th in the two individual events.

Luge – First entered in 2022, when they entered all four events, finishing 12th out of 14 in the mixed team relay.

Alpine Skiing – Have been entering since 1980, but their best four finishes all came in 2022. They came 15th in both the women's combined and mixed team events.

JAPAN   **Olympic Rank 10th**

Population: 123,719,238 (rank 11th)
Olympic rank/ population differential: +1
Population per gold: 665,157 (rank 46th)
Population per medal: 215,915 (rank 51st)

Summer: 169 gold, 150 silver, 178 bronze (total 497)
Winter: 17 gold, 28 silver, 31 bronze (total 76)
Total: 186 gold, 178 silver, 209 bronze (total 573)

Best sports: Skateboarding (3 golds, 75.00%, 1st)
Judo (48 golds, 31.58%, 1st)
Baseball/Softball (3 golds, 27.27%, 2nd)

Japan made their Olympic debut in 1912, and have entered every Games since, apart from 1948 (when they were banned from both Winter and Summer Games in the aftermath of the war) and 1980 (when they boycotted the Summer Games). Japan's first medals were two Tennis silvers in 1920. Their first golds came in 1928, one each in Athletics and Swimming. They have never failed to win a gold since, and in Tokyo 2021 they smashed all previous records. They won 27 golds (previous best: 16, both in 1964 and 2004), and they won 58 medals in total (previous best: 41, set in 2016). Their 3rd place finish emulated that of Tokyo 1964 and Mexico City 1968.

Their first Winter medallist was Chiharu Igaya (Alpine Skiing, 1956), and their only gold prior to 1992 came in the 1972 Ski Jumping (when Yukio Kasaya led a Japanese 1-2-3 in Sapporo). Their only top-10 medal table finish came in Nagano in 1998, when they came 7th after winning a record 5 golds. The most medals they have won in a Winter Games is 18, set in 2022.

Inevitably, all of Japan's most decorated Olympians have been gymnasts, although Kosuke Kitajima (Swimming) and Kaori Icho (Wrestling) can boast astonishing achievements in winning 4 golds each.

SUMMER
Skateboarding (3-1-1, 1st). In 2021, they won gold and silver in women's park, gold and bronze in women's street, gold in men's street, and came 14th in men's park.

Judo (48-21-27, 1st). Judo was introduced to the Games in Tokyo in 1964, and not surprisingly Japan have dominated, winning 48 golds, with France in second place with 16. They have won at least one gold at each Games, and won a record nine in the Tokyo 2021 Games. Their one three-time champion is Tadahiro Nomura, who won men's extra-lightweight in 1996, 2000 and 2004.

Baseball/Softball (3-2-3, 2nd). After Baseball silver in 1996, and bronzes in 1992 and 2004, they won gold in 2021. In Softball, they won silver in 2000 and bronze in 2004, and golds in 2008 and 2021.

Karate (1-1-1, 1st). Ryo Kiyuna won men's kata in 2021. Japan also took silver in women's kata, and bronze in men's >75kg. They finished top-eight in all 8 events.

Volleyball (3-3-3, 4th). The women won gold in 1964 & 1976, the men in 1972. Seven of their nine medals came between 1964 and 1976; the only medal this century is a 2012 bronze for the women. The men's best this century is 7th.

Gymnastics (33-34-36, 3rd). Sawao Kato is the only male gymnast ever to win 8 Olympic golds (he won 12 medals in all, 1968-76). Akinori Nakayama won six golds (1968-72). Japan have medalled in the men's team event in 14 of the last 17 Games (missing out only in 1996 & 2000 as well as the 1980 boycott). They have only ever won two women's medals (both bronze – team in 1964 and floor in 2021).

Wrestling (37-22-17, 3rd). Particularly adept in freestyle, Japan's last Greco-Roman gold came in 1984. They have been hugely dominant in women's Wrestling, winning 15 of the 24 titles (and medalling in five more) since its introduction in 2004. Kaori Icho won four in a row (middleweight & welterweight), from 2004 to 2016.

Swimming (24-27-32, 6th). There has been a regular stream of Japanese medallists, the pick of whom has been Kosuke Kitajima, who won the men's 100m/200m breaststroke double in both 2004 & 2008, and three medley medals too.

Table Tennis (1-3-4, 3rd). Won their first medal in 2012, and their first gold (mixed doubles) in 2021, beating China in the final – the first gold China have not won in any Table Tennis event since 2004.

Badminton (1-1-2, 5th). Won women's doubles gold in 2016. Their first medal came in 2012.

Boxing (3-0-5, 23rd). Three medals in the 1960s, including gold for Takao Sakuri. The other medals have all been since 2012, including golds for Ryota Murata (2012) and Sena Irie (2021).

Weightlifting (2-3-10, 23rd). Yoshinobu Miyake won Japan's first Weightlifting medal – silver in 1960. He then won golds in 1964 & 1968. Just one silver and two bronzes this century.

Athletics (7-10-10, 25th). Japan have been largely disappointing in Olympic Athletics. They won 13 medals between 1928 and 1936, but only another five after that until the end of the century – none of them gold, and all of them in marathons. Their only three post-war golds have been in the women's marathons of 2000 and 2004, and the men's hammer of 2004 (after the original gold medallist was stripped of his title due to doping).

Equestrianism (1-0-0, 19th=). Takeichi Nishi took individual jumping gold in 1932. Their best since then is 4th place in individual three-day eventing in 2021.

Fencing (1-2-0, 19th). Yuki Ota took men's individual foil silver in 2008. Japan then took men's team foil silver in 2012, and men's team épée gold in 2021.

Shooting (1-2-3, 28th=). Takeo Kamachi won the men's rapid-fire pistol in 1984. The most recent medals came in 1992.

Sport Climbing (0-1-1, 3rd). Japan took silver and bronze in the 2021 women's, and came 4th in the men's.

Surfing (0-1-1, 3rd). Japan took silver in the 2021 men's event, and bronze in the women's.

Artistic Swimming (0-4-10, 5th). Have won medals at all Games since 1984, other than 2012 and 2021. The silvers came in the events in 2000 & 2004.

Golf (0-1-0, 6th=). Mone Inami took women's silver in 2021. Japan came 8th in the men's.

Archery (0-3-4, 15th). Five of the medals came in men's individual, ranging from 1976 to 2021.

Football (0-1-1, 23rd=). The men took bronze in 1968, and finished 4th in 2012 & 2021. The women came 4th in 2008, and took silver in 2012.

Tennis (0-2-1, 21st). Japan won silvers in men's singles and doubles in 1920, and men's singles bronze (for Kei Nishikori) in 2016.

Basketball (0-1-0, 13th=). The women took silver in 2021. The men have entered 7 times since 1936, but have never reached the top eight. Japan came 5th and 6th in the two 3x3 events in 2021.

Hockey (0-1-0, 13th=). The men claimed silver in 1932. As hosts in 2021, the men participated for the first time since 1968. The women came 8th in 2004.

Cycling (0-2-3, 30th). Won their first medal in 1984. Took silvers in men's team sprint (1984) and women's omnium (2021).

Taekwondo (0-0-1, 37th=). Women's welterweight bronze in 2000. No man has yet finished in the top eight.

Sailing (0-1-1, 32nd=). Women's 470 silver in 1996; men's 470 bronze in 2004.

Canoeing (0-0-1, 35th=). Men's C1 slalom bronze in 2016. Their flatwater best is 5th in 2008.

Diving – The Japanese Diving best remains the two 4th places achieved in 1936 by Tsuneo Shibihara (men's springboard) and Reiko Osawa (women's platform). 5th places have been achieved in 2000 and twice in 2021.

Beach Volleyball – Two quarter-final appearances, both for the women. They came in 1996 and 2000, the latter of which saw Japan finish 4th, losing the bronze match to the Brazilian pair.

Rugby – In 2016, the men beat New Zealand and France, but had to settle for 4th place in the end. It remains their only top-eight finish.

Water Polo – In the 1932 men's event, they lost their three matches 10-0, 18-0 and 10-0, but finished 4th out of 5 after Brazil were withdrawn from the competition. Their next best finish is 9th (2021 women's event).

Handball – The best two performances both came in 1976 – 5th for the women and 9th for the men. In 2021, as hosts, they competed for the first time since 1988.

Triathlon – Their only top-eight finish so far was 5th for Juri Ide in the 2008 women's event.

Rowing – Finished 6th three times – men's coxed pairs (1932) and lightweight double sculls (2000 and 2004).

Modern Pentathlon – Japan finished 8th in the now-defunct team event in 1964, and 7th in 1968. Their best in an individual event is 12th (women's in 2016).

PWDS – never entered

WINTER

Ski Jumping (4-6-4, 5th). Having only ever previously won one Winter medal (and not in Ski Jumping), Japan completed a 1-2-3 in the 1972 men's normal hill, Yukio Kasaya taking gold. Kazuyoshi Funaki won large hill and team golds (and normal hill silver) in 1998, and Ryoyu Kobayashi took gold and silver in 2022.

Nordic Combined (2-3-2, 5th). Men's team golds in 1992 and 1994. Four medals this century, all involving Akito Watabe (three silvers and a bronze, 2014 to 2022).

Figure Skating (3-4-4, 9th). Golds for Shizuka Arakawa (2006 women's) and Yazuru Hanyu (men's in 2014 & 2018).

Speed Skating (5-10-11, 9th). Golds in 1998, 2022 and three in 2018. Sisters Nana and Miho Takagi have won an individual gold each as well as a team gold.

Snowboarding (1-3-3, 9th). Ayumu Hirano took men's halfpipe silver in 2014 & 2018, and gold in 2022.

Freestyle Skiing (1-0-4, 12th). Tae Satoya won women's moguls in 1998.

Short Track Speed Skating (1-0-2, 9th). Takafumi Nishitani took men's 500m gold in 1998. No medals this century.

Curling (0-1-1, 8th). Women's bronze in 2018 and silver in 2022. The men's best is 5th (1998).

Alpine Skiing (0-1-0, 19th=). Men's slalom silver in 1956. Two top-eight finishes this century, both in the same event (2006 men's slalom).

Luge – In 1972 at home, Yuko Otaka came 5th in the women's singles, and the men's doubles team came 4th. Japan's next best in Luge is a mere 12th.

Nordic Skiing – Five top-eight finishes; the best is 5th for Masako Ishida in the women's 30km in 2010.

Ice Hockey – The women have come 6th three times – 1998, 2018 and 2022. The men's best is 8th in 1960.

Biathlon – Ryoko Takahashi finished 6th in the women's 15km in 1998, their best finish so far.

Skeleton – One top-eight finish – 8th for Kazuhiro Koshi in the 2002 men's event.

Bobsleigh – Their best finish was 12th in the four-man event in 1972, on home ground in Sapporo.

SOUTH KOREA   **Olympic Rank 16th**
Population: 51,966,948 (rank 28th)
Olympic rank/ population differential: +12
Population per gold: 402,845 (rank 35th)
Population per medal: 141,986 (rank 45th)

Summer: 96 gold, 91 silver, 100 bronze (total 287)
Winter: 33 gold, 30 silver, 16 bronze (total 79)
Total: 129 gold, 121 silver, 116 bronze (total 366)

Best sports: Short Track Speed Skating (26 golds, 40.00%, 1st)
                                   Archery (27 golds, 38.03%, 1st)
                                   Taekwondo (12 golds, 25.00%, 1st)

Korea was ruled by Japan until 1945; indeed, the Korean winner of the 1936 men's marathon was forced to represent Japan in doing so. After the war, South Korea gained independence, and first entered both Summer and Winter Olympics in 1948. Since then, they have missed only the 1952 Winter Games, and the 1980 Summer Games (which they boycotted).

They had a slow start – they won 12 medals between 1948 and 1972, but none of them were gold. Their first Olympic champion was wrestler Yang Jung-mo in 1976. However, since 1984, they have won at least 6 golds at each Games, with a best of 13 in both 2008 and 2012. Their highest overall medal total was 33, set on home soil in 1988; 12 of these were gold, giving them their highest medal table finish of 4th. They have been top-10 finishers in all but two of the Games since 1984.

It was a similar story in the Winter Games, where they didn't even manage a medal until 1992, 44 years after their debut. Not surprisingly, this coincided with the advent of Short Track Speed Skating in the Olympics – 73 of their 79 medals have come either in this or in the longer form of Speed Skating. They won 6 golds in both 2006 and 2010 (finishing 5th in the latter), and won a record 17 medals in total in 2018 (again on home soil).

Their most successful Olympians have been Jin Jong-oh (Shooting), Kim Soo-nyung (Archery) and Chun Lee-kyung (Short Track Speed Skating), winning four golds each.

SUMMER
Archery (27-9-7, 1st). South Korea took until 1984 to win an Archery medal, but they have won 27 of the 39 golds on offer since then., including 4 out of 4 in 2016, and 4 out of 5 in 2021. They are particularly dominant on the women's side, having won 18 of the 19 golds on offer since 1984 (but only a mere silver in the 2008 women's individual). Leading the way is Kim Soo-nyung, winning 4 golds, a silver and a bronze (1988-2000).

Taekwondo (12-3-7, 1st). Since the sport was first included in 2000, South Korea have won twice as many medals as any other country – not surprising given they invented the sport. Hwang Kyung-seon won bronze in women's welterweight in 2004, and gold in both 2008 and 2012. In 2021, South Korea shockingly failed to win a Taekwondo gold for the first time.

Badminton (6-7-7, 3rd). Kim Dong-moon won mixed doubles gold in 1996, and men's doubles bronze in 2000 and gold in 2004. South Korea have won medals at every Games since the sport was first included in 1992.

Golf (1-0-0, 3rd=). Park In-bee won the women's title in 2016. The other top-eight finish was in the same event.

Baseball/Softball (1-0-1, 4th). Baseball bronze in 2000 and gold in 2008. They have never entered Softball.

Table Tennis (3-3-12, 2nd). Two golds on Table Tennis's debut in 1988; they then briefly broke China's domination with Ryu Seung-Min's victory in the 2004 men's singles.

Handball (2-4-1, 5th). The women won gold in 1988 & 1992; their last medal was a bronze in 2008. The men's only medal was a silver in 1988.

Judo (11-17-18, 4th). South Korea have won Judo medals every time they've entered. Their 11 golds have been won by 11 different people.

Wrestling (11-11-14, 10th). Sim Kwon-ho won golds in 1996 & 2000 in men's Greco-Roman light-flyweight and flyweight. 16 of their medals came in 1984 and 1988. They have yet to win a women's medal.

Shooting (7-9-1, 11th). Jin Jong-oh won four golds and two silvers in men's pistol events (2004-16).

Fencing (5-3-8, 7th). All the medals have come since 2000. Golds have been won in foil, épée and sabre.

Weightlifting (3-6-6, 17th). Golds for Chun Byung-kwan (1992), and Sa Jae-hyouk and Jang Mi-ran (2008).

Boxing (3-7-10, 17th). One gold in 1984, and two in Seoul in 1988, including one for Park Si-hun, whose "victory" in the final over Roy Jones Jr was the result of some infamously scandalous flawed voting.

Gymnastics (2-4-5, 24th). The first three medals (1988-96) all came in men's long horse vault, as have both golds (Yang Hak-seon in 2012 and Sin Jea-hwan in 2021). That same year saw the first women's medal.

Swimming (1-3-0, 27th). All four medals went to Park Tae-hwan, two each in men's 200m and 400m freestyle (2008 & 2012), including a 2008 gold in the 400.

Athletics (1-1-0, 57th=). Hwang Young-cho won the men's marathon in 1992, 56 years after his compatriot Sohn Kee-chung won the 1936 event, but was forced to do so whilst representing Japan. South Korea's only other medal was in the same event in 1996. Their best in any other event is 4th (men's high jump, 2021).

Hockey (0-3-0, 12th). Silvers for the women in 1988 & 1996, and the men in 2000.

Volleyball (0-0-1, 17th=). Women's bronze in 1976. They have also come 4th in 1972, 2012 & 2021. The men came 5th in 1984.

Basketball (0-1-0, 13th=). Women's silver in 1984. They also came 4th in 2000. The men came 8th in 1948, and last entered in 1996.

Football (0-0-1, 32nd=). The men beat Japan in a local grudge match to take bronze in 2012. They have entered 11 times, but the women never have.

Modern Pentathlon (0-0-1, 20th=). Bronze for Jeon Ung-tae in 2021 (men's). No woman has yet entered.

Diving – Both top-eight finishes were achieved in 2021 – 4th for Wu Ha-Ram in the men's springboard, and 7th in the men's synchronized platform, also involving Wu.

Cycling – Only three top-eight finishes; the best was 4th for Jo Ho-Seong in the men's points race in 2000.

Karate – Only one entry when the sport was introduced in 2021 – Park Hui-Jun came 6th in the men's kata.

Equestrianism – Just two top-eight finishes – 7th in the team three-day eventing in 1988 (they were last out of those that finished), and 8th in the team show jumping in 2004.

Sailing – Ha Ji-Min came 7th in the men's laser in 2021, his country's first ever top-eight finish in the sport.

Sport Climbing – On the sport's 2021 debut, South Korea came 8th in the women's competition (Seo Chae-Hyun) and 10th in the men's.

Rowing – South Korea have never had a top-eight finish in Rowing; the women's coxed four came 9th in 1984.

Canoeing – A best of 9th place in the K2 200m event for men in 2016.

Artistic Swimming – Came 11th in the duet in both 1988 and 2000.

Rugby – They made their debut in the men's competition in 2021, and came 12th after losing every game.

Water Polo – Only one entry – the men's competition in 1988, as hosts. They lost every game and came 12th.

Tennis – Have reached the last 16 four times, but never won a set in that round (men's singles, women's singles and women's doubles in Seoul in 1988, and men's doubles in 2000).

Triathlon – Only one entry – the men's event in 2012. They came 54th.

Beach Volleyball, Skateboarding, Surfing , PWDS – never entered

WINTER
Short Track Speed Skating (26-16-11, 1st). South Korea have won 26 of the 65 Short Track events since its introduction in 1992, winning at least two golds in each Games. Chun Lee-kyun won four golds and a bronze in women's events in 1994 & 1998. Amongst those who have won three golds for South Korea is Ahn Hyun-soo, who later won another three for Russia, having defected there.

Skeleton (1-0-0, 7th=) Yun Seong-bin won the 2018 men's title. The highest women's position is 15th.

Speed Skating (5-10-5, 10th). Despite the sport being part of the Olympics since 1924, South Korea didn't win a medal until 1992. All their golds have come since 2010 – two each for Lee Seung-hoon (men's) and Lee Sang-hwa (women's), and one for Mo Tae-bum.

Figure Skating (1-1-0, 14th=). Both medals went to Kim Yu-na (women's gold in 2010 and silver in 2014).

Curling (0-1-0, 9th=). Women's silver in 2018; also 7th in men's and 5th in mixed doubles in the same year.

Snowboarding (0-1-0, 19th=). Silver for Lee Sang-ho (men's parallel giant slalom, 2018).

Bobsleigh (0-1-0, 11th). Silver in the four-man bob in 2018; came 6th in the two-man, also in 2018.

Ski Jumping – One top-eight finish (8th in the men's team event, 2002). Their best in an individual event is 30th.

Luge – German-born Aileen Frisch was invited to claim South Korean citizenship ahead of the 2018 Pyeongchang Games. She finished 8th in the women's singles – the country's only top-eight finish.

Ice Hockey – Only participated when hosting the Games in 2018. The women's team (though not the men's) was a combined North/South Korea team as a result of a historic agreement. However, both the men and women finished last after losing every game – the men came 12th and the women 8th.

Freestyle Skiing – Choi Jae-U came 12th in the men's moguls in both 2014 and 2018. This remains South Korea's best.

Alpine Skiing – Came 14th out of 16 in the mixed team event in 2018. Their best individual position is 21st.

Nordic Skiing – Finished 15th out of 16 in the men's 4x10km relay in both 1988 and 1992, beating Great Britain and Greece respectively. Their best in an individual event is 33rd.

Biathlon – Three 16th-place finishes – one in a team event in 1988 and two in individual events in 2018.

Nordic Combined – Entered for the first time in 2018; their best finish is 42nd (men's normal hill in 2022).

NORTH KOREA   **Olympic Rank 41st**

Population: 26,072,217 (rank 55th)
Olympic rank/ population differential: +14
Population per gold: 1,629,514 (rank 56th)
Population per medal: 457,407 (rank 63rd)

Summer: 16 gold, 16 silver, 23 bronze (total 55)
Winter: 0 gold, 1 silver, 1 bronze (total 2)
Total: 16 gold, 17 silver, 24 bronze (total 57)

Best sports: Weightlifting (5 golds, 2.17%, 11th)
             Judo (2 golds, 1.32%, 17th)
             Gymnastics (3 golds, 0.78%, 21st=)

Unusually North Korea's first Olympic appearance was at the Winter Olympics in 1964; they didn't enter the Summer Games for another eight years. They have missed various Games since then; they missed the Summer Games of 1984, 1988 (boycotting due to it being hosted by South Korea) and 2021 (when they cited covid concerns). They also missed the Winter Games of 1968, 1976, 1980, 1994, 2002, 2014 and 2022 (when they were banned following their no-show at the previous year's Summer Games).

North Korea have won medals at every Summer Games in which they have competed. The most golds they have won is four, both in 1992 (4 golds and 5 bronzes) and 2012 (4 golds and 3 bronzes). The nine medals won in 1992 is a national record, as is their 16th place in that year's medal table. The fewest medals they have won in a Summer Games is two (a gold and a silver) in 1976. There have been three Games in which they have failed to win a gold – 1980, 2000 and 2004. Their worst record in these years was in 2000 (one silver and three bronzes).

Recent years have been dominated by Weightlifting. In 2012 and 2016, nine of their 14 medals came in the sport, including four of their six golds. They have won at least one medal in the sport in each of their appearances since 1980, although they didn't win a gold until 2008. Rim Jong-sim won the women's light heavyweight in 2012 and heavyweight in 2016, making her the second North Korean to win two Olympic golds. Her success is something of an anomaly, in that most of the country's best Weightlifting performances have come in the lighter weight categories.

In all, North Korea have won 18 medals in Weightlifting. The next most have come in Wrestling (10), Judo (8) and Boxing (8). In Wrestling, North Korea have had 18 top-eight finishes, all of them in light flyweight, flyweight or bantamweight, and 17 of them in freestyle (just one in Greco-Roman). Their three golds all came in 1992 and 1996, including one in each year for Kim Il in the men's freestyle light flyweight. He was thus North Korea's first two-time Olympic gold medallist.

Three of North Korea's eight Judo medals have been won by Kye Sun Hui, making her the only North Korean with three Olympic medals. She got heavier each time – winning gold in 1996 (extra lightweight), bronze in 2000 (half lightweight) and silver in 2004 (lightweight). An Kum Ae won their other Judo gold, in the women's half lightweight in 2012. The last of their eight medals in Boxing was won in 2004; they have not even reached a quarter-final in any event since then. The last of their two golds came in 1992.

In Gymnastics, North Korea have won three medals, all of them gold. They came in 1992 (men's pommel horse), 2008 (men's vault) and 2016 (women's vault). The only other sport to produce a gold medal was Shooting (Li Ho-Jun in the men's small-bore rifle (prone) in 1972). Four medals have been won in women's Table Tennis, and one (a 1972 bronze) in women's Volleyball (the only time they participated in the sport).

North Korea's Athletics record is bizarre. They have had multiple marathon participants in every Games they have entered, but have only ever entered any other event once (the women's long jump in 1992, when they came 25th). Their marathon bests are 6th and 8th in the women's of 1992 and 2000 respectively. Their best in the men's is 12th. They have never taken part in Olympic Swimming.

They have had five top-eight finishes in Winter Olympics, three in Speed Skating (all in 1964) and two in Short Track Speed Skating (1992 and 1998). They have won two medals – a silver for Han Pil-Hwa in the women's 3000 metres in 1964 and a bronze for Hwang Ok-Sil in the women's 500 metres (short track) in 1992. Their best in any other sport is 13th in Figure Skating.

CHINESE TAIPEI   **Olympic Rank 56th**

Population:	23,588,613 (rank 57th)
Olympic rank/ population differential:	+1
Population per gold:	3,369,802 (rank 67th)
Population per medal:	655,239 (rank 72nd)
Summer:	7 gold, 11 silver, 18 bronze (total 36)
Winter:	*no medals (best finish: 15th)*
Total:	7 gold, 11 silver, 18 bronze (total 36)
Best sports:	Taekwondo (2 golds, 4.17%, 7th)
	Badminton (1 gold, 2.56%, 6th)
	Weightlifting (4 golds, 1.74%, 16th)

Chinese Taipei have probably the most complicated political history of participation in the Olympic Games of any country (if indeed one can call them a country). In 1949, the Republic of China saw their government forced out to the island of Taiwan. They continue to see themselves as the continuation of China, but the Chinese mainland (known as the People's Republic of China) see it differently. In Olympic terms, both were able to represent China in 1952, though the ROC (Taiwan) withdrew in protest. From then on, only the Taiwanese represented China, so the Olympic history of Chinese Taipei begins in 1956 (known as the Republic of China). They have competed in all Summer Games since, apart from 1976 and 1980. Finally, in 1981, an agreement was signed which gave the team their new, deliberately ambiguous, name of Chinese Taipei, and allowed them to compete alongside mainland China. They compete under a manufactured flag which includes the Olympic rings.

Four of Chinese Taipei's seven gold medals have come in Weightlifting, and we should start with their only multiple gold medallist. Competing in the women's featherweight category, Hsu Shu-ching actually secured her two golds a few months apart. Having easily won gold at Rio in 2016, she then discovered that her 2012 silver was to be upgraded to gold after the original gold medallist, a Kazakh, was retroactively disqualified for doping. Disappointingly, Hsu has been involved in doping controversy herself, although her two golds stand. In fact, nine of Chinese Taipei's ten Weightlifting medals have come in women's events, including a 2016 bronze and 2021 gold for their other Weightlifting multi-medallist, Kyo Hsing-chun (lightweight). Indeed, 21 of their 36 medals overall in the Olympics have come in women's events (and one in mixed).

Proportionally speaking, it is Taekwondo and Badminton that have produced most Taiwanese success, with both sports providing a number of top-eight finishes, and Chinese Taipei are in the top 10 of both sports' medal tables. These three sports are the only which have produced gold medals, but they have also won medals in Archery (four), Table Tennis (three), Athletics (two), and one each in Baseball, Boxing, Golf, Gymnastics, Judo and Karate. They have also had top-eight finishes in Cycling, Shooting, Softball and Tennis. One sport missing from that list is Swimming – their best finish in that sport is ninth, achieved in 1968 (women's 200m freestyle) and again in 1996 (women's 800m freestyle).

Prior to 1984, Chinese Taipei had only won two Olympic medals, and both were in Athletics. They were a silver for Yang Chuang-Kwang in the 1960 men's decathlon, and a bronze for Chi Cheng in the 1968 women's 80m hurdles (before the event was lengthened to 100 metres). But, after that auspicious start, none of the country's subsequent 34 medals have come in Athletics. The Sydney 2000 Games saw Chinese Taipei win more than one medal for the first time, winning a silver and four bronzes. Four years later, they saw gold for the first time. Chen Shih-Hsien won the women's flyweight Taekwondo and, remarkably, her compatriot Chu Mu-Yen won the men's equivalent later the same day. Prior to 2021, their best medal haul at any Games had been five, but they beat that record comfortably with the 12 they accrued in Tokyo – two gold, four silver and six bronze. It put them 34th in the medal table, three places lower than their best position, achieved in Athens in 2004, the only other occasion they have managed two golds at one Games.

In the Winter Games, they have of course been much less successful. They have actually entered every Games since 1972, with the exception of 1980 in Lake Placid. In that time, they have entered more than half of the sports on offer – namely Alpine Skiing, Nordic Skiing, Luge, Biathlon, Bobsleigh, Figure Skating, Short Track Speed Skating and Speed Skating. But they have never come close to a medal – their best three finishes in all that time have been in varied sports: 15th (1988 Bobsleigh), 17th (1992 Figure Skating) and 20th (2018 Speed Skating).

MONGOLIA   **Olympic Rank 75th**

Population:	3,255,468 (rank 134th)
Olympic rank/ population differential:	+59
Population per gold:	1,627,734 (rank 55th)
Population per medal:	108,516 (rank 40th)
Summer:	2 gold, 11 silver, 17 bronze (total 30)
Winter:	*no medals (best finish: 20th)*
Total:	2 gold, 11 silver, 17 bronze (total 30)
Best sports:	Judo (1 gold, 0.66%, 21st)
	Boxing (1 gold, 0.38%, 33rd)
	Wrestling (4 silvers, 6 bronzes, 37th)

Mongolia have won 30 Olympic medals in all, but only two of them have been gold – at 6.67% this is the lowest proportion of golds to medals of any country that has won at least one gold. Both of their golds were won in 2008, prior to which they had won 5 silvers and 10 bronzes. Their best Games in terms of overall medals has been 2012 (2 silvers and 3 bronzes). Their highest medal table position came in 1980 (2 silvers and 2 bronzes placing them 27th in the boycott-affected Moscow Games).

Mongolia's Olympic debut came in 1964, entering both Winter and Summer Games that year. Since then, they have missed only the 1976 Winter Games and 1984 Summer Games. Their 30 medals have come in four sports – Judo (1 gold, 4 silver, 6 bronze), Boxing (1-2-4), Wrestling (0-4-6) and Shooting (0-1-1). In their first Summer Games, they came nowhere near a medal, but in 1968 they opened their medal account with a silver and 3 bronzes, all in Wrestling. They won more Wrestling medals in 1972 and 1976, and again in 1980, when they won two Judo medals as well. Prior to their 1984 boycott, 8 of their 10 medals were in Wrestling, but the sport has provided only 2 of their 20 medals since (both bronze).

They have had a total of 97 top-eight finishes. There have been 47 in Wrestling (45 Greco-Roman and just 2 freestyle, of which their highest finish was 5th), 26 in Judo, 14 in Boxing and 6 in Shooting. Four of the six in Shooting were achieved by Otryadyn Gundegmaa, who finished 5th, 6th and 6th in the women's sport pistol from 1996 to 2004, before taking silver in 2008. Her 6th place in 2000 was Mongolia's best finish that year – it is the only time since 1964 (other than the 1984 boycott) that Mongolia have failed to medal at a Summer Games. The same event also saw a bronze in 1992 for Dorjsurengiin Monkhbayar – the first Mongolian woman to win an Olympic medal. There have also been three top-eights in Weightlifting (one in 1980 and two for the same woman in 2016 and 2021), and an 8th place (out of 8) in the inaugural 3x3 Basketball competition in 2021 for the women's team.

Mongolia's first Olympic champion was Naidangiin Tuvshinbayar, who beat Kazakhstan's Askhat Zhitkeyev to win the men's half-heavyweight Judo title in 2008. Later in the same Games, Enkhbatyn Badar-Uugan comprehensively won gold in the men's bantamweight Boxing – the closest of his five bouts was in the last 16, when he won 9-2. Since 2008, Mongolia have added 4 silvers and 7 bronzes, but no further golds. One of those silvers was won in 2012 by Tuvshinbayar, making him the only Mongolian ever to win two Olympic medals. He received various state honours for his achievement, but in 2022 he was sentenced to 16 years in prison after a drunken brawl with a childhood friend, who subsequently died from his injuries.

In Athletics, Mongolia competed from 1964 to 1972, and then in all Games from 1992 onwards. Fifteen of their 19 entries since 1992 have been in the marathon, although their best finishing position in a marathon so far is 45th. Their best position in any Athletics event is 12th (Dashzevgiin Namjilmaa in the women's discus in 1968). Mongolia have participated in Swimming in all Games since 2000. Their highest finish so far is 45th (women's 100m breaststroke in 2012).

Mongolia have participated in just four Winter sports – Nordic Skiing, Speed Skating, Short Track Speed Skating, and Biathlon (the latter not since 1968). Nobody has yet bettered Tsedenjavyn Lkhamjav's 20th place in the 1964 women's 3000m Speed Skating.

HONG KONG Olympic Rank 78th

Population:	7,288,167 (rank 105th)
Olympic rank/ population differential:	+27
Population per gold:	3,644,084 (rank 69th)
Population per medal:	809,796 (rank 76th)

Summer:	2 gold, 3 silver, 4 bronze (total 9)
Winter:	*no medals (best finish: 18th)*
Total:	2 gold, 3 silver, 4 bronze (total 9)
Best sports:	Sailing (1 gold, 0.52%, 27th)
	Fencing (1 gold, 0.43%, 22nd=)
	Swimming (2 silvers, 39th=)

Having first entered the Olympics in 1952, Hong Kong have entered every Summer Games since, with the exception of 1980. They failed to medal at all in their first ten appearances. A Hong Kong pair did manage to finish third in the Badminton mixed doubles in Seoul in 1988, but unfortunately Badminton was only a demonstration sport at that time. Their first medal came eight years later in Atlanta, courtesy of Lee Lai Shan, who added Olympic gold to her numerous world championship achievements in Sailing (women's windsurfing). With Hong Kong returning from Britain to China the following year, that was the only medal Hong Kong won as a British colony.

Over the following five games, only two further medals were added – a silver in men's doubles Table Tennis in 2004, and a bronze in women's keirin Cycling in 2012 for Sarah Lee (aka Lee Wai-sze). But in Tokyo in 2021, they trebled their all-time medal haul from three to nine. Lee added another bronze in Cycling (this time in the sprint), and there were also bronzes in women's kata (Karate) and the women's team Table Tennis. Siobhan Haughey, born to an Irish father and Hongkonger mother shortly after the 1997 handover, won her nation's first two Swimming medals – silvers in the 100m and 200m freestyle, behind Australians Emma McKeon and Ariarne Titmus respectively. Haughey thus joined Lee as Hong Kong's two multi-medallists in Olympic history.

The crowning achievement of the 2021 Games for Hong Kong, though, came in the men's foil Fencing event, where Edgar Cheung (aka Cheung Ka Long) came from 4-1 down in the final to defeat the Italian reigning gold medallist 15-11 to claim Hong Kong's second ever Olympic gold. These six medals helped Hong Kong to 49th place in the Tokyo medal table.

Besides their six medal-winning sports, other top-eight finishes have been accrued in Badminton and Weightlifting (though they managed no top-eight finishes at all until 1992, when they managed a couple of quarter-finalists in Table Tennis). In Athletics, though, they have had no success at all – their best finish is 14th (out of 16 – the other two were disqualified), in the men's 4x100m relay in 2012. They also came 17th out of 32 in the 2016 men's long jump.

In the Winter Olympics, Hong Kong's interest has been limited to just two sports. They made their Winter debut in 2002, entering Short Track Speed Skating. They stuck to just this until 2018, when their sole entrant was in Alpine Skiing instead. In 2022, they entered both sports. Their best finish so far is the 18th place achieved by Short Track exponent Han Yue Shuang in the 2006 women's 1000m.

CHAPTER TWENTY-SIX - South-Eastern Asia (Thailand, Indonesia, Philippines, Vietnam, Singapore, Malaysia, Myanmar, Cambodia, Laos, Timor-Leste, Brunei)

THAILAND	**Olympic Rank 51st**
Population:	69,794,997 (rank 20th)
Olympic rank/ population differential:	-31
Population per gold:	6,979,500 (rank 80th)
Population per medal:	1,994,143 (rank 99th)
Summer:	10 gold, 8 silver, 17 bronze (total 35)
Winter:	*no medals (best finish: 38th)*
Total:	10 gold, 8 silver, 17 bronze (total 35)
Best sports:	Weightlifting (5 golds, 2.17%, 14th)
	Taekwondo (1 gold, 2.08%, 14th=)
	Boxing (4 golds, 1.51%, 15th=)

Thailand has had independence for centuries, and they first took part in Olympic competition in 1952. They have entered every Summer Games since then, with the exception of the 1980 Moscow boycott. They won no medals between 1952 (when they entered only Athletics) and 1972. Their first top-eight finish came in Weightlifting in 1968 (8th place). A 7th in Weightlifting and an 8th in Boxing followed in 1972, before their first medal was won in 1976, a bronze for Payao Poontarat in men's light flyweight Boxing. Thailand have won at least one medal in all of their Games since then. After one medal in each of 1984, 1988 and 1992 (all in Boxing), their first gold came in 1996, again in Boxing. It was won in men's Featherweight by Somluck Kamsing, who went on to become a singer and film actor. Having won that first gold, Thailand have won at least one gold at every Games since, with the exception of 2012, when they had to settle for two silvers and two bronzes. The 2004 Athens Games were their most successful, garnering them their most golds (3), their most medals overall (8), and their highest medal table position (25th).

All 35 of Thailand's medals have come in just three sports. Boxing has provided 15 (4 gold, 4 silver and 7 bronze); 9 of them came between 1996 and 2008. Weightlifting has provided the most golds (5), along with 2 silvers and 7 bronzes (all between 2000 and 2016). However, Thailand agreed not to enter Weightlifting in 2021 after being embroiled in numerous doping cases in the sport. As a result of not taking part in probably their best sport, they won only 2 medals that year (1 gold, 1 bronze) – their lowest medal total since 1996 (also 2).

Their other 6 medals (1 gold, 2 silver, 3 bronze) have come in Taekwondo. All six have come in flyweight (one in men's, five in women's). The one gold was won by Panipak Wongpattanakit in 2021; she had also won bronze in 2016. All ten of Thailand's Olympic gold medals have been won by different people, but two of them are multi-medallists. Wongpattanakit is one, the other is Manus Boonjumnong in men's light welterweight Boxing (gold in 2004, silver in 2008). Two female lightweight weightlifters have also won two medals each (Wandee Kameaim with bronzes in 2004 and 2008, and Pimsiri Sirikaew with silvers in 2012 and 2016). Of Thailand's 35 medals, 32 of them have come in weight categories of welterweight or lighter. The only three exceptions are light middleweight (one), middleweight (one) and heavyweight (one, a gold in women's weightlifting in 2004 for Pawina Thongsuk).

Those three sports account for 62 of Thailand's 82 top-eight finishes. A further 10 have come in Badminton (nine quarter-finals and one 4th place), 6 in Shooting (including one 4th place), two quarter-finals in women's doubles Tennis in 1996 and 2000, one in Golf in 2016, and one in Athletics. The one in Athletics was by default, missing the men's 4x100m relay final in 2008 after finishing 9th in the semi-finals, but eventually moving up a place following Jamaica's doping violation. Almost all of Thailand's highest Athletics finishes have come in the relays. Their best Swimming finish is 12th, in the 1996 men's 400m individual medley.

Thailand first entered the Winter Olympics in 2002, and have attended all Games since, other than 2010. They have competed only in Nordic Skiing and Alpine Skiing, and their best finish is 38th (men's Alpine Skiing giant slalom in 2022). Their most notable competitor, though, is Singapore-born Vanessa Vanakorn, who finished 67th in Alpine Skiing in 2014; she is better known as world-famous violinist Vanessa-Mae.

INDONESIA Olympic Rank 52nd

Population:	279,476,346 (rank 4th)
Olympic rank/ population differential:	-48
Population per gold:	34,934,543 (rank 97th)
Population per medal:	7,553,415 (rank 119th)

Summer:	8 gold, 14 silver, 15 bronze (total 37)
Winter:	*never participated*
Total:	8 gold, 14 silver, 15 bronze (total 37)
Best sports:	Badminton (8 golds, 20.51%, 2nd)
	Weightlifting (7 silvers, 8 bronzes, 43rd)
	Archery (1 silver, 21st)

Indonesia gained independence from the Dutch (they had previously been known as the Dutch East Indies) in 1949, and they took part in the Olympics for the first time three years later. Since then, they have missed only two Summer Games – 1964 (due to political disagreements with the IOC) and 1980 (joining the large boycott). The fourth most populous nation in the world, Indonesia are by far the most populous never to have competed in the Winter Olympics.

Only three Indonesians competed on their debut in 1952 – one each in Athletics, Swimming and Weightlifting. They have branched out since then, entering a number of sports, but almost all their success has come in just a small handful. Between 1952 and 1984, Indonesia managed only five top-eight finishes, and no medals. Their first medal came in 1988, a silver in women's team Archery (they finished well behind South Korea, but just held off both the USA and USSR for silver). But then in 1992, Badminton was introduced to the Games, and it transformed Indonesia's fortunes. All their medals since then have come in just two sports.

Badminton is far and away Indonesia's most successful sport. It has provided all eight of their gold medals, and 21 of their 37 medals in total. Although China can boast more than double that on both counts, Indonesia are the second most successful country in the history of Olympic Badminton; the only other country that comes close is South Korea (6 golds, 20 medals in total). No other country has more than 2 golds, or more than 9 medals in total.

Indonesia's first Olympic champion was Susi Susanti in the 1992 women's singles. Later that same day, her compatriot Alan Budikusuma won the men's singles. The two married soon after, and have gone on to have three children. Taufik Hidayat won the men's singles in 2004, whilst Indonesia have also won the men's doubles in 1996, 2000 and 2008, and the mixed doubles in 2016. They then won the women's doubles in 2021 to become the only country besides China to win all five events over the course of Olympic Badminton history. No Indonesian has yet won more than one gold; Liliyana Natsir is the only one to win a gold and a silver (mixed doubles silver in 2008 and gold in 2016). The 1992 Games is still the only one to have seen two Indonesian golds (it put them in a national best 24th place in the medal table), but each Games since has seen one gold, with the exception of 2012. The most medals in a Games is six, achieved both in 2000 and 2008.

The 2012 Games were, in fact, something of a disaster for Indonesian Badminton – they didn't win a medal at all, and were also involved in a match-fixing scandal (along with China and South Korea). The only two medals they did win that year were both in Weightlifting. That sport has provided 15 medals in total, but no golds (7 silvers and 8 bronzes instead). The first came in 2000, and they have won medals in every Games since. Eko Yuli Irawan won men's bantamweight bronze in 2008, before switching to featherweight and taking another bronze in 2012, and silvers in both 2016 and 2021. His four medals is an Indonesian record.

Indonesia have had 82 top-eight finishes in Olympic history, with 46 of them in Badminton and 28 in Weightlifting. Of the other eight, four have been in Archery (most recently in the 2021 mixed team event) and three in Boxing (most recently in 1996). The other was in Football – Indonesia have only participated in the sport once, in 1956, when their first-round opponents South Vietnam withdrew, and they reached the quarter-finals by default, taking the Soviet Union to a replay before losing 4-0.

Indonesia's best Athletics attempts have come in sprinting. The men's 4x100m relay team came 12th in 1984, and Mardi Lestari came 13th in the men's 100 metres in 1988. Their best in Swimming is 14th (women's 200m breaststroke in 1956). Their only other top-16 finish in the sport came in 2021.

PHILIPPINES   Olympic Rank 85th

Population:	116,434,200 (rank 13th)
Olympic rank/ population differential:	-72
Population per gold:	116,434,200 (rank 101st)
Population per medal:	8,316,729 (rank 121st)

Summer:	1 gold, 5 silver, 8 bronze (total 14)
Winter:	*no medals (best finish: 19th)*
Total:	1 gold, 5 silver, 8 bronze (total 14)
Best sports:	Weightlifting (1 gold, 0.43%, 36th=)
	Boxing (4 silvers, 4 bronzes, 41st)
	Swimming (2 bronzes, 47th)

The Philippines made their Olympics debut as far back as 1924, when David Nepomuceno contested the 100-metre and 200-metre events. He did not progress beyond the first round of either event, but he was a noted athlete of the era nonetheless. Their first medal came in 1928, a bronze for swimmer Teofilo Yldefonzo in the 200m breaststroke. He also won a bronze in the same event in 1932, and reached the final again in 1936 – no Filipino has reached a Swimming final since.

Athletics is another sport where the Philippines won medals pre-war (bronzes in the 1932 men's high jump and 1936 men's 400m hurdles), but have not finished in the top eight of any event since.

By far their most prolific source of medals has been Boxing. They have won eight medals in total, of which three were won in Tokyo in 2021. Of their four silvers, the one which was closest to gold was that of Anthony Villenueva in the 1964 featherweight division – he lost a split 3-2 decision to his Soviet adversary.

Having won ten medals between 1928 and 2016, the Philippines finally celebrated their first gold in 2021. The person who achieved national glory was featherweight weightlifter Hidilyn Diaz. She had first entered the Olympics as a 17-year old in 2008, finishing 10th. She failed to register a valid clean & jerk lift in 2012, and won silver in 2016, before finally taking gold in 2021, for which she was awarded a house and a huge cash sum by the Philippine government. Although the Philippines had been coming close in Weightlifting ever since 1948, Diaz's medals are still the only two the Philippines have won in that sport.

The Philippines have also finished fourth in Shooting (men's small-bore rifle, prone, in 1936) and Gymnastics (men's long horse vault in 2021). They have also managed top eight finishes in Basketball, Judo, Skateboarding and Taekwondo.

They have twice won more than one medal in the same Games – three bronzes in 1932 (which gave them their highest ever medal table finish of 25th), and a gold, two silvers and a bronze in 2021. Their other medals have been spread fairly evenly down the years – they have entered every Games since their debut, with the exception of 1980.

The Philippines first entered the Winter Olympics in 1972, but only entered twice more (1988 and 1992) prior to 2014. Their best two finishes in Winter events have both been achieved by figure skater Michael Christian Martinez (19th in 2014 and 28th in 2018). Luge (once) and Alpine Skiing (several times) are the only other winter sports they have entered.

VIETNAM   **Olympic Rank 86th**
Population: 104,799,174 (rank 16th)
Olympic rank/ population differential: -70
Population per gold: 104,799,174 (rank 100th)
Population per medal: 20,959,835 (rank 132nd)

Summer: 1 gold, 3 silver, 1 bronze (total 5)
Winter: *never participated*
Total: 1 gold, 3 silver, 1 bronze (total 5)

Best sports: Shooting (1 gold, 0.33%, 35th)
                     Weightlifting (1 silver, 1 bronze, 49th=)
                     Taekwondo (1 silver, 29th=)

Vietnam first took part in the Olympic Games in 1952. They took until 2000 to win a medal, but their performances have been hugely improved since then. Their first appearance, in 1952, took place before the partition of the country; the "State of Vietnam" was owned by France at the time, and they sent participants in Athletics, Swimming, Boxing, Cycling and Fencing. After the 1954 partition into North Vietnam (backed by the Soviets) and South Vietnam (backed by the US), the North never participated in the Olympics, whilst the South competed in all Summer Games from 1956 to 1972, never coming close even to a top-eight finish in any event.

The country missed the 1976 Games, but took part in 1980, the first time they competed as Vietnam in their current guise. They missed 1984, but have entered all Summer Games since. Vietnam have never, in any form, entered the Winter Olympics. Up until 1996, they entered a variety of Summer sports, but never managed a top-eight finish in any of them.

The Sydney 2000 Games saw Vietnam emerge as a contender on the Olympic stage. That year, they managed their first two top-eight finishes, both in women's Taekwondo. In the featherweight, Tran Hieu Ngan reached the final with a 9-6 win over her Dutch opponent, but lost 2-0 to South Korea's Jeong Jae-Eun and settled for silver. This remains Vietnam's only Taekwondo medal, but they have had five top-eight finishes in the sport, four of them for women, and all five in flyweight or featherweight.

The sport to have provided the most top-eight finishes for Vietnam (seven) is Weightlifting. There has been at least one at each Games since 2004. Again, all of them have been in the lighter weight categories (middleweight and downwards). Their two medals in the sport have both come in men's bantamweight – a silver for Anh Tuan Hoang in 2008, and a bronze for Tran Le Quoc Toan for the 2012 Games (although it wasn't awarded until 2019, following the disqualification of the original Azerbaijani bronze medallist for doping offences).

So Taekwondo and Weightlifting have accounted for 12 of Vietnam's 15 top-eight finishes. The other three have come in Shooting, all for the same man. In the men's free pistol final in 2012, Hoang Xuan Vinh was 2.7 points clear of his Chinese rival for bronze with two shots left, but a stunning turnaround left him in an agonising 4th place. But on the first full day of the Rio 2016 Games, he produced a final-shot turnaround of his own, coming from behind to win gold in the air pistol with a 10.7 (the highest score possible being 10.9). It was all the more impressive as he did it in front of a partisan home crowd, who were cheering on his Brazilian rival Felipe Wu. It made him Vietnam's first – and so far only – Olympic champion. Four days later, he added a silver in the free pistol, making him Vietnam's only multi-medallist in the Olympics as well.

Vietnam's best Swimming finish has been 9th in the women's 400m individual medley in 2016. In Athletics, their best is 18th, by Quach Thi Lan in the 2021 women's 400m hurdles.

SINGAPORE   **Olympic Rank 89th**
Population: 5,975,383 (rank 113th)
Olympic rank/ population differential: +24
Population per gold: 5,975,383 (rank 79th)
Population per medal: 1,195,077 (rank 84th)

Summer: 1 gold, 2 silver, 2 bronze (total 5)
Winter: *no medals (best finish: 28th)*
Total: 1 gold, 2 silver, 2 bronze (total 5)

Best sports: Swimming (1 gold, 0.17%, 35th=)
                    Table Tennis (1 silver, 2 bronzes, 7th=)
                    Weightlifting (1 silver, 54th=)

Singapore made their Olympic debut in 1948, at which time they still came under British rule. They have entered every Summer Games since then, with the exception of 1964 (at this point, they were legally part of Malaysia, who entered a combined team that year, with Singapore gaining full independence the following year), and 1980 (due to the large-scale boycott).

By far Singapore's most successful sport on the international stage is Table Tennis. Illustrative of this is the fact that the sport is responsible for 57 of the 108 Commonwealth Games medals that Singapore has ever won (and 25 of its 41 golds). In the Olympics, the sport has provided three of its five medals, and sees Singapore 7th equal in the medal table. It has also provided 15 of its 24 top-eight finishes. Of these, 14 of the 15 have come in women's events, including all three of its medals – a bronze for Feng Tianwei in the 2012 women's singles, and team silver and bronze in 2008 and 2012 respectively. On all three occasions, China won the gold.

That 2008 medal was only Singapore's second Olympic medal ever. The first had come 48 years earlier, with a silver medal in men's lightweight Weightlifting for Tan Howe Liang (also known as "Tiger" Tan). Interestingly, the man he narrowly pipped in the battle for silver and bronze (the gold medal-winning Soviet finished well clear) was Iraq's only ever Olympic medallist. Weightlifting has provided four top-eight finishes for Singapore, all of which were between 1952 and 1960.

Singapore's fifth and most recent medal is also their only ever gold. Joseph Schooling had slowly been building a name for himself in the 100m butterfly, but it was still a shock when he beat the more renowned Michael Phelps, Chad le Clos and Laszlo Cseh (all of whom tied for silver) in the Rio final in 2016. Schooling was given a victory parade on his return to Singapore. The nation's only other top-eight finish in Swimming had come in the women's 100m butterfly in 2008.

Besides these three sports, the only other top-eight finishes Singapore have accrued have come in Badminton (in 2004 and 2008) and Hockey (in 1956). In Athletics, their best finish remains that of Lloyd Valberg, who came 14th equal in the men's high jump in 1948. Valberg was, in fact, Singapore's first ever Olympian – the only person to compete for the country on their debut in 1948, and remarkably, he was the great-uncle of Joseph Schooling (although he died in 1997, when Schooling was not yet two).

Meanwhile, Singapore have only ever had one Winter Olympic entry – Cheyenne Goh came 28th in the women's 1500m Short Track Speed Skating in 2018.

MALAYSIA Olympic Rank 103rd

Population:	34,219,975 (rank 43rd)
Olympic rank/ population differential:	-60
Population per gold:	n/a
Population per medal:	2,632,306 (rank 103rd)

Summer:	0 gold, 8 silver, 5 bronze (total 13)
Winter:	*no medals (best finish: 25th)*
Total:	0 gold, 8 silver, 5 bronze (total 13)
Best sports:	Badminton (6 silvers, 3 bronzes, 8th)
	Diving (1 silver, 1 bronze, 14th=)
	Cycling (1 silver, 1 bronze, 32nd=)

By far Malaysia's most successful Olympic sport is Badminton. It has provided six of their eight silver medals, three of their five bronzes, and 18 of their 42 top eight finishes in the Olympics. Malaysia have won by far the most medals (13) of any nation without any golds; the next most is Kyrgyzstan with seven. If the Olympic medal table was calculated on medals rather than golds, they would rank 72nd rather than 103rd. And only three countries have won more medals than Malaysia in Badminton – China, Indonesia and South Korea.

Three of Malaysia's silver medals have been won by a single man – Lee Chong Wei, who lost three men's singles finals in a row from 2008 to 2016, all to Chinese players. The closest he came to gold was in 2012 – losing 21-19 in the deciding set. The Malaysian pair in the 2016 men's doubles final came even closer – losing 23-21 in the deciding set; again China took the gold. Malaysia have, in fact, never failed to reach at least the last eight of the men's doubles since it began in 1992.

In Diving, Malaysia have been particularly strong in the women's synchronised events, whilst in Cycling all their top eight finishes have come in the men's sprint and keirin events. The other sports in which Malaysia have achieved top eight finishes are Archery, Hockey, Taekwondo and Weightlifting. Their Athletics best is 13th (men's 4x100m relay in 1968) and their Swimming best is 14th (men's 4x100m medley relay in 1964).

They first entered the Olympics in 1956, competing in two teams as Malaya and North Borneo. They first competed as Malaysia in 1964, and have competed in all Summer Games since, except for 1980. They won medals in 1992, 1996 and in all Summer Games since 2008. They first entered the Winter Games in 2018; in that year, figure skater Julian Yee finished 25th, which remains their best Winter finish.

MYANMAR Olympic Rank 140th

Population:	57,970,293 (rank 26th)
Olympic rank/ population differential:	-114

Summer:	*no medals (best finish: 4th)*
Winter:	*never participated*
Best sports:	Weightlifting
	Boxing
	Football

Myanmar have competed in every Summer Olympics since 1948, other than 1976, but have never won a medal. Prior to 1992, they were known as Burma. They have never competed in the Winter Games. The closest they came to a medal was in the 2000 women's flyweight Weightlifting competition, where Win Kay Thi came fourth in a close contest. The nation has also finished fifth (twice), sixth, seventh and eighth in Weightlifting events over the years, but are still waiting for that elusive first medal. Certainly Weightlifting remains very much their best chance. Two competitors from Myanmar/Burma have reached the quarter-finals in Boxing events, but that was back in 1960 and 1964.

No other athlete from the country has achieved a top-eight finish. Their best achievement in any sport besides Weightlifting and Boxing was in the 1972 Football competition, where narrow defeats to the USSR and Mexico were followed by a win over Sudan, meaning they exited with the ninth-best record in the competition. They have also finished inside the top 16 in events in Judo, Archery, Sailing and Shooting in the past.

CAMBODIA   Olympic Rank 182nd
Population: 16,891,245 (rank 72nd)
Olympic rank/ population differential: -110

Summer: *no medals (best finish: 11th)*
Winter: *never participated*

Best sports: Boxing
                   Taekwondo
                   Wrestling

Cambodia's first foray into the Olympics came at the 1956 Equestrian events, held in Stockholm five months before the main Games in Melbourne (which Cambodia didn't enter). After not entering in 1960, they entered Boxing, Sailing and Cycling in 1964. They again missed out in 1968, returning in 1972, where they made their debuts in Athletics and Swimming. But then the Khmer Rouge seized power in Cambodia, and it would be two decades of unimaginable tragedy before the nation was ready to return to the Olympics. They did so in 1996, and have entered all Summer Games since. In that time, they have added Wrestling, Judo and Taekwondo to their repertoire. They have never entered the Winter Games.

They have had only five top-16 finishes; the highest of all being 11th. That was the finishing position of Khieu Soeun, who gained a knockout win in the first round of the 1964 men's featherweight Boxing, but lost narrowly in round two. They also had a 15th-place finish in light-welterweight in the same year. Their next best finish was 13th out of 16 for Sorn Davin, losing narrowly in the first round of the women's heavyweight Taekwondo in 2012, Cambodia also finished 15th in the same event four years later. Finally, in 2016, Cambodia managed a 16th-place finish (out of 18) in women's Wrestling. In Athletics, they have never progressed through a round. In Swimming, their best finish is 17th out of 17 in the 1972 men's medley relay; their best that wasn't last was 31st.

LAOS   Olympic Rank 199th
Population: 7,852,377 (rank 103rd)
Olympic rank/ population differential: -96

Summer: *no medals (best finish: 17th)*
Winter: *never participated*

Best sports: Boxing
                   Judo
                   Athletics

Laos made their Olympic debut in 1980, when they entered a number of events in Athletics, Boxing and Shooting. They then missed the 1984 Games, but have returned for all Summer Games since 1988 (they have never entered the Winter Games). Since their 1988 return, they have fielded much smaller teams than they did in 1980. They have debuted in a handful of other sports – Swimming (2000), Archery (2004), and Judo and Cycling (2016).

Three of Laos's four highest Olympic finishes have come in Boxing, all in 1980. Singkham Phongpratith came 21st out of 22 in the light-flyweight (lasting just two seconds longer than the boxer from Ethiopia), Souneat Ouphaphone came 24th out of 33 in bantamweight, and M. Kampanath (first name unknown(!)) lost by the smallest possible margin in his light-welterweight bout against a Syrian opponent, coming 17th out of 30 (both were favoured by two judges each, whilst the other scored it level but leant the Syrian's way in the tie-breaker). In addition, Soukphaxay Sithisane came 21st out of 23 in the men's extra-lightweight Judo in 2021.

In Athletics, no Laotian has ever progressed beyond a heat. Thipsamay Chanthaphone finished 25th in the men's 20km walk in 1980, finishing higher than nine non-finishers, though over half an hour slower than all the other finishers. This is the highest position they have ever achieved in Olympic Athletics. In Swimming, they have never swum further than 50 metres in an Olympic race; their best event ranking is 56th in the men's freestyle in 2012.

TIMOR-LESTE   Olympic Rank 200th

Population: 1,476,042 (rank 154th)
Olympic rank/ population differential: -46

Summer: *no medals (best finish: 20th)*
Winter: *no medals (best finish: 43rd)*

Best sports: Weightlifting
Cycling
Boxing

Timor-Leste, often known as East Timor, gained its independence from Indonesia in 2002, following a transitional period from 1999 to 2002. During this period, four Timorese competitors participated in the Sydney Olympics, competing as "Individual Olympic Athletes". Two of these were marathon runners who finished well down the pack. The other two were weightlifter Martinho de Araujo, who finished 20th out of 22 (one was disqualified and one failed to produce a valid lift), and boxer Victor Ramos who finished 28th out of 28, after being stopped in round two of his first bout.

Unimpressive as those two performances might sound, their finishing positions have never been bettered by any athlete since Timor-Leste began competing under their own flag. They have participated in every Games since 2004. In the first three, they only entered the marathons where, due to the large number of entries, they have come nowhere near finishing 28th. In 2016, their three competitors were two 1500 metres runners, and a mountain biker, Francelina Cabral, who finished 28th out of 29 (the other failed to finish). Finally, in 2021, they entered another 1500 metres runner plus, for the first time, two swimmers – both of whom competed in the 50 metres freestyle, and finished 72nd and 78th.

Timor-Leste have also had one Winter Olympian, Alpine skier Yohann Goutt Goncalves, who has competed in 2014, 2018 and 2022, with a best finish of 43rd (out of 61, but slowest of those who finished) in the 2014 slalom.

BRUNEI   Olympic Rank 206th

Population: 484,991 (rank 171st)
Olympic rank/ population differential: -35

Summer: *no medals (best finish: 37th)*
Winter: *never participated*

Best sports: Badminton
Athletics
Swimming

It's probable that most people wouldn't guess that the only country which has never finished in the top 32 of any Olympic event in its history is Brunei. On their debut in 1996, they had only one entrant – skeet shooter Prince Abdul Hakeem Jefri Bolkiah, nephew of the Sultan of Brunei. He returned in 2000, along with a single 100-metre runner. In 2004, they had a single 1500-metre runner. In 2008, they didn't turn up, allegedly due to an injury to one of their two intended entrants. They returned in 2012 with two athletes and one swimmer; in 2016 they entered two athletes and one Badminton player, and in 2021 they had one athlete and one swimmer.

Their best finish in Swimming was 40th (out of 40) in the men's 200 metres freestyle in 2012 (their swimmer in 2021 finished 47th out of 49, with two disqualifications). The Prince's best Shooting display was in 2000, when he finished 45th out of 49. In Athletics, they have had two 38th places – 38th out of 38 in the men's 1500 metres in 2004, and 38th out of 48 for Maziah Mahusin in the women's 400 metres in 2012. But the honour of being Brunei's highest Olympic finisher of all time goes to Jaspar Yu Woon Chai, his nation's only Olympian in Badminton. He lost his two group matches 21-16 21-15 and 21-12 21-10 in the men's singles in 2016, but that was enough to finish 37th out of 41 in the overall rankings; his points difference of -31 being better than the competitors from Mexico (-33), Austria (-57) and Suriname (-68), and he also ranked higher than the Guatemalan entrant, who failed to finish.

Brunei have never competed in the Winter Olympics.

CHAPTER TWENTY-SEVEN - Australasia & Melanesia
(Australia, New Zealand, Fiji, Papua New Guinea, Solomon Islands, Vanuatu)

AUSTRALIA   **Olympic Rank 12th**
Population: 26,461,166 (rank 54th)
Olympic rank/ population differential: +42
Population per gold: 152,955 (rank 20th)
Population per medal: 45,505 (rank 20th)

Summer: 164 gold, 173 silver, 213 bronze (total 550) *(plus Australasia: 3-4-5 tot 12)*
Winter: 6 gold, 7 silver, 6 bronze (total 19)
Total: 170 gold, 180 silver, 219 bronze (total 569) *(plus Australasia: 3-4-5 tot 12)*
              (plus mixed team: 0 gold, 0 silver, 0.5 bronze (total 0.5))

Best sports: Rugby (2 golds, 25.00%, 2nd=)
                                     Skateboarding (1 gold, 25.00%, 2nd)
                                     Swimming (71 golds, 11.81%, 2nd)

Australia, despite having only limited self-governance from Britain prior to 1901, entered the 1896 Olympics, albeit with just one competitor – Edwin Flack, who won golds in the men's 800 and 1500 metres, as well as a bronze in doubles Tennis (with a British partner). In 1900, only two Australians went, and again both won medals. Australia have, in fact, never failed to win a medal at an Olympics – the closest they came was in 1936, when they won a single bronze (in triple jump). In 1908 and 1912, they competed alongside New Zealand as part of a combined Australasian team.

Only once since the war have they failed to win a gold – that was in 1976. Their best Games were the Melbourne Games of 1956, when they finished 3rd in the medal table with 13 golds (8½% of all available golds that year). They came 4th in Sydney 2000 (16 golds) and Athens 2004 (17 golds), and also secured 17 golds in 2021. Their highest medal total was 58, in 2000. They have finished in the top 10 in every Games since 1992.

Australia only fielded one Winter Olympian prior to 1952 – a speed skater in 1936. They took until 1994 to win a medal – a Short Track Speed Skating relay bronze. They have won medals at every Games since, with their first golds coming in 2002.

SUMMER
Rugby (2-0-0, 2nd=). Australasia beat Great Britain 32-3 in the only match of 1908 to win gold. Australia then beat New Zealand to win the inaugural women's Sevens in 2016.

Skateboarding (1-0-0, 2nd). Keegan Palmer won the men's park in 2021.

Swimming (71-73-78, 2nd). Australia have won medals in every Games other than 1896 and 1936. There has been a long line of stars. Murray Rose won three golds in Melbourne in 1956, Dawn Fraser won the women's 100m freestyle three times in a row (1956-64) and Shane Gould won three golds in 1972. But in more recent years, Australia have got even better, and two swimmers – Ian Thorpe (2000-04) and Emma McKeon (2016-21) have won five golds each. McKeon has won 11 medals in total; both are Australian records across all sports.

Hockey (4-4-5, 4th). The men won gold in 2004, and have only missed the medals once since 1992. The women have only won three medals – all of them gold (1988, 1996 & 2000).

Triathlon (1-2-2, 3rd). All five medals came in women's, including gold for Emma Snowsill in 2008. The men's best is 4th in 2004.

Beach Volleyball (1-1-1, 4th). Natalie Cook and Kerri-Ann Pottharst won gold in 2000, having taken silver in 1996. The bronze came in 2021. The men's best is 4th in 2004.

Sailing (13-8-8, 6th). Australia have been particularly adept at the 470 class, winning men's gold in 2000, 2008, 2012 & 2021, and women's gold in 2000 & 2008. Malcolm Page and Matthew Belcher won two golds each.

Cycling (15-19-20, 8th). Australia's best Games were in 2004, when they won 11 medals, including 6 golds (they had only ever won 7 golds prior to that, and have only won 2 since).

Rowing (13-15-16, 8th). Only three Rowing golds before 1992, but ten since. Drew Ginn and James Tomkins, who combined for pairs gold in 2004, have won three golds each.

Equestrianism (6-4-4, 9th). All 14 medals have been in three-day eventing. Lawrence Morgan (1960) and Matthew Ryan (1992) have taken individual gold, whilst Australia won the team title in 1960, 1992, 1996 & 2000. Andrew Hoy was involved in the last three of those, as well as taking individual silver (2000) and bronze (2021, at the age of 62). Australia have best finishes of 4th in show jumping and 6th in dressage.

Water Polo (1-0-2, 11th=). The women took gold in 2000, and bronzes in 2008 & 2012. The men's best is 5th.

Modern Pentathlon (1-0-0, 10th=). Chloe Esposito won the 2016 women's title. The men's best is 4th in 1964.

Diving (3-3-8, 7th). Dick Eve won the plain high dive in 1924, Australia's only Diving medal prior to 2000. Chantelle Newbery won women's platform in 2004, and Matthew Mitcham took men's platform in 2008.

Taekwondo (1-1-0, 16th=). Both medals came in 2000, including gold for Lauren Burns in women's flyweight.

Canoeing (5-8-14, 14th). Australia won a bronze in 1956, but no other medals until 1980. Clint Robinson took the first gold, in 1992; others have followed in 2008, 2012 and 2021 (twice).

Athletics (21-27-31, 12th). Australia's most successful athlete was Betty Cuthbert, who won golds in the women's 100m, 200m and 4x100m relay in 1956, followed by 400m gold eight years later. Australia have won medals at all post-war Games except for 1976. Their last golds came in 2012.

Shooting (5-1-5, 16th). All their medals, other than 3 bronzes, have come in trap and double trap. Michael Diamond won the former in 1996 & 2000. The first medal was in women's sport pistol in 1984.

Archery (1-0-2, 12th). Simon Fairweather took gold in 2000, and bronzes have been won in 2004 & 2016.

Tennis (1-1-5.5, 12th). Both the gold (1996) and the silver (2000) were won by the all-conquering "Woodies", Todd Woodbridge and Mark Woodforde, in men's doubles. Only two singles medallists – Anthony Wilding (a New Zealander representing Australasia) in 1912, and Alicia Molik in 2004.

Weightlifting (1-1-2, 34th). Dean Lukin won men's super-heavyweight gold in 1984. Stefan Botev, who won bronze for Bulgaria in 1992, then switched to Australia and won bronze again in 1996, their most recent medal.

Surfing (0-0-1, 5th). Men's bronze for Owen Wright in 2021; Australia came 5th in the women's.

Baseball/Softball (0-2-3, 5th). Australia were shock Baseball silver medallists in 2004. They also won Softball silver the same year, as well as bronzes in 1996, 2000 & 2008.

Basketball (0-3-3, 8th). The women won medals at every Games between 1996 and 2012. The men won their first medal (a bronze) in 2021.

Boxing (0-2-4, 44th). Silver for Snowy Baker for Australasia in 1908 and Grahame Cheney in 1988. The bronzes came in 1956, 1960 (twice) and 2021.

Judo (0-0-2, 44th=). Bronzes in men's open in 1964 and women's lightweight in 2000.

Wrestling (0-1-2, 41st=). The medals came in 1932 (bronze) and 1948 (silver and bronze). The last top-eight finish was a 6th place in 1992. All 15 top-eight finishes have come in freestyle.

Gymnastics (0-1-0, 34th=). Australia's only Gymnastics medallist is Ji Wallace in men's trampolining in 2000. The best finish in artistic Gymnastics is 5th (women's floor, 2012 and men's horizontal bar, 2021).

Football – Two 4th place finishes – losing bronze to Ghana in 1992 (men) and the USA in 2021 (women).

Badminton – Three quarter-final appearances (1992 women's singles for Anna Lao, and women's doubles in 1992 and 2012). They ranked 5th in each of the doubles.

Golf – Marcus Fraser (2016 men) and Hannah Green (2021 women) both tied for 5th.

Fencing – Greg Benko came 6th in men's foil in 1976. Last top-eight finish in 2000, and last entry in 2008.

Artistic Swimming – Regular competitors, but Australia's best remains 7th in the 2008 team event.

Table Tennis – One quarter-final appearance, coming 8th in the women's doubles in 2000. Both of the Australian pair were born in China.

Handball – Entered only as hosts in 2000, when both the men and women lost every game.

Karate – The only entrant, Japanese-born Tsuneara Yahiro, finished last in his 10-man field in 2021.

Sport Climbing – 20th in the men's event in 2021, and 19th in the women's.

Volleyball – Made their debut as hosts in 2000. The men beat Spain and Egypt to reach the quarter-finals and finished 8th, Australia's best finish. The women finished 10th. The men have since returned in 2004 and 2012.

PWDS – never entered

WINTER
Freestyle Skiing (4-3-2, 5th). Golds for Alisa Camplin (2002) and Lydia Lassila (2010) in women's aerials, Dale Begg-Smith (2006) in men's moguls, and Jakara Anthony (2022) in women's moguls.

Snowboarding (1-3-2, 10th). Torah Bright won women's halfpipe gold in 2010 (and silver in 2014).

Short Track Speed Skating (1-0-1, 10th). Australia won relay bronze in 1994, their first ever Winter medal. One of that team, Steven Bradbury, then won a famous gold in the 2002 men's 1000m when his rivals all collided, allowing the outclassed Bradbury, who was so far behind that he avoided the crash, to sweep through for the win (the same thing had also happened in the semi-final).

Skeleton (0-1-0, 10th=). Jackie Narracott won women's silver in 2022; Australia's next best finish is 10th.

Alpine Skiing (0-0-1, 22nd). Zali Steggall won women's slalom bronze in 1998. Australia's next best is 9th.

Bobsleigh – They had never finished higher than 14th prior to a 5th place in the 2022 women's monobob.

Speed Skating – Colin Hickey (1956) and Colin Coates (1976) have two top-eight finishes each. The best was 6th, by Coates in the men's 10000 metres in 1976.

Biathlon – One top-eight finish, Kerryn Rim came 8th in the women's 15km in 1994.

Ice Hockey – Only one entry – the men's event in 1960. They finished 9th out of 9 after losing every game.

Figure Skating – Two 10th places, half a century apart, in the men's singles of 1952 and 2002.

Curling – Just one entry – finishing 10th and last in the 2022 mixed doubles, despite 2 wins out of 9.

Nordic Skiing – Australia are regular competitors. Their best finish is 12th (in the women's team sprint in 2018). Their best in an individual event is 31st.

Luge – Various singles entries since 1992; their best finish is 16th in the men's event in 2022.

Nordic Combined – Only entered once, coming 31st out of 33 (of which 31 finished) in the men's event in 1960. Their entrant was Norwegian-born.

Ski Jumping – never entered

NEW ZEALAND   **Olympic Rank 24th**
Population: 5,109,702 (rank 125th)
Olympic rank/ population differential: +101
Population per gold: 92,904 (rank 10th)
Population per medal: 35,732 (rank 14th)

Summer: 53 gold, 33 silver, 51 bronze (total 137)
Winter: 2 gold, 2 silver, 2 bronze (total 6)
Total: 55 gold, 35 silver, 53 bronze (total 143)

Best sports: Rugby (1 gold, 12.50%, 5th)
                                   Triathlon (1 gold, 7.69%, 4th=)
                                   Rowing (14 golds, 5.11%, 6th)

New Zealand initially took part in the Olympics as part of a combined Australia & New Zealand (Australasia) team in 1908 and 1912, despite both countries being independent by this time. The first New Zealand-born medallist was Harry Kerr, with a bronze in the men's 3500m walk in 1908. Anthony Wilding won a bronze in men's indoor singles Tennis in 1912, and in the same year swimmer Malcolm Champion became New Zealand's first Olympic champion, as part of the men's 4x200m freestyle relay.

New Zealand have competed in all Summer Games since 1920. Their most successful showing was in 1984, when they won 8 golds and came 8th in the overall table. Their total of 11 medals that year was their best at the time, but they have bettered it four times since, with their current best being the 20 medals (7 gold, 6 silver, 7 bronze) that they won in Tokyo in 2021. They have only twice failed to win a medal at the Summer Games – 1948 (best finish 8th) and 1980 (best finish 7th). The first person to win a gold whilst representing New Zealand was boxer Ted Morgan in 1928. The next three Games produced only one gold between them, but New Zealand have won golds at all Games since 1952 (with the exception of 1980).

New Zealand's two greatest Olympians are both canoeists. Ian Ferguson won four golds (and a silver) in 1984 and 1988 – a record he held until Lisa Carrington won golds in the women's K1 200m, K1 500m and K2 500m in 2021, bringing her overall haul since 2012 to five golds and a bronze. Between them, Ferguson and Carrington have won nine of New Zealand's ten Canoeing golds. Two other New Zealanders have won five medals in total – Ferguson's teammate Paul MacDonald (3 gold, 1 silver, 1 bronze, 1984-88) and three-day event legend Mark Todd. Todd won individual golds in 1984 and 1988 (he was the first person to retain the title), and team bronzes in 1988, 2000 and 2012. He was 56 in the latter Games, and went onto compete again, aged 60, in 2016, coming 4th in the team event and 7th in the individual. It was his seventh Games.

The sport for which New Zealand are most internationally renowned is Rugby (in fact it was an All Blacks Rugby tour to South Africa which was the catalyst for the mass Olympic boycott of 1976). They did not compete in its early Olympic outings, but since returning in Sevens form in 2016, they have won a gold (the 2021 women's team) and two silvers. Hamish Carter's gold in the 2004 men's Triathlon ensured its entry in the "best sports" list; they also won a silver in 2004 and bronzes in 2008 and 2021. However, the four sports with most golds overall are Rowing (14), Athletics and Canoeing (10 each) and Sailing (9). No other sport has produced more than three. Eighteen of their 29 Rowing medals (including 11 golds) have come since 2000. Georgina and Caroline Evers-Swindell (double sculls), Eric Murray and Hamish Bond (pairs), and Mahe Drysdale (single sculls) have won two golds each. Athletics was lucrative for New Zealand until the mid-70s, particularly the middle distances, which provided three golds for Peter Snell in 1960 and 1964, and one each for Jack Lovelock (1936) and John Walker (1976). Only two golds have been won since, both by shot putter Valerie Adams, who also has a silver and a bronze (in four consecutive Games, 2008-2021). The Sailing medals have been won regularly since 1956; perhaps the most notable champions are two windsurfers, Bruce Kendall (1 gold, 1 bronze, 1984-88) and his sister Barbara (1 gold, 1 silver, 1 bronze, 1992-2000). Up to 1988, New Zealand had only won three Swimming medals, all of them bronze. Since then, they have three more, 2 golds and a silver, all for Danyon Loader (1992 and 1996). They have yet to win a Swimming medal this century.

Despite their geographical position, New Zealand have competed in the Winter Games in 1952, 1960, and all of them since 1968. They didn't manage a top-eight finish prior to 1992, but in Albertville that year Annelise Coberger won a silver in the women's Alpine Skiing slalom, making her the first person from the Southern Hemisphere ever to win a Winter medal. Hers would remain New Zealand's only Winter medal until 2018, but there have been five since – a gold and bronze for Nico Porteous (Freestyle Skiing) and a gold, silver and bronze for Zoi Sadowski-Synnott (Snowboarding).

FIJI **Olympic Rank 84th**

Population: 947,760 (rank 162nd)
Olympic rank/ population differential: +78
Population per gold: 473,880 (rank 39th)
Population per medal: 315,920 (rank 57th)

Summer: 2 gold, 0 silver, 1 bronze (total 3)
Winter: *no medals (best finish: 55th)*
Total: 2 gold, 0 silver, 1 bronze (total 3)

Best sports: Rugby (2 golds, 25.00%, 1st)
Weightlifting
Judo

Fiji made their Olympic debut as long ago as 1956, making the short trip to Australia. Since then, they have only missed two Summer Games – in 1964 and 1980. For many years, it looked difficult to see where a medal might come from – and then Rugby Sevens was introduced to the Games.

They have competed in Athletics on every appearance, as well as Swimming (1984 onwards), Sailing (1956, 1984-2000, 2021), Judo (since 1984), Cycling (1984 only), Weightlifting (1996 to 2016), Shooting (2004 to 2016), Archery (2004, 2012, 2016), Boxing (1956, 1988, 2016), Rugby Sevens (2016 & 2021), Table Tennis (2016 & 2021), and Football (2016).

Their bests in each sport have been 5th in Weightlifting (Maria Liku, middleweight, 2012 – this is their only top-eight finish outside of Rugby), 9th in Judo (Josateki Basalusalu, middleweight, 1988), 10th in Sailing (Tony Philp, windsurfing, 1992 & 2000), 12th in Athletics (Leslie Copeland, men's javelin, 2012), 13th in Shooting (Glenn Kable, trap, 2008), 26th in Swimming (Sharon Pickering, 200m individual medley, 1984), and 32nd in Cycling. In Boxing in 1956, they had a first-round defeat, but only 16 boxers entered the event. They qualified for the men's Football in 2016, but lost 8-0, 5-1 and 10-0 to finish 16th out of 16. They have never breached the top 32 in Archery or Table Tennis.

When Rugby Sevens came into the Olympics in 2016, it immediately gave Fiji a great chance to break their medal duck, as it is the sport with which they have always been most associated. Sure enough, their men's team won gold in Rio, thrashing Great Britain 43-7 in the final. This result also acted as a bit of revenge for the fact that their women's team was denied a medal when Great Britain beat them in the quarter-finals. Not only that, but Fiji's Prime Minister declared a national holiday to celebrate.

Five years later, in Tokyo, the Fiji women beat Great Britain in the bronze medal play-off to earn their first medal, whilst the men retained their gold with a comfortable win over the only team who can really match them in the sport historically – New Zealand. The Fiji men have thus won all 12 matches they've played in Olympic Rugby Sevens thus far. Jerry Tuwai is the only player who was in both gold medal-winning squads.

Incongruous as it may seem, Fiji have also competed in the Winter Olympics on three non-consecutive occasions – 1988, 1994 and 2002. Only two people have competed for them in that time – Rusiate Rogoyawa in Nordic Skiing in 1988 and 1994, and Laurence Thoms in Alpine Skiing in 2002. The Fijian best finish of 55th was achieved by Thoms in the giant slalom. Surprisingly, perhaps, both Thoms and Rogoyawa were Fiji born and bred; Thoms had been sponsored by a Swiss businessman living in Fiji, whilst Rogoyawa learnt skiing whilst studying in Oslo.

PAPUA NEW GUINEA   Olympic Rank 151st

Population: 9,819,350 (rank 93rd)
Olympic rank/ population differential: -58

Summer: *no medals (best finish: 6th)*
Winter: *never participated*

Best sports: Weightlifting
Swimming
Boxing

Papua New Guinea first entered the Olympics in 1976. They have entered every Summer Games since, with the exception of 1980, when they joined the anti-Soviet boycott. They have participated in eight sports in that time: Athletics (all 11 times), Weightlifting (nine times), Boxing (seven times), Swimming (six times), Sailing and Taekwondo (three times each), and Shooting and Judo (twice each). They have yet to enter the Winter Games.

By far their most successful sport has been Weightlifting, which has been responsible for their three highest placings. Dika Toua finished sixth in women's lightweight in 2004, and seventh in 2008 (despite lifting more weight than she had done four years earlier), whilst Morea Baru finished sixth in men's lightweight in 2016. Toua is also a former Commonwealth Games gold medallist, whilst Baru has won Commonwealth silver.

In Swimming, Papua New Guinea's best six finishes have all been achieved by Ryan Pini, whose events have spanned backstroke, butterfly and freestyle. In 2008, he reached the final of the 100m butterfly, finishing eighth. Three PNG boxers have reached the last 16, although only one did so without receiving a walkover in the last 32. None of their participants in Sailing, Shooting or Judo have finished in the top 16. No PNG Olympian has won a fight in Taekwondo. Finally, PNG's best Athletics finish is 19th, courtesy of both Iammogapi Launa in the 1984 women's heptathlon (19th out of 23), and Rellie Kaputin in the 2021 women's long jump (19th out of 30).

SOLOMON ISLANDS   Olympic Rank 180th

Population: 714,766 (rank 166th)
Olympic rank/ population differential: -14

Summer: *no medals (best finish: 11th)*
Winter: *never participated*

Best sports: Weightlifting
Judo
Boxing

The Solomon Islands have participated in every Summer Games since their first appearance in 1984.
They have participated in Athletics on nine of their 10 Games, and Weightlifting in eight.
The only other sports in which they have participated are Archery (1988), Boxing (1988), Judo (2012) and Swimming (2021).

The highest-placed finisher in Solomon Islands history is their one judoka, Tony Lomo. In the extra-lightweight competition in 2012, he defeated his opponent from Mozambique in the first round, before losing in the round of 16. Of the eight losers in that round, his defeat was the third-narrowest, putting him in 11th place.

Wendy Hale also finished in 11th for the Solomon Islands – in her case, it was in women's lightweight Weightlifting in 2008. However, unlike Lomo, she didn't defeat anybody at the Games. There were 12 competitors, of whom one (the original bronze medallist) failed a drugs test. Hale lifted a total of 173kg; the next-to-last weightlifter lifted 192kg.

The best Solomon Islands weightlifter who actually lifted more than a fellow competitor is Jenly Tegu Wini. Again competing in women's lightweight, she was well adrift of the field in 2012 after the snatch section, but rose up to 15th after two competitors failed to register a lift in the clean & jerk, and another two failed drugs tests. In 2016, she finished 15th again, this time beating one competitor who completed a valid total.

None of the Solomon Islands competitors in Athletics, Archery, Boxing or Swimming have progressed beyond the first round. They have never entered the Winter Games.

VANUATU   ***Olympic Rank 202nd***
Population: 313,046 (rank 177th)
Olympic rank/ population differential: -25

Summer:	*no medals (best finish: 26th)*
Winter:	*never participated*
Best sports:	Athletics
	Boxing
	Judo

Vanuatu have entered all Summer Games since their debut in 1988, though they have never entered the Winter Olympics. They have entered six sports in that time. Probably their greatest Olympian is Mary-Estelle Kapalu. She entered the women's 400m hurdles in 1992, 1996 and 2000, only beating another finisher once (in 1996), but finishing 26th, 28th and 32nd – the former was Vanuatu's joint best finish in an Olympic event.

Also finishing 26th was Boe Warawara, who lost in the first round of the men's bantamweight Boxing in 2016, but by a smaller margin than two other boxers in the 28-man field. He was one of only two ni-Vanuatu boxers in the Olympics – the other was in 1988. They entered Athletics every time until 2012, but have surprisingly not entered since. They are also one of the very few nations to have also never entered Swimming. They have been entering Judo since 2012, losing in the first round every time, but with a best finish of 27th. They have entered five Table Tennis events since 2008, but have yet to win a match – or even a single game (the closest they came was losing a game 12-10). They entered Archery in 2000, finishing 61st out of 64, and have entered Rowing twice, finishing 30th out of 32 and 30th out of 31.

CHAPTER TWENTY-EIGHT - Micronesia & Polynesia (Samoa, Tonga, American Samoa, Nauru, Micronesia, Kiribati, Cook Islands, Marshall Islands, Tuvalu, Palau, Guam)

SAMOA	**Olympic Rank 125th**
Population:	207,501 (rank 180th)
Olympic rank/ population differential:	+55
Population per gold:	n/a
Population per medal:	207,501 (rank 49th)
Summer:	0 gold, 1 silver, 0 bronze (total 1)
Winter:	*never participated*
Total:	0 gold, 1 silver, 0 bronze (total 1)
Best sports:	Weightlifting (1 silver, 54th=)
	Taekwondo
	Boxing

Samoa have been competing in the Olympics since 1984 (though never the Winter Games). By far their most successful sport in that time has been Weightlifting. Super-heavyweight Ele Opeloge finished 4th in 2008 and 6th in 2012. However, re-testing of doping samples some years later led to numerous disqualifications, and as a result Opeloge was elevated in late 2016 to a 2008 silver medal and a 2012 fifth place. It remains Samoa's only ever Olympic medal – what a dreadful shame that she was robbed of her medal rostrum moment in Beijing.

There have been three other top-eight finishes for Samoa – an 8th place for male featherweight weightlifter Vaipava Ioane, and a couple of 8th places in Taekwondo where, in both cases, 8th place was achieved purely due to losing in the first round to an eventual finalist. Samoa's best in Athletics is 17th in the men's discus in 1984. They only entered Swimming in 2016, with a best finish of 32nd in the women's 100m backstroke. They have had five last-16 appearances in Boxing, although only one of those had to win a last-32 bout to get that far. They have also entered Judo, Wrestling, Canoeing, Cycling, Archery and Sailing.

TONGA	**Olympic Rank 127th**
Population:	105,221 (rank 186th)
Olympic rank/ population differential:	+59
Population per gold:	n/a
Population per medal:	105,221 (rank 39th)
Summer:	0 gold, 1 silver, 0 bronze (total 1)
Winter:	*no medals (best finish: 32nd)*
Total:	0 gold, 1 silver, 0 bronze (total 1)
Best sports:	Boxing (1 silver, 54th=)
	Taekwondo
	Weightlifting

Tonga made their Olympic debut in 1984 with a team made up entirely of boxers, two of whom reached the quarter-finals (although one of them didn't have to win a match to get there). They have entered all Summer Games since. In the 1996 men's super-heavyweight category, Paea Wolfgramm reached the final, losing to future world champion Wladimir Klitschko of Ukraine. Nonetheless, his achievements were marked by a national holiday. The only other top-eight finishes for Tonga all came in 2021, when they had two in Taekwondo (both times by default, following heavy defeats), and an 8th place finish in Weightlifting as well.

Tonga's best Athletics finish is 21st (women's discus in 1988), and in Swimming it is 41st (men's 100m breaststroke in 2012). They have also entered Judo and Archery. Tonga have, remarkably, entered the Winter Olympics twice. In 2014, Fuahea Semi, competing under the alias Bruno Banani due to a marketing ploy by a German underwear company, finished 32nd out of 39 in men's singles Luge, and Pita Taufatofua finished 110th in Nordic Skiing in 2018 – Taufatofua has also competed in Olympic Taekwondo in 2016 and 2021 and has famously been the Tongan flagbearer, whilst topless and slathered in oil, at all three of those Games.

AMERICAN SAMOA   **Olympic Rank 162nd**
Population: 44,620 (rank 198th)
Olympic rank/ population differential: +36

Summer: *no medals (best finish: 8th)*
Winter: *no medals (best finish: 19th)*

Best sports: Boxing
                              Weightlifting
                              Athletics

American Samoa first sent a team to the Olympics in 1988, and have entered every Summer Games since. Their highest finish in any event in that time is 8th – achieved by light-middleweight boxer Maselino Masoe, who got through two rounds before losing in the quarter-finals. His brother Mika has the country's second-highest finish, finishing 9th in the light-heavyweight in 1992.

Heavyweight weightlifter Tanumafili Jungblut finished 13th in 2021 – American Samoa's highest non-Boxing finish. The best they have done in Athletics is 14th by Lisa Misipeka in the women's hammer in 2000 (she won a world championship bronze the previous year). The best in Swimming is 32nd (women's 100m breaststroke in 2021). Other sports they have entered have been Wrestling, Judo, Sailing and Archery.

American Samoa have entered the Winter Games twice – finishing 39th out of 43 in the two-man Bobsleigh in 1994, and 19th out of 25 in the men's Skeleton in 2022 (the latter was achieved by Nathan Crumpton, a Kenyan-born US citizen with little or no links to American Samoa prior to seeking citizenship).

NAURU   **Olympic Rank 163rd**
Population: 9,852 (rank 205th)
Olympic rank/ population differential: +42

Summer: *no medals (best finish: 8th)*
Winter: *never participated*

Best sports: Weightlifting
                              Judo
                              Athletics

Nauru have only ever entered three sports in their Olympic history, but their performances in one of them are highly commendable. They have only been competing since 1996, entering all Summer Games, but no Winter Games, since then. Yukio Peter finished 8th in the men's lightweight Weightlifting in 2004. They have also finished 10th in Weightlifting three times.

The most famous Nauruan sportsman is another weightlifter – Marcus Stephen – who represented Samoa in 1992 due to Nauru not having an Olympic Committee at the time. He finished 9th on that occasion, and went on to lift for Nauru in 1996 (failing to finish) and 2000 (finishing 11th). He then served as President of Nauru, no less, from 2007 to 2011.

They only entered Athletics for the first time in 2021, with Jonah Harris clocking 11.01 secs in his preliminary round heat in the 100 metres. Their other sport has been Judo, where they have had one win and two defeats in their three bouts so far.

MICRONESIA   Olympic Rank 172nd
Population: 100,319 (rank 190th)
Olympic rank/ population differential: +18

Summer: *no medals (best finish: 9th)*
Winter: *never participated*

Best sports: Weightlifting
                     Boxing
                     Wrestling

The Federated States of Micronesia, to give them their full name, have participated in every Summer Games since their first appearance in 2000. They have participated in Athletics and Swimming in all six of their Games. They also competed in Weightlifting in each of their first four Games, as well as Wrestling (2012) and Boxing (2016) once each. In Athletics, Swimming, Wrestling and Boxing, none of their participants have ever progressed beyond the first round.

Their best success has come in Weightlifting. On all four occasions, their representative was Manuel Minginfel. In 2000, in bantamweight, he failed to complete the snatch section, and finished last. In 2004, switching to featherweight, he finished 10th out of 20 (of whom one was disqualified and four failed to register sufficient valid lifts). He dropped back a place to 11th in 2008, but achieved his (and his nation's) best finish in 2012, reaching 9th out of 15 (of whom one was disqualified and one failed to register sufficient valid lifts).

Minginfel's Olympic achievements should make him a national hero, but instead he was subsequently jailed following a conviction of child sexual abuse.

KIRIBATI   Olympic Rank 173rd
Population: 115,372 (rank 184th)
Olympic rank/ population differential: +11

Summer: *no medals (best finish: 9th)*
Winter: *never participated*

Best sports: Weightlifting
                     Judo
                     Athletics

Kiribati is famous for a few pieces of trivia – it is surprisingly pronounced *Kiribas*, it is a collection of tiny islands spread over a vast area in the Pacific Ocean, and part of it comprises the first place on Earth to welcome each new day.

In the Olympics, they have a positive differential entirely because of one sport – Weightlifting. Their main star is David Katoatau. In 2008 he finished 12th in light-heavyweight; he then finished 9th in middle-heavyweight in 2012 and 14th in heavyweight in 2016. In 2021, his younger brother Ruben finished 12th in lightweight. All five of Kiribati's Weightlifting entries have resulted in top 14 finishes. In 2012, David initially finished 17th, only for no fewer than eight of those finishing above him to be disqualified for doping. In 2014, he won Kiribati's first (and so far only) ever Commonwealth Games medal – and a gold at that.

Other than Weightlifting, the only other sports in which they have ever competed are Judo (once only) and Athletics. Their one Judo entry resulted in a first-round exit. In Athletics, they have only ever entered the 100m (both men's and women's) – they have never had a sprinter finishing better than sixth in a first-round heat.

COOK ISLANDS   **Olympic Rank 179th**
Population: 7,939 (rank 206th)
Olympic rank/ population differential: +27

Summer: *no medals (best finish: 11th)*
Winter: *never participated*

Best sports: Weightlifting
                                          Boxing
                                          Canoeing

The Cook Islands, who have the smallest population of any of the 206 Olympic nations, made their Olympic debut in 1988, and have competed in all Games since. They have competed in six sports – Athletics (all nine times), Weightlifting (seven times), Sailing & Swimming (four times each), Canoeing (three times) and Boxing (once).

Five of their six top 16 finishes have come in Weightlifting. Rarotonga-born Luisa Peters has the honour of their highest finish of all. In 2012, she came 11th out of 14 in women's super-heavyweight (one did not finish, and one was disqualified). She came 14th four years later. Father and son Sam Nunuke Pera and Sam Pera also finished 14th and 12th respectively in the 2004 heavyweight and 2008 super-heavyweight events.

The best performance from a non-weightlifting Cook Islander was in the 1988 featherweight boxing. Richard Pittman received a bye in the first round, and beat a Swazi boxer in the second to reach the last 16. The Cook Islands' best performances in the other sports are 18th in Canoeing, 20th in Sailing, 30th in Swimming (men's 400m freestyle in 2021), and 36th in Athletics (both in the 2008 women's discus and the 2021 men's 800m).

MARSHALL ISLANDS   **Olympic Rank 185th**
Population: 80,966 (rank 193rd)
Olympic rank/ population differential: +8

Summer: *no medals (best finish: 11th)*
Winter: *never participated*

Best sports: Weightlifting
                                          Taekwondo
                                          Athletics

The Marshall Islands have participated in every Summer Games since their first appearance in 2008.
They have participated in Swimming in all four of their games, and Athletics in the first three.
Besides these, the only sports in which they have participated are Taekwondo (2008) and Weightlifting (2016), once each.

In Athletics, Swimming and Taekwondo, none of their participants have ever progressed beyond the first round.

Their best success, by far, came in their one participation in Weightlifting. Mathlynn "Mattie" Sasser won numerous medals in Oceanian and Pacific competitions, and competed in the 2016 Games in the women's lightweight event. All 16 competitors finished the event, and Sasser finished 11th, beating lifters from Sweden, Ukraine, Australia, the Solomon Islands and the United Arab Emirates. She then moved to North Carolina, and switched allegiance to the United States.

TUVALU   **Olympic Rank 187th**
Population: 11,639 (rank 204th)
Olympic rank/ population differential: +17

Summer: *no medals (best finish: 11th)*
Winter: *never participated*

Best sports: Weightlifting
                        Athletics

Tuvalu, who have of course never entered the Winter Olympics, first entered the Summer Games in 2008. They are the only one of the IOC's 206 countries to have achieved fewer than three top-40 finishes. They have only ever entered nine events – the men's 100 metres four times (2008 to 2021), the women's 100 metres three times (2008, 2012 and 2021), and two Weightlifting events (2008 and 2012).

In the men's lightweight Weightlifting in 2008, Logona Esau finished 21st out of 30. Two were disqualified, six failed to complete sufficient valid lifts, and Esau lifted more than one fellow finisher, from Tajikistan. Four years later, Tuau Lapua Lapua finished 11th out of 15 in the men's featherweight category (one DNF, one DQ, and two lifters, from Uganda and Palau, lifting less weight). Their best finish in any of the 100-metre events they have entered is a rather dismal 69th (Tavavele Noa coming home in 11.55 seconds).

PALAU   **Olympic Rank 192nd**
Population: 21,779 (rank 203rd)
Olympic rank/ population differential: +11

Summer: *no medals (best finish: 13th)*
Winter: *never participated*

Best sports: Weightlifting
                        Wrestling
                        Canoeing

Palau made their Olympic debut in 2000, having gained full independence in 1994. They have entered all Summer Games since, but no Winter Games. They have participated in Athletics and Swimming every time, as well as Wrestling (2004, 2008, 2016), Weightlifting (2000, 2012), Judo (2012) and Canoeing (2016). In Judo, they lost in the first round. In Canoeing, their one entrant, Marina Toribiong, finished 24th out of 28 in the women's K1 200m and 27th out of 27 in the K1 500m. In Swimming, their best is 47th in the women's 100m freestyle in 2000 (the only time they have entered a race longer than 50 metres).

In Athletics, they have only ever entered 100 and 200-metre races. They have only progressed from a heat once (a preliminary round heat in 2016). In Wrestling, they have contested five bouts and lost the lot, although the ranking system saw Florian Temengil come 15th out of 20 in the men's freestyle super-heavyweight in 2008.

Their best finisher in an Olympic event is weightlifter Stevick Patris, who finished 13th in the men's featherweight in 2012. The two who finished below him outperformed him comfortably, though one failed to complete a valid lift in the clean & jerk and the other was disqualified. Their other weightlifter, Valerie Pedro in the women's light-heavyweight in 2000, also came last of those who finished, 14th out of 15 with one non-finisher behind her.

GUAM   **Olympic Rank 194th**
Population: 169,330 (rank 181st)
Olympic rank/ population differential: -13

Summer: *no medals (best finish: 14th)*
Winter: *no medals (best finish: 71st)*

Best sports: Judo
                                   Wrestling
                                   Weightlifting

Guam, unusually, made their Olympic debut in the Winter Games – in Calgary in 1988. They first entered the Summer Games later that same year, and have attended every Summer Games since, though they have never yet returned to the Winter equivalent. Their only Winter athlete has been Judd Bankert, who came 71st in the men's 10km sprint Biathlon event.

Guam are one of the few non-independent nations that compete in the Olympics. As an overseas US territory, they have entered a wider variety of sports than most nations of comparable population. They have entered ten different Summer sports in all – Athletics and Swimming (every time), Wrestling (all except 2000 and 2016), Judo (1988, 1992, 2008, 2012, 2021), Cycling (1992, 2000, 2012, 2016), Sailing (1988-2000), Weightlifting (1988, 1992, 2000), Boxing (1988), Archery (1992) and Canoeing (2008).

In Athletics, their best finish is 34th in the women's 800 metres in 2012; in Swimming, their best finish is 16th in the men's 4x100m freestyle relay in 1992 (they beat two countries in this event – Guatemala and the UAE). They have done better than 16th in four Olympic events thus far – 15th in women's Weightlifting (2000) and men's Judo (2008), and 14th for Erin Lum in the women's middleweight Judo (1992) and Rckaela Aquino in the women's freestyle featherweight Wrestling (2021).

CHAPTER TWENTY-NINE - Other Teams

In 2016, the IOC inaugurated a new tradition of including a Refugee Team at the Summer Games. The first such team included 10 athletes, originally from South Sudan, Syria, Congo DR and Ethiopia, competing in Athletics, Swimming and Judo.

The team was expanded in 2021 to include 29 athletes, including a number from Afghanistan and Iran, amongst others. They entered 12 different sports, and secured their first three top-eight finishes. Best amongst them were Kimia Alizadeh, who came 5th in women's featherweight Taekwondo, and Hamoon Derafshipour, who came 5th in men's <67kg Karate. Both were originally Iranian.
**

There have been various occasions when athletes have competed in the Olympics as Independent Olympic Participants, as follows:
1992 Summer   Yugoslavia and Macedonia
2000 Summer   Timor-Leste
2012 Summer   Curacao and South Sudan
2014 Winter   India
2016 Summer   Kuwait

In addition, Russian athletes have competed as independents in the 2018 Winter Games, and as representatives of the ROC (Russian Olympic Committee) rather than Russia itself at the 2021 and 2022 Games.

These situations have occurred when the country in question has either not yet formed its National Olympic Committee, or it has been suspended for various reasons.

In each case, I have worked in contravention of the IOC, and have allocated all medals won to the country involved because, whether they are allowed to use their own flag or not, if a Russian wins a medal at the Olympics, the viewing public will, by and large, view it as a Russian medal.
**

Here is a list of all mixed-team medals from the early Olympic Games:
Medals awarded to the majority country:
1900 Athletics (5000m team race)	gold	Great Britain (one member was Australian)	
1904 Athletics (4 mile team race)	silver	United States (one member was French)	
1904 Fencing (team foil)	gold	Cuba (one member was American)	
1900 Football (men's)	bronze	Belgium (one member was British)	
1904 Gymnastics (team)	gold	United States (one member was Austrian)	
1900 Polo (men's)	gold	Great Britain (two members were American)	
	silver	Great Britain (one member was American)	
	bronze	France (one member was British)	
1900 Rowing (coxed pairs)	gold	Netherlands (the cox was French)	
1906 Rowing (coxed pairs)	silver	Belgium (the cox was Greek)	
1900 Sailing (2-3 ton, race 1)	gold	France (one member was British)	
1900 Sailing (2-3 ton, race 2)	gold	France (one member was British)	
1904 Tug of War	bronze	United States (one member was German)	
1906 Tug of War	gold	Germany (one member was Swiss)	
1900 Water Polo	bronze	France (one member was British)	

Medals split between countries:
1896 Tennis (men's doubles)	gold	Germany & Great Britain	
	bronze	Australia & Great Britain	
1900 Tennis (men's doubles)	silver	France & United States	
1900 Tennis (mixed doubles)	silver	France & Great Britain	
	bronze	Bohemia & Great Britain	
	bronze	Great Britain & United States	
1900 Tug of War	gold	Denmark & Sweden (3 members each)	
1906 Football	silver	Great Britain (0.4), France (0.4), Greece (0.1), Turkey (0.1)	

CHAPTER THIRTY - Top 5s

In the tables below, the number next to each country denotes number of gold medals won. Ties are separated by number of silver and, if still tied, bronze medals. The number next to each sport denotes the total number of events that have been contested in that sport (normally, that would tally with the number of golds awarded; however, there have been occasions where there has been a tie for gold, as well as a smaller number of occasions where gold has not been awarded at all, for example if it was stripped due to a doping violation and not re-allocated). As is the case throughout this book, medals awarded to now-defunct countries (e.g. USSR, East Germany, Yugoslavia) have been re-allocated to their modern-day equivalent on the lists by sport, although they have been kept under their original countries for the lists by year.

Sport	1st	2nd	3rd	4th	5th
Athletics 1047	United States 355	Russia 90	Germany 73	Great Britain 59	Finland 49
Swimming 598	United States 259	Australia 71	Germany 56	Hungary 30	Russia 25
Wrestling 432	Russia 103	United States 55	Japan 37	Turkey 29	Sweden 28
Gymnastics 363	Russia 107	United States 38	Japan 33	China 33	Romania 25
Shooting 299	United States 57	Russia 31	China 26	Germany 18	Italy 16
Rowing 274	Germany 64	United States 33	Great Britain 31	Romania 20	Italy 15
Cycling 270	France 42	Great Britain 40	Italy 38	Germany 26	Netherlands 23
Boxing 265	United States 50	Cuba 41	Russia 25	Great Britain 20	Italy 15
Canoeing 242	Germany 54	Russia 32	Hungary 28	Sweden 15	Czech Republic 12
Fencing 231	Italy 49	France 47	Hungary 38	Russia 35	Germany 15
Weightlifting 229	Russia 48	China 38	United States 16	Bulgaria 12	Germany 9
Sailing 194	Great Britain 30	United States 19	France 17	Norway 17	Denmark 13
Equestrian 152	Germany 44	Sweden 18	France 15	Great Britain 13	United States 11
Judo 152	Japan 48	France 16	Russia 12	South Korea 11	China 8
Diving 130	United States 48	China 47	Russia 8	Germany 8	Sweden 6
Tennis 75	United States 21	Great Britain 17½	France 8	Germany 4½	Russia 4
Archery 71	South Korea 27	United States 14	Belgium 11	France 7	Italy 2
Taekwondo 48	South Korea 12	China 7	United States 3	Great Britain 2	Russia 2
M Pentathlon 42	Hungary 9	Russia 9	Sweden 9	Great Britain 4	Poland 3
Badminton 39	China 20	Indonesia 8	South Korea 6	Denmark 2	Japan 1
Table Tennis 37	China 32	South Korea 3	Japan 1	Sweden 1	Germany 0
Football 35	United States 4	Hungary 3	Great Britain 3	Brazil 2	Germany 2
Hockey 35	India 8	Netherlands 6	Germany 5	Australia 4	Great Britain 4
Basketball 34	United States 26	Russia 5	Serbia 1	Argentina 1	Latvia 1
Water Polo 34	Hungary 9	Serbia 5	United States 4	Italy 4	Great Britain 4
Volleyball 30	Russia 8	Brazil 5	United States 4	Japan 3	China 3
Handball 26	Russia 7	France 4	Denmark 4	Serbia 3	South Korea 2
Artistic Swim 19	Russia 12	United States 5	Canada 3	China 0	Japan 0
Beach V'ball 14	United States 7	Brazil 3	Germany 2	Australia 1	Norway 1
Triathlon 13	Great Britain 3	Switzerland 2	Australia 1	New Zealand/ United States 1	
Baseb'l/Softb'l 11	United States 4	Japan 3	Cuba 3	South Korea 1	Australia 0
Golf 8	United States 5	Great Britain 1	Canada/ South Korea 1		New Zealand 0
Karate 8	Japan 1	Spain 1	Egypt/ Italy 1		Bulgaria/ France/ Iran/ Serbia 1
Rugby 8	Fiji 2	Australia 2	United States 2	France 1	New Zealand 1
Skateboarding 4	Japan 3	Australia 1	Brazil 0	United States 0	Great Britain 0
Sport Climbing 2	Slovenia/ Spain 1		Japan 0	United States 0	Austria 0
Surfing 2	Brazil/ United States 1		Japan 0	South Africa 0	Australia 0
PWDS 25	Great Britain 10	France 4	United States 3	Canada 2	Argentina 2
Speed Skating 201	Netherlands 48	United States 30	Norway 28	Russia 27	Germany 25
Nordic Skiing 181	Norway 52	Russia 46	Sweden 32	Finland 22	Italy 9
Alpine Skiing 164	Austria 40	Switzerland 27	United States 17	Germany 17	France 16
Biathlon 97	Germany 24	Norway 22	Russia 20	France 12	Sweden 6
Figure Skating 95	Russia 31	United States 16	Germany 8	Austria 7	Canada 6
Short Track SS 65	South Korea 26	China 12	Canada 10	United States 4	Italy 3
Freestyle Ski 57	Canada 12	United States 11	Switzerland 6	China 5	Australia 4
Ski Jumping 54	Norway 12	Finland 10	Germany 9	Austria 7	Japan 4
Bobsleigh 51	Germany 22	Switzerland 10	United States 8	Canada 5	Italy 4
Luge 51	Germany 38	Italy 7	Austria 6	Russia 1	United States 0
Snowboarding 51	United States 17	Switzerland 8	Canada 5	Austria 5	France 4
N'dic Comb'd 40	Norway 15	Germany 12	Finland 4	Austria 3	Japan 2
Ice Hockey 32	Canada 14	Russia 9	United States 4	Sweden 2	Czech Republic 1
Curling 17	Canada 6	Sweden 4	Great Britain 3	Switzerland 1	Norway 1
Skeleton 14	United States 3	Great Britain 3	Germany 2	Canada 2	Russia 1

1896 Athens	United States 11	Greece 10	Germany 6.5	France 5	Great Britain 2.5
1900 Paris	France 31	United States 19	Great Britain 18	Belgium 6	Switzerland 6
1904 St Louis	United States 77	Germany 4	Canada 4	Cuba 4	Hungary 2
1906 Athens	France 15	United States 12	Greece 8	Great Britain 8	Italy 7
1908 London	Great Britain 56	United States 23	Sweden 8	France 5	Germany 3
1912 Stockholm	United States 25	Sweden 23	Great Britain 10	Finland 9	France 7
1920 Antwerp	United States 41	Sweden 19	Finland 15	Great Britain 14	Belgium 14
1924 Paris	United States 45	Finland 14	France 13	Great Britain 9	Italy 8
1928 Amsterdam	United States 22	Germany 10	Finland 8	Sweden 7	Italy 7
1932 Los Angeles	United States 41	Italy 12	France 10	Sweden 9	Japan 7
1936 Berlin	Germany 33	United States 24	Hungary 10	Italy 8	Finland/ France 7
1948 London	United States 38	Sweden 16	France 10	Hungary 10	Italy 8
1952 Helsinki	United States 40	USSR 22	Hungary 16	Sweden 12	Italy 8
1956 Melbourne	USSR 37	United States 32	Australia 13	Hungary 9	Italy 8
1960 Rome	USSR 43	United States 34	Italy 13	Germany 12	Australia 8
1964 Tokyo	United States 36	USSR 30	Japan 16	Germany 10	Italy 10
1968 Mexico City	United States 45	USSR 29	Japan 11	Hungary 10	East Germany 9
1972 Munich	USSR 50	United States 33	East Germany 20	West Germany 13	Japan 13
1976 Montreal	USSR 49	East Germany 40	United States 34	West Germany 10	Japan 9
1980 Moscow	USSR 80	East Germany 47	Bulgaria 8	Cuba 8	Italy 8
1984 Los Angeles	United States 83	Romania 20	West Germany 17	China 15	Italy 14
1988 Seoul	USSR 55	East Germany 37	United States 36	South Korea 12	West Germany 11
1992 Barcelona	Unified Team 45	United States 37	Germany 33	China 16	Cuba 14
1996 Atlanta	United States 44	Russia 26	Germany 20	China 16	France 15
2000 Sydney	United States 37	Russia 32	China 28	Australia 16	Germany 13
2004 Athens	United States 36	China 32	Russia 28	Australia 17	Japan 16
2008 Beijing	China 48	United States 36	Russia 24	Great Britain 19	Germany 16
2012 London	United States 48	China 39	Great Britain 29	Russia 18	South Korea 13
2016 Rio de Jan.	United States 46	Great Britain 27	China 26	Russia 19	Germany 17
2021 Tokyo	United States 39	China 38	Japan 27	Great Britain 22	Russia 20
1924 Chamonix	Norway 4	Finland 4	Austria 2	Switzerland 2	United States 1
1928 St Moritz	Norway 6	United States 2	Sweden 2	Finland 2	Canada/ France 1
1932 Lake Placid	United States 6	Norway 3	Sweden 1	Canada 1	Finland 1
1936 Garmish-P	Norway 7	Germany 3	Sweden 2	Finland 1	Switzerland 1
1948 St Moritz	Norway/ Sweden 4		Switzerland 3	United States 3	France 2
1952 Oslo	Norway 7	United States 4	Finland 3	Germany 3	Austria 2
1956 Cortina d'A	USSR 7	Austria 4	Finland 3	Switzerland 3	Sweden 2
1960 Squaw V	USSR 7	Germany 4	United States 3	Norway 3	Sweden 3
1964 Innsbruck	USSR 11	Austria 4	Norway 3	Finland 3	France 3
1968 Grenoble	Norway 6	USSR 5	France 4	Italy 4	Austria 3
1972 Sapporo	USSR 8	East Germany 4	Switzerland 4	Netherlands 4	United States 3
1976 Innsbruck	USSR 13	East Germany 7	United States 3	Norway 3	West Germany 2
1980 Lake Placid	USSR 10	East Germany 9	United States 6	Austria 3	Sweden 3
1984 Sarajevo	East Germany 9	USSR 6	United States 4	Finland 4	Sweden 4
1988 Calgary	USSR 11	East Germany 9	Switzerland 5	Finland 4	Sweden 4
1992 Albertville	Germany 10	Unified Team 9	Norway 9	Austria 6	United States 5
1994 Lillehammer	Russia 11	Norway 10	Germany 9	Italy 7	United States 6
1998 Nagano	Germany 12	Norway 10	Russia 9	Canada 6	United States 6
2002 Salt Lake C	Norway 13	Germany 12	United States 10	Canada 7	Russia 5
2006 Turin	Germany 11	United States 9	Austria 9	Russia 8	Canada 7
2010 Vancouver	Canada 14	Germany 10	United States 9	Norway 9	South Korea 6
2014 Sochi	Norway 11	Russia 10	Canada 10	United States 9	Netherlands 8
2018 Pyeongchang	Norway 14	Germany 14	Canada 11	United States 9	Netherlands 8
2022 Beijing	Norway 16	Germany 12	China 9	United States 8	Sweden 8
Total (summer)	United States 1074	Russia 608	Germany 441.5	Great Britain 294.5	China 264
Total (winter)	Germany 163	Norway 148	Russia 142	United States 113	Canada 78
Grand Total	United States 1187	Russia 750	Germany 604.5	Great Britain 307.5	China 286

Smallest population per gold
Liechtenstein 19,997　　　Norway 26,530　　　Finland 37,936　　　Bahamas 44,814　　　Sweden 48,893

Smallest population per medal
Liechtenstein 3,999　　　Norway 9,821　　　Finland 11,600　　　San Marino 11,631　Sweden 15,193

Least populous countries with a gold medal (population to the nearest thousand)
Liechtenstein 40k　　　Bermuda 73k　　　Grenada 114k　　　Bahamas 359k　　　Suriname 640k

Least populous countries with a medal (population to the nearest thousand)
San Marino 35k　　　Liechtenstein 40k　　Bermuda 73k　　　US Virgin Is 105k　　Tonga 105k

Best Olympic rank/ population differential *(ie. rank in medal table compared to rank in population)*
Bahamas +122　　　Liechtenstein +118　Estonia +115　　　Norway +109　　　Jamaica +105

Most populous countries without a gold medal (population to the nearest million)
Bangladesh 167m　　　Congo DR 112m　Tanzania 66m　　Myanmar 58m　　　Sudan 49m

Most populous countries without a medal (population to the nearest million)
Bangladesh 167m　　　Congo DR 112m　Myanmar 58m　　Angola 36m　　　Yemen 32m

Worst Olympic rank/ population differential
Bangladesh -189　　　Congo DR -162　　Yemen -131　　　South Sudan -125　Angola/ Benin -116

Worst highest finish in an Olympic event
Brunei 37th　　　South Sudan 32nd　Eq'trl Guinea 32nd　Maldives 26th　　　Vanuatu 26th

Countries who have never won an Olympic medal, but have had a 4th-place finish
Albania, Myanmar, Nicaragua, Congo, Honduras, British Virgin Islands

CHAPTER THIRTY-ONE - Full Olympic Rankings

Rankings determined by most gold medals, then most silver, then most bronze, then most 4th places, then most 5th places etc.

102 nations have won at least one gold:

1. United States   1187 golds
2. Russia   750 golds
3. Germany   604.5 golds
4. Great Britain   307.5 golds
5. China   286 golds
6. France   283 golds
7. Italy   266 golds
8. Sweden   215.5 golds
9. Norway   211 golds
10. Japan   186 golds
11. Hungary   185 golds
12. Australia   173 golds
13. Canada   149 golds, 183 silvers
14. Netherlands   149 golds, 156 silvers
15. Finland   148 golds
16. South Korea   129 golds
17. Switzerland   120 golds
18. Austria   94 golds
19. Romania   90 golds
20. Cuba   85 golds
21. Czech Republic   80 golds
22. Poland   79 golds
23. Bulgaria   55 golds, 90 silvers
24. New Zealand   55 golds, 35 silvers
25. Denmark   51.5 golds
26. Spain   49 golds
27. Belgium   48 golds
28. Greece   43 golds
29. Turkey   41 golds
30. Ukraine   38 golds
31. Brazil   37 golds
32. Kenya   35 golds
33. Serbia   34 golds
34. South Africa   27 golds
35. Jamaica   26 golds
36. Iran   24 golds
37. Ethiopia   23 golds
38. Belarus   21 golds, 37 silvers
39. Argentina   21 golds, 26 silvers
40. Croatia   18 golds
41. North Korea   16 golds
42. Kazakhstan   15 golds
43. Slovakia   14 golds, 18 silvers
44. Estonia   14 golds, 11 silvers
45. Mexico   13 golds
46. Slovenia   12 golds
47. Ireland   11 golds, 10 silvers
48. Uzbekistan   11 golds, 6 silvers
49. Georgia   10 golds, 12 silvers
50. India   10 golds, 9 silvers

51. Thailand — 10 golds, 8 silvers
52. Indonesia — 8 golds, 14 silvers
53. Egypt — 8 golds, 11 silvers
54. Bahamas — 8 golds, 2 silvers
55. Azerbaijan — 7 golds, 14 silvers
56. Chinese Taipei — 7 golds, 11 silvers
57. Morocco — 7 golds, 5 silvers
58. Lithuania — 6 golds
59. Latvia — 5 golds, 14 silvers
60. Colombia — 5 golds, 13 silvers
61. Portugal — 5 golds, 9 silvers
62. Algeria — 5 golds, 4 silvers
63. Tunisia — 5 golds, 3 silvers
64. Uganda — 4 golds
65. Nigeria — 3 golds, 11 silvers
66. Venezuela — 3 golds, 7 silvers
67. Trinidad & Tobago — 3 golds, 5 silvers, 11 bronzes
68. Dominican Republic — 3 golds, 5 silvers, 4 bronzes
69. Zimbabwe — 3 golds, 4 silvers
70. Pakistan — 3 golds, 3 silvers
71. Ecuador — 3 golds, 2 silvers
72. Israel — 3 golds, 1 silver, 9 bronzes
73. Cameroon — 3 golds, 1 silver, 2 bronzes
74. Kosovo — 3 golds, 0 silvers
75. Mongolia — 2 golds, 11 silvers
76. Armenia — 2 golds, 8 silvers
77. Chile — 2 golds, 7 silvers
78. Hong Kong — 2 golds, 3 silvers
79. Puerto Rico — 2 golds, 2 silvers, 6 bronzes, 4 fourths
80. Uruguay — 2 golds, 2 silvers, 6 bronzes, 1 fourth, 1 fifth
81. Liechtenstein — 2 golds, 2 silvers, 6 bronzes, 1 fourth, 0 fifths
82. Qatar — 2 golds, 2 silvers, 4 bronzes
83. Bahrain — 2 golds, 2 silvers, 0 bronzes
84. Fiji — 2 golds, 0 silvers
85. Philippines — 1 gold, 5 silvers
86. Vietnam — 1 gold, 3 silvers, 1 bronze
87. Luxembourg — 1 gold, 3 silvers, 0 bronzes, 5 fourths
88. Peru — 1 gold, 3 silvers, 0 bronzes, 4 fourths
89. Singapore — 1 gold, 2 silvers
90. Ivory Coast — 1 gold, 1 silver, 2 bronzes, 3 fourths
91. Costa Rica — 1 gold, 1 silver, 2 bronzes, 1 fourth, 2 fifths
92. Syria — 1 gold, 1 silver, 2 bronzes, 1 fourth, 1 fifth
93. Tajikistan — 1 gold, 1 silver, 2 bronzes, 0 fourths
94. Jordan — 1 gold, 1 silver, 1 bronze, 1 fourth, 1 fifth
95. Grenada — 1 gold, 1 silver, 1 bronze, 1 fourth, 0 fifths
96. Burundi — 1 gold, 1 silver, 0 bronzes
97. Kuwait — 1 gold, 0 silvers, 4 bronzes
98. Panama — 1 gold, 0 silvers, 2 bronzes
99. Bermuda — 1 gold, 0 silvers, 1 bronze, 1 fourth, 4 fifths
100. Mozambique — 1 gold, 0 silvers, 1 bronze, 1 fourth, 3 fifths
101. United Arab Emirates — 1 gold, 0 silvers, 1 bronze, 1 fourth (next best is 7th)
102. Suriname — 1 gold, 0 silvers, 1 bronze, 1 fourth (next best is 8th)

27 nations have never won a gold, but have won at least one silver:
- 103. Malaysia — 8 silvers
- 104. Namibia — 5 silvers
- 105. Kyrgyzstan — 3 silvers
- 106. Moldova — 2 silvers, 4 bronzes
- 107. Iceland — 2 silvers, 2 bronzes, 3 fourths
- 108. Saudi Arabia — 2 silvers, 2 bronzes, 2 fourths
- 109. Lebanon — 2 silvers, 2 bronzes, 1 fourth
- 110. Tanzania — 2 silvers, 0 bronzes, 0 fourths, 2 fifths
- 111. Sri Lanka — 2 silvers, 0 bronzes, 0 fourths, 1 fifth
- 112. Ghana — 1 silver, 4 bronzes
- 113. San Marino — 1 silver, 2 bronzes
- 114. Botswana — 1 silver, 1 bronze, 1 fourth
- 115. North Macedonia — 1 silver, 1 bronze, 0 fourths, 1 fifth (next best 6th, then 7th)
- 116. Niger — 1 silver, 1 bronze, 0 fourths, 1 fifth (next best 6th, then 10th)
- 117. Haiti — 1 silver, 1 bronze, 0 fourths, 1 fifth (next best 7th)
- 118. Zambia — 1 silver, 1 bronze, 0 fourths, 0 fifths
- 119. Guatemala — 1 silver, 0 bronzes, 3 fourths, 1 fifth
- 120. Montenegro — 1 silver, 0 bronzes, 3 fourths, 0 fifths
- 121. Senegal — 1 silver, 0 bronzes, 2 fourths, 3 fifths
- 122. Cyprus — 1 silver, 0 bronzes, 2 fourths, 1 fifth
- 123. Turkmenistan — 1 silver, 0 bronzes, 1 fourth
- 124. Sudan — 1 silver, 0 bronzes, 0 fourths, 1 fifth (next best 7th)
- 125. Samoa — 1 silver, 0 bronzes, 0 fourths, 1 fifth (next best 8th)
- 126. Paraguay — 1 silver, 0 bronzes, 0 fourths, 0 fifths (next best 6th)
- 127. Tonga — 1 silver, 0 bronzes, 0 fourths, 0 fifths (next best 7th)
- 128. US Virgin Islands — 1 silver, 0 bronzes, 0 fourths, 0 fifths (next best 8th)
- 129. Gabon — 1 silver, 0 bronzes, 0 fourths, 0 fifths (next best 10th)

9 nations have never won a gold or silver, but have won at least one bronze:
- 130. Afghanistan — 2 bronzes
- 131. Barbados — 1 bronze, 2 fourths
- 132. Eritrea — 1 bronze, 1 fourth, 1 fifth
- 133. Iraq — 1 bronze, 1 fourth, 0 fifths (next best 6th)
- 134. Djibouti — 1 bronze, 1 fourth, 0 fifths (next best 8th)
- 135. Mauritius — 1 bronze, 0 fourths, 0 fifths (next best 6th)
- 136. Guyana — 1 bronze, 0 fourths, 0 fifths (next best 7th)
- 137. Burkina Faso — 1 bronze, 0 fourths, 0 fifths (next best 8th)
- 138. Togo — 1 bronze, 0 fourths, 0 fifths (next best 10th)

31 nations have never won a medal, but have had at least one top-eight finish:
- 139. Albania — best finish 4th, then 5th, 5th, 5th
- 140. Myanmar — best finish 4th, then 5th, 5th, 6th
- 141. Nicaragua — best finish 4th, then 6th, 7th
- 142. Congo — best finish 4th, then 6th, 12th
- 143. Honduras — best finish 4th, then 7th
- 144. British Virgin Islands — best finish 4th, then 12th
- 145. Mali — best finish 5th, then 6th
- 146. Sierra Leone — best finish 5th, then 7th, 9th
- 147. Seychelles — best finish 5th, then 7th, 10th
- 148. El Salvador — best finish 5th, then 8th
- 149. Liberia — best finish 5th, then 11th
- 150. Bosnia & Herzegovina — best finish 6th, then 6th, 6th
- 151. Papua New Guinea — best finish 6th, then 6th, 7th, 8th
- 152. St Kitts & Nevis — best finish 6th, then 6th, 7th, 10th
- 153. Monaco — best finish 6th, then 10th

154. Somalia — best finish 6th, then 15th
155. St Lucia — best finish 6th, then 18th
156. Nepal — best finish 7th, then 7th
157. Angola — best finish 7th, then 8th
158. Guinea-Bissau — best finish 7th, then 9th, 11th
159. Lesotho — best finish 7th, then 9th, 15th
160. Malta — best finish 8th, then 8th
161. Madagascar — best finish 8th, then 9th, 9th
162. American Samoa — best finish 8th, then 9th, 13th
163. Nauru — best finish 8th, then 10th, 10th
164. Cayman Islands — best finish 8th, then 10th, 12th, 13th
165. Central African Republic — best finish 8th, then 10th, 12th, 16th
166. Libya — best finish 8th, then 10th, 14th
167. Oman — best finish 8th, then 10th, 19th
168. Malawi — best finish 8th, then 13th
169. Rwanda — best finish 8th, then 14th

37 nations have never finished in the top eight of any Olympic event:

170. Andorra — best finish 9th, then 9th, 11th, 11th
171. Antigua & Barbuda — best finish 9th, then 9th, 11th, 12th
172. Micronesia — best finish 9th, then 10th
173. Kiribati — best finish 9th, then 12th, 12th
174. Chad — best finish 9th, then 12th, 15th
175. Mauritania — best finish 10th, then 10th
176. Congo DR — best finish 10th, then 11th
177. Dominica — best finish 10th, then 12th
178. Yemen — best finish 10th, then 14th
179. Cook Islands — best finish 11th, then 12th
180. Solomon Islands — best finish 11th, then 13th, 14th, 15th, 15th
181. Gambia — best finish 11th, then 13th, 14th, 15th, 17th
182. Cambodia — best finish 11th, then 13th, 15th
183. Eswatini — best finish 11th, then 14th
184. Aruba — best finish 11th, then 15th
185. Marshall Islands — best finish 11th, then 16th
186. St Vincent/ Grenadines — best finish 11th, then 19th
187. Tuvalu — best finish 11th, then 21st
188. Belize — best finish 12th, then 12th
189. Guinea — best finish 12th, then 13th
190. Benin — best finish 13th, then 13th, 13th
191. Bolivia — best finish 13th, then 13th, 15th
192. Palau — best finish 13th, then 14th
193. Palestine — best finish 13th, then 27th
194. Guam — best finish 14th, then 14th
195. Cape Verde — best finish 14th, then 15th
196. Sao Tome and Principe — best finish 14th, then 16th
197. Bangladesh — best finish 16th
198. Bhutan — best finish 17th, then 20th
199. Laos — best finish 17th, then 21st
200. Timor-Leste — best finish 20th
201. Comoros — best finish 21st
202. Vanuatu — best finish 26th, then 26th
203. Maldives — best finish 26th, then 32nd
204. Equatorial Guinea — best finish 32nd, then 32nd, 36th
205. South Sudan — best finish 32nd, then 32nd, 40th
206. Brunei — best finish 37th

CHAPTER THIRTY-TWO - Summary of Olympic Games

Ancient Olympics
- The Ancient Olympic Games traditionally date from 776BC, and were held every four years in Olympia, Greece. They were held in honour of Zeus, king of the Gods, on Mount Olympus. Initially, there was only one event (a running race), and the 776BC champion was Koroibos, a cook from Elis. Other events were subsequently added, including Boxing, Wrestling, Pankration (a sort of mixed martial art) and Chariot Racing, as well as other Athletics events including discus and long jump. The games lasted for over a thousand years, and were last recorded in 393AD.
- The most-decorated ancient Olympian on record was Leonidas of Rhodes, who won a total of twelve events between 164BC and 152BC. This record stood for 2168 years, until broken by Michael Phelps in 2016. His triumphs came in three events which he won four times each – the stade (c.200m in the nude), diaulos (c.400m in the nude) and hoplitodromos (c.400m in armour).
- Various sporting festivals using the term "Olympic" were being documented in the British Isles from the mid-17th century, and were gaining traction in the mid-1800s. Around this time, there was interest in Greece in the idea of resurrecting the Games, but it was French aristocrat Baron Pierre de Coubertin who was the driving force in turning this into reality. He founded the International Olympic Committee, who first met in 1894.

Summer Games

1896 Athens, Greece   **43 events, 14 nations**
- Athens was deemed to be the obvious choice to host the first reincarnation of the Olympic Games of Ancient Greece. Nine sports were included, all open to men only: Athletics, Swimming, Gymnastics, Cycling, Shooting, Fencing, Tennis, Weightlifting and Wrestling. James Connolly from Massachusetts won the triple jump to become the first modern Olympic champion. Carl Schumann (Germany) won three events in Gymnastics and one in Wrestling; he also competed in Athletics and Weightlifting. Spyridon Louis, a Greek water carrier, won the most prestigious event – the marathon. Gold medals were not awarded at the time, however (winners received a silver medal). All in all, the Games were a great success, but de Coubertin resisted calls to make Athens the permanent hosts.

1900 Paris, France   **95 events, 24 nations**
- Paris were agreed as 1900 hosts at the same 1894 meeting that had decided on Athens for the 1896 Games. However, the 1900 Games were linked to a prestigious world's fair, were stretched over six months, and were relegated to a sideshow. Many of the events were not specified as Olympic at the time, and many competitors never realised they were Olympians. There is still some dispute as to which events should be included in the records. Sailing, Archery, Rowing, Equestrianism, Football, Water Polo, Golf, Rugby, Croquet, Pelota, Polo, Cricket and Tug of War were all added. Wrestling and Weightlifting were dropped. Women competed for the first time, and Swiss sailor Helene de Pourtales became the first female champion. Alvin Kraenzlein won four golds in Athletics in individual events – still the only person ever to do so at a single Games.

1904 St Louis, United States   **95 events, 12 nations**
- The 1904 Games had been awarded to Chicago. However, St Louis were hosting a world's fair in 1904, and demanded that the Olympics become part of it. Eventually, with the support of US President Theodore Roosevelt, they got their way and thus all the worst mistakes of 1900 were repeated. Due to the paucity of European representation, the 1904 Games were actually even worse. Many events were effectively US national championships, if that, and the men's marathon was an extraordinary shambolic affair. Wrestling and Weightlifting returned. Boxing, Diving, Lacrosse and Roque were introduced. Sailing, Equestrianism, Shooting, Rugby, Croquet, Pelota, Polo and Cricket were dropped.

1906 Athens, Greece (intercalated, unofficial)   **74 events, 20 nations**
- The Greeks planned to host "intercalated Games" every four years, in the mid-years between the regular Games. Due to instability in the Balkan region, the 1910 Games were dropped, and the plan was never pursued. The IOC do not recognise the 1906 Games; however, they certainly should – but for the 1906 Games, the whole Olympic movement may have collapsed, such were the disasters of the 1900 and 1904 Games. Shooting returned. Archery, Boxing, Golf, Water Polo, Lacrosse and Roque were dropped.

1908 London, Great Britain   **109 events, 22 nations**

- The 1908 Games had been awarded to Rome, but in 1906 Mount Vesuvius erupted, and the nearby city of Naples desperately needed funds. The Italians were struggling to meet the costs of the Olympics anyway, and withdrew from hosting. London willingly stepped in, building the White City Stadium in a matter of months. Once again, the Games dragged on over several months, but were more successful than 1900 or 1904. Ray Ewry completed his haul of 10 golds (including two from 1906), all in the now-defunct standing jump events. The Games were marred by several disputes between Britain and the US. Archery, Boxing, Lacrosse, Polo, Rugby, Sailing and Water Polo all returned. Hockey, Jeu de Paume, Motor Boating, Rackets and Figure Skating were introduced. Weightlifting was dropped.

1912 Stockholm, Sweden   102 events, 28 nations
- Stockholm were selected as hosts unopposed, and oversaw by far the most successful Games yet. The Games were dominated by Jim Thorpe, who won golds in the pentathlon and decathlon. In 1913, though, he was stripped of his titles on a dubious charge of professionalism; they were posthumously returned in 1983, and he was restored as sole champion in both events in 2022. Boxing, Archery, Hockey, Rugby, Rackets, Jeu de Paume, Polo, Motor Boating, Lacrosse and Figure Skating were dropped. Equestrianism returned, and Modern Pentathlon was introduced.

1920 Antwerp, Belgium   155 events, 29 nations
- Antwerp were awarded the 1920 Games in 1914. Following the devastation of Belgium throughout the ensuing Great War, they were given the option of pulling out but, in 1919, decided to press on, and produced a remarkable Games in the circumstances. Willis Lee (USA, Shooting) and Nedo Nadi (Italy, Fencing) won five golds each. Oscar Swahn, aged 72, won silver in Shooting. Archery, Boxing, Figure Skating, Hockey, Polo, Rugby and Weightlifting returned, and Ice Hockey was introduced. These Games saw the introduction of the Olympic Flag.

1924 Paris, France   126 events, 44 nations
- Paris was awarded the 1924 Games at the request of retiring IOC President Baron de Coubertin. It made France the first country to host the Games twice (excluding Greece's hosting in 1906). Archery, Hockey and Tug of War were dropped, Figure Skating and Ice Hockey were moved to the Winter Games, and the Sailing and Shooting programmes were hugely reduced. The "Flying Finn" Paavo Nurmi won five golds, and his compatriot Ville Ritola won four. British Athletics champions Harold Abrahams and Eric Liddell were later immortalised in the film *Chariots of Fire*.

1928 Amsterdam, Netherlands   109 events, 46 nations
- After agreeing to stand aside for Paris in 1924, Amsterdam were given the 1928 Games. The number of events again decreased; Polo, Rugby, Shooting and Tennis were all dropped, but Hockey returned. Also making its belated debut were women's Athletics and Gymnastics. Paavo Nurmi won the 10,000 metres, his ninth Olympic gold. The Games were peaceful and serene, unlike many that followed.

1932 Los Angeles, United States   116 events, 37 nations
- Due to the Great Depression and cost of travel, the 1932 Games saw fewer than half the number of competitors as had taken part in 1928. Shooting returned to the Games, though Football was omitted. The Los Angeles Coliseum, an enormous venue, saw numerous world records set on the track. The greatest athlete of the Games was American Babe Didrikson, who was only allowed to enter three events, winning two and controversially being demoted to silver in the other. She would likely have won several other golds given the chance, and was also world-class in Basketball, Baseball and Golf.

1936 Berlin, Germany   129 events, 49 nations
- The 1936 Games are synonymous with two men – Adolf Hitler, who didn't compete, and Jesse Owens who, to Hitler's disappointment, won an iconic haul of four golds in Athletics. Berlin had been scheduled to host the 1916 Games, which were cancelled due to war, and were awarded the 1936 Games ahead of Barcelona; the vote taking place two years before Hitler's rise to power. Threats of boycotts from the likes of the USA, Great Britain and France never materialised. Football and Polo returned, and Basketball, Canoeing and Handball were introduced.

1948 London, Great Britain   136 events, 59 nations
- London had previously been awarded the 1944 Games, which were cancelled due to war. They agreed to host in 1948, despite the ravages of war. The "Austerity Games" went well, with army barracks and colleges being used instead of an Olympic Village. Polo and Handball were dropped. Fanny Blankers-Koen, mother to two young children, won four Athletics golds, becoming the star of the Games.

1952 Helsinki, Finland   **149 events, 69 nations**
- Helsinki won the bid ahead of various US venues, and hosted the first "Cold War" Games, as the Soviets took part for the first time since the last Russian entry in 1912. The opening ceremony was graced by the presence of Finnish hero Paavo Nurmi in the torch relay. The star of the Games, though, was Emil Zatopek, who completed an extraordinary golden treble of 5000m, 10000m and marathon.

1956 Melbourne, Australia   **151 events, 72 nations**
- Melbourne beat Buenos Aires by a single vote (21-20) to host the Games. The IOC did not realise at the time that Australian quarantine regulations would preclude them from hosting Equestrianism – these events were held six months earlier in Stockholm. Soon after the Soviet invasion of Hungary, the two nations met in Water Polo in a violent affair that left the water blood-red in places. At the suggestion of an Australian schoolboy, the athletes of all nations paraded together at the closing ceremony – a tradition that has stuck.

1960 Rome, Italy   **150 events, 83 nations**
- Rome beat Lausanne to host the Games, 52 years after having to pull out in 1908. It produced some marvellous sights, including Wrestling at the ancient Basilica di Maxentius, and Abebe Bikila's barefoot marathon victory in torchlight along the Appian Way. Cassius Clay won gold in Boxing, and the Games were largely free of political controversy. But there was tragedy, in the death of a Danish cyclist during the team road time trial amidst unconfirmed allegations of doping.

1964 Tokyo, Japan   **163 events, 93 nations**
- Tokyo easily won the bid, thus becoming the first Asian host of an Olympic Games. Judo and Volleyball were introduced, both of which saw predictable Japanese success. Indonesia, North Korea and South Africa were all barred from competing for various reasons, but the Games went well. Soviet gymnast Larisa Latynina brought her Olympic tally to 9 golds, 5 silvers and 4 bronzes – her total of 18 remains the most for anybody other than Michael Phelps.

1968 Mexico City, Mexico   **172 events, 112 nations**
- Mexico City won the bid with just over half the votes, ahead of Detroit and Lyon, despite misgivings about the altitude. The altitude led to slow times in the longer distance events, but helped Bob Beamon set a legendary long jump world record of 8m90. Dick Fosbury's revolutionary "Fosbury Flop" technique won him the high jump, and Al Oerter won men's discus for the fourth time in a row. Drug testing was introduced. Judo was dropped. The Games were marked by political protest – hundreds of students were killed by police during a demonstration against the cost of the Olympics, and two black Americans famously raised a black-gloved fist during the medal ceremony of the men's 200 metres.

1972 Munich, West Germany   **195 events, 121 nations**
- Munich won ahead of bids from Montreal and Madrid, and hoped to use the Games to banish the memory of the 1936 Nazi-dominated Games. But the Games would be remembered for a horrendous tragedy, when Palestinian terrorists stormed the Israeli team's accommodation and, following a disastrous rescue attempt, 11 Israelis were murdered. The Games were suspended for a day, but then controversially resumed. Judo returned, as did Archery (last seen in 1920) and Handball (last seen in 1936). Mark Spitz won all seven Swimming events he entered, all in world-record time. Meanwhile, the USA's winning streak in Basketball was ended in highly controversial fashion when the USSR were given an extra three seconds to make the winning score in a 51-50 victory.

1976 Montreal, Canada   **198 events, 92 nations**
- Montreal won the bid, while its two rivals, Moscow and Los Angeles, went on to host the following two Games. The Games were a disaster for Canada, who went way over-budget in organising the Games (which they were still paying off years later), and who became the only Summer hosts in history not to win a single gold medal (they won 5 silvers and 6 bronzes). A total of 26 nations (mostly African) boycotted the Games in protest at New Zealand's participation, given that their Rugby team had recently toured the international pariah state of South Africa (this despite Rugby having no connection to the Olympics at the time). Gymnast Nadia Comaneci became the darling of the Games, whilst East Germany, who had never previously won a gold medal in women's Swimming, won 11 out of 13 this time, raising deep suspicions of doping, which were only proved decades later.

1980 Moscow, USSR   **203 events, 80 nations**

- Moscow saw off their only rivals, Los Angeles, to host the Games. Over 60 countries then joined a US-led boycott protesting the Soviet invasion of Afghanistan in late 1979. Some countries, such as Great Britain, boycotted some sports but not others. All in all, many of the events, and subsequently the medals, were hugely devalued. Despite that, the Games were well run, and the action is possibly best remembered for the duals of Sebastian Coe and Steve Ovett, who each won the other's favoured event.

1984 Los Angeles, United States   221 events, 140 nations
- Los Angeles was effectively the only bidder for the 1984 Games, confirmed in 1978. In May 1984, the USSR withdrew, citing safety concerns due to "anti-communist" activity in Los Angeles. Clearly a "revenge" boycott due to 1980, they were joined by several other countries that would have won a lot of medals, including East Germany, Cuba and Bulgaria. Two Eastern European nations, Romania and Yugoslavia, did compete, being roundly lauded for doing so, and all in all the Games attracted more nations than ever before. Synchronized Swimming (later renamed Artistic Swimming) was introduced. Carl Lewis emulated Jesse Owens in 1936 by winning the same four golds. Perhaps most importantly, the Games had been completed well within budget, which helped future Games attract more bidders.

1988 Seoul, South Korea   237 events, 160 nations
- Seoul surprisingly beat Nagoya (Japan) to win the bid, despite South Korea being under a military dictatorship at the time (democracy – of sorts – eventually returned in 1987). North Korea and Cuba boycotted, but the boycotts were on nothing like the scale of the previous three Games. Unfortunate headlines were made when the most prestigious gold medallist of the Games, Ben Johnson (men's 100 metres), turned out to be a drugs cheat. Florence Griffith Joyner broke records in the women's sprints. Kristin Otto won six Swimming golds (only the second Olympian ever to win six golds in one Games), and Matt Biondi five. Table Tennis was introduced, and Tennis returned for the first time since 1924.

1992 Barcelona, Spain   257 events, 169 nations
- The first post-Cold War Games, and the first entirely boycott-free Games for 20 years, were a magnificent affair, from the moment an archer lit the Olympic flame with a bow and arrow, all to the soundtrack of Freddie Mercury and Montserrat Caballe's spectacular theme song "Barcelona", in honour of the city that had won the bid ahead of Paris, amongst others. Relaxed eligibility rules meant the US could call upon all their NBA stars to create Basketball's "Dream Team". Gymnast Vitaly Scherbo, competing for the post-Soviet "Unified Team" (he was from Belarus) won six golds. Badminton and Baseball were introduced. South Africa returned to their first Games since 1960.

1996 Atlanta, United States   271 events, 197 nations
- With these Games marking the centenary of the first modern Games, it was widely assumed that they would return to Athens. But the IOC made the shocking decision to award the Games to Atlanta, which was not even in the top 25 of largest cities in the US. The decision was seemingly motivated by commercial concerns (Atlanta is the home of major Olympic sponsor Coca-Cola). The Games were massively over-commercialised, and remembered with little fondness, especially given that a domestic bomb in the Olympic Park killed two people one night during the Games. Nonetheless, for the first time, every country in the IOC attended the Games. Michael Johnson's world record in the 200 metres was perhaps the highlight of the action. Beach Volleyball and Softball were introduced.

2000 Sydney, Australia   300 events, 199 nations
- Sydney beat Beijing 45-43 in a close vote, and proceeded to host arguably the best Games yet. National hero Cathy Freeman, Aboriginal by heritage, lit the flame, and went on to win the women's 400 metres – a glorious moment for the host nation, who were making a concerted effort to atone for their past mistreatment of Aboriginal people. Again, no countries were missing. Taekwondo and Triathlon were introduced. Freeman apart, the two biggest stars were Australian swimmer Ian Thorpe (three golds) and US sprinter Marion Jones (three golds, but later unmasked as a drugs cheat, and her medals stripped).

2004 Athens, Greece   301 events, 201 nations
- Eight years later than expected, the Games returned to Athens, after they saw off several rival bids, in particular Rome. There were serious concerns that construction was being left until the last minute, but it all came together in the end, and the Games were memorable. The shot put competitions took place in ancient Olympia – the first Olympic action there for 1,611 years. The Panathenaic Stadium, made of marble for the 1896 Games, hosted the Archery and the climax of the marathons. Gold medal winners in all events were crowned with olive wreaths, as in the ancient Games. Michael Phelps attempted to

win eight Swimming golds, but had to settle for a mere six (and two bronzes). On a personal note, these were the first Games I attended, having become obsessed with the Olympics years earlier as a child.

2008 Beijing, China　　　　　　　　　　　　**302 events, 204 nations**
- Having narrowly missed out on hosting in 2000, Beijing won this time, beating Toronto and others. Serious concerns in the build-up, including human rights issues and internet censorship, were largely forgotten once the Games got underway with a no-expense-spared spectacular opening ceremony. Michael Phelps smashed almost every record going in claiming eight golds in the pool, bringing his career total to 14. But perhaps even he was overshadowed by Usain Bolt, who broke the 100-metre world record despite jogging over the finish line. Great Britain began their domination of track Cycling, and China topped the medal table for the first time, having been getting gradually closer over the previous few Games.

2012 London, Great Britain　　　　　　　　**302 events, 204 nations**
- London won a close bidding race against pre-vote favourites Paris. As with most Games, there were concerns in the build-up, including going well over budget, and problems with the designated security company, meaning that police and troops needed to step in at late notice. But, helped by an army of superb volunteers, London 2012 was an absolute joy from the moment Queen Elizabeth II "parachute-jumped" her way into the stadium to open the Games. Even the weather largely complied, and demand for tickets went through the roof. Michael Phelps won another four golds, and Usain Bolt another three. The hosts' "face of the Games" Jessica Ennis won gold, as did Mo Farah (twice). Baseball and Softball were dropped, but the programme was otherwise largely unchanged.

2016 Rio de Janeiro, Brazil　　　　　　　　**306 events, 206 nations**
- Rio comfortably beat Madrid in the 2009 vote, bringing the Games to South America for the first time. But the intervening years saw financial and political problems in Brazil which, together with fears over "Zika" virus, led to many people writing the Games off before they'd begun. But, like Greece and others before them, Rio rose to the challenge and hosted a successful Games. Golf and Rugby Sevens were introduced. For the third Games in a row, the biggest stars were Michael Phelps and Usain Bolt. Phelps won another five golds, bringing his final Olympic tally to 23, and 28 medals in total – outrageous totals that dwarf anything anybody else has ever done. Bolt won all three sprint events yet again. And Brazilian superstar Neymar scored the winning penalty as his nation won men's Football gold for the first time, gaining some revenge on Germany for their World Cup humiliation in 2014.

2021 Tokyo, Japan　　　　　　　　　　　　**339 events, 205 nations**
- Tokyo beat Istanbul and Madrid to be named hosts for the 2020 Games. Little did they know then that their big moment would be virtually destroyed by the coronavirus pandemic. In March 2020, the IOC bowed to the inevitable and delayed the Games by one year. They made it clear that the Games would either be held in 2021 or not at all. Just months before the Games, vaccination rates in Japan were still minimal, but eventually the Games went ahead, albeit in a terribly sterile atmosphere given the lack of spectators, and the extremely rigid isolation measures in place for all athletes. Baseball and Softball returned, and four new sports were introduced: Karate, Skateboarding, Sport Climbing and Surfing, which created some fresh excitement. Australian swimmer Emma McKeon won 7 medals, 4 of them gold, making her the rather under-publicised star of the Games.

2024 Paris, France　　　　　　　　　　　　**329 events scheduled**
- When Paris and Los Angeles were left as the only two remaining bidders for 2024, the IOC agreed to award them the 2024 and 2028 Games respectively. Breaking is to be introduced, with Baseball and Softball once again dropped, along with Karate, making it the first Games since 1960 with fewer events than the preceding one. The Surfing is scheduled for Tahiti, over 15,000km away from Paris.

2028 Los Angeles, United States
- Los Angeles were confirmed unanimously as 2028 hosts in 2017. It will be the fifth Summer Olympics held in the USA, and the third in Los Angeles.

2032 Brisbane, Australia
- Brisbane were named as the IOC's "preferred bid" in 2021, and confirmed as hosts later that year. It will be the third Games held in Australia, following Melbourne 1956 and Sydney 2000.

Winter

1924 Chamonix, France   16 events, 16 nations
- Following the successful inclusion of Figure Skating in the Summer Games of 1908 and 1920, and Ice Hockey in 1920, there was a push for a Winter Olympics. The Nordic countries were reluctant for their own Nordic Games to be overshadowed, but the IOC agreed to sponsor a "Winter Sports Week" in Chamonix in 1924. A year after the event, they were retrospectively recognised as the first Winter Olympics. As well as Figure Skating and Ice Hockey, they included seven other sports – Nordic Skiing, Nordic Combined, Ski Jumping, Biathlon, Speed Skating, Bobsleigh and Curling. Clas Thunberg of Finland entered all five Speed Skating events, winning 3 golds, 1 silver and 1 bronze.

1928 St Moritz, Switzerland   13 events, 25 nations
- St Moritz's world-famous resort needed little work in order to host the Games, though they did install the world's highest ski jump. Biathlon and Curling were dropped, but Skeleton was brought in, to be contested on the famed Cresta Run. The weather, particularly a strong wind, hampered the Games, and thawed ice led to the cancellation of one Speed Skating event.

1932 Lake Placid, United States   14 events, 17 nations
- As 1932 Summer hosts, the US were given hosting rights to the Winter Games too. However, at the height of the Great Depression, few countries made the trip; more than half of the competitors were from the US and Canada. The programme was similar to 1928, though with Skeleton dropped. There was controversy between the European and American ways of contesting Speed Skating. Eddie Eagan, a 1920 Boxing gold medallist, became the only person ever to win Summer and Winter golds when he was part of the winning team in the four-man Bobsleigh.

1936 Garmish-Partenkirchen, Germany   17 events, 28 nations
- Germany became the last country to host Winter and Summer Games in the same year. Sonja Henie won her third successive gold in Figure Skating, and Britain scored a stunning victory in Ice Hockey, aided by several "imported" Canadians (who were British-born). Alpine Skiing was finally introduced, despite the objections of the Nordic countries, who preferred their own cross-country style.

1948 St Moritz, Switzerland   22 events, 28 nations
- Following the end of the war, the Games were hastily arranged and returned to St Moritz, as all the venues from 1928 were still available. Switzerland's neutrality during the war was also to their benefit. Germany and Japan were excluded from entering. Alpine Skiing introduced downhill and slalom events, and Skeleton returned.

1952 Oslo, Norway   22 events, 30 nations
- The first Scandinavian Winter Games, they were followed by enthusiastic supporters throughout, and dominated largely by Norwegian athletes. Fears about Norway's ability to host the Games proved unfounded. Skeleton was once again dropped, but the programme remained largely unchanged.

1956 Cortina d'Ampezzo, Italy   24 events, 32 nations
- Cortina had been due to host the Games in 1944, which were cancelled due to war. When their chance finally came, they made a huge success of it. They were the first Winter Games to be widely televised. The Soviet Union made their debut, and immediately topped the medal table, but the star of the Games was Austrian downhill skier Toni Sailer, who won three golds.

1960 Squaw Valley, United States   27 events, 30 nations
- Squaw Valley in California was awarded the Games ahead of Innsbruck, despite consisting of virtually nothing but a small hotel at the time of the bid. It was deemed too expensive to build a Bobsleigh track, so the sport was dropped; however, Biathlon made its debut. Despite European reservations, the Games were well-run, and the opening and closing ceremonies were organised by Walt Disney himself. In 2021, the resort was renamed Palisades Tahoe, in order to appease modern sensitivities.

1964 Innsbruck, Austria   34 events, 36 nations
- Having narrowly lost their 1960 bid, Innsbruck easily won this time, and hosted a marvellous Games, drawing in more than a million spectators. Bobsleigh returned to the programme, and Luge was introduced. Lidiya Skoblikova won all four women's Speed Skating golds, whilst Eugenio Monti was feted for his sportsmanship in lending mechanical help to rival bobsledders, who duly beat him to gold.

1968 Grenoble, France   **35 events, 37 nations**
- Grenoble beat Calgary to the bid, but the Games suffered various issues, including venues and accommodation being widely spread out, and controversy over advertising on the skiing kits. Local boy Jean-Claude Killy was the hero of the Games, winning all three men's Alpine Skiing golds, although this too was controversial, with two skiers having beaten him in the slalom only to be disqualified. The only addition to the programme was a Biathlon relay.

1972 Sapporo, Japan   **35 events, 35 nations**
- The controversy over commercialisation and amateurism continued, with IOC president Avery Brundage singling out Austrian medal favourite skier Karl Schranz, and disqualifying him from competing due to commercial activity – others had done the same thing but not been disqualified. Sapporo was a surprise choice over the Canadian resort of Banff, but hosted an extravagant Games.

1976 Innsbruck, Austria   **37 events, 37 nations**
- In 1970, these Games were awarded to Denver, USA. However, the citizens of Denver voted in a 1972 referendum against hosting the Games, citing issues over cost and environmental impact. Denver withdrew, and 1964 hosts Innsbruck stepped in to save the day. In his retirement speech, former IOC president Avery Brundage had expressed his hope that the Winter Games would be scrapped forever; the great success of Innsbruck ending up saving the Winter Olympics. The most popular gold medal was that of Austrian Franz Klammer in the men's downhill Skiing.

1980 Lake Placid, United States   **38 events, 37 nations**
- Lake Placid had hosted the Games in 1932, and were effectively unopposed in their bid for 1980. However, the Games had grown massively, and the small upstate New York venue was no longer ideally suited to host such a big event. The build-up was also overshadowed by politics – the US talked openly in the build-up of boycotting the 1980 Summer Games in protest at the Soviet invasion of Afghanistan, and Taiwan withdrew after being forced to call themselves Chinese Taipei (as opposed to Republic of China). Cheerier headlines were made by Eric Heiden, who swept all five Speed Skating golds, and the US ice hockey team, who secured a famous win over the USSR (the "Miracle on Ice").

1984 Sarajevo, Yugoslavia   **39 events, 49 nations**
- Sarajevo seemed an unlikely host, but their main rivals, Sapporo, had already hosted the Games only a few years before the bid. The Games were staged quietly but effectively – the first to be held in a communist country. The IOC made one last attempt to preserve amateurism, banning some prominent skiers on those grounds. But they did also provide financial help to many smaller nations to enable them to enter for the first time. Torvill & Dean's "Bolero" routine was perhaps the highlight of the Games. Much of the Olympic infrastructure was destroyed in the Yugoslav Wars a decade later.

1988 Calgary, Canada   **46 events, 57 nations**
- The Winter Games finally came to Canada after years of trying. Calgary won the bid ahead of Falun in Sweden, and staged a hugely successful Games. Matti Nykanen (Ski Jumping) and Yvonne van Gennip (Speed Skating) won three golds each, but perhaps more remembered are Eddie "the Eagle" and the Jamaican Bobsleigh team, both of whom performed relatively appallingly, but would have films made about their exploits. Canada repeated their 1976 embarrassment of failing to win a single home gold.

1992 Albertville, France   **57 events, 64 nations**
- 1968 Olympic star Jean-Claude Killy successfully organised the third Winter Games to be held in France. Lyubov Yegorova, a Nordic skier representing the "Unified Team" of former Soviet republics, won three golds and two silvers. The Biathlon events were doubled from three to six (with women competing for the first time), and Freestyle Skiing and Short Track Speed Skating were introduced.

1994 Lillehammer, Norway   **61 events, 67 nations**
- The 1994 Winter Games were the first to be held in a different year to the Summer Games. The build-up was marred by various tragedies, including the death of medal favourite Ulrike Maier, as well as the dramatic attack on skater Nancy Kerrigan by associates of her rival Tonya Harding. But the small town of Lillehammer (having narrowly beating Ostersund in Sweden to the bid) staged a wondrous Games, notable for their environmentally-friendly construction. Professionals were now allowed full entry. In 1984, speed skater Dan Jansen had been favourite for gold, only to fall just hours after learning of his sister's death from leukaemia. Ten years later, his gold was the most popular of the Games.

1998 Nagano, Japan   **68 events, 72 nations**

- Nagano narrowly beat Salt Lake City to the bid, and organised the Games well, although they were hampered by the weather – heavy snow, freezing rain and even a minor earthquake. Snowboarding was introduced for the first time, as was women's Ice Hockey, and Curling ended a 74-year absence. Nordic skier Bjorn Dahlie finished his Olympic career with 8 golds and 4 silvers, a Winter record at the time.

2002 Salt Lake City, United States   **78 events, 78 nations**

- Having failed in four previous bids, Salt Lake City easily won the rights to the 2002 Games. Allegations soon surfaced that IOC members had been effectively bribed, leading to a number of resignations, although it appeared no law had actually been broken. Security was tight, just months after the 9/11 attacks in the US, but the Games passed off well. Skeleton returned to the Games for the first time since 1948. The biggest story was the scandalous voting in the pairs Figure Skating, which eventually led to two golds being awarded, and the scoring system being overhauled. Ole Einar Bjorndalen won all four men's golds in Biathlon.

2006 Turin, Italy   **84 events, 80 nations**

- Turin prevailed over the pre-bid favourite, Sion in Switzerland, to host the Games. The Games passed off with no major problems, although with fewer memorable moments than most Games. Perhaps the most memorable was when snowboarder Lindsey Jacobellis lost a certain gold when she fell whilst showboating, yards from the finishing line. She would eventually win Olympic gold 16 years later.

2010 Vancouver, Canada   **86 events, 82 nations**

- Vancouver narrowly defeated Pyeongchang to host the Games. They began dreadfully with the death of a luger in practice, technical difficulties in lighting the flame, and a lack of snow. But by the end they were a huge triumph, not least for the hosts. Canada had failed to win a single gold in their Montreal or Calgary Games, but won 14 here, topped the medal table, and even won the ones they wanted most – the men's and women's Ice Hockey, in which they defeated the Americans in both finals.

2014 Sochi, Russia   **98 events, 88 nations**

- Again, Pyeongchang missed out in a tight vote, and the Games went to Russia. It was a surprise choice, as Sochi was a summer resort. The Games were also marred by unrest over the Putin regime, and in particular the recently-passed anti-homosexuality legislation. But the action was exciting. Women's Ski Jumping was introduced, Ole Einar Bjorndalen ended his Olympic career with 8 golds, 4 silvers and 1 bronze, and the Dutch enjoyed huge domination in Speed Skating.

2018 Pyeongchang, South Korea   **102 events, 92 nations**

- Third time lucky for Pyeongchang. The build-up to the Games was overshadowed by scandalous revelations of widespread doping and cover-ups by the Russian Olympic authorities, and by increased tensions between the US and North Korea. The Games went well, though, with North and South Korea even agreeing to field a combined team in the women's Ice Hockey. Norwegian Nordic skier Marit Bjorgen brought her Olympic tally to an all-time Winter record of 8 gold, 4 silver and 3 bronze.

2022 Beijing, China   **109 events, 91 nations**

- 2008 Summer hosts Beijing became the first city to host both Summer and Winter Games. Almaty (Kazakhstan) had been the only other contenders, after Oslo pulled out in disgust at the demands of the IOC for luxury treatment of its members. Coronavirus restrictions took much of the fun out of the Games, and there were uncomfortable scenes involving 15-year old Russian figure skater Kamila Valiyeva, who had failed a doping test, been cleared to compete anyway, and then bullied in public by her coaches. Biathlete Johannes Thingnes Bo won four golds and a bronze. Freestyle Skiing now had 13 medal events (up from just six in 2010); only Speed Skating now had more events.

2026 Milan-Cortina, Italy   **116 events scheduled**

- Defeating a Stockholm/Are bid, 1956 hosts Cortina d'Ampezzo will host the Games again, in conjunction with Milan, which is over 400km away, in the first official dual-hosting in Olympic history. For the first time since 1998, an entirely new sport will be introduced – Ski Mountaineering.

2030 TBC

- At the time of writing, the hosts are due to be announced in 2024. Salt Lake City, the 2002 hosts, would seem to be favourites, as Sapporo, the 1972 hosts, have "paused" their bid. Sweden, Switzerland and France have expressed interest too.

Printed in Great Britain
by Amazon